FUNDAMENTALS OF CRITICAL ARGUMENTATION

Fundamentals of Critical Argumentation presents the basic tools for the identification, analysis, and evaluation of common arguments for beginners. The book teaches by using examples of arguments in dialogues, both in the text itself and in the exercises. Examples of controversial legal, political, and ethical arguments are analyzed. Illustrating the most common kinds of arguments, the book also explains how to evaluate each kind by critical questioning. Douglas Walton shows how arguments can be reasonable under the right dialogue conditions by using critical questions to evaluate them. The book teaches by example, both in the text itself and in exercises, but it is based on methods that have been developed through the author's thirty years of research in argumentation studies.

- Represents the state of the art in the methods and techniques of argumental and informal logic.
- Uses realistic dialogues featuring examples from political, scientific, and legal argument that will be familiar to students from their university and everyday experiences.
- Draws students into thinking and arguing.
- Offers objective guidelines for evaluating the strengths and weaknesses of an argument by critical questioning.
- Clear writing style and use of everyday examples make the subject easily understandable for students and makes evident the importance of the subject.

Douglas Walton is professor of philosophy at the University of Winnipeg. He is the author of thirty-three books and many articles on aspects of critical argumentation. He received the ISSA Prize from the International Society for the Study of Argumentation for his contributions to research on fallacies, argumentation, and informal logic.

For Karen, with love

CRITICAL REASONING AND ARGUMENTATION

General Editors
Douglas Walton, *University of Winnipeg*
Hans V. Hansen, *University of Windsor, Ontario*

This series is aimed at introductory students in the field of argumentation, informal logic, and critical thinking. Informed by research in linguistics, communication, artificial intelligence, and pragmatics, as well as philosophy, books in this series are up to date in method and presentation, particularly in their emphasis on dialogue and rhetoric, which contrasts with the traditional "go it alone" approach. Each book is designed for use in a one-semester course and includes exercises.

FUNDAMENTALS OF Critical Argumentation

Douglas Walton
University of Winnipeg

CAMBRIDGE
UNIVERSITY PRESS

CAMBRIDGE UNIVERSITY PRESS
Cambridge, New York, Melbourne, Madrid, Cape Town, Singapore, São Paulo

Cambridge University Press
40 West 20th Street, New York, NY 10011-4211, USA

www.cambridge.org
Information on this title: www.cambridge.org/9780521823197

First published 2006

Printed in the United States of America

A catalog record for this publication is available from the British Library.

Library of Congress Cataloging in Publication Data

Walton, Douglas N.
Fundamentals of critical argumentation / Douglas Walton.
p. cm. – (Critical reasoning and argumentation)
Includes bibliographical references and index.
ISBN 0-521-82319-6 (hardback) – ISBN 0-521-53020-2 (pbk.)
1. Reasoning. I. Title. II. Series.
BC177.W3235 2005
160–dc22 2005000190

ISBN-13 978-0-521-82319-7 hardback
ISBN-10 0-521-82319-6 hardback

ISBN-13 978-0-521-53020-0 paperback
ISBN-10 0-521-53020-2 paperback

Contents

Preface

Critical argumentation is a practical skill that needs to be taught, from the very beginning, through the use of real or realistic examples of arguments of the kind that the user encounters in everyday life. In this introductory textbook of critical argumentation an example-based method of teaching is therefore used. All points covered are introduced and illustrated through the use of examples representing arguments, or problems of various kinds that arise in argumentation, of a kind that will be quite familiar to readers from their own personal experiences. Exercises appended to each section of the book are designed to give practice in putting these skills to work.

As well as being a skill, critical argumentation is an attitude. It is an attitude that is useful in working your way through a problem or making a thoughtful decision. But it is most useful when you are confronted by an argument and you need to arrive at some reasoned evaluation of it on a balance of considerations in a situation where there are arguments on both sides of an issue. A purpose of this book therefore is to sharpen this critical attitude, which we all already have to some degree, to focus and heighten it in a constructive way, by providing an introduction to its basic methods. The methods presented are based on the latest state-of-the-art techniques developed in argumentation theory and informal logic. This book is meant to be an advance over the many other textbooks on the market today that lack the kind of depth needed by a textbook that is based on an established scholarly discipline.

Since this textbook is meant to be a basic entry-level introduction to fundamentals, it concentrates primarily on argument identification and analysis, confining argument evaluation mainly to identifying missing or weak points in an argument that calls for the asking of critical questions. Subsequent textbooks in the series, especially the one on fallacies, will go more deeply into argument evaluation. The perspective of this foundational first volume is that before any argument can be evaluated as strong or weak, reasonable or fallacious, it has to be identified. One needs to know how to classify it as type of argument and how to identify its premises and conclusion. And it has to be analyzed. One needs to know what its nonexplicit premises are and how it fits into other arguments it is connected to in a given case. Thus identifying and analyzing the most common kinds of arguments are the tasks that will take up most of this book. However, from time to time, comments are made on evaluation. For example, it is helpful to the reader even at this early point to have some idea of how a given type of argument that is often reasonable can sometimes be used fallaciously.

The approach to argument analysis presented in this book makes the assessment of any argument turn on three factors. The first factor is the structure of the reasoning on which the argument is based. Three kinds of reasoning are studied in chapters 2, 3, and 4, respectively: deductive reasoning, inductive reasoning, and defeasible reasoning. The structure represents the link between the premises and the conclusion. The second factor is the acceptability of the premises. This factor is judged in relation to the commitments of the two parties – the proponent and the respondent – who are involved in the argument. The third factor is the relevance of the argument. Relevance is seen as a matter of where the argument is leading in a dialogue. To be relevant it must be a chain of reasoning that leads toward the ultimate conclusion at issue in a dialogue. The second and third factors are explicitly dialectical, meaning that they involve a dialogue between two parties (in the simplest case) called the proponent and the respondent. The line of exposition of this approach in the book is divided into stages. The first stage starts from the basic building block of inference, where a conclusion is drawn from a given set of propositions called premises. Then reasoning is defined as a chaining together of inferences. This approach, while somewhat novel from the point of view of traditional logic, fits in with the view of reasoning that has been adopted in recent work in computer science, and especially in artificial intelligence. Readers taking courses in computer-related subjects will be familiar with this view of reasoning. The next stage is on arguments. Argument is defined as the use of reasoning in different types of goal-directed conversational exchanges called dialogues. The dialectical nature of the approach to critical argumentation advanced in this book becomes evident when the distinction between reasoning and argument is explicitly based on the purpose that reasoning is used for in a dialogue exchange between two parties. This new dialectical approach enables students to handle problems of argument evaluation in a way that they will not find confusing or simply unbelievable, as has been the case with previous textbooks in logic. The new dialectical approach provides a much more useful tool for identifying, analyzing, and evaluating common arguments than has been possible in the past.

A striking asset of the new dialectical approach to critical argumentation used in this book is that relevance can be defined with respect to how an argument has been used in a given case. Relevance is judged in relation to the type of dialogue the participants are supposed to be engaged in, and the issue they are supposed to be arguing about in that dialogue. Thus, for the first time, an account of relevance is presented in a critical argumentation textbook that really is helpful in giving practically useful guidance to students on how to judge whether something is relevant or not, in a conversational argument exchange, judging by the context (as known) for the case. Other chapters deal with the familiar topics of critical argumentation by showing how to deal with the use of plausible reasoning in an argument and how to evaluate certain common kinds of arguments, such as argument from analogy, appeal to expert opinion, appeal to popular opinion, use of personal attack in argument, and the slippery slope argument. This book teaches a range of other important skills of critical argumentation needed to evaluate an argument contextually, as it is given in a particular case, based on the textual evidence supplied in the case. As the book proceeds, it focuses less on individual inferences or types of arguments and more on how to evaluate critically certain properties of how a line of argumentation needs to be judged in a global perspective, in a case as a whole. One of these important properties is bias or slanting in an argument. Another skill is how to identify and reconstruct a longer chain of argumentation as used in a given case, identifying the "missing" premises and conclusions that have not been stated explicitly. Other skills taught in this part are how to deal with problems in arguments that arise from language, such as ambiguity and the use of definitions, and how to learn critical argumentation skills of questioning and answering.

The material in this book is meant to be flexible, so that it can be used alongside other textbooks in the series that go into more detailed treatments of different aspects of critical argumentation. Each chapter is based on the presumption that the student's comprehension will be sharpened through having mastered the material in the previous chapters. All the material is easily readable, and examples are freely used to illustrate every point. Thus chapters can be skipped by an instructor who wants only to cover selected topics. I would recommend covering at least the first chapter, and then picking out other chapters according to interest. The use of examples throughout the book is meant to make the material easier to grasp and more interesting for students. But the instructor can also use these cases to generate discussion in the classroom or in a seminar. It may be a good strategy of teaching to make the cases focal points of a lecture, as well. Also, the cases, along with the exercises at the end of each section, can be used to generate further assignments or test questions, in what should essentially be a hands-on learning experience for the students.

Acknowledgments

The support, encouragement, and advice of the late Terry Moore were important factors in the launching of this new series. Hans V. Hansen has also had much input into what is treated in this first volume of the series, and how it is treated. I honestly cannot remember whose idea the series was in the first place, but it doesn't really matter. Terry made everything possible, and all decisions have come from discussions among the three of us. Without the practical problem solving and advice of Terry and Hans, this book would never have overcome the many problems along the bumpy road to its current state of development. In recent years there has been a cross-fertilization of research between work on artificial intelligence and argumentation theory, to the benefit of both fields. New and useful tools incorporated into this textbook have been derived from tutorials at the Symposium on Argument and Computation held at Bonskeid House in Perthshire, Scotland, in June and July of 2000. I would especially like to thank Tim Norman and Chris Reed for organizing the conference. I would also like to thank the following conference participants for lectures and discussions that have influenced the model of argumentation presented in this book: Trevor Bench-Capon, Daniela Carbogim, Jim Crosswhite, Aspassia Daskalopulu, John Fox, Jim Freeman, Janne Maaike Gerlofs, Michael Gilbert, Rod Girle, Floriana Grasso, Leo Groarke, Corin Gurr, David Hitchcock, Hanns Hohmann, Erik Krabbe, Peter McBurney, Henry Prakken, Theodore Scaltsas, Simone Stumpf, and Bart Verheij. The techniques taught by the participants at this conference influenced various revisions during the refinements developed during the rewriting of the book. Among the colleagues in philosophy with whom I have worked, whose ideas and conversations have strongly influenced the direction of my work on critical thinking, I would especially like to thank

Tony Blair, Maurice Finocchiaro, Dov Gabbay, Ralph Johnson, Henry W. Johnstone, Jr., Jim Mackenzie, Michael Scriven, and John Woods. Colleagues in the communication field whose discussions influenced the book include Frans van Eemeren, Jean Goodwin, Sally Jackson, Scott Jacobs, and Mike Leff. I would also like to thank Anahid Melikian for help with proofreading and Rita Campbell for the index.

ONE Arguments and Dialogues

The three goals of critical argumentation are to identify, analyze, and evaluate arguments. The term "argument" is used in a special sense, referring to the giving of reasons to support or criticize a claim that is questionable, or open to doubt. To say something is a successful argument in this sense means that it gives a good reason, or several reasons, to support or criticize a claim. But why should one ever have to give a reason to support a claim? One might have to because the claim is open to doubt. This observation implies that there are always two sides to an argument, and thus that an argument takes the form of a dialogue. On the one side, the argument is put forward as a reason in support of a claim. On the other side, that claim is seen as open to doubt, and the reason for giving the reason is to remove that doubt. In other words, the offering of an argument presupposes a dialogue between two sides. The notion of an argument is best elucidated in terms of its purpose when used in a dialogue. At risk of repetition, the following general statement about arguments is worth remembering throughout chapter 1 and the rest of this book. The basic purpose of offering an argument is to give a reason (or more than one) to support a claim that is subject to doubt, and thereby remove that doubt.

Chapter 1 presents several key examples of dialogues in which one side makes a claim and the other expresses doubts about it. In this chapter it is shown how argument is based on a dialogue framework. In the dialogues, there are many specific arguments, and they are connected together with other arguments. The examples will show how argumentation takes the form of a chain made up by linking several specific arguments together. The word "argumentation" denotes this dynamic process of connecting arguments together for some purpose in a dialogue. The internal core of an argument is a reason, or set of reasons, offered to support a claim, called the conclusion of the argument. This set of statements is the internal core of the argument. But around this core there is also a framework of argument use, in which argumentation is used for some purpose in a dialogue. Chapter 1 fits the internal core into the framework of dialogue, giving the reader an integrated introduction to the notion of argument that fits both components together, gaining an integrated perspective, that helps him or her to grasp the concept of reasonable argument at the core of critical argumentation.

ONE Dialogues

A dialogue is a type of goal-directed conversation in which two participants (in the minimal case) are participating by taking turns. At each move one party responds to the previous move of the other party. Thus each dialogue is a connected sequence of moves (speech acts) that has a direction of flow. Dialogues are conventional frameworks that make rational argumentation possible. Dialogues do not contain only arguments. They can also contain explanations, instructions on how to do something, and so forth. But often they do contain argumentation. And when they do, if the argumentation is to be successful, it is important that the participants take turns, each giving the other party a fair chance to state his or her argument. If a participant, for example, uses force to shut the other party up, that kind of move is an obstruction to the success of the dialogue. To present a typical example of argumentation, consider a situation where two people, Helen and Bob, have a difference of opinion during a dinner party. Helen is against tipping. She has had difficulties with tipping in restaurants in the past and thinks that tipping is generally a bad kind of practice that should not be continued. Bob, on the other hand, thinks that tipping is a good practice that should be retained. The group decides that Bob and Helen should try to resolve their difference of opinion by having a discussion about it after dinner. To help us keep track of what was said at each move, for later discussion, the moves are numbered below.

The Dialogue on Tipping

Helen (1): A problem with tipping is that sometimes it's very difficult to know how much to tip taxi drivers, hotel bellhops, or waiters or waitresses in restaurants.

Bob (1): It's not so difficult. If you got excellent service, give a tip. Otherwise don't give a tip at all.

Helen (2): But how much should one give? And how can you judge whether service is excellent?

Bob (2): You just have to use common sense.

Helen (3): Come on Bob, that's no answer! Common sense is often wrong, isn't it? What kind of criterion for good judgment is that?

Bob (3): Like most things in life, if you want to do something good, like reward excellence of service, you have to use common sense.

Helen (4): With tipping, common sense leaves too much open to uncertainty. Because of this uncertainty, both individuals involved can be offended. If the tipper gives too little, the receiver is embarrassed and uncomfortable. If the tipper gives too much, she can be embarrassed and uncomfortable. Thus the practice of tipping leads to embarrassment and discomfort.

Bob (4): A lot of students depend on tips to help pay their tuition costs. University education is a good thing. Discontinuing tipping would mean that fewer students could afford it.

Helen (5): That's no problem. All we need to do is to raise the minimum wage.

Bob (5): That might just put a lot of restaurants out of business, with a resulting job loss for students and others.

The dialogue might have gone on much longer, but we will only consider the five moves above, in the discussion that follows. First of all, let's look over the dialogue as a whole. If we examine the tipping dialogue given above, we can identify its five main characteristics as a type of dialogue containing argumentation.

1. **The Issue.** There is a central pair of propositions at issue here. The dialogue above is on the issue of whether tipping is a good practice that should be continued. The issue is made up of two statements called theses. One thesis is the statement that tipping is a good practice of the kind that should be continued. The other is that tipping is a bad practice that should not be continued. It is unsettled which is true and which is false.
2. **The Viewpoints of the Participants.** There are two key participants, called the proponent and the respondent. Each has a point of view (viewpoint) on the issue. Bob is for tipping. His could be called the pro point of view on tipping. Helen is against tipping. Hers could be called the contra point of view on tipping.

3. **The Characteristic of Civility.** The two participants take turns, and neither tries to prevent the other from expressing his or her point of view by dominating the dialogue or attacking the other party either verbally or physically. This characteristic could be called civility or politeness.
4. **The Opposition of Viewpoints.** The two points of view are opposed, resulting in a conflict of opinions about the issue. In the dialogue on tipping, Bob's thesis is the opposite, or negation of Helen's. This means that the one thesis can be true only if the other is not.
5. **The Use of Arguments.** The two participants make various kinds of moves. For example, they ask questions, and then at the next move, the other party is expected to answer, or at least reply to the question. But one of the most important kinds of move is the putting forward of an argument. The purpose of making such a move is to get the other party to change his or her point of view and come to accept the arguer's point of view instead of the one previously accepted.

As far as we can tell from the conversation recorded in the dialogue on tipping, neither participant was successful in using argumentation to get the other side to change his or her viewpoint. This would be the goal of both in the dialogue. But even though neither achieved that goal, and there was no winner or loser, the dialogue still had benefits. The participants themselves could learn something about their opposed viewpoints. Each could deepen his or her viewpoint on the issue. This can be achieved in several ways. Helen had to articulate her reasons supporting her own viewpoint more clearly, in response to questions and objections. This made her supporting arguments stronger. She could have to take the counterarguments of the other side into account. This could not only strengthen her arguments, but might even make her refine her viewpoint, by adding qualifications and clarifications to it. And most importantly, by coming to understand the reasons given in the arguments of the other side, she might deepen her own understanding of the issue and its ramifications. This deepens her viewpoint and sharpens the argumentation supporting it. And anyone who reads the dialogue learns more about the tipping controversy, especially if he or she hadn't thought very deeply about it before or seen it as an issue. Thus as a venue for expressing arguments, and allowing them to interact with opposed arguments, the dialogue can have significant benefits, even if the conflict of opinions is not resolved decisively, one way or the other. It all depends on how the arguments are put forward, and how the other side reacts to them.

TWO Arguments

Consider the last part of the dialogue on tipping once again as a sequence of moves where Bob and Helen exchanged opposed arguments.

Bob (4): A lot of students depend on tips to help pay their tuition costs. University education is a good thing. Discontinuing tipping would mean that fewer students can afford it.

Helen (5): That's no problem. All we need to do is to raise the minimum wage.

Bob (5): That might just put a lot of restaurants out of business, with a resulting job loss for students and others.

Here Bob began the exchange by putting forward an argument. As shown above, his argument can be expressed as a set of premises that support a conclusion that he is arguing for. Bob made a statement when he said that a lot of students depend on tips to help pay their tuition costs. Then he made two more statements. First he said that university education is a good thing. And then he stated that discontinuing tipping would mean that fewer students could afford it. To structure Bob's statements as an argument, we could paraphrase it by stating the general premise first. His first premise is the statement that university education is a good thing. His next two statements are additional premises. Bob uses these three premises to support a conclusion. Let's set out the premises and conclusion of his argument.

PREMISE: University education is a good thing.

PREMISE: A lot of students depend on tips to help pay their tuition costs.

PREMISE: Discontinuing tipping would mean that fewer students could afford a university education.

CONCLUSION: Therefore, tipping is a good practice that should be continued.

Helen replied with another argument, saying, "That's no problem. All we need to do is to raise the minimum wage." The problem Bob posed in his argument is that discontinuation of tipping would interfere with students' being able to afford a university education. Helen's argument addresses this problem. Her solution is to raise the minimum wage. Presumably, this would solve the problem, because students would no longer have to depend on tips. Let's express Helen's argument in the form of a set of premises and a conclusion.

PREMISE: If we raise the minimum wage, students would not have to depend on tips to afford tuition costs.

PREMISE: If students wouldn't have to depend on tips to afford tuition costs, it would not be necessary for them to rely on tips to afford a university education.

CONCLUSION: Students would be able to afford a university education even if the practice of tipping were to be discontinued.

Her first premise introduces a new assumption into the argumentation in the dialogue. Based on this assumption as a premise, and also on the other premise stated above, Helen arrived at a conclusion. Her conclusion supports her viewpoint that tipping should be discontinued. She agrees with Bob's statement that a university education is a good thing, or at any rate, she does not want to dispute it. But even so, she can now argue that her viewpoint in the dialogue on tipping is not in conflict with this statement.

Bob's argumentation fits in with his viewpoint in the dialogue on tipping. If students couldn't afford to pay tuition costs that would be a bad thing, because it would mean that they couldn't go to university. And since university education is a good thing, it follows that discontinuing tipping is a bad thing. So we can see how Bob's argument links up with his ultimate thesis in the dialogue, the proposition that tipping is a good practice that ought to be continued. Thus his argumentation is relevant to the issue that Bob and Helen are discussing. Because Bob's argument above is relevant, it offers reasons to support the claim that tipping is a good practice, and thus it has some value in the dialogue. Similarly, Helen's argument is relevant to her viewpoint.

Arguments like Bob's are made up of statements called premises and conclusions. A statement, or proposition (we will use the terms interchangeably), is a sentence that is true or false. Premises are statements that offer reasons to support a conclusion. A conclusion is a statement that expresses a claim made by one party in a dialogue in response to doubt about the claim made by the other party. The conclusion of an argument can often be identified by an expression such as 'therefore' or 'thus'. Such words are called conclusion indicator words. They include the following.

Conclusion Indicators
therefore
thus
hence
consequently
we may conclude that
so
it follows that
accordingly

Premises can often be identified by expressions in the following list.

Premise Indicators
since
for
because
given that
for the reason that
seeing that

The ability to identify an argument by stating its premises and conclusions is a very valuable skill of critical argumentation. Only when an argument has been thus identified can it be critically examined in a clear and objective fashion. However, the list of premise and conclusion indicators given above is not complete, and such indicators are not sufficient as means to identify premises, conclusions, and arguments in natural language discourse. One sometimes has to recognize the kind of argument involved, and this ability will increase as we identify many kinds of arguments in this book.

EXERCISE 1.2

1. Find two more examples where an argument was put forward in the dialogue on tipping. Identify the premises and conclusion in each argument.

2. Show how Helen's argument on page 6 is relevant to her viewpoint in the dialogue on tipping.

THREE Questions and Statements

In the dialogues above, it was shown how the dialogue is held together by the sequence of moves. Each party takes turns making a move that responds to the previous move of the other. To respond to another party's argument in a dialogue, an arguer needs to do more than put forward more arguments. She also needs to ask questions that express doubts. Arguments are made up of premises and conclusions, as we saw, and these are statements. But asking a question is different from making a statement. When you make a statement, you are committed to that statement. You have gone on record as stating it. But when you ask a question, you may not be committed to anything, in the way you are when you make a statement. When you ask a question, you are merely expressing your doubt that something is true or asking for a clarification of it. This kind of move is different from that of putting forward an argument made up of statements.

Speech acts are forms of expression representing the various kinds of moves made in a dialogue. One kind of speech act that is very important is the making of a statement. In this book, as indicated above, we will take the terms 'proposition' and 'statement' to be equivalent. A proposition (statement) is something that is true or false. For example, if I say, "Madrid is in Spain," I am making the statement that Madrid is in Spain. Another way to put it is that I am asserting that the proposition, 'Madrid is in Spain' is true. We will take all the following speech acts as equivalent.

Saying that Madrid is in Spain.

Asserting that Madrid is in Spain.

Asserting the proposition that Madrid is in Spain.

Asserting the proposition that Madrid is in Spain is true.

Making the statement that Madrid is in Spain.

Making a statement is a bold move in a dialogue, because you are claiming that the statement is true, and thus incurring a commitment to that statement. Another type of speech act that is very important is the asking of a question. If I say, "Is Madrid in Spain?" I am asking a question. Asking a question is different from making a statement. When I make a statement, as indicated above, I am making a claim that it is true. Such a claim has a burden of proof attached to it, meaning that if I am challenged, I must either support the claim by an argument or give it up. This notion of burden of proof will be taken up in chapters 5 and 6. For the moment, we need only to recognize that when somebody makes a claim in argumentation, by stating that a proposition is true, she should be held to be putting forward an argument that gives evidence for the claim, meaning an argument that supports it. If her claim is questioned by a respondent, and she cannot give an argument to support it, she should give up the claim. This need to give evidence to support one's claims is an important requirement of critical argumentation.

Another type of speech act is a directive – such as "Pass the salt!" – which directs the listener to carry out an action. A directive is expressed in an imperative sentence, one that has the form of a command. An imperative sentence does not assert a proposition that is true or false. If I express the imperative sentence, "Shut the door!" to you, it would not be appropriate for you to reply, "That's true" or "That's false." You might reply, for example, "There's no need – the door is already closed." But that would be different from saying, "The directive 'Shut the door!' is false" – a reply that would make no sense. On the other hand, a directive can be associated with a proposition that asserts that carrying out an action imperative is recommended. Associated with the imperative "Shut the door!" is the proposition, 'Shutting the door is a recommended action.' Thus although directives are associated with, and could be said to contain, propositions of a sort, they do not express propositions in the same direct way that assertions do. More lessons about directives containing practical recommendations for action will be learned in the chapter on practical reasoning. In the present chapter, our primary concern is with propositions of the kind contained in assertions.

The concept of a proposition is fundamental to critical argumentation, because arguments are made up of premises and conclusions that are propositions. A proposition has two defining characteristics. First, it is something that is, in principle, true or false. But something can be a proposition even if we do not know whether it is true or false. For example, the sentence, 'Hannibal wore a beard on the day of the Battle of the Trasimene Lake' is a proposition. It expresses a claim that is true or false, even though we do not know, in fact, whether it is true or false. No reliable pictures or visual representations of Hannibal survive, and it is not known whether he wore a beard or not on that day. So although propositions have the identifying characteristic of being true or false, we may not in fact know whether a proposition is true or false.

A second characteristic of a proposition, as noted above, is that it is typically contained in a special kind of speech act. It is contained in a sentence that makes an assertion. For example, if I assert that Madrid is in Spain, then the proposition 'Madrid is in Spain' is contained in my assertion. But there is a difference between a sentence and a proposition. Two different sentences can contain the same proposition. For example, 'Snow is white' and 'Schnee ist weiss', the one in English, the other in German, are different sentences, but both (we can presume) express the same proposition. Ambiguous sentences are not propositions. An ambiguous sentence such as "Elizabeth Taylor Loses Appeal" (a headline found in a tabloid) is that it could express either of two propositions.

1. Elizabeth Taylor appealed a court ruling, and the appeal court ruled against her.
2. Elizabeth Taylor has a less attractive appearance than she did at some previous time.

One cannot tell from the headline sentence by itself which one of these two propositions represents the meaning of the sentence. Thus one cannot tell whether this sentence is true or false. Indeed, the sentence itself is not true or false. Once its meaning has been disambiguated, then one can perhaps see whether the contained proposition meant to be asserted is true or false.

Ambiguous sentences do contain propositions. But an ambiguous sentence is not itself a proposition. The reason is that it does not have the property, by itself, of being true or false. The problem with an ambiguous sentence is that it contains more than one proposition. Hence one of these contained propositions might be true, while the other is false. Thus for purposes of critical argumentation, it is important to distinguish between sentences and propositions. Propositions are contained in sentences, but they are not the same as sentences. The notion of a proposition is a kind of philosophical abstraction. It represents the meaning contained in a sentence, especially a sentence making an assertion. Of course the concept of meaning is hard to define, and philosophical theories disagree about what meaning is or where it is. Nevertheless, the concept of a proposition is very useful in critical argumentation, and we will often refer to it.

Sentences containing incomplete referring expressions do not express propositions. For example, the sentence 'She wore jelly shoes during the Folk Festival, for the whole month of July, 1993' contains the incomplete referring expression 'she'. This expression is incomplete because, although it refers to a female person, it is not specified which female person the property of wearing jelly shoes during the whole month of July, 1993, refers to. The sentence is (presumably) true of one such individual.

For example it could be true if 'she' refers to Shirley Smith. But it could be false if 'she' refers to Shirley Jones. Until it is specified who the individual is, the sentence itself is not true or false. Incomplete referring expressions are familiar in algebra, where variables x, y, . . . , are used to stand in for numbers. The sentence 'x is a prime number', for example, is not a proposition, because the variable x is incomplete. Any number could be put in for x. If some numbers are put in for x, the resulting proposition is true. For example, '3 is a prime number' is true. But if other numbers are put in for x, the resulting proposition is false. For example, '9 is a prime number' is false. So sentences containing variable (incomplete) referring expressions are not propositions, as they stand. But if a specific individual is put in the place of the variable referring expression, the resulting sentence is a proposition.

EXERCISE 1.3

Determine whether or not each of the following sentences is a proposition. Justify your determination by showing why the sentence expresses a proposition or, for some particular reason, does not express a proposition.

(a) Japan invaded Korea in 1948.
(b) What is the atomic weight of aluminum?
(c) What a lovely baby!
(d) Flattering women amused him.
(e) Everyone who fails to tell the truth is a liar.
(f) Never take your good health for granted.
(g) She ran toward the plane rolling along the runway.
(h) When did you stop cheating on your income tax returns?
(i) Take three capsules every day.

FOUR Arguments in Dialogues

Let's look at another example of a dialogue containing arguments. In this example, Bob and Alice have two young children named Ted and Kearney. One day Ted and Kearney got into a discussion about Santa Claus. Kearney was at an age where she was starting to be skeptical about whether Santa Claus exists. Ted told Kearney, "Santa Claus doesn't really exist; that's just something adults tell you." Kearney was very upset that her belief in Santa Claus had been shaken. When Bob and Alice overheard this conversation between Ted and Kearney, they started to wonder whether they might have been wrong to tell the children that it was Santa Claus who brought their presents. As they were decorating the Christmas tree, they had the following discussion.

The Santa Claus Dialogue

Alice (1): Well I think that lying is wrong. It's an ethical rule that lying is always wrong.

Bob (1): Well yes, I agree that lying is wrong as a general rule, but surely it's not wrong in all cases. Take the rule that everyone has a right to his or her property.

Alice (2): That's a general rule, so it holds for everyone, just as the rule states.

Bob (2): Well, yes, generally, but there are exceptions. Suppose my neighbor has given me his rifle to lock up securely in our basement, because he has small children. Smith comes to the front door one day, demanding that I return his rifle to him. It happens that I know that Smith is being treated for side effects of a malaria drug that he had to take during military service, and is capable of extreme acts of violence when not on his medication. It looks from his appearance that he may not be on his medication. He asks, "Do you still have my rifle?" How should you answer? In my opinion it would be permissible in a case like this to tell him that you no longer have the rifle. This would be a lie. But in this case the purpose of the lie is to prevent harm, possibly even deaths. Therefore in such a case lying could be justified. I think it follows that lying is not always wrong.

Alice (3): Well yes, you might be right. Lying may not always be absolutely wrong, but as a general principle you can assume that it is wrong unless the circumstances are exceptional. In the case of Santa Claus, I think lying is wrong.

Bob (3): Can you remember back when you were a child and your parents told you about Santa Claus? Didn't it give you a lot of pleasure to think that Santa Claus had given you these presents at Christmas?

Alice (4): Yes, it did, and I admit that it was a pleasant experience. But I still think that, in general, lying is wrong, because lying is conveying false information, and this is confusing to children. When children become confused in this way, it is hard for them to distinguish between fantasy and reality. Hence they are in a state where they are confused and out of touch with reality. Being in that state is a bad thing for anyone.

Bob (4): I don't think it's such a bad thing. It's normal for children to have fantasies and to believe stories that aren't true. In many cases, telling children these stories can have beneficial effects, because it can teach them all kinds of moral lessons even though the story isn't based on reality. It's similar to adults reading a fictional story. The fictional story can contain moral lessons or have great benefits in teaching the reader different things, even though the story is not true in reality. It may not be historically accurate or a story about something that really happened.

Alice (5): Kids are disappointed when they find out that Santa Claus does not really exist. The child reasons that if her parents lied about Santa Claus, they are probably lying about other things. Such a child may become skeptical and mistrustful, or even morally confused. She may lose self-esteem, and her grades in school may suffer.

Bob (5): Well, I think children are smarter than that. They know the Santa Claus story is just a "white lie," a sort of fiction that adults use in order to help make Christmas a more exciting time for children. The deception isn't permanent, and children realize that it isn't meant to deceive them about the facts, but merely to entertain them during a time of their life when they need such stories to perk them up.

Alice (6): I can see that the lie about Santa Claus is a relatively harmless one, but I still think that a lie is a lie. It's the principle of the thing. Once you allow lying of any sort, it could become a habit. It could be easy to start lying about anything, to get what you want. You could become one of these manipulative slippery people who lie their way out of anything. We've got enough of these people in high political office already.

Bob (6): Telling kids a story about Santa Claus isn't really a lie. It's just a way of stimulating a child's power of imagination, like telling a bedtime story about fictional events. It doesn't count as a lie, except maybe as a "white lie" of a kind that is sometimes necessary if we are to be diplomatic and polite. It's just a kind of harmless fiction.

Alice (7): Bob, a lie is lie. If you tell a child that Santa Claus exists, when in fact Santa Claus doesn't exist, you are telling the child something false. You know that the statement you made to the child is false, and you did it intentionally. That counts as a lie, because that's what a lie is. It's intentionally saying something that you know is false.

Bob (7): Well yes, OK, literally it is a lie. But as I said before not all lies are equally serious. Some lies are not harmful, and are necessary in order to prevent people from suffering the harm that telling them the literal truth might cause.

In this dialogue, like the one on tipping, the original dispute is not resolved. Alice and Bob still disagree about the issue when the dialogue ends. What prompted the dialogue in the first place was a difference of opinion. Alice took the view that lying to children about Santa Claus is wrong, while Bob took the opposite view. This difference of opinion is the issue that the dialogue was aimed at resolving.

The Santa Claus dialogue did not resolve the original difference of opinion expressed by Alice and Bob. Still, their arguments were interesting and revealed something about the viewpoints of both on the ethical issue of lying. The dialogue was about the specific issue of lying to the children about Santa Claus, but it quickly ascended to a higher level of generality. Much came to turn on the more general issue of whether lying is always wrong. Of course both Alice and Bob accepted the proposition that lying is generally wrong. But each of them viewed this as a different sort of statement. Alice saw it as an absolute claim, while Bob saw it as a proposition that holds generally, but is subject to exceptions in specific cases. Alice's viewpoint could be called that of an ethical absolutist. On this view, ethical rules cover all cases, without exception, and are binding on all actions that fit the rule. For her, all cases of lying are wrong. Bob's viewpoint could be called that of an ethical relativist, or situationalist. From his standpoint, lying is generally wrong, but that generalization is subject to exceptions in some situations. According to Bob's view, the general rule needs to be considered in light of the specific situation of a case. It may hold in many cases even though it fails to apply to some.

Bob and Alice use some other kinds of arguments that are interesting. At move 4, Bob compared the case of telling a story to a child to the case of an adult reading fiction. Such a comparison is called an analogy, and the type of argument based on it is called argument from analogy. At move 6, Alice and Bob argue about the meaning of the term 'lie'. Disputing about how to define terms is also an important kind of argumentation in dialogues. Both kinds of argument will be studied in chapter 3. As in the dialogue on tipping, Alice and Bob have a productive dialogue because they not only present arguments that are relevant to the issue but reply to each other's arguments in a thoughtful way. They don't just attack each other, ignore the arguments the other party has put forward, or prevent the other party from expressing his or her viewpoint. Thus even though the dialogue does not lead to agreement, it is productive in the sense that it does give insight into the argumentation on the issue.

EXERCISE 1.4

1. Identify and describe the five main characteristics of the Santa Claus dialogue as a type of dialogue containing argumentation.

2. In the dialogue at move 4, Alice admitted to Bob that when her parents told her about Santa Claus, it gave her a lot of pleasure to think that Santa Claus had given her Christmas presents. Bob, at his move 4, put forward an argument depending on this statement and on several other assumptions. Express Bob's argument at move 4 as a set of premises and a conclusion.

3. At move 4, Alice argued that, in general, lying is wrong. Display her argument in the form of a set of premises and a conclusion. Is her argument relevant in the Santa Claus dialogue? If so, explain why.

FIVE Generalizations

One very common way of giving a reason to support a conclusion is to offer a generalization that the conclusion falls under. For example, suppose a geometry student doubts that the triangle he is working with has three sides. The teacher may prove that it has three sides simply by stating the generalization, 'All triangles have three sides'. This statement is called a universal generalization because it ascribes a property to all triangles. A generalization is a type of statement that ascribes some property to a group of individual things, as opposed to a particular statement about a specific thing. Sometimes a generalization is called a rule, or general rule, because it states how things generally go in a wide range of specific cases. There are different kinds of generalizations, and how they work is best illustrated by discussing some aspects of the Santa Claus dialogue.

The Santa Claus dialogue starts out with a discussion of an ancient problem. This problem could be expressed in the old saying that for every general rule there is an exception. Alice said that it's an ethical rule that lying is always wrong. Bob replied to this claim by using an example of the sort called a counter-example. A counter-example is a specific case in which the general rule fails. Suppose, for example, that you make the statement that all frogs are green. Let's say that you mean this statement to be taken as an absolute generalization. In other words, what you're saying is that all frogs, without exception, are green. But then suppose I present you with a brown frog. It's a frog, and it's not green. This is a counter-example to your general rule that all frogs are green. In his argument in the beginning of the Santa Claus dialogue, Bob has presented Alice with a counter-example. He asks her to suppose that his neighbor, a man known to be capable of extreme acts of violence when not on his medication, comes to her door asking for his rifle. It is clear in this case that what Alice should do is to keep the rifle from this man, even if it means lying to him. The reason, as Bob said, is that this act of lying may prevent harm, even save lives. What Bob's counter-example shows is that the generalization that lying is always wrong does not always hold. But then another point is made in Alice's reply. In the face of Bob's counter-example she admits that lying may not always be absolutely wrong. In other words, she is saying that her generalization is not an absolute one that holds in all situations. Instead she is now presenting it as a general principle that holds as a rule, but is subject to exceptions in special cases. However, Alice did not entirely concede to Bob's argument. She admitted that lying could be justified in the case of the violent neighbor, but she still maintains, "in the case of Santa Claus, I think lying is wrong." What has happened here is that Alice has admitted that her general principle can fail in some cases, but this concession opens the possibility that the generalization could apply in some cases, but not in others. And so Alice is arguing that although her generalization fails in the case of the violent neighbor, it still may hold in the case of Santa Claus.

A counter-example is a specific statement of a kind called singular, because it is about a single, particular instance. A singular statement is a proposition that says something about only one individual. By contrast, a generalization is a proposition that goes beyond saying something about just one individual and says something that extends over a wider group or population of individuals. An example of a singular statement is the proposition 'Socrates was a courageous person'. This proposition says something about the individual Socrates, a Greek philosopher who lived in the fifth century B.C., and so it is classified as a singular statement. An example of a generalization is the proposition 'All philosophers are courageous'. This particular type of generalization, containing the word 'all', is a universal generalization, a proposition that is falsified by even a single counter-instance. All you have to do to prove the generalization is false is to find a single instance of a philosopher who is not courageous.

Another type of proposition is the existential statement, which asserts that some individuals have a certain property. For example, the proposition 'Some frogs are green' is an existential statement. Are existential statements generalizations? At first, it might seem that they are, because they do say something about a wider group of individuals than just one. But traditionally in logic, existential statements, such as 'Some frogs are green', are taken literally as meaning only 'At least one frog is green'. Such a statement can be proven true by citing only one instance of a green frog. Hence generally in logic, existential statements are not classified as generalizations. On the other hand, they are not singular statements, either.

One of the most common kinds of arguments familiar in logic is that where a generalization or an existential statement is linked with a singular statement to form an argument for a conclusion. For example, consider the argument 'All frogs are green. This creature is a frog. Therefore this creature is green'. Here the universal generalization is linked with a singular statement, and the two of them together proved an argument that supports the conclusion. Many examples of such arguments are examined in chapter 4, sections 2 and 4.

A universal generalization is absolute in nature, because it says something about each and every individual of the given kind, and no exceptions are tolerated, unless the generalization is appropriately qualified. For example, in the proposition 'All frogs except tree frogs and burrowing frogs live at ground level', two qualifications have been inserted. But this statement is still classified as a universal generalization, because it makes a claim about all frogs except tree frogs and burrowing frogs. And a single instance of a frog that is not a tree frog or a burrowing frog that does not live at ground level falsifies the statement.

Some generalizations, however, are not absolute in nature, and are not classified as universal generalizations. One type is the inductive generalization, which states that a certain number of individuals (a number that may be specified exactly or not) have a certain property. Examples would be the statements 'Most frogs are insect-eaters' or '76.8 per cent of frogs are insect-eaters'. An inductive generalization like the latter, which has an exact number specifying the extent of the generalization, is a statistical generalization. An inductive generalization like the former, that uses a non-specific inductive term such as 'most' or 'many', is classified as a non-statistical inductive generalization. A non-statistical inductive generalization can be converted to a statistical one by inserting an exact figure for the non-specific inductive term in the generalization, making the generalization more precise.

Another type of generalization that is non-absolute in nature is the presumptive defeasible generalization, which says that some kinds of individuals generally have a certain property, subject to exceptions. For example, the defeasible generalization 'Birds fly' says something generally about the birds. But unlike an absolute universal generalization, it is not subject to defeat by a single counter-instance. The general statement 'Birds fly' is true, even though there are some birds, such as penguins and ostriches, that do not fly. Such generalizations make a claim about the way things typically or generally go in a standard or normal case, but they are subject to exceptions. They have the property of being defeasible, that is, they are subject to defeat in special cases, even though the generalization still holds for the standard or typical case. This type of generalization is also presumptive, meaning that it holds only provisionally as an assumption tentatively agreed to by both parties in a dialogue. Later on in the dialogue, if an exception is found, the generalization may have to be given up. Sometimes the types of exceptions are known and predictable, but sometimes they are not. For example, it is well known that certain types of birds do not fly. But there are other kinds of exceptional cases that may not be predictable. For example, a bird may have a broken wing. So even though it is true generally that birds fly, and even true that this type of bird normally flies, it may not be true that this particular bird flies. Thus the exceptions that may be encountered in particular cases are not generally predictable in presumptive defeasible generalizations. Note that this statement is itself a presumptive defeasible generalization.

To sum up, then, there are three types of generalizations. The first is the universal generalization. It may be called "strict" or "absolute," because it admits of no exceptions. Inductive generalizations are less strict, because they are based on probability. But probability can be calculated exactly using numerical data. Thus inductive inferences can be judged numerically. Presumptive defeasible generalizations are the least strict, because they are based on what is assumed to be a familiar or typical situation, but one where there is inexact and incomplete knowledge on how things might go. For short, let us adopt the practice of calling presumptive defeasible generalizations simply 'defeasible generalizations'.

The precise nature of the difference between inductive and defeasible generalizations has been a matter of considerable controversy recently. Some think that defeasible generalizations are a special subtype of inductive generalization, while others think they are a separate type of generalization in their own right. The basic difference is that inductive generalizations are about the number of instances or proportion of instances to non-instances of a property, while defeasible generalizations are about how things can normally be expected to go in an ordinary or familiar situation. In defeasible generalizations, the exact number of positive versus negative instances is generally impossible to anticipate or calculate. In defeasible reasoning, there can be huge masses of data, the probabilities can be unknown, and the situation can change rapidly. The best we can do is to list all the arguments on both sides and then decide which side plausibly has the stronger case. When it is said that they are defeasible, it is meant that they have exceptions that cannot, in many instances, be predicted or even categorized in advance. Hence arguments containing them cannot be evaluated in the same numerical or statistical way that inductive arguments can. We have to keep an open mind about such arguments because they are based on assumptions that are subject to default as new information comes in. We must be open to giving them up.

Using defeasible generalizations in argumentation is necessary but dangerous. One of the problems is that there is a natural tendency in some cases to over-generalize or to make hasty generalizations that are not really warranted by the evidence. But the amount of evidence needed to support a generalization depends on the type of generalization (supposedly) being made in a given case. Strict universal generalizations are the hardest to prove, because they make a claim about all instances. Many universal generalizations even refer to future events that cannot be known yet or predicted with certainty. Such generalizations cannot be proved with absolute certainty, because the future is not known. Inductive generalizations are generally easier to prove, and defeasible generalizations require even less evidence, because they are weaker in nature and allow for exceptions.

A common error of reasoning in connection with the use of defeasible generalizations is the fallacy of ignoring qualifications. It is also sometimes called the fallacy of hasty generalization. It occurs in cases where exceptions to a defeasible generalization are overlooked and not properly taken into account when a conclusion based on that generalization is drawn. We have already seen how exceptions to a generalization can be controversial in the Santa Claus dialogue, where a general rule cited was that you should return somebody's property if that person requests it. But suppose someone ignored the exception to the rule, arguing in a dialogue as indicated below. Let's say that at some point in an ongoing dialogue, a participant drew a conclusion based on the following argument.

ARGUMENT AT ONE POINT IN THE DIALOGUE

PREMISE: Everyone has a right to his or her property.

PREMISE: Smith is demanding that I return his rifle to him.

PREMISE: Smith's rifle is his property.

CONCLUSION: I should return Smith's rifle to him.

This argument is reasonable, so far. The generalization in the first premise is defeasible. But there is no exception to it so far – let's say, as far as either participant knows at this point. But then new information about the particular situation becomes known, in the form of two new facts.

NEW FACT: Smith is known to be mentally ill and to be capable of extreme acts of violence when not on his medication.

NEW FACT: Smith is not on his medication.

The right way to proceed in the face of this new evidence about the situation is to retract the former conclusion in the defeasible argument accepted at the earlier point. This argument has now been defeated. But what if the proponent of the earlier argument refuses to retract and sticks with the conclusion, 'I should return Smith's rifle to him'? The problem with this dialogue is that although the conclusion follows from the first two premises of the original argument by defeasible reasoning, the two new facts of the case pose exactly the right kind of exception to defeat that argument. So anyone who sticks with the original conclusion, based on the support given to it by the first two premises, ignores the qualifications that should be part of the generalization. Such an arguer commits the fallacy of ignoring qualifications (hasty generalization).

A serious problem with argumentation based on generalizations is that some people who are passionately committed to a viewpoint tend to overlook qualifications that are needed in a specific case. They persist in treating the generalization as absolute or universal in nature, as though no qualifications to it are necessary. Such a lack of flexibility in argumentation and insensitivity to a possible need for qualifying a generalization is at the root of the rigid stereotyping that is characteristic of fanatical and dogmatic arguers who are intensely committed to their convictions. Such arguers want to see everything in a black-and-white, polarized kind of way that rigidifies defeasible generalizations into universal generalizations, even when such an absolutistic view of things is impractical and cannot be adequately supported by the evidence that is available. They may even see all critics or opponents of their viewpoint as evil people who can never be trusted to tell the truth. They operate on the principle, "If you aren't for us, you are against us." Thus they are closed to critical argumentation that asks questions that raise doubts about their views. It tends to be futile to use rational argumentation when engaging in dialogue with such persons. They may appear to listen to your arguments and even to acknowledge them or argue against them, but they always come back to their same fixed viewpoint. Thus defeasible generalizations are dangerous. But they are also necessary, if we are to deal with argumentation in a world of uncertainty and lack of knowledge, where we have to operate on the basis of presumptions in order to draw intelligent conclusions in argumentation about controversial matters of values and public policy, such as genetically modified foods and euthanasia.

EXERCISE 1.5

1. Classify the following as a singular statement, an existential statement, or a generalization. If it is a generalization, identify what type it is.

(a) Some Parisians who live on the Left Bank are intellectuals.
(b) Opinion polls are not reliable.
(c) John F. Kennedy was assassinated in Dallas.
(d) All creatures that have hearts have kidneys.
(e) In 1994, 78 percent of buyers of diapers bought disposable diapers.
(f) Sea lions are mammals.
(g) Sea lions live in these caves.
(h) Xerxes was a king in ancient Persia.
(i) Electrons have negative charges, unlike protons, which have positive charges.
(j) Bachelors are male persons.
(k) Most apartment buildings in Fresno are made of concrete blocks.
(l) Nearly all deaths that occur in vehicles with air bags occur in cases where the occupants were not wearing seat belts.

2. State a counter-example to the following generalizations.

(a) All the astronauts on the shuttle were Americans.
(b) Radioactive fallout always follows a nuclear explosion.

3. Judge whether the fallacy of ignoring qualifications has been committed in any of the following arguments.

(a) All except students are invited. Bob is a student. Therefore Bob is not invited.
(b) Most scouts sell cookies. Wilma is a scout. Therefore Wilma sells cookies.
(c) Generally, hummingbirds are attracted to bright flowers. Here comes a hummingbird. It would be a good guess that it will approach those bright flowers in the garden.
(d) Strenuous exercise is healthy. Jim ought to engage in strenuous exercise because he has a heart condition that is unhealthy.
(e) Aspirin is good for people who have a heart condition. Sue has a heart condition and also stomach problems. So Sue should take aspirin.

(f) Dogs are generally friendly, and you should pat them. Here comes a little dog. It looks like a pit bull. It is growling and foaming at the mouth. You should pat it.

SIX Chaining of Arguments

In the dialogue on tipping, Helen put forward a chain of argumentation that could be summed up as follows. She argued that it is difficult to know how much to tip, and because of this uncertainty, the practice of tipping leads to embarrassment and discomfort. She used this chain of argumentation to support her ultimate conclusion (thesis) in the dialogue as a whole. This ultimate conclusion is the statement that tipping is a bad practice that should be discontinued. At a global level, the argumentation in the dialogue on tipping on Helen's side can be seen as moving toward this ultimate conclusion. But we can also pinpoint parts of it at a local level.

Let's identify a specific argument in Helen's chain of argumentation, by indicating the premises and conclusion in it. These premises are statements put forward by Helen as reasons to try to get Bob to accept the conclusion stated below.

FIRST ARGUMENT IN THE CHAIN

PREMISE 1: With tipping, common sense leaves too much open to uncertainty.

PREMISE 2: If the tipper gives too little, the receiver is embarrassed and uncomfortable. If the tipper gives too much, she can be embarrassed and uncomfortable.

PREMISE 3: Because of this uncertainty, both individuals involved can be embarrassed and uncomfortable.

CONCLUSION: The practice of tipping leads to embarrassment and discomfort.

It looks like premise 2 is a reason that supports premise 3. Based on this support, premise 3 is then linked to premise 1, and they together support the conclusion.

Let's consider another argument in Helen's chain of argumentation. It can be expressed in a format of three statements. Two of these statements represent premises, statements offered to support a conclusion, a claim made by Helen. This claim is Helen's ultimate conclusion in the dialogue on tipping.

SECOND ARGUMENT IN THE CHAIN

PREMISE 1: If a practice leads to embarrassment and discomfort, it is a bad policy and should be discontinued.

PREMISE 2: The practice of tipping leads to embarrassment and discomfort.

CONCLUSION: Tipping is not a good policy and should be discontinued.

This argument is used by Helen to try to remove Bob's doubts about its conclusion, which is her ultimate conclusion in the dialogue as a whole.

Now we can put these two arguments together in a chain of argumentation. The conclusion of the first one acts as a premise in the second one. Thus we can see that the first argument represents a backup support for the second. If Bob expresses doubts about premise 2 in the second argument, Helen can bring in the first argument as backup to support premise 2. In the dialogue as a whole, Bob doubts Helen's ultimate conclusion. He is for tipping. But once Helen brings forward the second argument, he has to deal with it, in order to defend his view. Premise 1 in the second argument seems hard to question. Few of us would have any doubts about it. But premise 2 seems more questionable. Bob could certainly ask Helen to give some evidence to support that claim before he could be talked into accepting it. Helen can then bring the first argument forward to support the premise that Bob expressed doubt about. Thus it is natural to see how argumentation in a dialogue forms a chain made up of smaller arguments.

In previous examples, an argument was a single step from one set of premises to a conclusion. But even in very simple examples of arguments, it is common to have a chain of specific arguments combined together. For example, in the cold weather example below, statement 2 is drawn by an inference from statement 1. In this part of the argument, 2 is the conclusion. But then, at the next step, 2 is used as a premise in another argument.

THE COLD WEATHER EXAMPLE

1. The temperature is 33° below (Celsius) today.
2. Therefore, it is cold outside today.
3. Therefore, it would be a good idea to wear a parka.

Here we have an intermediate statement, 2, that is used as the conclusion in the first argument, but then used as a premise in the second one. Thus the chain of argumentation goes from the initial premise 1 through the intermediate statement 2 to the final conclusion 3. This structure is called a chain of argumentation, where the conclusion of one inference functions as the premise of another inference. Such a chain can be quite lengthy. Consider the kind of reasoning used in a game of chess, for example. One has to think several moves ahead. The way to do this is to construct a chain of argumentation.

Chains of argumentation often contain inferences that have more than one premise at a given step. Let us consider an example of a more lengthy chain of argumentation.

THE BERMUDA EXAMPLE

1. All persons born in Bermuda are British subjects.
2. Harry was born in Bermuda.
3. Therefore Harry is a British subject.
4. All British subjects have the right to reside in Britain.
5. Therefore Harry has the right to reside in Britain.

The first local argument in this chain has a one-step structure. The two premises are the propositions 1 and 2, and the conclusion is proposition 3. But this argument is combined with another one, the argument from premise 4 to the conclusion 5. But premise 4 by itself is not much support for conclusion 5. The previous conclusion 3 needs to be added in as another premise. Once statement 4 is linked to statement 3, the two together as premises provide quite a strong argument in support of 5. Thus 3 performs two roles in the chain of argumentation. First it functions as a conclusion of one argument, and then it functions as a premise in the next one. In general, then, we can see how chains of argumentation are made up of smaller arguments that are connected together. The conclusion of one inference becomes a premise in another one.

Once we understand the idea of a chain of argumentation we can ask what such a chain would be used for in a dialogue. Asking this question leads us to the notion of argumentation. Typically, a chain of argumentation is used to prove or give evidence to justify some ultimate conclusion that is the end point of the chain. The chain is aimed at this end point. Thus rational argumentation can be defined as the chaining of argumentation towards some ultimate end point. An argument purports to give reasons to support a conclusion, and thus to remove doubts about the truth or acceptability of that conclusion expressed by a dialogue partner. But a chain of argumentation, made up of smaller arguments connected together, always has an aim or direction. It is aimed at proving or justifying some statement that is in doubt or is unsettled in a dialogue.

To better understand the term 'argument', it is necessary to see that it has two uses in logic. In traditional logic, the term is typically taken to refer to a single, one-step argument like that in so many previous examples above. This represents an argument at the local level, meaning that it is used at one particular point, as part of an exchange of questions and replies that is much longer. In contrast, you can also think of an argument at the global level as a lengthy sequence of connected argumentation composed of many smaller arguments chained together over the longer sequence of a dialogue. An argument at the global level connects a local-level argument back to the original issue that is to be settled by the dialogue as a whole. In the dialogue on tipping, the issue to be settled is whether tipping is generally a good practice or not. Bob's thesis is that tipping is generally a good practice. Helen's is that tipping is generally a bad practice. Thus at the global level, Helen's and Bob's theses are in opposition to each other. The issue between them is unsettled.

EXERCISE 1.6

In each of the examples below, make a list, numbering all the statements that are made. In the case of a single argument, identify each statement as a premise or conclusion. In the case of a chain of argumentation, show how the smaller arguments are combined into the longer chain. In either case, show how the premises could provide support for the conclusion in a dialogue about some controversial issue.

(a) Smoking is bad for your health, because it destroys the healthy functioning of your lungs. Anything that destroys healthy functioning of your lungs is bad for your health.

(b) Euthanasia leads to loss of respect for human life. Anything that leads to loss of respect for human life is dangerous. Therefore euthanasia is dangerous.

(c) Punishment does not deter crime unless it is swift and certain. Punishment is not swift and certain in the justice system of North America. Therefore punishment does not deter crime in the justice system of North America.

(d) Holland is susceptible to flooding. What evidence do we have to support that claim? Holland is below sea level in many areas, and any area below sea level is susceptible to flooding. The reason is that water always exerts pressure on its container. If released, it flows downward to occupy an empty space.

(e) God is good, even though some skeptics deny this claim. A good being would not cause pain and suffering for no reason. Therefore, God would not cause pain and suffering for no reason. But God does cause pain and suffering in plagues, wars, and natural disasters. Hence God must have a reason. Consequently, there must be some reason for plagues, wars and natural disasters. Thus plagues, wars, and natural disasters are not sufficient reasons for thinking that God is not good.

SEVEN Criticizing by Questioning or Rebuttal

There is a distinction that is fundamental to critical argumentation that will run through this whole book. This is the distinction between asserting a proposition and questioning a proposition. When you assert a proposition, you are claiming that it is true. You are making a definite claim. You are saying that you are for the proposition, meaning that you are expressing a pro point of view with respect to it. This assertion represents a commitment to the proposition asserted. So you have to stand behind that claim in a dialogue if you wish to continue to maintain it in the face of questioning or objections that arise as the dialogue proceeds. Questioning a proposition is a different matter. When you question a proposition, you are not necessarily making a claim that the proposition is false, or that it is true. Questioning expresses a neutral point of view if it is merely an expression of doubt. For doubt does not need to imply belief or commitment. Questioning is, at least very often, a suspension of one's opinion or claim about truth or falsehood. A question typically says, "I don't know whether this proposition is true or false," so it makes no claim that the proposition is true or that it is false. In other words, questioning a proposition represents a weaker kind of commitment than asserting it. When you make a statement, you are staking out a claim, so to speak, and you have to defend it if you want to maintain it. But you are free to question any proposition without committing to it as something you hold to be true or false.

This distinction between asserting and questioning has fundamental implications about how moves in a dialogue are related to previous moves. Let's say that there are two participants in a dialogue called White and Black. White moves first and puts forward an argument. At his next move, Black can react critically to the argument. He can put forward an opposed argument, meant to attack the prior argument by giving a reason to think that its conclusion is not true. In other words, he can put forward a new argument that has a conclusion that is the opposite of White's conclusion. This kind of move is called presenting a counter-argument (or rebuttal) to the original argument. Such a rebuttal would (presumably) show that White's argument is wrong. Or at least it would offer a reason to show that White's argument does not prove what she supposed it to prove. If it does not present a reason, then Black can attack it by simply pointing that out. Another way Black can react critically is to question White's argument, but without presenting a reason to show its conclusion is false. He can raise a question about the argument, perhaps by finding some weak point in it, representing some aspect in which it is open to doubt. Thus there are two basic ways to attack an argument. One is to present a rebuttal or counter-argument, a comparatively strong form of attack. The other is to ask questions that raise doubts about the argument but not going so far as to rebut it by putting forward a counter-argument.

For example, suppose White asserted that Uranus is the seventh planet in orbit around the sun, because it said so in a newspaper. Black might question this argument, asking, "Is that newspaper a reliable source?" Here Black is not offering a counter-argument, but only asking a question that raises doubt about some aspect of the argument. On the other hand, Black might take the stronger stance of putting forward an opposed argument, such as, "It says in my astronomy textbook that Venus is the seventh planet in orbit around the sun." The conclusion of this argument, 'Venus is the seventh planet in orbit around the sun', is opposed to the conclusion of White's argument, 'Uranus is the seventh planet in orbit around the sun'. They are opposed in the sense that both cannot be true. If the one proposition is true, the other is false. Thus Black has made an opposed claim, and presented a counter-argument to back it up. Since an astronomy textbook is generally a more reliable source than a newspaper, Black's argument is the stronger of the two. It is a rebuttal of White's argument.

Consider the last part of the dialogue on tipping once again as a sequence of moves where Bob and Helen exchanged opposed arguments.

Bob (4): A lot of students depend on tips to help pay their tuition costs. University education is a good thing. Discontinuing tipping would mean that fewer students could afford it.

Helen (5): That's no problem. All we need to do is to raise the minimum wage.

Bob (5): That might just put a lot of restaurants out of business, with a resulting job loss for students and others.

Here Bob began this exchange by putting forward an argument. As shown above, his argument can be expressed as a set of premises that support a conclusion that he is arguing for. Let's sum up the main thrust of his argument as follows.

PREMISE: University education is a good thing.

PREMISE: A lot of students depend on tips to help pay their tuition costs.

PREMISE: Discontinuing tipping would mean that fewer students could afford a university education.

CONCLUSION: Discontinuing tipping would be a bad thing.

Helen replied with another argument, saying, "That's no problem. All we need to do is to raise the minimum wage." She put forward another argument opposed to Bob's, and thus her move is classified as a rebuttal. A rebuttal occurs, as defined above, where one argument has been put forward by one party in a dialogue, and another argument with the conclusion opposite to that of the first argument is put forward by the other party. The way such rebuttal works is that it undermines the support given by the premises for the conclusion of the first argument, often by introducing a new premise. Helen's rebuttal can be put in the form of an argument as follows.

PREMISE: If we raise the minimum wage, students would not have to depend on tips to afford tuition costs.

PREMISE: If students didn't have to depend on tips to afford tuition costs, it would not be necessary for them to rely on tips to afford a university education.

CONCLUSION: It's not true that discontinuing tipping would be a bad thing.

Her first premise introduces a new assumption into the argumentation in the dialogue. Based on this assumption as a premise, and also on another premise, as indicated above, Helen arrived at a conclusion. The conclusion is the opposite of Bob's conclusion in his prior argument above. The premises of Bob's argument supported the conclusion. But Helen's new argument, which was introduced into the dialogue at the next move, gave a reason to support its conclusion, the opposite of Bob's. Thus Helen's argument is a rebuttal of Bob's previous argument.

We noted above that relevance is an important property of argumentation and that an argument is relevant if it leads to an arguer's thesis that he or she is supposed to prove in a dialogue. But there is another factor that is crucial to relevance. This is the relationship of one argument to the next argument, or move made by the other party, that makes a dialogue hang together and makes it productive as a dialogue. Bob's argument responds to Helen's, and then her rebuttal responds to his last one. Thus the dialogue as a whole has a certain connectivity of argumentation. One move is relevant to the next one. The whole chain of argumentation hangs together and leads in a certain direction, toward the resolution of the central issue. Looking at an argument from a local viewpoint is very useful when we want to isolate the specific premises and conclusion for analysis and evaluation, and see how one move is related to a next move. But it can also be useful to look at an argument from a global viewpoint, especially where the argument is a long one and we know more about the context of how it is being used and where it is leading.

EXERCISE 1.7

1. Find an example in the Santa Claus dialogue where one party rebuts the previous argument of the other party. Express each argument as a set of premises and a conclusion.

2. Find an example in the Santa Claus dialogue where one party questions the previous argument of the other party but makes no attempt to rebut it.

3. Find a chain of argumentation in the Santa Claus dialogue and identify all the premises and conclusions in the chain.

EIGHT Criticizing an Argument by Asking Questions

In the dialogue on tipping, Alice asks Bob the question, "How can you judge whether service is excellent?" Bob answers by saying, "You just have to use common sense." Helen replies, "That's no answer." What we see here is a typical kind of exchange in a dialogue. Helen claimed that Bob did not answer the question. But she didn't mean that literally. What she meant is that she found Bob's answer questionable. She didn't accept his answer that common sense can be used as a criterion of whether service is excellent. She replied, "Common sense is often wrong, isn't it?" Helen made the nature of her objection clearer a little later when she said, "With tipping, common sense leaves too much open to uncertainty." This example shows that the asking of a question can be backed up by an argument. It also illustrates another aspect of the distinction between rebutting an argument and asking a question about it. The speech act of asking a question may not be entirely neutral. It may be a critical question that may undercut or undermine a previous argument of the other party in a dialogue. In such a case, merely asking a question is a serious criticism of a previous argument. Such a criticism is an attack on the argument, just as a rebuttal is an attack. For exposing genuine doubt about an argument can be a reason for no longer accepting it.

To illustrate how a question can be an attack on an argument, and to introduce some new kinds of arguments, consider the following dialogue on genetically modified foods. Genetically modified foods come from plants that have been modified in the laboratory to enhance desired traits, such as resistance to herbicides. Geneticists can isolate genes, such as the one responsible for drought tolerance, and then create a plant with that exact gene. Genetically modified plants grow faster and are more resistant to pests and can be created in such a way that they are more nutritious. For these reasons, genetically modified foods are becoming more widespread in grocery stores. Many plants, such as soybeans, sugar beets, and tomatoes, as well as processed foods, such as vegetable oils and breakfast cereals, now contain some percentage of genetically modified ingredients. Mark and Sarah are discussing this subject. He argues that we ought to continue this process of introducing genetically modified foods into the human food supply. Against this view, environmental activists and public interest groups have raised questions about whether this introduction of genetically modified foods might be harmful. Sarah adopts a skeptical view in the dialogue below, raising critical questions about Mark's arguments.

The Dialogue on Genetically Modified Foods

Mark (1): There are starving people in many countries of the world today. The world population is predicted to double in the next fifty years. Hence the problem of people dying from starvation will be much more serious in future years. Genetically modified foods can help to solve this problem.

Sarah (1): The long-term effects of genetic modification have not yet been tested. For all we know, reliance on genetically modified crops could destroy the environment, including all plant life, making the problem of starvation even worse. Thus it is doubtful whether they are safe.

Mark (2): According to Monsanto, the world's leading biotechnology company, genetically engineered foods are safe for the environment. They are the experts who know all about these products.

Sarah (2): They stand to profit from producing these new foods. Can we trust them to give an unbiased view? I doubt it. This is the company that produced Agent Orange and DDT.

Mark (3): No harmful effects of people eating genetically modified foods have been verified, as far as we know. Since there is no evidence that they are harmful, it is best to operate on the presumption that they are not harmful.

Sarah (3): That's just arguing from ignorance, isn't it? Can you argue from lack of evidence? Isn't it better to argue from the positive knowledge we have?

Mark (4): What we do know is that farmers now use many tons of chemical pesticides every year in the crops they produce. Food treated with pesticides is a health hazard. Thus, the crops produced by farmers right now are a health hazard. Also, agricultural wastes from pesticides and fertilizers are poisoning the water supply. Thus, current agricultural practices are producing serious harm to the environment and to human health. Growing genetically modified crops requires fewer pesticides and fertilizers. It is less hazardous than what we are doing right now.

Sarah (4): I doubt it, because there are also environmental hazards of genetically modified foods that are occurring as a result of what we are doing right now. Scientists have shown that the high mortality rates currently suffered by monarch butterflies are caused by pollen from genetically modified corn. Pollen from the corn blows onto neighboring fields, the monarch caterpillars ingest it, and they die in huge numbers.

Mark (5): Well, that's only an appeal to authority. Can you trust it?

Sarah (5): The findings were published in the scientific journal *Nature*.

Mark (6): Even granting your point, there are always two sides to the use of pesticides. Right now, we know that crop losses from insect pests can be enormous. As the world population grows, resulting in more and more shortages of land suitable for food production, we will need to grow plants in areas where it would be impossible without genetically modified foods.

Sarah (6): What if the genetically modified plants currently being engineered transfer their genes into weeds that become impervious to herbicides? Superweeds could be created. And as I said above, the future consequences could be the creation of new genetically modified species that could destroy all the crops. Herbicides could become ineffective against these superweeds. Their pollination around the world would create much more widespread starvation than we have now. I think this poses a problem for your argument.

Mark (7): A solution is to create buffer zones around fields of genetically modified crops. This would prevent gene transfer to weeds or other crops.

Sarah (7): How feasible is this plan? What if it doesn't work? Many children have developed life-threatening allergies to peanuts and other foods. The introduction of genetically modified foods will create new allergens, causing allergic reactions that could make these health problems much worse.

Mark (8): Increases in allergies could be caused to a significant extent by the herbicides that are currently used in crop cultivation. The new genetically modified plants are more resistant to pests even when herbicides are not needed to protect them. Thus the advent of genetically modified foods may not have the effect of increasing allergies in children. As I mentioned, no harmful effects of eating genetically modified food have been proven so far. I think we have to move ahead unless we have a definite problem.

Sarah (8): As I said before, I think we need to argue from knowledge and what has been proven, not just move ahead on the basis of ignorance. For all we know, all kinds of horrible things could happen if we continue this process of introducing more and more genetically modified foods into the human food supply. Now we are incorporating more and more genetically modified foods into our diet. These foods are gradually becoming more and more accepted by consumers and food regulatory agencies. But it's a huge experiment. Biotech engineers are tinkering with the fundamental building of life. For example, they have produced Frankenfish that grow four times faster than normal fish. What's this kind of experiment going to lead to? We don't know, do we? The marketing of such products moves relentlessly ahead, because corporations are driven by short-term gains, the so-called bottom line. If we keep moving ahead, won't we reach a point where we won't be able to turn back? We don't know what the ultimate outcome of all this might be. Couldn't it be a wholesale destruction of plant and animal life, in effect a devastation of all life on the planet?

At his first move in the dialogue on genetically modified foods, Mark presented an argument. The word 'hence' indicates that the statement following this word is a conclusion. Marks said, "Hence the problem of people dying from starvation will be much more serious in future years." The two statements just before this conclusion appear to be the premises of Mark's argument. One is the statement that there are starving people in many countries of the world today. The other is the statement that the world population is predicted to double in the next fifty years. When you put these two statements together they give a reason to support Mark's conclusion that the problem of people dying from starvation will be much more serious in future years. The one premise says that there are starving people in many countries today. The other premise extrapolates forward from the present situation to the prediction that in the next fifty years the population will double. These two premises work together to support Mark's conclusion because they indicate that the present problem is likely to grow much worse. Finally, there is an additional statement added to Mark's argument. This is the statement that genetically modified foods can help to solve this problem. This statement provides a bridge between the conclusion of Mark's argument and his ultimate conclusion to be proved in the dialogue, the thesis that we ought to continue the process of introducing genetically modified foods into the human food supply. Thus it is easy to see the link between Mark's thesis and the conclusion of his argument in move 1 that genetically modified foods can help to solve the problem of starvation. Obviously, if genetically modified foods can help to solve the problem of starvation, that would be a reason for continuing the process of introducing such foods into the human food supply.

In answer to Mark's argument, Sarah, at her first move, presents a rebuttal, an argument that moves toward a conclusion that is opposed to Mark's. The conclusion of her argument, indicated by the word 'thus', is that it is doubtful whether introducing genetically modified foods into the human food supply is safe. She gives two reasons to support this conclusion. The first is that the long-term effects of genetic modification have not yet been tested. The second is that reliance on such crops could destroy the environment, including all plant life, making the problem of starvation even worse. So, according to her argument, introducing genetically modified crops could, for all we know, make the problem of starvation even worse. This claim is opposed to Mark's previous argument that genetically modified foods could help to solve the problem of starvation. Sarah's argument at move 1 is thus a rebuttal to Mark's argument at move 1.

At move 2, Mark brings forward a different kind of argument, based on appeal to expert opinion. He argues that a leading biotechnology company, Monsanto, has said that genetically engineered foods are safe for the environment. Why should we think that this statement is true just because Monsanto says it is true? Mark gives the following reason: "They are the experts who know all about these products." At move 2, Sarah offers a rebuttal to Mark's argument, saying that Monsanto stands to profit from producing these new foods. Based on this observation she asks a question, "Can we trust them to give an unbiased view?" By asking this critical question she has suggested that Monsanto could be biased. In other words they could have a reason for making this claim other than the truth of the claim. That reason is that they would stand to profit from making such a claim. Sarah backs up this argument with still another one that appears strongly to condemn Monsanto as a reliable source. She says that this is the company that produced Agent Orange and DDT. These products turned out to be destructive to human life. They turned out to be highly unsafe. Thus Sarah's argument suggests that Monsanto does not have a good track record concerning their statements that their products are safe. Once again, this suggests that this company is biased and not a reliable source to make claims about which foods are safe for the environment.

At move 3, Mark introduces an interesting type of argument. He argues that there are no harmful effects on people eating genetically modified foods that have been verified so far. After this sentence, he draws an inference: Since there is no evidence that these foods are harmful, it is best to operate on the presumption that they are not harmful. The conclusion of this inference is that we should accept the statement that eating these foods is not harmful. But as Sarah points out, this is an argument on the basis of ignorance or lack of knowledge. She asks whether it may not be better to argue from positive evidence rather than from a lack of evidence. Her remark is puzzling. Somehow it seems wrong that we should argue from a lack of evidence. But very often we do lack evidence, because we have to move forward and make a decision under conditions of uncertainty. In such cases, then, we are arguing from ignorance. Is that inherently wrong? Mark and Sarah seem to have a difference of opinion on this issue. Mark uses the argument from lack of evidence to support his conclusion that eating genetically modified foods can be presumed to be safe. But Sarah questions this argument, arguing that because it is simply based on ignorance, it must therefore somehow be faulty.

At move 4, Mark puts forward a lengthy argument based on a number of premises he asserts as factual. His conclusion is stated at the very end of his move. This conclusion is the statement that growing genetically modified crops is less hazardous than what we're doing right now. His reason is that what we're doing right now is using all kinds of fertilizers and pesticides, and, as he argues, these pesticides and fertilizers are health hazards. Sarah replies at move 4 that she is doubtful about Mark's argument. The reason she gives is that genetically modified foods are also being used right now, and their use is also contributing to environmental hazards. She cites the example of high mortality rates currently suffered by monarch butterflies. As Mark observed at move 5 in his response to this argument, it is based on appeal to expert opinion. That was a form of argument that Mark had just used at move 2 above. Sarah criticized it there by arguing that Monsanto cannot be trusted to give an unbiased opinion. Now Mark uses a similar form of attack when he questions Sarah's use of the appeal to expert opinion. He says, at move 5, that this form of argument is only an appeal to authority, suggesting that such a form of argument could be illegitimate. But, one might think, appeals to expert opinion are very common, for example in legal argumentation. Legal evidence, for example, ballistics evidence and DNA evidence, is often based on the authority of expert witnesses. Such cases suggest that appeal to expert opinion could be a reasonable form of argument in collecting evidence. Also, Sarah has a good reply to Mark's question. Sarah's reply at move 5 backs up the legitimacy of the appeal to expert opinion as a form of argument by citing an authoritative source. She states that the findings about monarch butterflies were published in the scientific journal *Nature*. This journal is a good source, and therefore Sarah's appeal to expert opinion seems like quite a strong argument. It is possible for Mark to question her, asking who the authors of the article were, and what were their qualifications. But despite this lack of detailed support, her appeal to expert opinion is not without worth. It may not be conclusive, but it does provide a reason supporting her claim. Thus Sarah's counter-argument, based on appeal to expert opinion, is a rebuttal to Mark's prior argument.

EXERCISE 1.8

1. Express Mark's point of view and Sarah's point of view in the dialogue on genetically modified foods by identifying each attitude and each proposition in the point of view. How are the two points of view opposed?

2. Write out Mark's argument at move 1 as a set of premises and a conclusion. Write out Sarah's argument at move 1 as a set of premises and a conclusion. How is the conclusion of the one argument related to the conclusion of the other?

3. Represent Mark's argument at move 2 as a set of premises and a conclusion. Show how, at move 2, when Sarah questions this argument, her questioning takes the form of an attack on it. How does she back up the attack with an argument? Identify its premises and conclusion.

4. Identify the premises and conclusion of the argument Mark presents at move 3. Is Sarah's reaction to it a rebuttal or merely a questioning of his argument? Give a reason to support your answer.

NINE Disputes and Dissents

As noted above, there is a fundamental difference between arguing that a proposition is false and merely questioning whether it is true. The first expresses a contra point of view, while the second may represent a neutral point of view. Offering a rebuttal is a stronger form of attack on an argument than merely raising doubt about some aspect of it by asking a critical question. This difference, as noted above, can be found at many points in a dialogue where a specific argument has been put forward or where a specific question has been asked. However, this difference is also very important when it comes to looking at the dialogue as a whole. Every dialogue containing argumentation is based on a difference of viewpoints on some central issue. It is this issue that gives the argumentation in the dialogue an aim and direction. Each party has a thesis, and the thesis of the one party is opposed to the thesis of the other. But there are two kinds of opposition that can be found in a dialogue.

In the dialogue on tipping, we described Helen's thesis in negative terms, as the proposition that tipping is not a good practice. Assuming 'bad' is the negation of 'good', we could say that Bob's and Helen's viewpoints are strongly opposed, meaning that the thesis contained in one is the opposite of the thesis contained in the other. It is also possible to suppose that, in another kind of case, the conflict between Bob and Helen could be a weaker kind of opposition. Suppose that Bob took as his thesis the proposition that tipping is a good practice, but Helen took only the skeptical position of not being convinced, one way or the other, whether tipping is good or bad. Here Helen's opposition is of a weaker sort. Helen doubts whether tipping is a good practice, but she does not go so far as to claim it is definitely bad.

In dialogues containing a conflict between the viewpoints held by the two participants, the mode of opposition can take a stronger or weaker form. In the stronger kind of opposition, called a dispute, the one party has a thesis, and the other holds the opposite thesis. In the weaker form of opposition, called a dissent, the one party holds the viewpoint that a particular thesis is true, while the other only doubts whether this proposition is true, but does not hold the viewpoint that it is false. In some cases, it is clear whether a dialogue is a dispute or a dissent. In other cases, it may start out one way, and then shift to the other way. When a particular case is being analyzed, especially if it is a longer dialogue, the analyst needs to examine the details at the various moves, as well as the dialogue as a whole. The opposition between the two parties should be described as a dispute only if there is clear evidence that the respondent is arguing for his own thesis. That is, the respondent must be declaring that his thesis is true and presenting argumentation to prove it is true. Unless the evidence on this point is clear, the case should be classified as a dissent.

In the next dialogue, Cassie and Fred have just read the news report about a retired Michigan pathologist, Dr. Jack Kevorkian, who used a machine he had invented to help a patient with Alzheimer's disease end her life. This machine connects a container holding lethal chemicals to a patient through an intravenous line. When the patient pushes a button, the chemicals are released and go into the patient's bloodstream. A question posed by this widely publicized case is whether Dr. Kevorkian violated the code of ethical conduct for physicians (not meaning any actual 'code', or official set of rules, but only what one should take such rules to be, ethically speaking). In this case, Dr. Kevorkian was reported to have pushed the button himself. Thus the case is classified as one of active euthanasia, as opposed to passive euthanasia, in which the physician lets the patient with a terminal illness die by withholding or withdrawing treatment. It is one thing to allow a patient to die by discontinuing treatment that he no longer wishes to have, but it is quite another to actively intervene to bring about the death of a patient by carrying out actions that will cause that patient's death. After reading about this case, Cassie and Fred expressed a disagreement on whether Dr. Kervorkian had violated the code of ethical conduct for physicians.

The Euthanasia Dialogue

Cassie (1): I think he did violate the code of ethical conduct for physicians, because he pushed the button himself. If the patient had pushed the button instead of Dr. Kevorkian, I would say that the doctor did not violate the code.

Fred (1): I find this view highly dubious. What's the difference whether he pushed the button, or just set the whole thing up so the patient could push the button?

Cassie (2): It's the difference between active and passive euthanasia. Active euthanasia is causing an outcome to occur, whereas passive euthanasia is merely not intervening to prevent it. That's why active euthanasia is always wrong, while passive euthanasia is not.

Fred (2): I don't see how one can be wrong and the other not, because both lead to the death of the patient. Anything that leads to the death of the patient is against human life. Anything that is against human life is wrong. It follows that both active and passive euthanasia are wrong. Anything that is wrong should not be allowed in any code of ethical conduct for physicians. Thus I think that both should be against the code of ethical conduct for physicians.

Cassie (3): I don't think that both should be against the code of ethical conduct for physicians, because I think there is a morally significant difference between active and passive euthanasia. In passive euthanasia the patient voluntarily carries out the act of killing himself. That's suicide, and it's no fault of the physician. However, if a physician were to kill the patient by administering the lethal drug himself, that would be murder.

Fred (3): Legally, there may be a difference, but ethically I don't see that there is. Both acting and not acting can lead to the death of a patient. Since both can lead to the same outcome, death, surely both kinds of actions are equally serious and are morally equivalent. So what's the difference?

Cassie (4): Now wait a minute Fred! There is a difference here. Let's begin with a case where I shoot you. That is quite different, ethically speaking, from a case where I fail to save you from another party who shoots you. In the one case I am directly responsible for your death because I personally carry out the action that causes it. In the other case I merely stand by and fail to intervene, failing to prevent your death. My responsibility for your death is quite different in the two cases.

Fred (4): I don't see the difference. If you fail to intervene when you could have, and I die, then you are responsible for my death.

Cassie (5): Let's look at this in a different way. Suppose a cancer patient is suffering terrible pain, and there is no hope she will recover by continuing chemotherapy. Suppose she asks that the chemotherapy be discontinued. Shouldn't her doctor be allowed to carry out her wishes? I think he should be allowed to stop treatment, according to the code of ethics for physicians. But I don't think he should be allowed to give her a lethal injection.

Fred (5): But how does your argument fit with the view that human life is sacred? Taking a human life should never be allowed, even if it is only a matter of collaborating in a killing, as opposed to actually carrying it out.

Cassie (6): Think of the case of animals. When your dog gets very old, and is suffering terribly, you take it to the humane society and have it put down. Are you saying that there is a difference between human life, which is sacred, and animal life, which is not? This position is 'speciesism', the view that human life is special and uniquely valuable, simply because we are members of the human species.

Fred (6): Giving it a negative-sounding name doesn't make it wrong. What about the differences between dogs and humans? A human is a rational being with free choice, rights, and responsibilities. Dogs are dependent on us to make decisions for them.

One interesting thing about the euthanasia dialogue is that the argumentation gets hung up on a linguistic difficulty. At her first move in the dialogue, Cassie gives a reason to support her view that Dr. Kevorkian did violate the code of ethical conduct for physicians. The reason she gave is that he pushed the button himself. Fred is skeptical about this argument and subjects it to questioning. He asks what the difference is between Dr. Kevorkian's pushing the button and the patient's pushing it. To answer this question Cassie (at move 2) cites a distinction between active and passive euthanasia. She offers a definition of each term. She says that active euthanasia is causing an outcome to occur. She defines passive euthanasia, by contrast, as not intervening, meaning not causing the outcome. On the basis of this distinction, she argues for her conclusion that active euthanasia is always wrong, while passive euthanasia is not. It is not difficult to see how this conclusion is relevant to her thesis in the euthanasia dialogue. She is contending that what a physician did can be classified as passive euthanasia as long as he did not push the button. Based on her argument just stated, passive euthanasia is not always wrong. Thus she can argue that what a physician might do by setting up his euthanasia machine was not wrong, if that's all he did. What Cassie's argument shows is that how terms are defined can be very important in argumentation.

At his move 2, Fred rebuts Cassie's argument by presenting another argument that has the conclusion opposite to Cassie's argument at her move 2. Fred's argument has two premises, both generalizations.

FIRST PREMISE: Anything that leads to the death of a patient is against human life.

SECOND PREMISE: Anything that is against human life is wrong.

CONCLUSION: Both active and passive euthanasia are wrong.

Fred uses this argument for two purposes. The first is indicated in his remark at move 2: "I don't see how one can be wrong and the other not, because both lead to the death of the patient." In other words, Fred is giving a reason to support his skeptical remark that he doesn't see how one type of euthanasia, active euthanasia, could be wrong, while the other, passive euthanasia, might not be wrong. This is interesting because it shows that Fred is using an argument to back up his questioning of Cassie's previous argument. In other words, what he is doing is not rebutting her argument but using an argument to question it. The second thing he is doing is using his argument to lead to another argument, thus producing a chain of argumentation. The conclusion of his first argument was the statement that both active and passive euthanasia are wrong. This statement is now used as a premise along with an additional premise. The additional premise is the statement that anything that is wrong should not be allowed in any code of ethical conduct for physicians. These two generalizations, taken together, support the conclusion that Fred asserts. Fred says, "Thus I think that both [active and passive euthanasia] should be against the code of ethical conduct for physicians." This statement is clearly relevant in the dialogue, as it goes directly against Cassie's viewpoint.

At her move 4, and then again at her move 5, Cassie uses an argument based on an example. Using an example can be a reasonable form of argument, because it not only illustrates your point but can show how it is applicable to a particular case. If the respondent is convinced that the generalization you are arguing for is true in this case, then he may be convinced to accept it. But, of course, simply using one case as your evidence is a weak form of argument if it is supposed to support a wide generalization. Thus argument from example, even if it is a weak form of argument, can still be a reasonable argument that carries some weight.

Another argument that Cassie uses at move 6 is an argument from analogy. She draws a comparison to the kind of case where your dog is suffering and you take it to the Humane Society to have it put down. Still another kind of argument that she uses at move 6 is based on her assertion that Fred's argument can be defined as speciesism. Once again, the argument is interesting because it derives from the use of language. She is using what is often described as emotively loaded language. In other words, she uses a term that makes Fred's view sound somehow unreasonable or wrong. Fred responds at move 6 by pointing out that such a negative use of language doesn't necessarily prove that his argument is wrong. He backs up his point by putting forward another argument based on the statement that human beings are different from animals.

EXERCISE 1.9

1. Classify the following cases as a dissent or a dispute, giving your reasons to support your classification.

(a) Tom thinks that doctors who have the AIDS virus should be allowed to practice, while Tara has some reservations about this policy.

(b) Max and Melissa are arguing about the existence of God. He is a believer and she is an agnostic.

(c) Sandra and Scott are arguing about the existence of God. She is a believer and he is an atheist.

(d) Bruno and Barbara are arguing about abortion. He thinks that abortion is always wrong and she thinks that a decision about abortion should be the woman's choice.

(e) Elsa and Ed are opposed on the question of whether Howard should have a Harley Davidson. Ed thinks he should have one but Elsa doubts that it would be a good idea.

2. Classify the euthanasia dialogue as a dispute or a dissent, giving reasons to support your classification.

3. Classify the dialogue on genetically modified food as a dispute or a dissent, giving reasons to support your classification.

4. In the euthanasia dialogue, show how Cassie's argument at her move 3 is a rebuttal of Fred's previous argument (at his move 2). What are the premises and conclusion of Cassie's argument? What is special about Cassie's argument that makes it similar to her earlier argument at move 2?

TEN Summary

An argument is made up of statements called premises and a conclusion. The premises give a reason (or reasons) to support the conclusion. The conclusion of an argument that has been put forward is a claim made by the arguer, meaning she has a pro point of view to the statement contained in the conclusion. A point of view is a statement and an attitude toward it, pro, contra, or neutral. Generally, an argument is a set of statements put forward by one party in a dialogue in reply to an expression of doubt posed by the questioning or opposed argument of the other party in the dialogue. Thus, an argument presupposes a dialogue with two participants (in the minimal case), called the proponent and the respondent. A dialogue is a verbal exchange between two parties where they take turns making moves that can be classified as speech acts. Putting forward an argument is only one type of speech act. Another important speech act is that of questioning the other party in a dialogue. Asking a question is one type of move, while putting forward an argument is another. When a party makes a statement or puts forward an argument, she incurs commitments. These are moves that have a burden of proof attached. Asking a question, in contrast, doesn't always commit the questioner to propositions that have to be defended. There are two basic ways to criticize an argument. One is to offer a rebuttal or counter-argument. The other is to merely ask critical questions that express doubt about the argument, indicating weak points in it.

Arguments can be connected together to form a chain of argumentation. Thus, there are two ways to view an argument in a dialogue, locally or globally. Viewed locally, an argument is a set of premises with a single conclusion. Viewed globally it is a chain of argumentation used in a context of dialogue to contribute, at some stage of the dialogue, to the settling of the central issue. The distinction between presenting an argument and merely asking a question is also important at the global level of a dialogue. If something is an argument, it is to be presumed that there is some issue in a dialogue in which it appears and that the argument is being used to settle that issue. In a dispute, the proponent makes a statement identified as her thesis, and the respondent has a thesis that is the opposite of the proponent's. The issue to be resolved is which one of this opposed pair of statements is better supported by the argumentation in the dialogue. In a dissent, the proponent has a thesis, but the respondent has no thesis. His function is merely to express doubts about the proponent's thesis. Both questions and arguments should be relevant. To be relevant, an argument must play some part in helping to settle the central issue of a dialogue. The issue, it is presumed, has been made explicit at an early stage of the dialogue or can be made explicit by examining what was said. In a dissent, the purpose of one party's putting forward an argument is to remove the doubt expressed by the other party's questioning of a specific statement at issue, called his or her thesis. In a dispute, the purpose of one party's putting forward an argument is to rebut the other party's thesis by using rational argumentation to show it is false.

TWO Concepts Useful for Understanding Arguments

This chapter introduces fundamental concepts needed to identify, analyze, and evaluate arguments. It is most vital to be able to recognize deductive arguments and to be able to contrast them with two other types of arguments. One is the inductive type of argument based on probability. The other is the presumptive type of argument based on plausibility. It is necessary to begin with deductive arguments, as these are the kind that have been most intensively studied in logic and about which most is known. From there, the chapter goes on to examine the distinction between an explanation and an argument. Mainly in this book we are concerned with arguments. But there is a common tendency to confuse arguments and explanations, and the problem of distinguishing between the two has to be dealt with if we are to avoid the error of treating something as an argument when it is not. The chapter begins with the notion of inconsistency and its role in argumentation. This notion is fundamental to defining and recognizing deductive arguments as a distinctive type.

There can also be much confusion in mixing up the three kinds of arguments, and the clues in a dialogue on which type was meant to be put forward can be subtle. Even so, one can begin to get a good fundamental grasp of how to recognize each type of argument by learning about its success criteria. Each type of argument has a distinctive structure. If we learn to recognize common and readily identifiable structures and get some grasp of how each has standards for correct use, we are on a good footing. We at least have some basis for identifying common arguments of the three types, and this basis is extremely helpful to prevent confusion. It is a great help to the beginning student of argumentation to be able to identify these three different kinds of arguments. It will enable him or her to apply the evaluative criteria appropriate for each kind of argument.

ONE Inconsistency

Inconsistency is a very important notion for analyzing and evaluating argumentation in dialogues. Suppose that in the dialogue on tipping in chapter 1 Helen has argued for her thesis that tipping is a bad practice. But then suppose that later in the dialogue she brings forward an example, from her own experience, where she tipped a taxi driver who had gotten her to the airport on time. She was happy to give him a tip, and she admitted that in this particular case, giving him a tip was a good thing. Let's suppose that when Helen argued for her thesis that tipping is a bad practice, she meant this statement to be an absolute generalization. In other words, she was meaning to say that all cases of tipping fall under the heading of something that is a bad practice. But then later in the dialogue, when describing this example, she admitted that giving the tip was a good thing. Something being a good thing is the opposite of its being a bad thing. Therefore, it seems that in this dialogue, Helen's earlier statement was inconsistent with her later statement. The reason is that it is not logically possible for both statements to be true. Inconsistency can be defined as follows. Two statements are inconsistent if it's not logically possible for both of them to be true. By 'inconsistent' we mean logically inconsistent and not just practically or physically inconsistent. 'Bob is a sixty-nine-year-old man' may be practically or physically inconsistent with 'Bob can run a mile in under four minutes', but the two statements are logically consistent with each other. However, 'Bob is a sixty-nine-year-old man' is logically inconsistent with 'Bob is not a sixty-nine-year-old man'. In the dialogue, it seems to be a bad thing that Helen has committed herself to an inconsistency. So we have to ask: What is wrong with inconsistency when it occurs in argumentation?

Inconsistency is very common, especially in long and complex arguments where we tend to lose track of our previous arguments. Thus, in a way, inconsistency in argumentation is quite understandable. But the problem is that when you have an inconsistent pair of statements, it is not possible for them both to be true. Thus, in order to maintain truth, in such a case, an arguer has to give up the one statement or the other. Suppose, for example, that Bob, in the dialogue on tipping, says that Helen's two statements are inconsistent. In other words, suppose that Bob points out that Helen had earlier maintained that tipping is not a good practice, but then in her later example she had maintained that tipping is a good practice. Suppose that Bob said, "Look Helen, you can't have it both ways, either tipping is a good practice or it is not." What Helen has to do in such a case is to make a retraction. She could do this in various ways. She could say, for example, "I didn't really mean to say that all cases of tipping are bad. All I meant to say was that tipping is generally a bad practice, subject to exceptions." Or she could retract her later statement. She could say, "Well I didn't really mean to say in this example that my tipping the taxi driver was a good thing. I still maintained that all tipping is a bad practice, but in this case I just wanted to make the point that sometimes the tip can be deserved, and that the act of tipping can be good in certain respects, even though looking at it from an overall point of view, it is a bad practice." We can see here that Helen has retracted the inconsistency by clarifying what she was trying to say. Although inconsistency can in many cases be understood and can be resolved, in general it is something that has to be addressed in argumentation once it has been discovered. The reason, once again, is that when you have an inconsistent set of statements, not all of them can be true.

A very simple case of inconsistency, called a contradiction, occurs when one statement is the direct opposite of another. The following two statements, taken together, constitute a contradiction.

Mount Lemmon is in Arizona.

Mount Lemmon is not in Arizona.

In this case it is clear that the one statement is the direct opposite of the other. One is the negation of the other, indicated by the word 'not' appearing in the second statement. Because of this word, it is immediately evident that it is not possible for both statements to be true.

In other cases of inconsistency, one statement is not the negation of the other, yet it is clear that one asserts what the other denies. For example, consider the following set of statements, where 'all' is taken as an absolute universal generalization.

(a) All wolves are pack animals.

(b) Some wolves are pack animals.

(c) Some wolves are not pack animals.

(d) No wolves are pack animals.

(e) Not all wolves are pack animals.

(f) It is false that some wolves are not pack animals.

(g) All wolves are not pack animals.

It is clear enough that (a) is consistent with (b). Two statements are consistent if it is possible for both to be true. But is (a) consistent with (c)? No, it would seem not, for it is not logically possible for both statements to be true. If all wolves are pack animals, with no exceptions, the possibility that some are not is ruled out. (a) is the direct opposite of (d). What one asserts the other denies. Hence, (a) and (d) are inconsistent. On the other hand, (a) is consistent with (f). But (c) is not, for (c) is the direct opposite of (f). And clearly, (a) is inconsistent with (f), for it is not possible that both could be true. In contrast, (b) is consistent with (c), because it is possible that both are true. So we see that in many cases of inconsistency, there is no direct contradiction, but one can still determine that a pair of propositions is inconsistent by asking whether it is possible for both to be true.

In still other cases, we are confronted with a set of statements, often more than two, that are collectively inconsistent. In many of these cases, one cannot prove that they are inconsistent so easily, and more work is involved. One has to draw out the contradiction by analyzing the argumentation. For example in the tipping case above, we have to show that the statement that a thing is bad is inconsistent with the statement that it is good. We can easily draw out this assumption by observing that part of the meaning of the term 'bad' is that something is being condemned as 'not good'.

It is also common to have cases where there is no direct contradiction, but where a set of propositions is collectively inconsistent. Consider the following set of statements. Let's assume that the universal generalization in the first premise is absolute.

All police chiefs are honest.

John is a police chief.

Taking a bribe is dishonest.

John took a bribe.

If you consider all four statements together as a set, it is clear that not all of them can be true. They contain an inconsistency. Hence at least one is false. But there is no direct contradiction. There is no one statement that is the opposite of another one in the set. However, a contradiction can be derived from the set by a chain of argumentation. Consider the first pair of statements in the set. From them, the conclusion follows that John is honest, by the following argument.

PREMISE: All police chiefs are honest.

PREMISE: John is a police chief.

CONCLUSION: John is honest.

Next, consider the last two statements. Let's assume that the first of the pair is an absolute generalization. By expressing it in this way, as below, the following argument is produced.

PREMISE: All persons who took a bribe are dishonest.

PREMISE: John took a bribe.

CONCLUSION: John is dishonest.

The conclusion of the second argument is the opposite of the conclusion of the first one. The reason is that 'dishonest' means 'not honest'. Thus, it has been revealed that if you consider the whole set of four statements together, you can show by a chain of argumentation that they lead to a direct contradiction. If someone engaging in argumentation in a dialogue were to state all four of these propositions as part of his argument, and the other party in the dialogue showed that they are collectively inconsistent, then the party who stated them would have to resolve the inconsistency. The obvious way to do this would be for him to give up one of the propositions in the set.

To review the basic definition of inconsistency, a set of statements is said to be inconsistent if it is not logically possible for all of them to be true. Then we can say that a set of statements is consistent if it is logically possible that all of them could be true. Finally, let's note that propositions can be consistent with each other even if they do not appear to be related to each other in any way. For example, consider the following two statements.

Genetically modified foods cause increases in allergies.

Tipping is a bad practice.

In this case, the two statements are consistent, because it is possible for both to be true. The evidence for such a claim in this case is that the one statement is not relevant to the other. This implies that you can use one to prove the opposite of the other. Generally speaking, then, if one statement is not relevant to another one, the two must be consistent with each other. However, the subject of relevance will not be taken up until chapter 7.

All 'consistency' means is that it is possible for both statements to be true. It doesn't mean that either of the statements actually is true. But a finding of inconsistency in a set of statements means that one of them has to be false. The basic problem with an inconsistent set of assertions in argumentation is that it is not possible for all of them to be true. Hence the allegation that an arguer has put forward a set of assertions that contains an inconsistency is a powerful and important kind of criticism. If an arguer in a dialogue has committed herself to a set of statements that are inconsistent, and the other arguer in the dialogue points out the contradiction, then the first arguer must deal with that criticism right away. The usual way to deal with it is to retract one of the statements. Although inconsistency is often quite understandable and can be fairly common in argumentation, it is something that has to be dealt with once it has been pointed out. If someone's argument has been shown to be inconsistent, it does not necessarily mean it is entirely worthless and beyond repair. But it does mean that the argument is not acceptable as it stands. The arguer must deal with the criticism of inconsistency if her argumentation is to move forward successfully in the dialogue.

The finding of inconsistency is vitally important in legal argumentation. If a witness offers an account that contains an inconsistency, the cross-examining questioner in court can tear the story to shreds. Unless the witness can resolve the inconsistency, her credibility may be destroyed. The finding of inconsistency is also important in scientific argumentation where, for example, a theory may be shown on careful analysis to contain a hidden inconsistency. By finding and dealing with such inconsistencies, scientific discovery and theory formation is able to move forward.

EXERCISE 2.1

1. Determine which propositions are inconsistent with others, and which are not, among the following sets of propositions.

(a) Some peacocks are afraid of kangaroos.
(b) No peacocks are afraid of kangaroos.
(c) All peacocks are afraid of kangaroos.
(d) It is false that all peacocks are afraid of kangaroos.
(e) Some peacocks are not afraid of kangaroos.
(f) No kangaroos are afraid of peacocks.

(g) At least one peacock is not afraid of kangaroc
(h) It is false that at least one peacock is afraid of

2. Prove that the following set of statements is inco contradiction that can be derived from the argument

(a) All romantic idealists love poetry.
(b) All persons who love poetry are affectionate.
(c) All affectionate persons love pets.
(d) Sam is a romantic idealist.
(e) Sam is afraid of my pet snake.
(f) No person who is afraid of my pet snake loves pets.

TWO Three Kinds of Arguments

There are three kinds of arguments, and each of them differs from the others in virtue of having a different standard of strictness. In a deductively valid argument, if the premises are true, the conclusion must be true (by logical necessity). Thus, in a deductive inference, the link between the premises and the conclusion is strict. For example, consider the following argument, where the first premise is taken to be an absolute universal generalization with no exceptions.

PREMISE: All police chiefs are honest.

PREMISE: John is a police chief.

CONCLUSION: John is honest.

In this argument, there is no room for doubting that the conclusion is true, once the premises have been accepted as true. The reason stems from the word ‘all’ in the first premise of the inference. Presumably, ‘all’ means ‘all without exception’. If so, the statement in the first premise is an absolute universal generalization. Thus, the conclusion follows by logical necessity from the premises. If both the premises are true, then the conclusion has to be true.

Deductive validity can be defined in another way that offers an even more useful criterion to recognize it in an argument. To say that an argument is deductively valid means that it is logically impossible for all the premises to be true and the conclusion false. In other words, in a deductively valid argument, the claim that the premises are true and the conclusion false is inconsistent. For example, let’s consider three statements comparable to the argument above, with the first two the same as the premises, but with the third as the opposite of the conclusion.

FIRST STATEMENT: All police chiefs are honest.

SECOND STATEMENT: John is a police chief.

THIRD STATEMENT: John is not honest.

This set of three statements is collectively inconsistent. You cannot maintain all three at the same time without being inconsistent. This observation leads to the best test to identify deductive validity in an argument. If the premises, taken together, are inconsistent with the negation of the conclusion, the argument is deductively valid.

In an inductive argument, the link is not so strict. If the premises are true, the conclusion is probably true, but it could possibly be false. Determining whether a given argument is meant to be deductive or inductive, as used in a given case, can be quite difficult in some cases and requires consideration of several criteria and several kinds of evidence. One of the main criteria is the nature of the inferential link between the premises and the conclusion. It is this link that determines whether the argument is a successful deductive argument as opposed to being a successful inductive argument. To give the beginner an entry point into grasping the distinction between inductive and deductive as types of arguments, here we concentrate exclusively on the nature of this link. Inductive arguments are based on probability. An example is the following argument.

Most swans are white.

This bird is a swan.

Therefore, this bird is white.

In this argument, the first premise is an inductive generalization. It is not said to be true of all swans, but only of most of them. In this case, if the premises are accepted as true, then the conclusion is probably (but not necessarily) true. It could be that this bird is one of those black swans. What makes such an argument inductive rather than deductive is the link between the premises and the conclusion. But the fact that one premise is an inductive rather than a universal generalization is a good indicator that the argument is inductive. Such an inductive premise, in the sample argument above, limits the conclusiveness or strength of the argument. It cannot be used to show that the conclusion follows from the premises necessarily, but only inductively, as a matter of probability.

Inductive arguments are based on probability[1] and statistics. The support for an inductive argument is typically given by gathering empirical evidence. In the basic cases, the evidence takes the form of enumerating or counting objects or polling individuals. The outcomes are expressed in numbers that are processed, by the methods currently in use in statistics, to generate an inference evaluated as a probability. The following is a typical example of a numerical inductive argument.

Seventy percent of residents of Tutela Heights vote Conservative.

Ned is a resident of Tutela Heights.

Therefore (probably) Ned will vote Conservative.

In this argument, the conclusion has a certain degree of probability relative to the premises. A contrasting deductive argument would be the following case, where the warrant is absolute. Let's say, at any rate, for purposes of illustration, that the word 'all' in the first premise is taken to mean 'absolutely all, with no exceptions.'

All residents of Tutela Heights reside in Brant County.

Ned is a resident of Tutela Heights.

Therefore, Ned is a resident of Brant County.

In this deductively valid argument, it is impossible for both the premises to be true and the conclusion false. The absolute generalization in the first premise excludes any possible contrary instances. However, in the inductive argument above, room is left for the possibility of the premises being true and the conclusion false. It could be that Ned is one of those residents of Tutela Heights who does not vote Conservative.

Deductive argument is a simple 'yes' or 'no' affair: Either the argument is deductively valid or not. If not, it is called invalid. Using the inductive method of evaluation, an inference is evaluated as inductively stronger or weaker to the degree that the premises would, if true, support the conclusion as true. The measure of probability used in inductive evaluation

[1] It is hard to define the term 'probability' precisely because there is disagreement among experts on exactly how to define it. Some think it should be defined as statistical frequency of the occurrence of an event. Others think it should be defined in terms of degrees of rational belief. Still others think it should be defined by axioms of the probability calculus. It would be a mistake to get worried about such subtleties at this point. It is enough for us to be aware that probability is calculated by statisticians by attaching numbers to statements (fractions between zero and one) that are supposed to measure the likelihood that such statements are true or false and numbers that measure confidence in inferences based on them.

makes the strength of support a matter of degree. The argument link could be very strong, if the premises support the conclusion with a higher degree of probability. Or the argument link could be weak, if the premises support the conclusion with only a low probability, as in the argument "Twenty percent of residents of Tutela Heights vote Conservative; Ned is a resident of Tutela Heights; therefore (probably) Ned will vote Conservative." Or the degree of inductive support could be somewhere in between. In many cases, this degree of support can be measured exactly by the methods currently used in statistics. Both deductive and inductive arguments can be evaluated using exact methods of calculation.

The third type of argument is less precise and reliable than the other two, but is often more useful and even necessary, in many cases in the practical conduct of affairs of everyday life. This type of argument leads to a conclusion that is plausible, and that may be provisionally acceptable as a presumption. To say that it is plausible means that it seems to be true, on the given appearances. Of course, appearances can be misleading in some cases. Thus such an inference is inherently subject to retraction. It is defeasible, meaning that it may turn out to fail (default) if new evidence comes in. The conclusion is indicated as presumably true on a basis of plausibility, and therefore tentatively acceptable, given that the premises are true. Consider the following argument.

> Where there's smoke there's fire.
>
> There is smoke in Buttner Hall.
>
> Therefore there is fire in Buttner Hall.

Notice that, in this case, the premise 'Where there's smoke there's fire' is not taken as an absolute universal generalization. It does not mean that all places where smoke is seen are places where there is fire. It is better taken as a defeasible statement meaning that generally, but subject to exceptions, if you see smoke someplace, you can presume that there is fire in that place. Even though both premises of the argument above are true, it is possible that the conclusion is false. It is possible that there is a column of smoke rising from Buttner Hall, but there might be no fire there, just a smoldering mass of some substance that gives off a lot of smoke. And it is not practical to try to judge the strength of the argument by numerical data about fires, because this case is an individual one with many circumstantial factors that are relevant. But in such a case, on grounds of safety, it may be prudent to operate on a presumption. It may be the right conclusion to draw by presumptive inference that there is a fire in Buttner

Hall. This can be the right conclusion to act on even though I don't know the probabilities and even if can I see no direct evidence of fire. For practical purposes, drawing the conclusion that there is or may be fire there is the sensible option, provided I have no evidence indicating otherwise, for example, a news bulletin that the smoke is being caused by a smudge pot as part of the making of a movie. The smoke rising from Buttner Hall can be good enough evidence of fire to justify calling the fire department in the absence of contra-indicating evidence. But, as noted, presumptive reasoning is inherently provisional in nature and should be used with caution. It is applicable where a conclusion needs to be drawn, yet not enough is known about a situation to use a more exact or reliable method of drawing it. It is appropriate where, for practical reasons, under conditions of uncertainty and incomplete knowledge, a tentative conclusion needs to be drawn as a provisional basis to continue a line of reasoning or adopt a policy for action.

These three types of argumentation are relatively independent of each other. If an argument is deductively valid, the (conditional) probability that the conclusion is true, given that the premises are true, is 1.0 (the highest possible probability value a proposition can have). So you could say that the argument is inductively strong. But judging such an argument by inductive standards and methods would not be particularly useful. It is more useful to simply say that the argument is deductively valid. If an inference to a conclusion can be supported or refuted very effectively by inductive methods, then the need or usefulness of judging it as plausible or not as a presumptive inference falls away. In general, if an argument can be evaluated on a basis of probability, then evaluating it as plausible or implausible becomes less useful. Methods of plausible reasoning give way to inductive evidence, if it is available. Similarly, inductive evaluation gives way to deductive logic, if it can be usefully applied to a case.

EXERCISE 2.2

Identify the premises and the conclusion in each of the following inferences. Identify the generalization in the inference, and judge whether the inference is of the deductive, inductive, or presumptive type.

(a) All swans are birds. Beverly is a swan. Therefore, Beverly is a bird.

(b) Anyone who fails to reply to this memo will be presumed to be in agreement. Bob failed to reply to this memo. Therefore, Bob is in agreement.

(c) The typical working person cannot afford to fly on the Concorde. Frank is a typical working person. Therefore, Frank cannot afford to fly on the Concorde.

(d) Cinnabar always contains mercury. This object is cinnabar. Therefore, this object contains mercury.
(e) Advocates of a cause do not find it easy to compromise their group interests. Helen is the advocate of a cause. Helen does not find it easy to compromise her group interests.
(f) Seventy percent of the birds in this zoo fly. Tweety is a bird in this zoo. Therefore, Tweety flies.
(g) Wayne normally takes his Jeep when he leaves home. Wayne's Jeep is not in the driveway. Therefore, Wayne is not home.
(h) Conservatives are against raising taxes. Bob is a Conservative. Therefore, Bob is against raising taxes.
(i) If Minnesota is in Canada, then it is north of the Canadian border. Minnesota is in Canada. Therefore, it is north of the Canadian border.
(j) Nancy is an honest person. Whatever an honest person says should be taken as true. Nancy said that Peter does not like Denise. Therefore, Peter does not like Denise.

THREE Syllogisms

One very common form of deductive argument that it is important to know about is called the syllogism. Aristotle constructed a system of evaluating syllogistic arguments as deductively valid or invalid, and this system was the backbone of logic in schools and universities for over two thousand years. A syllogism is a particular type of argument that always has two premises and a single conclusion, and all three statements are what are called categorical propositions. A categorical proposition is prefaced by the term 'all' or the term 'some'. The following argument is a syllogism.

All stunt pilots are daredevils.

Some stunt pilots are accountants.

Therefore, some accountants are daredevils.

A categorical proposition is made up of four components, the quantifier, the subject term, the copula, and the predicate term. A quantifier is of one of two types: the universal quantifier 'all' or the particular (existential) quantifier 'some'. A term is a word that stands for a class of individuals, called the 'extension' of that class. For example, the term 'stunt pilots' stands for the class of stunt pilots. A copula is a form of the verb 'is' or 'are' that joins one term to another. The subject term stands for a class said to belong, or not to belong, to another class, denoted by the predicate term. In the example above, ‘Some accountants are daredevils’ is a categorical proposition, because it can be paraphrased as ‘Some accountants are individuals who are daredevils’. Every syllogism must be made up of exactly three propositions, and each of these propositions must be a categorical proposition.

The negative expression ‘no’ is also allowed as a quantifier. So universal negative generalizations, such as ‘No stunt pilots are cowardly’, are categorical propositions. To express negative existential statements, the particle ‘not’ is attached to the copula. For example, the sentence ‘Some stunt pilots do not have life insurance’ is a categorical proposition of the negative existential type. This admission of negative as well as positive versions of the categorical propositions gives the theory of syllogistic inference a good generality. A syllogism, as a particular type of argument, however, is narrowly defined. There must be exactly three terms in it, and each term must occur exactly twice. One, the middle term, must occur once in each premise. The others, the end terms, must occur once in one of the premises only, and once in the conclusion. So the following inference is a syllogism, because it meets all of the above requirements.

All ducks are birds that have webbed feet.

All mallards are ducks.

Therefore, all mallards are birds that have webbed feet.

There are only four types of propositions recognized as categorical propositions in syllogistic reasoning. Where *F* and *G* are variables for terms, these four types are represented below.

A: All *F* are *G*: Universal Affirmative

I: Some *F* are *G*: Particular Affirmative

E: No *F* are *G*: Universal Negative

O: Some *F* are not *G*: Particular Negative

A universal proposition, such as ‘All men are mortal’ makes an assertion about each and every individual referred to by the subject term (in this case ‘men’). A particular proposition asserts literally that at least one thing is both an *F* and a *G*. Unlike conversational English, where saying ‘Some *F* are *G*’ suggests that there is more than one thing that is both an *F* and a *G*, in syllogistic reasoning all that is required to make the particular affirmative proposition true is one thing that has both properties *F* and *G*. The A proposition is the contradictory opposite of the O, and the I proposition is the contradictory opposite of the E.

Now that we understand A, I, E, and O propositions, an easy method of evaluating syllogistic inferences by means of diagrams, called Venn diagrams, can be set out. Since the word 'all' in syllogistic reasoning is taken to mean 'all without exception' (a strict generalization), a syllogism is structurally correct only when it is deductively valid. According to the definition of deductive validity, an inference is deductively valid if and only if it is logically impossible for the premises to be true and the conclusion false. In other words, to say that a syllogism is deductively valid is to say that if the premises are true, then the conclusion must be true too. Deductive inference, as noted above, is a kind of necessary inference, meaning that if the premises are true, no option is left but that the conclusion must be true as well. The mallards example is a valid syllogism because the premises are inconsistent with the opposite of the conclusion, 'Some mallards are birds that do not have webbed feet'.

Let's test the mallards example above for validity using a Venn diagram. We let *D* stand for ducks, *B* for birds with webbed feet, and *M* for mallards. Now we construct a Venn diagram with three intersecting circles, where each circle represents one term.

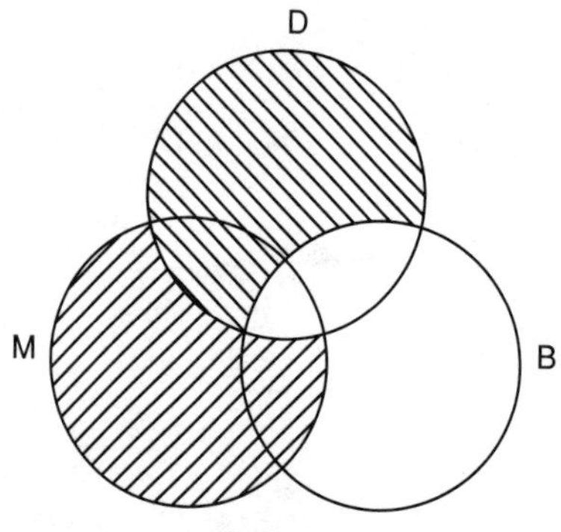

By convention, the middle term, the one occurring in both premises, is represented by the middle circle. Then we put each premise on the diagram, using shading to represent an empty class. Both premises have been marked on the diagram, using shading. Then we ask whether the conclusion also has to be represented on the diagram. It does, so we conclude that the argument is valid.

Next, let's test the stunt pilots argument above for validity.

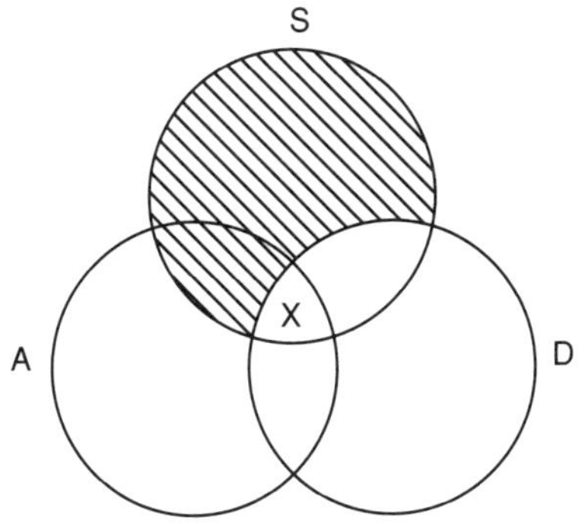

As above, both premises have been represented on the diagram. Then we have to ask whether the conclusion is also true, according to the diagram. We see that it is, so we conclude that the argument is valid.

Now let's test another syllogism for validity.

All neurotics exhibit deviant behavior.

All obsessive-compulsives exhibit deviant behavior.

Therefore, all neurotics are obsessive-compulsives.

Let's put both premises of this argument on the following Venn diagram.

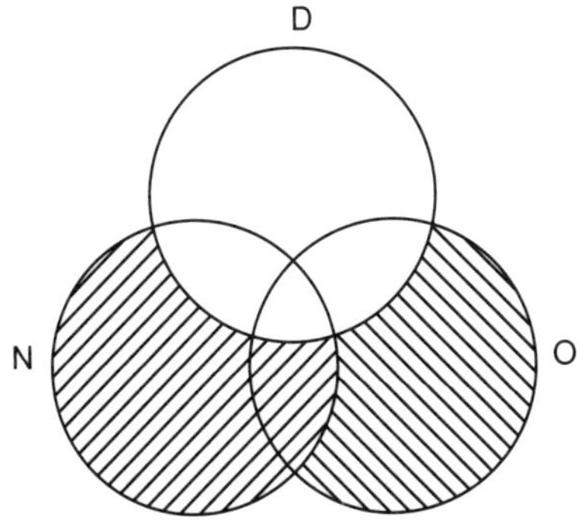

By examining the diagram, it can be seen that even though both premises are true, it is possible that the conclusion is false. Thus, this argument is invalid.

Note, however, that even though an argument is deductively valid, it is possible for one or more of the premises to be false. For example, consider the following argument.

All crocodiles are friendly.

All friendly animals make good pets.

Therefore all crocodiles make good pets.

This argument is deductively valid. If both premises are true, the conclusion has to be true too. It would be inconsistent to assert the following three statements.

All crocodiles are friendly.

All friendly animals make good pets.

Not all crocodiles make good pets.

Even though the argument is deductively valid, as shown by the inconsistency of the three statements above, the first premise is false. The important point illustrated here is that just because an argument is valid, it doesn't mean that the premises are true.

As can be illustrated by another syllogism, it is even possible to have a valid argument in which not only all the premises are false, but the conclusion is false too. Consider the following argument.

All crocodiles have six legs.

All animals with six legs make friendly pets.

All crocodiles make friendly pets.

Even though this argument is deductively valid, both premises and the conclusion are false statements.

There are three general lessons that can be drawn. One is that a valid argument is not necessarily one that is a good argument in every respect. It may have false premises or even a false conclusion. Another lesson is that validity of an argument has to do with the link between the premises and the conclusion. A third lesson is that there are two distinct ways to attack a deductive argument. One is to show that the argument is not valid. This way is to attack the link between the premises and the conclusion, arguing that the conclusion does not follow from the premises. The other way is to attack one or more of the premises individually, arguing that it is not true. In the example above, the first premise can be attacked as a generalization that does not hold.

EXERCISE 2.3

Use Venn diagrams to determine whether the following syllogistic arguments are valid or invalid.

(a) All chameleons are lizards. All lizards are cold-blooded animals. Therefore, all chameleons are cold-blooded animals.

(b) All ducks are birds. No birds like chocolate sauce. Therefore, no ducks like chocolate sauce.

(c) All manufactured foods have a prolonged shelf life. Some foods that have a prolonged shelf life are made from unhealthy ingredients. Therefore, some manufactured foods are made from unhealthy ingredients.

(d) Some budgies are birds that exhibit aggressive behaviors. Some birds that exhibit aggressive behaviors are dangerous to humans. Therefore, some budgies are dangerous to humans.

(e) Some mining companies are organizations that are concerned about the environment. Some organizations that are concerned about the environment approve of Greenpeace. Therefore, some mining companies are organizations that approve of Greenpeace.

FOUR Complex Propositions

The syllogism is one type of argument that can be proved to be deductively valid or invalid in a given case by specifying its form. There are also many other common forms of argumentation that display a deductively valid form that is easily recognizable. These forms of argument are built up of complex propositions of certain kinds. Some propositions are complex, in the sense that they are formed from simple propositions by certain logical operations. One of these operations we have already encountered above is negation. 'Snow is not white' is formed from the simple proposition 'Snow is white' by negation. If a proposition is true, its negation is false. And if a proposition is false, its negation is true. So the operation of negating a proposition gives the resulting (negated) proposition the opposite truth value. Another logical operation is that of conjunction, which takes two propositions and asserts that both are true. For example, the conjunctive proposition 'The book is on the table and the pencil is on the desk' takes the two component (simple) propositions, and forms their conjunction, using the word 'and'. A conjunctive proposition can also include a negated proposition, as in the sentence 'The book is on the table and the pen is not on the desk'. Another kind of logically complex proposition is formed by the disjunction of propositions. For example, the disjunctive proposition 'The book is on the table or the pencil is on the desk' takes two component (simple) propositions and forms their disjunction, using the word 'or'. Disjunctive propositions can also include negated propositions, as in the sentence 'The book is on the table or the pen is not on the desk'. A conjunctive proposition is only true if both (or all) the propositions contained in it are true. But a disjunctive proposition is true if either of the contained propositions is true. So generally speaking, conjunctive propositions are harder to prove than disjunctive sentences, because they claim that more is true.

Another kind of complex proposition that is very important in understanding logical reasoning is the conditional type of proposition. A conditional proposition (statement) is a proposition of the form 'If *A*, then *B*' where *A* and *B* are component propositions in the conditional proposition. The component that directly follows the 'if' (the *A*, in this case) is called the antecedent (hypothesis). The other proposition (the *B*, in this case) is called the consequent. An example is the statement:

If Bob is in Miami, then Bob is in Florida.

In this example, 'Bob is in Miami' is the antecedent, and 'Bob is in Florida' is the consequent. Conditional propositions, like conjunctive and disjunctive propositions, can include negated propositions. For example, the conditional proposition 'If Bob is in Miami, Bob is not in Texas' contains a negated proposition as its consequent.

In fact, conjunctive, disjunctive, negated, and conditional propositions can all be combined, as in the following proposition: If Bob is in Miami or Bob is in Tampa, then Bob is not in Texas and Bob is not in Vermont. In stating this complex conditional, we have written everything out explicitly, but normally the sentence would be expressed in a more compact form using the pronoun 'he': If Bob is in Miami or Tampa, then he is not in Texas and not in Vermont. In this case, the whole sentence has the form of a conditional proposition, but the antecedent part of the conditional is a disjunctive proposition, and the consequent part of the conditional is a conjunction.

The most important thing about conditionals is that the antecedent proposition is not (necessarily) being claimed (asserted) to be true. Generally, it is only an assumption or hypothesis. What is being claimed is that if the antecedent proposition is true, then the consequent proposition is true as well. Such a claim is hypothetical in nature. For example, if I say, 'If Bob is a gangster, then he should be prosecuted', I am not (necessarily) saying that Bob is a gangster. I am only claiming that if he is a gangster, then he should be prosecuted. The whole conditional proposition can be true, even if the antecedent proposition is false. Even if, in fact, it's not true that Bob is a gangster, it could still be true that if he is a gangster, then he should be prosecuted.

What is important to note is that there is a difference between assumptions and assertions. If I assume that a proposition is true, such an assumption is only a hypothesis, and if anyone questions it, I don't have to prove it. But if I assert that a proposition is true, I have made a claim. So if anyone questions this claim or asks me to prove it, then either I have to give reasons (evidence) that support it, or I have to give up my claim that it is true. So assumptions are 'free', whereas assertions have a 'cost' attached. You either have to prove (justify) them or give them up (as assertions). In this respect, assumptions are more like questions than assertions.

EXERCISE 2.4

Identify the simple propositions in the following complex propositions and show how the complex propositions are made up from the simple ones, identifying each logical operation used.

(a) If antibiotic use is not restrained, tuberculosis and polio will become impossible to control.
(b) If eating bran cereal every day reduces the chances of colon cancer, then not eating bran cereal every day is a way of decreasing longevity.
(c) Either Bob is a gangster or Bob is working for the FBI and is engaged in undercover work.
(d) Madagascar is south of the equator.
(e) Courage is a form of addiction to combative action, and it needs to be restrained, or it may threaten those who fear its dangers.
(f) If this object is metal, then it will be attracted by a magnetic coil, if one is placed in its vicinity.
(g) Some coins are made of silver and some are made of gold.
(h) Either Ted is not coming to the party, or Linda is staying home and waiting for a call from Bob.

FIVE Some Other Common Forms of Deductive Argument

In addition to syllogisms, there are certain other forms of argument that are very common and that can be evaluated as deductively valid. One commonly used form of argument has the following structure, where the capital letters *A*, *B*, and so forth, stand for statements.

MODUS PONENS

PREMISE: If A, then B

PREMISE: A

CONCLUSION: B

This structure of inference is called *modus ponens* (MP). It is a common form of valid argument. An example is the following argument.

> If Lugano is in Switzerland, then Lugano is in Europe.
>
> Lugano is in Switzerland.
>
> Therefore, Lugano is in Europe.

If the premises of this argument are both true, the conclusion must (by logical necessity) be true. To assume that both premises are true while the conclusion is false is a logical inconsistency. Thus, the argument is deductively valid. We may not even know whether both the premises are true. But we do know that if they are true, then the conclusion must be true as well. Thus the argument is valid.

Another example of an interesting form of argument is the following case.

PREMISE: If this iron bar is magnetized, it attracts nearby iron filings.

PREMISE: This bar does not attract nearby iron filings.

CONCLUSION: This bar is not magnetized.

If both premises are true, it follows necessarily that the conclusion is true. Hence the argument is valid. This form of argument is called *modus tollens* (MT).

MODUS TOLLENS

PREMISE: If A, then B.

Not-B.

CONCLUSION: Not-A.

This form of argument is valid, meaning that if the premises are accepted as true, then the conclusion has to be true as well. MP and MT are commonly used forms of argument that are deductively valid, meaning that if the premises are true (or reasonably acceptable), then the conclusion has to be true (or reasonably acceptable) as well. Using these forms of inference is a good way to be sure your reasoning meets standards of structural correctness appropriate for logical reasoning.

Another commonly used form of reasoning is the hypothetical syllogism (HS), of the following form, where two conditionals are combined.

HYPOTHETICAL SYLLOGISM

If *A*, then *B*.

If *B*, then *C*.

Therefore, if *A*, then *C*.

This kind of inference is frequently used in planning, while trying to predict possible future events, as in the following example.

PREMISE: If England increases military spending, then Germany will put an embargo on imported beef.

PREMISE: If Germany puts an embargo on imported beef, France will build more nuclear reactors near the German border

CONCLUSION: If England increases military spending, France will build more nuclear reactors near the German border.

If both premises are true, it follows that the conclusion is true as well. Here is an example from mathematical reasoning.

PREMISE: If the first triangle is congruent with the second triangle, then the second triangle is isosceles.

PREMISE: If the second triangle is isosceles, then two of its angles must be equal.

CONCLUSION: If the first triangle is congruent with the second triangle, then two of the angles of the second triangle must be equal.

Mathematical reasoning generally tends to be deductive in nature, because it is based on generalizations that are absolutely universal and on inferences that are strict.

When we come to evaluating inferences that have the forms (MP), (MT), and (HS), it is important to remember that there are two separate questions to be asked: (1) are the premises true, and (2) does the conclusion follow from the premises, by some standard of what constitutes a correct inference? If an inference has one of the forms (MP), (MT), or (HS), then it is deductively valid. Premises are often claimed to be true or to be supported as true by evidence, but not in all cases of arguments. In some arguments, the premises are merely assumed to be true but are not claimed to be true. For example, consider the following argument.

PREMISE: Bob is the murderer.

CONCLUSION: Bob would have to have been at the crime scene during the time the crime was committed.

This argument could be a reasonable one, even though no claim may be made that the premise is true. The only claim is that the conclusion is true if the premise is true (a hypothetical claim). So the premise of an argument is not necessarily a claim or assertion. A premise can also be an assumption. The reasonableness of the step from the premise(s) to the conclusion of an inference is independent of the reasonableness of the premise(s), as statements that are backed up by supporting evidence. Generally, then, in evaluating inferences, there are two separate factors to be considered: (1) whether or not the premises are true propositions, and (2) whether or not the conclusion follows from the premises. If an inference has the form (MP), (MT), or (HS), then the conclusion does follow from the premises according to the standard of correctness of inference appropriate for the given case. But that, of course, does not mean that the premises of the inference are true. For that is always a separate question.

EXERCISE 2.5

1. Determine whether the following inferences have the form of (MP) or (MT) or do not have either form of argument.

(a) If Socrates is a man, then Socrates is not female. Socrates is a man. Therefore, Socrates is not female.

(b) If Bob is in Germany, then Bob is not in Italy. Bob is in Germany. Therefore, Bob is not in Italy.

(c) If Bob is in Germany, then Bob is not in Italy. Bob is not in Italy. Therefore, Bob is in Germany.

(d) If Bob is in Germany, then Bob is not in Italy. Bob is in Italy. Therefore, Bob is not in Germany.

(e) If Boris is a tiger, then Boris is an animal. Boris is not an animal. Therefore, Boris is not a tiger.

2. Evaluate the following inferences by judging (1) whether the premises are true and (2) whether the inference is deductively valid.

(a) If the population continues to grow, there will be greater stress on the environment. If there will be greater stress on the environment, natural disasters will occur. So if the population continues to grow, natural disasters will occur.
(b) If equality of opportunity is to be achieved, then those people previously disadvantaged should now be given special opportunities. If people previously disadvantaged should now be given special opportunities, then some people will receive preferential treatment. Therefore, if equality of opportunity is to be achieved, some people will receive preferential treatment.
(c) If human actions are predictable, the universe is deterministic. If the universe is deterministic, free choice is an illusion. Therefore, if human actions are predictable, free choice is an illusion.
(d) If Bob cheated on his exam, then his honesty should be questioned. If Bob's honesty should be questioned, then charges should be laid against Bob. Therefore, charges should be laid against Bob.

SIX Probability and Inductive Argument

Deductive argumentation is based on propositions that are true or false. Inductive argumentation adds another dimension by introducing the idea that a proposition can be probably true or probably false. The science of the measurement of probability is statistics. Statistical probability is the measure of how probable or improbable a proposition may be calculated to be, on a scale of fractions between zero and one. In making estimates of the probability of a proposition being true (or false), statisticians also usually give a numerical measure of the probability of error, the proportion of times an estimate might turn out to be wrong. Critical argumentation is concerned not so much with the formulas and methods statisticians use to calculate numerical probabilities as with the application of these methods to drawing probable inferences used in everyday reasoning that influence our thinking and deciding about how to proceed in everyday affairs.

As noted in chapter 1, statistical generalizations have an exact number representing their probability value, but many inductive generalizations have no exact number attached. Instead, a proposition may be evaluated, in a less precise fashion, as having a 'high' or 'low probability'. Or equivalently, it may be said that an event is likely to occur, is unlikely to occur, is very likely to occur, and so forth. To say that a proposition has a high (low) probability is to say that a high (low) number, representing its statistical value, can be attached to it, even if that number has not yet been calculated.

Probability is a property not only of individual propositions, but also of arguments. An argument is inductively strong where it is improbable that the premises are true and the conclusion is false. 'Improbable' means that the probability is low (but it is not specified, in general, exactly how low). It is assumed, as well, that the argument is not deductively valid. Otherwise, deductively valid arguments would simply be a special case of inductively strong arguments where the probability that the premises are true and the conclusion is false would equal zero.

The following two arguments illustrate the difference between deductive and inductive argumentation.

PREMISE: All students who graduated from Godfrey College after 1995 took a course on critical thinking.

PREMISE: Bob was a student who graduated from Godfrey College after 1995.

CONCLUSION: Bob took a course on critical thinking.

This argument is deductively valid, provided, of course, that the first premise is taken as an absolute universal generalization. Now consider another argument.

PREMISE: Most students who graduated from Bohemond College after 1995 took a course on critical thinking.

PREMISE: Elaine was a student who graduated from Bohemond College after 1995.

CONCLUSION: Elaine took a course on critical thinking.

The second argument is different from the first in that the word 'most' is used instead of 'all', indicating a probabilistic (inductive) generalization, as opposed to a universal generalization. The second argument is inductively strong in the sense that if both premises are true, then it is probable that the conclusion is true. Or in other words, it is improbable that both premises are true and the conclusion false. Thus, inductive arguments are based on probability, not logical necessity. With an inductively strong argument, it is logically possible that all the premises are true and the conclusion false. It's just that it is not probable.

Whether one should take a particular inference[2] used in a given case of argumentation as inductive or deductive is sometimes difficult to judge, and one has to pay careful attention to the language used. But the criteria for success, and hence the internal structure of each of the two types of argument, is inherently different. This difference of structure is certainly one important indicator in helping us to identify both kinds of arguments. The structure of the argument is the inferential link that joins the premises to the conclusion, and as noted above, there can be two kinds of link. A deductive argument is meant to be strict or tight, implying logical necessity in the way the conclusion is supposed to be drawn from the premises. In contrast, an inductive argument, being based on probability rather than necessity, is not meant to be absolute or strict in the same way. An argument could be put forward as inductive, and even if it is very strong by that standard, it remains possible that the premises could turn out to be true and the conclusion false (even if that is improbable). So there is a clear structural difference between the two types of argumentation.

In many cases, the best way to distinguish between instances of the two types of inference is to look at the type of generalization each is based on. If an absolute generalization, such as 'all' or 'every', is used, then the inference is deductive in nature. If a statistical term giving a number representing a probability value is given, or if a term such as 'most', 'many', or 'very few' is given, then the inference is inductive in nature.

There is a common misconception that deductive argumentation is from the general to the specific, while inductive reasoning always goes from the specific to the general. Many inductive inferences, it is true, go from specific instances to a generalization, as in the following example.

PREMISE 1: Swan one is white.

PREMISE 2: Swan two is white.

PREMISE 3: Swan three is white.

PREMISE 4: These three swans are representative of the population of swans in this area.

CONCLUSION: It is probable that the population of swans in this area is white.

---

[2] An inference, in the technical meaning of the term, is the reasoning process within the argument. In a looser sense used here, the term 'inference' may be used interchangeably with the term 'argument'.

This argument represents a very common type of inductive reasoning from specific instances to a wider population of the sort that is called a sampling inference. The sampling inference is in fact so commonly used in and so typical of inductive reasoning that it is easy to presume that all inductive arguments are from specific premises to a generalization as the conclusion. But the example listed above about Bohemond College shows that, in other instances, an inductive argument can go from a general premise to a specific instance as the conclusion.

We have seen many examples above of deductive arguments that go from premises that are generalizations to a conclusion that is specific or from premises that are generalizations to a conclusion that is a generalization as well. Yet it is also possible to have cases of deductively valid arguments that have specific instances as premise and have a general statement as the conclusion.

PREMISE: This fox ran over that hill.

CONCLUSION: It is possible for foxes to run over hills.

This inference is deductively valid. It would be inconsistent for the premise to be true and the conclusion false. Yet the premise cites a specific instance, while the conclusion is about foxes and hills generally. Contrary to what one might expect then, not all deductive inferences go from the general to the specific. Some go from general premises to general conclusions, and some from particular premises to particular conclusions. Still others go from specific instances as premises to a general conclusion.

EXERCISE 2.6

Determine which of the following arguments are deductive in structure and which are inductive in structure.

(a) All super-heroes defeat nasty villains. Batman is a super-hero. Therefore, Batman defeats nasty villains.
(b) Most super-heroes have a faithful sidekick. Batman is a super-hero. Therefore, Batman has a faithful sidekick.
(c) Nearly all super-heroes have a fatal weakness. Superman is a super-hero. Therefore, Superman has a fatal weakness.
(d) Seventy-six percent of Zorro fans are under twelve years old. Ricardo is a Zorro fan. Therefore, Ricardo is under twelve years old.
(e) Every villain meets his match by encountering a good guy. When a villain meets his match by encountering a good guy, in most cases

that good guy is a super-hero. Brutus is a villain. Therefore, when Brutus meets his match by encountering a good guy, that good guy will be a super-hero.

(f) This parrot is yellow. This parrot is green. Therefore, some parrots are different in color than others.

(g) This parrot is yellow. That parrot is yellow. Therefore some parrots are yellow.

(h) This parrot is green. That parrot is green. This third parrot is also green. The color of these three parrots is representative of the color of parrots here. Therefore, it is likely that parrots here are green.

(i) Ten balls have been removed from this urn, and all of them are white. The color of the balls removed is representative of the color of the balls in the urn. Therefore, all of the balls in the urn are white.

SEVEN Plausible Argumentation

Plausible argumentation can best be explained by citing an ancient example. According to Plato,[3] this example came from Corax and Tisias, two Sophists (ancient Greek teachers of argumentation skills) who lived around the middle of the fifth century B.C.[4] The example is a legal case in which one man accused the other of assault. There had been a fight between two men, and the issue was who started it. One man was quite a bit smaller and weaker than the other. The smaller man's argument to the jury could be put in the form of a question. He asked whether it was plausible that he, the smaller and weaker man, would assault this visibly bigger and more powerful man? The argument could be spelled out as a set of premises and conclusion as follows.

PREMISE 1: Normally, a smaller and weaker man would not attack a larger and stronger man.

PREMISE 2: I am the smaller and weaker man.

PREMISE 3: The other man is the larger and stronger man.

CONCLUSION: It is implausible that I would attack him.

[3] *Phaedrus* 272d-273c. For example, at the present state of technology, the statement 'Henry is in Boise, Idaho, at a given time' is practically inconsistent with 'Henry is in Athens, Greece, five minutes after that time'. But the two statements are not logically inconsistent.

[4] Aristotle attributed the example to Corax (*Rhetoric* 1402a17–1402a28).

This argument could influence the jury's thinking on the case. It would appear to them unlikely that the smaller man would attack the larger. It was possible, of course, that he did. The first premise contains the qualifier 'normally', and thus it is subject to exceptions. But there were no witnesses. It was one man's word against the other. Under these conditions of lack of first-hand knowledge of what really happened, the plausibility of the argument above shifted the burden of proof to the other side in the trial, giving a reason that the smaller man was not the one who started the fight. The argument works because the jury can mentally put themselves in the place of the smaller man in the given situation. Each would realize that if he were the smaller man, he would not start such a one-sided fight.

The curious thing about this example is that the larger man used a matching plausible argument to rebut it.[5] He argued that since it was so obvious that he was the bigger and stronger man, it was apparent that if he were to attack this smaller and weaker man, he would realize how bad it would look, especially if the case went to court. Now, knowing this fact, is it plausible that he would attack the smaller man? The question raises an argument similar to the previous one.

PREMISE 1: Normally, a larger and stronger man would not attack a smaller and weaker man, especially if he were aware that the case might go to court.

PREMISE 2: I am the larger and stronger man.

PREMISE 3: The other man is the smaller and weaker man.

PREMISE 4: I was aware that the case might go to court.

CONCLUSION: It is implausible that I would attack him.

This argument matches the plausible argument of the weaker man, above. Thus the one plausible argument functions as a rebuttal of the other. This argument works pretty much the same way. The jury would find it plausible because they can mentally put themselves individually into the situation of the arguer. A person on the jury would be aware that the larger man would be putting himself in a bad position by assaulting the smaller man, and so they can easily see why the larger man would be reluctant to do so. By using this plausible counter-argument, the stronger man was able to cancel out the shift in the burden of proof that made him appear to be guilty.

[5] Aristotle, *Rhetoric* 1402a 11.

Plausibility is different from probability. Probability is determined by collecting data on the statistical chances of what happened, and then using that data to judge how likely a statement is to be true. Plausibility is a matter of whether a statement appears to be true in a normal type of situation that is familiar both to the participants and the onlookers. In the example of the smaller man's argument above, the onlookers can be expected to see that if he were to start such a fight, he would realize that the consequence would be a humiliating defeat. Judging by appearances and by what would normally happen in a situation the onlookers are familiar with, they conclude it is implausible that the smaller man would start the fight. Of course, this conclusion is based on other things being equal. Suppose it was shown by evidence in the trail that the smaller man was a skilled boxer and was generally aggressive. And suppose that further evidence was introduced showing that the larger man was clumsy and was not an aggressive person. These additional facts would mean that the conclusion drawn in the case might be quite different.

Another classic example of reasoning based on plausibility is the case of the snake and the rope.[6] A man sees a coil of rope in a dimly lit room. It looks like a snake, and not wanting to get bitten, he acts on the plausible assumption that it is a snake by jumping over it. When he turns back, however, he sees it did not move. He now reasons that it is not very plausible that it is a snake and that it is plausible that it is a rope. But, then again, he thinks, snakes are sometime motionless. So he carries out a test. He prods the object with a stick. It still fails to move, and he concludes that the object is a rope. In this case, initial appearances suggested that the object might be a snake or a rope. The man could not be sure. But since there was a danger of snakebite, he acted on the plausible assumption that it was a snake. He took care to jump over it. But then new information entered the case. He saw that the object failed to move when he jumped over it. This evidence indicated that it was probably not a snake. To get even more evidence, he carried out a test by prodding the object. The test confirmed the hypothesis that the object was a rope and not a snake.

Still another example shows how a statement that is implausible might turn out to be true. John Locke, an eighteenth-century philosopher, presented the example of the Dutch ambassador who was entertaining the king of Siam to illustrate plausibility.[7] The ambassador told the king

[6] This example, attributed to the Greek philosopher Carneades, can be found in a book by the skeptical philosopher Sextus Empiricus, *Against the Logicians*, 188.

[7] John Locke, *An Essay on Human Understanding*, 9th ed. (London: A. Churchill, 1726), pp. 275–76.

that water in the Netherlands would sometimes, in cold weather, be so hard that men could walk on it. He said that this water would even be so firm that an elephant could walk on the surface. The king found this story so strange that he concluded the ambassador had to be lying. The story makes the point that plausibility refers to an inference drawn on the basis of normal, commonplace expectations based on conditions that a person is familiar with. In the tropics, people were not familiar with freezing conditions, and hence the story of the freezing canal did not fit in with the normal expectations they had in their environment. They just found the ambassador's statements implausible and unconvincing.

Still another example of plausibility is a statement accepted on the basis of an appeal to expert opinion. If an expert asserts a statement as true, that is a plausible reason for thinking that the statement is true. It could turn out that this statement is not true. The expert could be lying or could just be wrong. But still, other things being equal, if a person is not an expert himself and lacks much knowledge about the subject in question, it could be wise to accept the opinion of an expert as plausible. It could be a plausible assumption to act on, as long as one is open to new evidence that might come in.

Inductive arguments are based on probability, in the statistical meaning of this term. Plausible arguments are based on presumption. A presumption is a qualified, tentative assumption of a proposition as true that can be justified on a practical basis, provided there is no sufficient evidence to show that the proposition is false. In computer science, this way of drawing an inference is called 'defeasibility'. Plausible inference is based on a generalization or a conditional premise that is of the defeasible type, where there are qualifications that need to be made and where it is not known whether these qualifications apply to the given case or not. Until such knowledge comes in, a tentative conclusion can be inferred by defeat. The classic case used in computer science to illustrate default is the Tweety example.

THE TWEETY EXAMPLE

Birds fly.

Tweety is a bird.

Therefore, Tweety flies.

The first premise in this argument is not a generalization that is meant to apply to all birds, without exception. The word 'generally' indicates that the first premise is not an (absolutely) universal generalization and makes room for exceptional cases of birds that do not fly. Nor is it a statistical or probabilistic generalization. It stands as a presumption subject to defeat. Hence the type of argument link in the Tweety case is presumptive. Suppose Tweety is a penguin. We know that no penguins fly. Thus we have a counter-example to the generalization in the first premise. We know that in this instance, Tweety does not fly. Thus, the argument in the Tweety example defaults. Of course, the statement 'Birds fly' allows for Tweety to be one of those exceptional cases. Tweety could be an ostrich or a penguin – a bird that does not fly. Before we knew that, the argument held. But once that new information came in, the Tweety argument defaulted.

A plausible argument is used to draw a provisional conclusion, based on an expectation of what would be normal in a familiar or known type of situation. The conclusion can be assumed provisionally as a guide to action, even where some of the particulars are not yet known in the form of hard evidence. Plausible argumentation in science is typical of the initial discovery stage of an investigation where a hypothesis is formed, even though it has not yet been verified by collecting enough data. At a later stage, once more information is in, testing and further verification of the initial hypothesis may lead to a point where it can be evaluated as probably true or probably false by inductive reasoning. Or still later, no reservations may need to be expressed, once a precise theory has been constructed and deductive arguments can be used to prove it. Plausible reasoning can be useful as a way to move forward provisionally and narrow down the number of hypotheses that need to be experimentally tested. Plausible reasoning is also very common in law. For example, the argument 'It looks like an affidavit, therefore it is an affidavit', could carry weight as legal evidence put forward in a trial.[8] Thus, a plausible inference is drawn for legal purposes even though the court might later reverse it, for example, if it can be proved that the notary's signature on the document was forged. How this works is that an inference is tentatively accepted as plausible based on what appears to be the case and as providing evidence to go ahead with, even if later it might be defeated by new evidence.

Both inductive and plausible arguments are non-absolute in nature. Both allow for contrary instances, and both are therefore subject to revision, should new information come into a case. The basic difference between them is that inductive reasoning is based on gathering positive

[8] An affidavit is a written statement, confirmed by oath, used as judicial evidence.

evidence that can (in the clearest cases) be counted or processed in some numerical way by statistical methods. Plausible argumentation is more practical in nature and is based on presumptions about the way things normally go, the way things normally appear, or practices that expedite ways of working together to perform smooth and efficient collaborative actions. Plausible argumentation is inherently negative in nature. It works by tentatively excluding certain conditions that are not known to obtain, in the given case. It is most useful to use plausible argumentation in cases where each individual situation is unique and unknown, even on a basis of probability. Because the resemblance of one case to another is not exact, plausible arguments are not (nonarbitrarily) subject to precise quantification. In contrast, deductive argumentation is absolute and precise. And inductive argumentation is positive and more precise than presumptive. Hence logic, in the past, has heavily emphasized deductive and inductive argumentation and tended to ignore plausible argumentation as too vague and unreliable. However, plausible argumentation is probably (or plausibly) the most common type of reasoning used in everyday deliberation, as well as in legal arguments, and it is vitally important for logic to evaluate it.

Although plausible argumentation is necessary for practical purposes, it is also dangerous. Because plausible argumentation is based on stereotypes, or assumptions about the way normal patterns or expectations work in practical experience, it is an inherently tentative and imperfect kind of reasoning that can turn out to be misleading or unwarranted in unanticipated or nonstandard situations. Therefore, an open-minded and cautious attitude is appropriate in using this kind of argumentation. When new information comes in, a presumptively reasonable argument that was plausible in the old situation may now have to be re-assessed as no longer plausible (by default). Hence it is important not to become too rigid or dogmatic in reliance on stereotypes in plausible argumentation. For example, if we do find that Tweety is a penguin, then sticking dogmatically to the absolute generalization 'All birds fly' and concluding (contrary to the facts) that Tweety must fly would not be reasonable. It would be a kind of prejudice or bias. The fallacy of hasty generalization (see chapter 1) is a danger here.

Plausible reasoning gives you some reason to think a proposition is true, provided you have no better reason to think it is false. For example, drawing a conclusion based on the testimony of a witness uses plausible reasoning. If you have no good reason to think that the proposition asserted by the witness is false, then the testimony gives you some reason to think it is true. But if you find out the witness has been bribed or threatened or if you find physical evidence (based on scientific tests, for example) that the proposition is false, then this is new information and you should withdraw your original conclusion. Plausible reasoning is of a kind that is inherently subject to default, should new evidence come into the picture. Therefore, assent to a conclusion drawn by plausible inference should always be tentative and subject to revision in the light of new information.

EXERCISE 2.7

Discuss the argumentation used in the following dialogues.

(a) Two soldiers see a dust cloud moving toward them from the east. One says to the other, "It must be an enemy tank column approaching."

(b) Bob says to his lawyer, "How do you know this thing is an affidavit?" His lawyer replies, "It looks like an affidavit to me."

EIGHT Arguments and Explanations

So far, in this chapter we have learned to recognize many different kinds of arguments, and we have begun to learn how to analyze and evaluate such arguments. Having advanced this far, there is a tendency to see arguments everywhere, and even to classify things as arguments that are not really arguments at all, though they may look like them. For example, sometimes a speaker is merely reporting a fact or belief but not arguing for it. One of the most common kinds of cases where something may be taken to be an argument when it is really not are those of explanations. For example, suppose Larry and Sandra see her dog scratching himself. He asks her, "Why is your dog scratching himself?" and she replies, "He is scratching himself because he has a flea." In this case Sandra has offered an explanation to Larry. They both see that the dog is scratching himself, and she explains why it is happening. Sandra's speech act is clearly meant to be an explanation. But in some ways it does look as if it could be an argument. She is giving a reason why the dog is scratching himself, and she even uses the word 'because', which might sometimes be an indicator word for an argument. How then can we identify explanations, as contrasted with arguments, and thereby prevent ourselves from confusing the two? After all, if something is not really an argument at all, it would be a serious mistake to criticize it as a bad argument on the basis that it fails to meet the standards required for a good argument.

It was shown in chapter 1 that the purpose of an argument is to give a reason to support a claim made by one party in a dialogue. The claim is something that is doubted by the respondent in the dialogue. It is a proposition that is at issue or is unsettled. An argument is supposed to present a good reason for the respondent to come to accept this proposition as true, thus removing the doubt. The purpose of an explanation is to help the questioner who doesn't understand something. Thus, the concept of explanation, like that of argument, is based on dialogue in the sense that it involves a conversational exchange between two participants. In the case of the offering of an explanation by a proponent to a respondent, a certain function should be performed. If the explanation is to be helpful, it should perform a clarifying function, meaning that it should help the respondent to come to understand something that he did not understand before. A useful explanation should make the thing queried clearer for the respondent, by expressing it in terms he is familiar with or already understands. In a dialogue, a request for an explanation takes the form of a question that asks for help with understanding something.

There are several different kinds of questions that characteristically function as requests for explanations. One is the how question. For example, if I don't understand how a certain computer works, I may ask someone, "How does it work?" and, in so doing, I would be asking for an explanation of how it works. I would not be asking the person to prove that it works or to use argument to show me that it works. Instead, I would be asking for help with understanding how it works. It is also often the case that why questions are used as prompts for explanations. For example, I might ask you, "Why does the sky appear blue from the earth's surface?" and then you might give me an explanation. You might say, for example: "The light rays from the sun are scattered by particles in the atmosphere in a certain way that activates the blue part of the spectrum when the light strikes our eyes as we look skyward." Such an explanation could be quite complicated and could involve quite a number of inferences from some propositions to other propositions that are connected to them.

In this way, then, explanations often appear to be quite similar to arguments. Both explanations and arguments consist of groups of statements where some of the statements are taken as starting points and lead to others as end points. However, when we are dealing with explanations, the terms 'premises' and 'conclusions' are not used. Instead, there is a proposition that is queried or that is supposed to be explained. The purpose of the explaining is not to give a reason for the other party to accept this proposition as true. The purpose of offering an explanation is to take this proposition that the explainee does not understand and clarify it, relating it to other propositions that the explainee is familiar with and can comprehend. Thus, explanations and arguments are different because each has a different purpose in a dialogue. The goal of an explanation is not to convince or persuade the party that a particular proposition is true but to express the queried proposition in some more familiar terms or relate it to another set of propositions that can be put together so that it is more familiar or comprehensible to him.

The Radiator Dialogue

Fred: Why are radiators usually located under windows, when windows are the greatest source of heat loss?

Donna: The windows are the coldest part of the room and that is why the radiators are placed underneath the windows. The air that comes in contact with the windows is cooled and falls to the floor. This creates a draft because the movement of air results in a convection current. If the radiator were placed at an inside wall, then the coldest part of the room, where the windows are, would stay colder and the warmest part, toward the inside, would stay warmer. This placement would not be a comfortable arrangement for habitation of the room. Therefore, the radiators are normally placed beneath the windows in a room.

In her reply to Fred's question, Donna is giving an explanation to him by showing what the outcome of putting the radiator next to an inside wall would be and showing why it would be undesirable. In this case, Fred asked a why question that expressed his puzzlement about the radiators being located in the area where there is the greatest source of heat loss. This placement would seem to be wasteful, and, therefore, it seems to him puzzling that, normally, radiators are placed under the windows in a room. If you look at the sequence of reasoning involved in Fred's question, the conclusion that is suggested is that the placement of the radiators is not practical because it is presumed that, normally, our purpose in constructing a house is to minimize unnecessary heat loss. Hence, locating the radiator under the window would appear to be impractical. Donna replied by citing another important factor to be considered: the comfort of the inhabitants of the room. The radiators are normally placed under the windows, she explains, because convection currents create a draft, so the cold part under the window needs to be heated. Of course, in designing a room, we want to avoid any situation where the person living in that room would be uncomfortable because of something like a draft or a severe difference in temperature between two parts of the room. Hence, as she explains, putting the radiator at the inner wall would be impractical.

In this case, the purpose of Donna's answer in the dialogue is not to produce an argument that would give Fred a reason to accept some proposition as true that he has expressed doubt about. For example, Donna is not trying to give Fred a reason to accept the doubtful proposition that radiators are located under windows. He does not doubt this proposition, nor is he expressing doubt about any other proposition. He is just puzzled why placing radiators under windows is the normal practice when it seems impractical for the reason he cited. Donna explained why this is the usual practice, by helping Fred to understand how convection currents are involved. Hence her reply to his question is an explanation, not an argument.

Explanations of human actions are similar to explanations of natural events, because both are attempts to help a questioner understand something.

The Motorist Example

A motorist spots an empty car with a missing tire parked on the shoulder of a highway. As the motorist drives further along the road, she sees a man rolling a tire along the edge of the highway. He is carrying a baby in the other arm, and three small children are following him. She explains what she sees by inferring that the tire the man was rolling along had been taken from the car by him. She inferred that the man was taking the tire to get it fixed. She also inferred that the man did not want to leave the children alone in the car.[9]

By observing the various events in sequence, the passing motorist drew inferences that explained these events. She had to know quite a bit about how cars function and how they can break down. The passing motorist assumed that the man with the children also knew about such things. This kind of common-sense knowledge about how things can normally be expected to go in a familiar kind of situation is often necessary for the one agent to be able to explain the actions of the other agent and for the two to engage in a dialogue together. It is also the basis of many common

[9] This example is taken from a book on computing: Sandra Carberry, *Plan Recognition in Natural Language Dialogue* (Cambridge, Mass.: MIT Press, 1990), p. 17.

cases of plausible arguments. But in this case, the passing motorist is not presenting an argument when she draws the three inferences cited in the motorist example. She is explaining what she sees. What she sees looks peculiar at first and calls for some sort of explanation. Why are the man and the children walking along the edge of the highway? She is able to explain the man's actions because she can draw plausible inferences about what he is trying to do, namely, to get his tire fixed without leaving the children alone, based on her own common-sense knowledge about how tires can be punctured and what one normally needs to do to fix them.

To distinguish between an argument and an explanation in a given case, you have to look not only at the context of dialogue, but also at the wording used in the reasoning in that text of dialogue. One criterion for recognizing an argument is the existence in the text of discourse of indicator words. As shown in the list of conclusion indicator words in chapter 1, section 2, certain words, such as 'therefore', 'hence', 'thus', and 'accordingly', typically indicate the conclusion of an inference. As shown in the list of premise indicator words in chapter 1, section 2, other kinds of words indicate the premise or premises of the inference. These include words such as 'since', 'because', 'as shown by', and 'the reason is that'. However, the indicator words are not sufficient by themselves to determine whether or not a sequence of reasoning is an argument, because many of the same indicator words, or very similar ones, are used in explanations. Therefore, in order to distinguish between whether a sequence of reasoning is used as an argument or an explanation in a particular case, we have to examine the text of discourse to try to determine the nature of the question that the reasoning was used to respond to. We have to try to determine, in the given case, what purpose the reasoning was used for.

The basic test for making this distinction in a given case is to focus on the proposition that is being explained or argued for, that is, to focus on the particular proposition that is either the proposition to be explained or the conclusion of the argument. If this proposition is presumed to be true by both parties to the dialogue, then the reasoning is being used as an explanation. If the proposition in question is in dispute, that is, if the one party is doubtful whether it is true or even clearly thinks it is false, then the reasoning is being used in an argument. For example, in the example above, where Helen used an argument of the form 'argument from consequences' to try to persuade Bob that tipping is a bad practice that should be discontinued, she is using the argument on the presumption that Bob does not accept the proposition that tipping is a bad practice that should be discontinued. In fact, we know from the context of the dialogue on tipping that this is the very proposition that Bob so actively opposes as his point of view in the dispute. So the reasoning in this case is clearly an argument.

Hence generally, in order to determine, in a particular case, whether a sequence of reasoning is being used as an argument or an explanation, we should ask what the purpose of the discourse is in which the reasoning is contained. Then, second, the best test is to focus on the conversational exchange at a more localized level to determine the nature of the question that was asked and what sort of response was given to it. In making such a determination, a key test is to focus on the particular proposition which is either the conclusion or the proposition to be explained and ask whether the participants appear to be presuming that it's true or not. If they are presuming that it's true, it's an explanation. If not, it's an argument. That is the test. However, there will be cases where we do not have enough information on the context of the conversation, or the text of discourse in a particular case, and we may not be able to tell then whether the reasoning is being used as an argument or an explanation. The best we can do, when evaluating such a case in logic, is to make a conditional evaluation. That is, we can say that if it's an argument, then it's a correct or incorrect argument in certain respects. Or, if it's an explanation, then it's a good explanation or not in certain respects. The mistake we must try to avoid is generally assuming that, because a text of discourse contains an inference or a sequence of reasoning, that it automatically must be an argument, and then set forward to evaluate it using methods of logic as a correct or an incorrect argument. The problem here is that, once students are taught to use logic to evaluate arguments, there is a tendency to use logical methods of evaluation wherever reasoning occurs in a text of discourse. But this can be a mistake because, if the reasoning was not being used as an argument at all but was being used as an explanation or perhaps as a description or some other type of speech act, then it is inappropriate to evaluate it as an argument. In particular, we wouldn't want to make the mistake of judging a sequence of reasoning to be a bad or fallacious argument when it really isn't even an argument at all.

EXERCISE 2.8

1. Determine whether the reasoning used in the following texts of discourse is an argument or an explanation, giving your reasons.
   (a) The U.S. dollar declined in value against the German mark and the Japanese yen in March 1995, because the U.S. spending deficit was thought by money traders to be too high.

(b) Free speech is a good thing, because if you don't allow free speech, irrational views that are out of touch with reality cannot be stated and criticized in public. And when such views are not stated and criticized in public, they can give a powerful appeal among those with hidden grievances.

(c) Kangaroos are frequently killed on the roads in Australia because they like to eat the short grass near the highways but have no sense of the danger of an approaching vehicle.

(d) Cows and sheep survive quite well on grass alone, whereas human beings do not. The reason is that cows and sheep have much more complex digestive systems than human beings do.

(e) Abortion is a woman's right. Therefore abortion is acceptable.

(f) Abortion is a killing of the fetus. The fetus is a person. Therefore abortion is unacceptable.

(g) Why does the classic Western movie always have a gunfight at the end, where the villain is killed? Such a climax is a required part of the ethical theme where there must be a struggle, and then good must triumph (narrowly) over evil.

(h) The Axis forces lost in World War II because, as in any war of attrition, they did not have enough human and material resources. Also, there was that factor that they did not develop an atomic bomb.

(i) Children should be immunized who are in day care because, if they are not, there is the danger of other children coming down with a contagious disease.

(j) In a university classroom, professors should not be allowed to argue for any viewpoint they happen to think is right, because arguing for that viewpoint may cause harm to persons in a group who have been singled out.

(k) The Cloudy Water Dialogue

NIGEL: Why is hot water cloudy when it first comes out of the tap?

MARY: The cloudiness is because of air bubbles in the hot water. As the cold water in the hot water tank heats up, it gives off the air that's dissolved in it.

NIGEL: But why would air bubbles, if they are just air, make the water appear cloudy?

MARY: The hot water system is closed, and the pressure that builds up prevents air from leaving the water. However, when the hot water flows out of the tap, the pressure is lessened, and the trapped air escapes, making the water cloudy.

(l) The First Crusade Dialogue

GREG: How is it that an army that began as some 50,000 Crusaders was successful in conquering Jerusalem in 1099, given that they faced so many obstacles and so many enemies and that most of them died before they even got there?

SOPHIE: Their religious idealism required that they liberate the holy places from the control of Islam. Pope Urban II promised "the remission of sin" to all who took up the cross. There was a religious enthusiasm sweeping the West at that time, and it was allied with the heroic and militant idea of knighthood, which took the liberation of the Holy Sepulcher in Jerusalem as a sanctified ideal appropriate for chivalry. Lust for booty was one factor, but the deeper allure of the East was as a religious quest for the knight.

NINE Summary

In this chapter it was shown how explanations are similar to arguments in certain respects and can easily be confused with them in some cases. Thus it is necessary to be careful to avoid the error of uncritically treating something as an argument if it was not really meant to be one by a speaker but was meant to be an explanation. For example, it would be unfair to criticize someone for having put forward a defective argument if they weren't even trying to argue at all, but merely trying to explain something. To avoid this error, we must be careful to examine the textual evidence and then arrive at a decision, based on the evidence, of whether to treat the given case as an argument or an explanation. As long as everyone involved is clear that we are not just uncritically assuming that something is an argument without even considering the possibility that it could be an explanation, the danger of error is avoided.

Some common kinds of arguments we need to be able to recognize can be evaluated according to various standards of structural correctness. In a deductively valid argument, if the premises are true, the conclusion must be true. The premises taken together with the negation of the conclusion is an inconsistent set of statements. A set of statements is inconsistent if it is not logically possible for all of them to be true. Syllogisms are common forms of deductive argumentation, with two premises and a conclusion made up of 'all' and 'some' statements. Other common deductive forms of argument are *modus ponens, modus tollens*, and disjunctive syllogism. A deductive argument is conclusive in the sense that if the premises are true, the conclusion must also be true. However, there are cases where the argument is deductively valid but the premises are false. Thus, in g there are two ways to criticize a deductive argument: You can argue it is invalid or you can argue that one or more of the premises are false.

In an inductively strong argument, if the premises are true, then it is probable (inductively likely) that the conclusion is true. Inductive arguments are based on probability and statistics. We are very familiar with these kinds of arguments, as they are often presented in polls and other statistical findings in the media.

The third type of argument is less reliable than the other two. But plausible arguments are also very common. It is often necessary for practical reasons to use them in science and law, as well as in everyday life, but they can be dangerous. They should never be accepted uncritically, and one must always be open-minded about them. One should be ready to give up an argument that seemed plausible if new evidence comes in that refutes it. In a plausible argument, if the premises are true, then a weight of plausibility is shifted to the conclusion. To say that a statement is plausible means that it seems to be true, based on the data known and observed so far in a normal kind of situation we are familiar with. But appearances can sometime be misleading, and when more is found out about the particular circumstances of a situation, a plausible inference can default. Many of the most serious problems of critical argumentation occur in cases where a person has become so strongly committed to an argument, because of financial interest or passionate belief in a cause, for example, that she cannot bring herself to give it up, even though new evidence has been discovered that shows it to be false.

ntation Schemes

Several distinct forms of argument are identified in chapter 3 that are not deductive or inductive in nature. These arguments are inherently presumptive and defeasible, and thus they are different in nature from deductive and inductive arguments. Each of the forms of argument described in this chapter is used as a presumptive argument in a dialogue that carries a weight of plausibility. If the respondent accepts the premises, then that gives him a good reason also to accept the conclusion. But it does not mean that the respondent should accept the conclusion uncritically. Matching each form of argument is a set of appropriate critical questions to ask. In a given case, there may be a balance of considerations to take into account. There may be some arguments in favor of the conclusion and some against it. These forms of inference are called argumentation schemes, and they represent many common types of argumentation that are familiar in everyday conversations. They need to be evaluated in a context of dialogue. They are used to shift a burden of proof to one side or the other in a dialogue and need to be evaluated differently at different stages of a dialogue. Only a few of the most important and familiar of these common types of argument are described in chapter 3. Others, such as argument from consequences, are described in chapter 4.

ONE Appeal to Expert Opinion

In a critical discussion, many different facts can be relevant to the dispute. For example, in a dispute on tipping, economic data on how tipping affects the economy or sociological data on how tipping affects job satisfaction may be very useful information to support or refute arguments on one or the other side. But citing such information always rests on quoting sources, such as books or articles, which is a form of argument called 'appeal to expert opinion.' It is frequently the case in personal, social, and political deliberations that one does not know all the relevant facts, but that even so, for reasons of time, costs, or pressing circumstances, one must make a choice between alternative courses of action. One possibility is to delay making a decision until more information can be collected. Frequently, this decision not to act is the most prudent course of action. But it is not always so, for delaying making a decision, by not taking any action, may itself be a course of action with significant (negative) consequences. What about the option of collecting more information? The more information one has about the alternatives, the situation, and the likely consequences of the available courses of action, the more informed and more practically wise one's conclusion on how to proceed is likely to be. But instead of trying to collect more information by doing original research, it might be practical to use sources.

There can be all kinds of sources of relevant information that would be helpful in a deliberation. One might have access to an encyclopedia, a dictionary, a manual, a reference book, or a computer data base. Or one may get information from another person who has the facts. For example, if one is deliberating on the best way to get to City Hall in an unfamiliar city, it may be very helpful to ask a passer-by who may be in a position to know this information. You can improve your chances of getting correct information by choosing a source you have reason to think is reliable. But to some extent, you will have to rely on presumption or trust that your source is knowledgeable and honest and is not misinforming you. So you may argue, to yourself or to your companion who is with you, "It looks as if this passer-by knows the streets, and she says that City Hall is over that way; therefore, let's go ahead and accept the conclusion that City Hall is that way." Based on that argument, you head in the direction indicated. In this kind of case, you have acted on the basis of position-to-know argumentation.

Where *a* is a source of information, the following argumentation scheme represents the form of position-to-know argumentation.

ARGUMENTATION SCHEME FOR ARGUMENT FROM POSITION TO KNOW

POSITION TO KNOW PREMISE: *a* is in a position to know whether *A* is true or false.

ASSERTION PREMISE: *a* asserts that *A* is true (false).

CONCLUSION: *A* may plausibly be taken to be true (false).

The form of argument can be plausible, but it is also defeasible. It can be critically questioned in a dialogue by raising doubts about the truth of either premise or by asking whether *a* is an honest (trustworthy) source of information. The following critical questions are appropriate for use in questioning a position-to-know argument.

1. Is *a* in a position to know whether *A* is true (false)?
2. Is *a* an honest (trustworthy, reliable) source?
3. Did *a* assert that *A* is true (false)?

The second critical question concerns the credibility of the source. For example, a lawyer, when cross-examining a witness in a trial, is allowed (within controlled limits) to raise questions about the character of the witness for honesty. If a witness has been known to lie in previous cases or can be generally shown to have bad judgment or a bad character for veracity, the lawyer is allowed to use or bring these sorts of concerns forward in her cross-examination. By raising such questions, the attorney could call the credibility of the witness into question, thereby influencing the jury to have doubts about the reliability of his testimony.

Much the same considerations apply in arguments outside a courtroom. Position-to-know reasoning is typically used in an information-seeking type of dialogue where one has to depend on a source. It is also frequently used in cases where having a high-quality deliberation dialogue depends on a prior information-seeking dialogue. In many cases of this sort, the use of information is helpful, because the information-seeking dialogue contributes to the goal of the deliberation by making the deliberation better informed. Such a deliberation is improved by additional relevant information because the deliberation is made more practical by better fitting it to the realities of a given situation.

The appeal to expert opinion, sometimes also called 'argument from expert opinion', is an important subspecies of position-to-know reasoning. It is based on the assumption that the source is alleged to be in a position to know about a subject because he or she has expert knowledge of that subject. Suppose in the context of the dialogue on tipping from chapter 1, Helen puts forward the following argument.

Dr. Phil says that tipping lowers self-esteem.

Dr. Phil is an expert psychologist, so Helen's argument is based on an appeal to expert opinion that can be stated as follows.

PREMISE: Dr. Phil says that tipping lowers self-esteem.

PREMISE: Dr. Phil is an expert in psychology, a field that has knowledge about self-esteem.

CONCLUSION: Tipping lowers self-esteem.

Helen's argument is a plausible one that rightly carries some weight to support her side in the dialogue on tipping. It is an argument that could be countered by Bob. For example, he might cite another expert in psychology who disagrees with what Dr. Phil says about tipping. Even so, unless Bob criticizes the argument, it does offer a reason in support of the conclusion. Such arguments from expert opinion are common and important as evidence in trials. For example, ballistics experts and DNA experts are often used to give expert testimony as evidence in trials.

ARGUMENTATION SCHEME FOR APPEAL TO EXPERT OPINION

MAJOR PREMISE: Source *E* is an expert in subject domain *D* containing proposition *A*.

MINOR PREMISE: *E* asserts that proposition *A* (in domain *D*) is true (false).

CONCLUSION: *A* may plausibly be taken to be true (false).

Appeal to expert opinion should, in most typical cases, at any rate, be seen as a plausible but defeasible form of argumentation. It is rarely wise to treat an expert as infallible, and indeed, taking that approach can be quite dangerous, for there is quite a natural tendency to respect experts and to defer to them unquestioningly.[1] For most of us, it is not easy to question the opinion of an expert. It tends to verge on the impolite and thus needs to be done in a diplomatic way. But it needs to be done, in many cases, because experts are often wrong. As a practical matter, for example, in matters of health and finance, you can do much better if you are prepared to question the advice of an expert in a critical but polite manner. Thus it is vital to see appeal to expert opinion as defeasible, as open to critical questioning.

1 The respect we have for authority was demonstrated by some famous experiments carried out by the psychologist Stanley Milgram. In these experiments, subjects were asked by an authoritative-looking scientist to administer severe electric shocks to other persons, and they often did so.

The six basic critical questions matching the appeal to expert opinion are listed below.[2]

1. **Expertise Question.** How credible is *E* as an expert source?
2. **Field Question.** Is *E* an expert in the field that *A* is in?
3. **Opinion Question.** What did *E* assert that implies *A*?
4. **Trustworthiness Question.** Is *E* personally reliable as a source?
5. **Consistency Question.** Is *A* consistent with what other experts assert?
6. **Backup Evidence Question.** Is *E*'s assertion based on evidence?

The idea behind using critical questions to evaluate appeals to expert opinion is dialectical. The assumption is that the issue to be settled by argumentation in a dialogue hangs on a balance of considerations. One can critically question an appeal to expert opinion by raising doubts about any of the premises. To be a genuine expert in a domain of knowledge or a technical skill, an individual must have the proper credentials and a record of experience. It is not enough, for example, that the person is a popular celebrity. With respect to the second question, one has to look at the exact wording of what the expert said (preferably, as quoted). With respect to the third question, one must be careful, for example, to check whether the expert may be an authority in one field (such as physics), while the proposition he is pronouncing on is in another field (such as religion). The sixth question cites the requirement that an expert should be able to back up her opinion with objective evidence. The two remaining critical questions relate to two other implicit assumptions. The fifth question relates to "maverick" opinions, especially on issues where experts disagree. One can pose the consistency question by comparing *A* with other known evidence (and, in particular, with what experts on *D* other than *a* say). One can pose the trustworthiness question by expressing doubts about whether the expert is personally reliable as a source. For example, one might question whether the expert is biased, for example, whether he has something to gain by making the claim put forward.

Using the appeal to expert opinion as an argument should not be seen as a substitute for getting factual evidence by scientific methods of data collection. It is a method of argument that can be abused. However, in many cases in deliberation and in other types of dialogue, this type of argument, despite its fallibility, can be a valuable way of collecting useful information and advice to solve a problem or make a decision. An example

[2] This set of critical questions is from Douglas Walton, *Appeal to Expert Opinion* (University Park: Penn State University Press, 1997), p. 223.

would be a case where a legislative assembly is having a discussion on a bill that would legalize marijuana. One of the arguments relevant to the debate would be the consequences of legalization. A powerful argument against legalization might be the slippery slope argument linking marijuana to increased addiction to harder drugs – a highly negative outcome, perceived as very dangerous. At this point what would very likely happen in the debate is that scientific experts would be brought in to testify on scientific findings concerning the linkages between marijuana use and the use of harder drugs. Experts might be brought in on both sides, and their testimony might conflict. Both sides in the debate could question the scientific experts, and the dialogue might be very helpful in making voting on the bill more informed and intelligent. Obviously, much would depend on how the expert testimony was presented and how it was critically questioned by the participants in the legislative assembly.

Perhaps the most familiar use of expert testimony is in the law, where it is a very important kind of evidence, for example, in criminal trials. A familiar type of expert witness is the ballistics expert or the forensic scientist who provides, for example, evidence on DNA tests of blood or hair found at the scene of a crime. Another familiar type of expert testimony in the criminal trial is that given by the psychiatrist or psychologist who is brought in to make a determination of a defendant's 'state of mind' when a plea of insanity has been made. Frequently, such cases turn into a "battle of the experts," because both sides are allowed to pay a fee for expert witnesses thought likely to support their side of a case. Such conflicts of expert testimony remind us that arguments based on appeal to expert opinion are inherently subjective and presumptive in nature and are rarely conclusive. Even so, they can be valuable guides to action in a deliberation or valuable sources of informed opinion in a persuasion dialogue. Appeals to expert opinion can, in some cases, be used fallaciously as well, to try to intimidate or silence one's partner in a dialogue by saying something like, "Well, you're not an expert, are you?" This tactic can be a fallacy where it is used to try to suppress or block off legitimate critical questioning of what the expert said.[3]

In summary, then, appeal to expert opinion is a defeasible type of argument that depends on trust in the honesty and competence of the

[3] As Locke (1690) put it, when an expert is "established in dignity," any questioning of what he says by a layman may be put down as "insolence" or showing insufficient respect for authority (Locke's *Essay*, as quoted by Charles Hamblin, *Fallacies* (London: Methuen, 1970), p. 160).

source that is consulted. If you have a choice between evidence based on the say-so of a source that is in a position to know and objective evidence based on scientific methods of observation, inquiry, and data collection, then it is best to give more weight to the objective evidence. But if you have to act in a deliberation, for practical reasons, and cannot delay any longer to collect objective information, it may be wiser to go with the say-so of a qualified expert, or someone who is in a special position to know, rather than throwing darts or relying on pure guesswork. It is a matter of striking a balance between qualified trust, or presumption of honesty and competence, on the one hand, and a skeptical attitude of doubt and critical questioning, on the other hand. The right balance should be decided by weighing each case individually, basing your judgment on balancing goals such as safety against the need to take positive action.

EXERCISE 3.1

Analyze the following arguments by identifying the argumentation scheme involved. Identify the premises and conclusion of the argument. If there are any questionable aspects of the argument that should be considered, identify critical questions that should be asked.

(a) Bob is lost in the jungle, in a country he is not familiar with. However, he knows that Tarzan is very familiar with the terrain in this area, and he asks Tarzan which is the best way to get to a mountain he wants to visit. Tarzan replies: "Don't go across that river. It is full of hungry crocodiles and dangerous hippos."

(b) You go to a new dentist to have your teeth cleaned, and he recommends that you have a root canal and to also consider having braces put on your teeth. He proposes to do both jobs immediately. This request seems odd to you, because you have had no problems with your teeth recently,

(c) Herman and Louise are Canadian tourists in Australia. As he is about to step off the curb, Herman asks: "Who has the right of way, the pedestrians or the motorists?" Louise replies, "I notice that all the other pedestrians are giving way to the cars."

(d) Gilbert and Joanne are having a critical discussion on the issue of whether HIV-infected surgeons ought to be allowed to operate. Joanne argues: "Doctor Dave says they ought to be allowed to, and since this issue is a medical question, I think he should have the last word! He is an expert."

(e) In the dialogue on genetically modified foods (chapter 1, section 8) Sarah cited the Prince of Wales as a source to support her point of view in the dialogue. She put forward the following argument:

"Prince Charles said that we need to rediscover a reverence for the natural world, and that science, which lacks a spiritual dimension, should not be used to change nature." She said, "He knows all about organic agriculture. He even has his own organic garden in Highgrove."

(f) Dr. Zorba, a cancer specialist, is testifying in court in the case of a man who was bruised by his seat belt when he was rear-ended by another car. The man later contracted testicular cancer. Dr. Zorba testified that, in his opinion, the bruise from the seat belt was a causal factor in the development of the man's testicular cancer. The physician for the insurance company testified that there is no established medical evidence that bruises or trauma caused by seat belt restraints cause cancer.

TWO Argument from Popular Opinion

The argument from popular opinion, or appeal to popular opinion, as it is commonly called, has the following form. If a large majority (everyone, nearly everyone, etc.) accepts *A* as true, as shown by a poll, say, this would be evidence that *A* is generally accepted. Or if *A* is common knowledge, meaning that it is an assumption that would not normally be disputed, then that is evidence that *A* is generally accepted. For example, in the contest of the dialogue on tipping, neither party would dispute the statement that the sky is blue or the statement that people often eat food in restaurants. If a statement is generally accepted, then that can be used as a plausible argument in favor of *A*.

ARGUMENTATION SCHEME FOR APPEAL TO POPULAR OPINION

GENERAL ACCEPTANCE PREMISE: *A* is generally accepted as true.

PRESUMPTION PREMISE: If *A* is generally accepted as true, that gives a reason in favor of *A*.

CONCLUSION: There is a reason in favor of *A*.

By itself, this type of argument is not very strong, as it is easily shown that the majority is often wrong. Still, it can make a claim plausible by giving a reason in favor of it in a dialogue in which there can be reasons both for and against it. Generally, the argument from popular opinion is weaker than the argument from expert opinion (though experts are often wrong, as well). Argument from popular opinion is best seen as expressing a limit on disputativeness. When you are arguing about a controversial issue, and some other proposition is relatively uncontroversial (because it is accepted by nearly everyone or by everyone that is party to the dialogue), then that proposition can be 'taken for granted', or accepted tentatively as uncontroversial. Such fine points of agreement help the dialogue go forward.

The following two critical questions match the argumentation scheme for appeal to popular opinion.

1. What evidence, such as a poll or an appeal to common knowledge, supports the claim that *A* is generally accepted as true?
2. Even if A is generally accepted as true, are there any good reasons for doubting it is true?

Although arguments from popular opinion are not very strong in themselves, they are frequently made stronger by being combined with 'position to know' arguments. The following case is an instance of argument from popular opinion, but its strength is reinforced by an implicit argument from position to know. Here is an example.

PREMISE: It is generally accepted by those who live in Cedar Rapids that the lake is a good place to swim in the summer.

CONCLUSION: The lake in Cedar Rapids is (plausibly) a good place to swim in the summer.

The implicit assumption that makes this appeal to popular opinion plausible is that since the people who live in Cedar Rapids are normally familiar with the area, they may be assumed to be in a position to know whether a particular lake in the area is a good place for swimming in the summer or not. Therefore, if the people who live in Cedar Rapids think that the lake is a good place to swim in the summer, it is a plausible and reasonably safe assumption (in the absence of any evidence to the contrary) that the lake is a good place to swim in the summer. This additional factor forms a chain of argumentation by joining argument from position to know to the appeal to popular opinion. Such a joining is called a bolstering of the appeal to popular opinion, meaning that the conjoined argument increases the plausibility of the appeal to popular opinion. An instance of bolstering can be identified by stating the implicit premise, as in the example below, relating to the argument just above.

IMPLICIT PREMISE: The people who live in Cedar Rapids are in a position to know whether the lake in Cedar Rapids is a good place to swim in the summer.

Of course, they could be wrong, because of some recent contamination of the lake that nobody knows about, for example. But in the absence of any countervailing developments of this sort, the conclusion that the lake is a good place to swim is a plausible presumption. It is often important to identify the implicit premise that bolsters the plausibility of the appeal to popular opinion, in order to be aware of what makes the argument plausible.

A practical form of the argument from popular opinion is called the argument from popular practice. This form of argument is connected to 'position to know' argumentation, because familiarity with a practice is a basis for being in a position to know whether it is generally acceptable or not.

ARGUMENTATION SCHEME FOR ARGUMENT FROM POPULAR PRACTICE

A is a popular practice among those who are familiar with what is acceptable or not with regard to *A*.

If *A* is a popular practice among those familiar with what is acceptable or not with regard to *A*, that gives a reason to think that *A* is acceptable.

Therefore, *A* is acceptable in this case.

An example of this type of argumentation is the following case, in which a husband and wife are visiting Holland for the first time and have rented bikes. They have started cycling along on a bicycle path in Holland. He is riding behind her, thinking that riding side-by-side is not allowed. She calls back to him, "Ride beside me, so we can talk." He replies, "I am not sure it is allowed." She replies, "Everyone else is doing it." The argument from popular practice in this example dialogue is made more plausible by the assumption that since the other couples are likely to be from the local area, and not all tourists, they would be likely to know what is generally accepted in practices of riding side-by-side on the bicycle paths. So the argument from popular practice is reinforced by an implicit position to know argument.

In still other cases, the argument from popular opinion is based not on a position to know argument but on an assumption that people have deliberated on a particular policy or practice and have come to accept it because they have found it a useful or good thing to do. Consider the following argument concerning the Golden Rule: Do unto others as you would they do unto you. In other words, treat others as you would like to be treated yourself.

PREMISE: The Golden Rule is basic to every system of ethics ever devised, and everyone accepts it in some form or other.

CONCLUSION: The Golden Rule is an established moral principle that has some weight of practical justification as a sound policy.

Here the assumption is that people have generally accepted the Golden Rule and even codified it in their systems of ethics. Such popular acceptance lends a certain weight of presumption in favor of the Golden Rule as an ethical principle to take seriously. It doesn't mean that the Golden Rule can't be questioned or criticized. It means only that the Golden Rule should be taken seriously in a discussion on ethical principles, because people have put some thought into such matters in the past, and their unanimity on accepting the Golden Rule indicates a presumption in its favor.

The two critical questions matching the argument from popular practice are the following.

1. What actions or other indications show that a large majority accepts *A*?
2. Even if a large majority accepts *A* as true, what grounds might there be for thinking they are justified in accepting *A*?

With respect to the first critical question, it is frequently problematic to determine, by asking a question, what a large majority really accepts as true or as representing their real opinion on a matter. Public opinion polls are often used, but much depends on how the question in the poll is worded. It may be better to go by evidence of how people act, in addition to going by what they say. But the uncertainty of verbal evidence is not the main problem with appeals to popular opinion generally. The main problem resides in the asking of the second critical question.

A typical problem with appeal to popular opinion is that in many instances no serious attempt is made to back up the first premise, by giving a real reason why everyone's accepting *A* is a good reason why you (the respondent) should accept *A*. Instead, the argument is used in such a way as to put pressure on the respondent to accept *A* or to feel left out of the popular group that accepts *A*. For example, consider the following argument.

> You ought to buy a sports recreation vehicle, as all members of the environmental off-road cool people now own one of these vehicles.

Instead of giving a reason why you should buy one of these cars, this argument tells the respondent that he will be left out of the "cool people" group if he does not buy one of these vehicles. This argument puts pressure on the respondent by appealing to his desire to be perceived as in some socially esteemed group unless he fails to take the action advocated. Such an argument appeals to his supposed desire to belong to some trendy group.

So arguments from popular opinion are variable. Although they are generally weak arguments, in some instances they can give good reasons to support a conclusion. In such cases, it would be unwise to ignore or reject them. But in other cases, arguments from popular opinion do not give the required support for their conclusion and instead appeal only to a wish for belonging to an esteemed group.

EXERCISE 3.2

Analyze the following arguments by identifying the argumentation scheme involved. Identify the premises and conclusion of the argument. If there are any questionable aspects of the argument that should be considered, identify critical questions that should be asked.

(a) A man is steering his sailboat into an unfamiliar harbor, and he has a choice of whether to turn left or right around a large rock. He has observed that all the sailboats entering the harbor before him have gone around to the left. He concludes that he should go around to the left.

(b) If we vote to return the death penalty, we, along with a few states, will be the only jurisdictions in the Western world with a death penalty. Not one country in Europe has a death penalty. Canada doesn't have it. New Zealand doesn't have it. Australia doesn't have it. It is on the books in Belgium, but there hasn't been an execution in that country since 1945. Therefore we should not vote to return the death penalty.

(c) In the dialogue on genetically modified foods (chapter 1, section 8), Mark supports his point of view by arguing: "People all over the planet have been genetically modifying animals and plants for centuries, nobody has worried about that, and even the scientists have long accepted it."

(d) Of course you should use Tartar Control toothpaste. A recent survey showed that 87 percent of people prefer Tartar Control toothpaste over other brands.

(e) I'm sure you will want to vote for my proposal. All highly educated professionals are in favor of it and always see the merit of it immediately.

(f) All the beautiful people who belong to the upper echelons of the rich and famous have Pilotage sunglasses. So you should buy Pilotage sunglasses too.

THREE Argument from Analogy

Argument from analogy is a very commonly used kind of case-based reasoning, where one case is held to be similar to another case in a particular respect. Since the one case is held to have a certain property, then the other case, it is concluded, also has the same property (because the one case is similar to the other). In outline, the argument from analogy has the following form.

ARGUMENTATION SCHEME FOR ARGUMENT FROM ANALOGY

SIMILARITY PREMISE: Generally, case C_1 is similar to case C_2.

BASE PREMISE: A is true (false) in case C_1.

CONCLUSION: A is true (false) in case C_2.

This form of argument is defeasible, because any two cases will be similar to each other in certain respects, but dissimilar to each other in other respects. So while one case may be generally similar to another, that does not mean that the two cases will be similar in every respect. If they were similar in every respect, they would be the same case. However, two cases can be generally similar, even though there are quite important differences between them.

In the dispute on tipping, Bob might use the following argument from analogy.

> Discontinuing tipping is like taking away an animal's source of food by destroying its natural habitat. Taking away an animal's source of food by destroying its natural habitat has the consequence that the animal will painfully die by starvation and disease. So discontinuing tipping will take away the income of people who are struggling

to survive in a weakening economy, with the same disastrous consequences.

In this argument, Bob compares two cases: the case of an animal struggling to survive in an endangered habitat and the case of a person struggling to survive in a weakening economy. He cites the bad consequences of destruction of habitat in the one case, and then postulates comparable bad consequences in the other case. Bob is using argument from consequences,[4] but this argument is built onto an argument from analogy, based on a comparison between the two cases. Of course, the two cases are different in certain respects, but by comparing them, Bob puts forward a plausible argument.

There are three critical questions that are appropriate for the use of argument from analogy.

1. Are there differences between C_1 and C_2 that would tend to undermine the force of the similarity cited?
2. Is A true (false) in C_1?
3. Is there some other case C_3 that is also similar to C_1, but in which A is false (true)?

In the example above, the second critical question is easy to answer, because the base premise of the argument – that taking away an animal's habitat has these bad consequences – is quite plausible. But asking the first critical question is a better avenue of criticism of the argument from analogy in this case. It could be argued that there is a difference between the two cases. If an animal loses its habitat, there may not be any other place it can go or be transferred where it will have adequate supplies of food available. But in the case of a person who loses tipping income, the additional money collected by charging the customer a higher price, once a tip is no longer required, could be used to provide higher salaries and benefits for the employee. At any rate, the citing of any difference of this kind can be used to raise doubts about the argument from analogy used in the example above.

Asking the third critical question is a very effective response in some cases, but it does not work well in all cases. The reason is that a certain thoughtfulness and cleverness to devise a suitable counter-analogy is

[4] This form of argument as a scheme used by Bob is to argue that an action or policy is bad because it has bad consequences. Argument from consequences is more fully explained in chapter 3, section 5.

required. But in some cases, use of a counter-analogy can be very effective. The following example is a classic case.

> Then President Ronald Reagan, in a speech for congressional funds to aid the Contra rebels in Nicaragua, compared the Contras to the American patriots who fought in the War of Independence. A speaker in Congress opposed to sending aid to the Contras compared the situation in Nicaragua to the war in Vietnam.

In using the argument from analogy, Reagan compared the case of the Contra rebels in Nicaragua to the case of American patriots who fought in the U.S. War of Independence. Since his audience would think the latter case represented a highly worthwhile cause, that was good to support, and that had good consequences, their policy on this case would presumably be one of overwhelming support for action. By the use of argument from analogy, Reagan hoped to transfer this positive attitude for support to the present case of the Contra rebels. But his opponent in Congress was able to counter Reagan's argument by posing another analogy that is also extremely powerful to the audience. Intervention in Vietnam had extremely bad consequences for the United States and was an experience that nobody would care to repeat. This case stands as a powerful lesson to the effect that intervention in a foreign war can lead to a messy situation that gets worse and worse, once the first steps to get involved in it are taken. Here, then, is a third case, which also appears to be similar to the Nicaragua case in certain respects, but the outcome of intervention was very bad.

In some cases, argument from analogy is used in an extremely aggressive way that packs all kinds of unstated and questionable assumptions into the argument. The following example is taken from a letter to *Chatelaine* magazine, May 1982.[5] Once the various implicit assumptions in the argument are identified, it can easily be shown that they are highly questionable and that the argument based on them is not justified.

> When a murderer is found guilty, he is punished regardless of his reasons for killing. Similarly, anyone partaking in an abortion is guilty of having deprived an individual of her or his right to life.

The implicit conclusion of this argument is the statement that anyone partaking in an abortion should be punished. Why? The argument is

[5] This example is from an article on arguments containing unstated assumptions: Douglas Walton and Chris Reed, "Argumentation Schemes and Enthymemes," *Synthese: An International Journal for Epistemology, Logic and Philosophy of Science*, to appear.

supported by the drawing of an analogy between two cases held to be similar. One is the case of one person murdering another person, a crime punishable by law. The other is the case of someone partaking in an abortion. The argument is that since the one type of case is similar to the other, something that is true of one should also be true of the other. The argument is therefore based on the argumentation scheme for argument from analogy. The argument is based on the assumption that since murderers are punished, regardless of the reason for killing, by analogy, abortion partakers should also be punished. As shown by applying the argumentation scheme for argument from analogy, this argument is based on an implicit premise that the two kinds of cases of murder and abortion are similar. But such an assumption is highly questionable. In law, murder is a crime in which a person is killed. But in law, a fetus is not a person and has no right to life in the way a person does. Of course, this distinction is a legal one, and there is a difference between law and morality. But even so, the assumption that anyone partaking in an abortion is depriving a person of his or her right to life is based on the further assumption that the fetus is a person. While pro-life advocates might accept such an assumption, pro-choice advocates would reject it. They would argue that the two cases of murder and abortion are dissimilar in this respect.

In general, the first critical question for the argument from analogy tends to be the most important one to focus on when evaluating arguments from analogy. If one case is similar to another in a certain respect, then that similarity gives a certain weight of plausibility to the argument from analogy. But if the two cases are dissimilar in some other respect, citing this difference tends to undermine the plausibility of the argument. So arguments from analogy can be stronger or weaker, in different cases.

EXERCISE 3.3

Analyze the following arguments by identifying the argumentation scheme involved. Identify the premises and conclusion of the argument. If there are any questionable aspects of the argument that should be considered, identify critical questions that should be asked.

(a) After ingesting one milligram of substance alpha per day for ninety days, white mice developed genetic abnormalities. Since white mice are similar in many ways to humans, it follows that substance alpha probably produces genetic abnormalities in humans.

(b) When an individual is diagnosed as having cancer, every effort is made to kill the cancerous growth, whether by surgery, radiation treatment, or chemotherapy. But murderers and kidnappers are cancerous growths on society. Therefore, when these criminals are apprehended and convicted, they should be treated like any other cancer and eliminated by capital punishment.

(c) When an elected political leader was subjected to extensive criticisms because of rising unemployment and a sagging economy, some argued that he should resign so that the party could select a new leader. Others said an election should be called. He replied: "People don't change doctors just because they're sick."

(d) Smokers should be allowed to smoke only in private where it does not offend anyone else. Would any smoker walk into a restaurant and start eating half-chewed food on someone's plate or drink a glass of water that previously held someone's teeth? Probably not, yet they expect non-smokers to inhale smoke from the recesses of their lungs. My privilege and right is to choose a clean and healthy life without interference.

(e) A doctor claimed that physicians should give a medical examination to every patient every year, using the following argument: "People take their car in for servicing every few months."

FOUR Argument from Correlation to Cause

Although scientists, particularly in the practical fields such as engineering and medicine, sometimes make claims about causal relationships, there is no settled scientific theory of causality (or philosophical theory, for that matter). It seems that the causal relationship is practical and contextual in nature. What it means to say that one state of affairs *A* causes another state of affairs *B* is that *A* is something that can be brought about, and when it is brought about (or stopped), then *B* is also brought about (or stopped).[6] At any rate, whatever causality means, the most important kind of evidence that *A* causes *B* in any particular case is that there is a statistical correlation between *A* and *B*. For example, if a significant statistical correlation is found between reduced incidence of heart attacks and drinking of red wine, the tentative conclusion may be drawn, as a hypothesis, that drinking red wine is the cause of the reduction in heart attacks. Recently, in fact, the causal conclusion has been drawn, based on such statistical findings, that drinking red wine with meals, as the French do, helps to prevent heart attacks.

As a presumptive form of reasoning, argument from correlation to cause has the following form.

[6] The variables *A* and *B* stand for states of affairs that are thought of as being like propositions because they can be made true (brought about) or made false by actions.

ARGUMENTATION SCHEME FOR ARGUMENT FROM CORRELATION TO CAUSE

CORRELATION PREMISE: There is a positive correlation between *A* and *B*.

CONCLUSION: *A* causes *B*.

A correlation is a purely statistical relationship, determined by counting up numbers where one event occurs in a case where another event also occurs. However, as noted above, causality is not a purely statistical relationship (or at least, if it is, it is a very complicated kind of one), so the inference from correlation to causation cannot be evaluated on a purely statistical or numerical basis. It is best seen as a presumptive and defeasible inference, subject to defeat as more data are collected.

One problem with arguments from correlation to cause is that there may not be a real correlation between two events, but only seem to be one. Consider the following example:

> Researchers at the Wellesley Central Hospital studied 18 patients with rheumatoid arthritis for more than a year, testing how changes in their symptoms were influenced by changes in the weather, but came up with no correlation between the two. "We hypothesize that this belief results, in part at least, from people's tendency to perceive patterns where none exist," Dr. Ronald Redelmeier of Wellesley writes in the abstract of the study published in the latest issue of the U.S. journal *Proceedings of the National Academy of Science*.... During his study of 18 arthritis patients at Wellesley, researchers gathered data on symptoms twice a month for 15 months. The patients rated the severity of pain themselves, while doctors evaluated the degree of joint tenderness, mobility and functioning in each patient at each assessment. The researchers also obtained local weather reports for several days around the time of each appointment. They interviewed the patients about their beliefs concerning arthritis pain, and all but two believed the effect of weather was strong. However, when researchers computed the correlations between pain and specific weather components mentioned by each patient, they found no pattern.[7]

[7] Jane Gadd, "Arthritis Study Rejects Weather Link," *Globe and Mail*, April 3, 1996, p. A5.

In this case there seemed to the arthritis sufferers to be a correlation between arthritis symptoms and weather changes. But Dr. Redelmeier's study raised doubts about whether such a correlation really exists.

Another problem is that a statistical correlation between two events can simply be a coincidence. A sophisticated statistical study by Steffie Woolhandler and David U. Himmelstein[8] citing figures from 141 countries found that the larger the percent of its gross national product a country spends on weapons, the higher is its infant death rate. Woolhandler and Himmelstein concluded that there is a plausible link between military spending and the infant death rate: "Our findings confirm what many have suspected – that militarism is deleterious to health even in the absence of overt hostilities" (p. 1378). However, critics questioned whether their finding represents anything more than a coincidence. Dr. John Bailar, a statistician at the Harvard School of Public Health, said that the same statistical approach could be used to show a causal link between infant mortality and the consumption of bananas.[9] He questioned whether statistical correlation between two things, in cases like these, is a reason to conclude that one thing causes the other.

Another critical question is whether both things correlated with each other are really caused by some common factor that is causing both of them. The following case is a classic example.[10]

> At a conference on the bond between humans and pets in Boston in 1986, researchers reported that pets can lower blood pressure in humans, improve the survival odds of heart patients, and even penetrate the isolation of autistic children. According to a report in *Newsweek* researchers at the conference reported on the beneficial effects of pet companionship. Studies showed that women who had owned dogs as children scored higher on self-reliance, sociability, and tolerance tests than petless women. Men who had owned a dog "felt a greater sense of personal worth and of belonging and had better social skills." Children with pets also showed greater empathy.

In this case, there was a genuine correlation between pet ownership and health improvement, but both factors could well be the result of the better

[8] "Militarism and Mortality," *The Lancet*, June 15, 1985, pp. 1375–1378.
[9] "Infant Death Link Found," *Winnipeg Free Press*, June 15, 1985, p. 70.
[10] Douglas Walton, *Informal Logic* (New York: Cambridge University Press, 1989), pp. 226–227.

than average social qualities of the people who acquire pets. This factor may lead to both pet ownership as well as better health. In a case like this, there may be a genuine correlation between two factors *A* and *B*, but the reason for the correlation is that some third factor *C*, is causing both *A* and *B*. In such a case, it is not correct to draw the conclusion that *A* causes *B*.

To sum up the lessons of these cases, the three main critical questions that should be asked, when an argument from correlation to cause is put forward, are the following.

1. Is there really a correlation between *A* and *B*?
2. Is there any reason to think that the correlation is any more than a coincidence?
3. Could there be some third factor, *C*, that is causing both *A* and *B*?

As an example of the third critical question, consider the correlation between drinking red wine every day with a meal and fewer heart attacks among men over forty. Subsequent studies showed that drinking alcohol of any sort (in moderation, meaning one or two drinks per day) was associated with significantly fewer attacks within this group. The latest finding suggested that it was the alcohol in the red wine that caused the outcome and that drinking beer or any kind of alcohol would have the same effect.

In short, argument from correlation to cause is a legitimate and correct type of inference of a presumptive and defeasible type, and it is extremely useful for practical purposes in guiding action in practical matters. But in many cases, there is a natural human tendency to leap too quickly to a causal conclusion once a correlation has apparently been observed. In such cases, it is better to ask appropriate critical questions before placing too much weight on an argument from correlation to cause.

Here is a final word of warning. All arguments based on the statistical claim of a correlation should be questioned regarding how the terms were defined in the survey. The red wine theory of heart disease prevention was recently questioned by a group of cardiologists who pointed out that while most countries require a specific cause of death to be stated, in France, many fatalities caused by cardiac arrest are officially put down to "sudden death."[11] This way of reporting medical statistics would mean that the findings reported would lessen the number of heart attacks.

[11] Bernard D. Kaplan, "The Attack on Red Wine's Hearty Reputation," *Globe and Mail*, September 16, 1994, p. A9.

EXERCISE 3.4

Analyze the following arguments by identifying the argumentation scheme involved. Identify the premises and conclusion of the argument. If there are any questionable aspects of the argument that should be considered, identify critical questions that should be asked.

(a) A report published in the *Journal of the American Medical Association* found a statistical relationship between typical "male pattern" baldness (spreading outward from the crown of the head) and heart attacks. Men with this type of baldness were found to be 30 to 300 percent more likely to suffer a heart attack than men with little or no hair loss. Researchers hesitated to draw the conclusion that baldness causes heart attacks, and some speculated whether stress or a common hormonal factor might be involved (David Gelman, Carolyn Friday and Shawn D. Lewis, "A Really Bad Hair Day," *Newsweek*, March 8, 1993, p. 62).

(b) A professor of medicine at the University of Toronto told a committee studying welfare programs in Ontario that children from poor families are twice as likely as children from more affluent families to die in infancy, or in accidents, and two and a half times as likely to die from infectious diseases. He concluded that poverty is an invisible killer that is more deadly than cancer (*The Winnipeg Free Press*, February 8, 1987, p. 10).

FIVE Argument from Consequences and Slippery Slope

One very common form of argumentation is used where one party in a dialogue says to the other, "This action would not be good, because it could have bad consequences." For example, suppose you are thinking of taking a certain medication and your doctor says, "You have high blood pressure, and taking this medication raises blood pressure, so in your case there would be a bad side effect of taking it." This form of argumentation is called *argumentum ad consequentiam*, or argument from consequences (literally, it means 'argument to consequence'). As a form of argumentation, it cites allegedly foreseeable consequences of a proposed action as the premise, and the conclusion is then inferred that this course of action is or is not recommended. This form of reasoning can be used in a positive or negative way, as an argument to respond to a proposal that has been put forward when two parties are having a dialogue on what to do. In argument from positive consequences, a policy or course of action is supported by citing positive consequences of carrying out this policy or course of action. In argument from negative consequences, a policy or course of action is argued against by citing negative consequences of carrying it out.

Argument from consequences is often used in economic and political deliberations where two parties (or groups) disagree on what is the best course of action to pursue. For example, suppose that two persons, Bob and Helen, disagree on whether tipping is generally a good custom or a good social policy that ought to be continued. Bob might use the following argument.

PREMISE: If the practice of tipping were discontinued, unemployment would result.

PREMISE: Unemployment is a bad thing.

CONCLUSION: It would not be a good idea to discontinue the practice of tipping.

In this instance, Bob has used an argument from negative consequences. By citing negative consequences of a certain policy or course of action, Bob has argued against this policy or course of action.

Argument from consequences can also be used in a positive form, to support a policy or action. For example, Helen might use the following argument.

PREMISE: If the practice of tipping were discontinued, service providers would have greater self-esteem.

PREMISE: Having greater self-esteem is a good thing.

CONCLUSION: The practice of tipping should be discontinued.

In this argument from consequences, Helen has cited positive consequences of a certain policy or course of action as a reason for supporting that policy or course of action as being a good idea. As the last two examples show, positive argument from consequences is often pitted against negative argument from consequences in argumentation.

Such conflicting arguments from consequences are common in political debates weighing up the alleged pros and cons of a course of action that is being contemplated. For example, in March 1995 voters in the province of Quebec were having town hall meetings deliberating on whether to have a referendum giving them a choice to leave Canada and form a separate country or stay as a province in Canada. Some argued that the economic consequences of separation from Canada would be highly negative for Quebec. Others argued that having a single French-speaking country separate from English-speaking Canada would have positive consequences for French culture in Quebec. In cases of this kind of political deliberation, typically the argument is about the future outcomes or possibilities of some course of action that is unique, at least in many respects, so that the likely consequences must be guessed or conjectured. The future can never be known with certainty, and guessing can be highly conjectural where many complex and changing variables of a real situation are involved. Hence argument from consequences is generally presumptive in nature as a kind of reasoning.

The argumentation scheme for argument from positive consequences is the following.

ARGUMENTATION SCHEME FOR ARGUMENT FROM POSITIVE CONSEQUENCES

PREMISE: If *A* is brought about, good consequences will plausibly occur.

CONCLUSION: *A* should be brought about.

The corresponding argumentation scheme for argument from negative consequences is the following.

ARGUMENTATION SCHEME FOR ARGUMENT FROM NEGATIVE CONSEQUENCES

PREMISE: If *A* is brought about, bad consequences will plausibly occur.

CONCLUSION: *A* should not be brought about.

There are the same three critical questions matching either of these argumentation schemes, whether it is the positive or negative variant.

1. How strong is the probability or plausibility that these cited consequences will (may, might, must) occur?
2. What evidence, if any, supported the claim that these consequences will (may, might, must) occur if *A* is brought about?
3. Are there consequences of the opposite value that ought to be taken into account?

Failure to answer any of these critical questions adequately, when asked by a dialogue partner or critic, casts an argument from consequences into doubt.

A slippery slope argument is a species of negative reasoning from consequences, used where two parties are deliberating together and one warns the other not to take a contemplated action, because it is a first step in a sequence of events that will lead to some horrible outcome. What is distinctive about the slippery slope argument as a special subtype of argument from consequences is that there is said to be a connected sequence of actions, such that once the first action in the series is carried out, a sequence of other actions will follow, so that once the sequence starts there is no stopping it, until (eventually) the horrible outcome comes about. This particularly horrible outcome is the final event in the sequence and represents something that would very definitely go against goals that are important for the participant in the deliberation who is being warned, for example, it might be his personal safety or security.

There are several types of slippery slope arguments, but the general form of the most common type of the slippery slope argument can be characterized by the following argumentation scheme. A slippery slope argument always has this recursive feature, meaning that it applies over and over again in a repeating process. This feature is defined in the recursive premise below.

ARGUMENTATION SCHEME FOR THE SLIPPERY SLOPE ARGUMENT

FIRST STEP PREMISE: A_0 is up for consideration as a proposal that seems initially like something that should be brought about.

RECURSIVE PREMISE: Bringing up A_0 would plausibly lead (in the given circumstances, as far as we know) to A_1, which would in turn plausibly lead to A_2, and so forth, through the sequence $A_2, \ldots, A_n$.

BAD OUTCOME PREMISE: A_n is a horrible (disastrous, bad) outcome.

CONCLUSION: A_0 should not be brought about.

The characteristic idea of the slippery slope argument is that once you take that first action in the sequence, it is like pushing off from the top of an Olympic ski-jump run. Once you have kicked off, turning back becomes harder and harder. At some ill-defined point or gray area, there is no turning back. Once you are into this area, there is only one way to go: faster and faster down the slope until you hit the bottom. So if you don't want to go careening down the slope out of control and hit the bottom (with disastrous consequences of personal injury), the message is that you had better not take that first step at all.

Slippery slope arguments are often used to give reason not to start taking drugs, because once you start taking an addictive substance, it gets harder and harder to stop. At some point that cannot be defined specifically for each individual, you are "hooked," and the outcome is that your life will be badly damaged or possibly even destroyed. Once a person begins to use drugs, physical dependency can make it very difficult to stop, and the sequence of subsequent outcomes can have all kinds of other bad consequences that eventually result in a painful life of substance dependency and eventually an unpleasant death. In this kind of case, the basis of the slippery slope is a physical addiction and dependency, caused by the body's reaction to the substance. As you consume more of the substance, you need more to keep up the habit. There are also variants on this argument that cite an alleged sequence leading from one addictive substance to another. Here the linkages are harder to prove, and debates about such arguments are highly controversial. One case of this sort is the argument that the decriminalization of marijuana would be the first step in a sequence that would lead to greater drug use and a progression to the use of harder drugs, such as heroin, and eventually to a society where the use of all kinds of drugs has become common and uncontrollable, with all the social problems attending widespread drug abuse.[12] A variant on this case with an even weaker linkage is the argument used when one person warns another not to start smoking, arguing it may lead to the use of other addictive substances, like marijuana, which in turn may lead to the use of harder drugs.

Slippery slope arguments are frequently used in disputes on ethics and public policy. In the case of *Texas v. Johnson* (1989) the issue concerned a man who burned an American flag during a political demonstration in Dallas to protest policies of the Reagan administration. The case of whether he should be convicted of "desecrating a venerated object" eventually went to the U.S. Supreme Court, where it was ruled that, in this case, the flag-burning was an "overtly expressive" act and was thus protected under free speech (First Amendment). Justice Brennan used a slippery slope argument as part of the rationale for his decision.

> We perceive no basis on which to hold that the principle underlying our decision in Schacht does not apply to this case. To conclude that

[12] Ralph Johnson and J. Anthony Blair, *Logical Self-defense*, 2nd ed. (Toronto: McGraw-Hill Ryerson, 1983), pp. 161–162.

> the Government may permit designated symbols to be used to communicate only a limited set of messages would be to enter territory having no discernible or defensible boundaries. Could the Government, on this theory, prohibit the burning of state flags? Of copies of the Presidential seal? Of the Constitution? In evaluating these choices under the First Amendment, how would we decide which symbols were sufficiently special to warrant this unique status? To do so, we would be forced to consult our own political preferences, and impose them on the citizenry, in the very way that the First Amendment forbids us to do so.[13]

The argument was that once the burning of the flag in a case such as the one above were prohibited by law, it would set a precedent for banning many other kinds of acts, such as burning other objects that represented federal or state governments. To have to enforce all these infringements would be costly, and the value of doing so seems dubious. It would lead to the imposition of political preferences in banning all kinds of expressive acts that would pose conflicts with the First Amendment.

In a Doonesbury cartoon[14] one character warned another of the perils of banning "physical desecration of the flag" by citing a number of more specific steps in the sequence of a slippery slope.

> ... "physical desecration" is a tricky business.... For instance, will it be illegal to burn a paper flag? Or to tear up a photo of a flag? How about cutting a cake decorated with a flag? And what about flag clothing? Are you a patriot if you wear a flag T-shirt, but a felon if you wear flag pants? And what does that make Uncle Sam? And what about art – who decides whether a flag painting is a desecration or an homage? Also, what about other national symbols, like the eagle or the Statue of Liberty? Or state flags? Or the confederate flag? All sacred to somebody – should they be protected? Also, since burning is the only sanctioned way of disposing of a worn-out flag, aren't we really outlawing an idea instead of an act? And, if so, what other ideas do we outlaw?

Here we can see that what propels the sequence of reasoning down the slope is not only the idea of setting a precedent, but also the linguistic difficulty of circumscribing a vague term such as 'physical desecration'. Once it has been applied to one object, like a flag, it is hard to stop it from also being applied to other objects, like a cake or a T-shirt. This vagueness is the gray area of the slippery slope.

[13] *Texas v. Johnson*, 1989, 10.
[14] G. B. Trudeau, August 12, 1989.

Slippery slope arguments conforming to the premises and conclusion of the argumentation scheme can be reasonable as presumptive arguments in a dialogue, provided all the connected steps in the sequences, linking the first step with the final (horrible) outcome, are adequately filled in and justified. In some cases, however, these links in the reasoning are not supported adequately, and the slope argument is not plausible. In some cases, it is even used unconvincingly as a fear appeal argument. The problem with fear appeal arguments is that they can easily backfire if the fear appeal is too exaggerated and unconvincing. For example, in the cult film *Reefer Madness*, teenagers were warned of the dangers of smoking marijuana, but the evidence was dubious, according to what was known at the time. Hence the argument was an unconvincing fear appeal argument that the audiences found funny. Generally, empirical evidence is needed to back up a slippery slope argument adequately. Since the period when this film was popular, considerable empirical evidence of the negative consequences of taking marijuana has been found. But how strong the link is between taking marijuana and progressing to harder drugs remains a subject of some controversy. Even so, drugs that are addictive are very dangerous for some people to try. So the burden of proof in such cases should be weighted toward caution. If even trying such a drug might be dangerous, urging a person to be cautious by not taking the first step could be a reasonable slippery slope argument.

Generally, in evaluating slippery slope reasoning, it is best to begin by identifying the three premises of the argument. The first-step premise postulates the first step in the sequence. The recursive premise describes the mechanism of the slope – the repeating or propelling factor that drives the sequence along past a point where the sequence can be stopped. The bad outcome premise cites the horrible outcome, supposedly the final event in the sequence. The most important appropriate critical questions for a slippery slope argument concern part 2, the sequence of steps in the argument.

1. What intervening propositions in the sequence linking up A_0 with A_n are actually given?
2. What other steps are required to fill in the sequence of events to make it plausible?
3. What are the weakest links in the sequence, where specific critical questions should be asked about whether one event will really lead to another?

How strong a slippery slope argument needs to be depends on how strong a claim is made in the conclusion – does it say that the horrible outcome may, will, or must occur? The stronger the claim, the stronger the argument needed to back it up. However, since slippery slope arguments are about the future, any of them that have a "must" in the conclusion (or any wording indicating inevitability) should be viewed very skeptically.

One must be very careful to distinguish between instances of arguments from negative consequences and instances of slippery slope arguments because, as indicated above, the slippery slope arguments described above are species of argumentation from negative consequences. What marks out the slippery slope argument as a special type of argument from negative consequences is that the slippery slope argument always has the characteristic recursive premise. This premise describes a sequence of actions where the argument moves forward from one step to the next by some repeating process of mechanism that drives the actions or consequences past the point where the sequence can be stopped. Many instances of argument from consequences do have such a recursive premise stated as part of the argument. If an argument from negative consequences does not have this recursive feature, it should not be classified as a slippery slope argument.

EXERCISE 3.5

Analyze the following dialogues, classifying the argument used by identifying its argumentation scheme. Identify the premises and conclusion of the argument. If there are any questionable aspects of the argument that should be considered, identify critical questions that should be asked.

(a) Pierre and Mary are arguing about the issue of Quebec separating from the rest of Canada. Pierre maintains that separation would be a good thing, because it would preserve the Francophone cultural heritage. Mary argues that if Quebec separates, there would be massive unemployment, especially in Quebec, where there are many federal government employees.

(b) Bob is about to try to fix his radio by picking up a live wire. Jane warns him, "I wouldn't do that. You could get a nasty shock!"

(c) Anne and Fred are arguing about the issue of whether scientists should get permission to do laboratory research on human embryos. Fred argues: "We must stop all research with human embryos immediately, because it will lead to more and more experimental research on human fetuses, and eventually, the harvest of human aborted fetuses will become such a resource for treatment of diseases like Parkinson's disease and muscular dystrophy, there will be no turning back."

(d) John and Louise are discussing the issue of whether physician-assisted suicide should be allowed in cases of terminal illness. Louise argues: "Once you allow it in cases of terminal illness, it will lead to euthanasia of the disabled. That will mean that anyone who is regarded as troublesome will be eliminated as 'unfit' by the state. Ultimately, the only citizens who will be allowed to live are those who fit the current concept of an ideal healthy person."

(e) In a debate on whether the practice of not allowing prayers in the schools should be continued, some participants worried that different religions might want to have special prayers representing their own religious practices and views. One participant argued that with all the different minority groups, once you accept one kind of religion as legitimate, you are going to have to accept many other kinds of religious groups as having a legitimate right to have prayers or religious services in the classroom. This participant said: "It's a Pandora's box. You know that Satanism is a religion too!"

(f) Trevor and Mary are arguing about the issue of whether drivers' licenses should have photographs on them. Trevor argues: "It would be the first step toward a police state!"

SIX Argument from Sign

In many cases of argumentation, data observed in a case are taken as a sign of something that fits a familiar pattern. Drawing an inference from a patient's symptom taken as a visible sign of a disease or some other known condition is a very common form of reasoning in medical diagnosis. For example, suppose a patient who is feeling ill has yellow skin. Such an observation may be taken by the physician as a sign or indicator that the patient has hepatitis. Of course, such a provisional diagnosis is only a hypothesis. The patient may have some other liver disease or may have a skin disease that does not affect the liver. This form of argumentation is defeasible at the first stages and may lead only to a plausible conclusion in the form of a tentative hypothesis. It may lead to further observations and tests that can be carried out. The hypothesis may be tested, for example, by analyzing a sample of the patient's blood. Argument from sign is typically a defeasible argument in an investigation that leads to the collection of further evidence. The following classic example illustrates argument from sign.

> Travis and Lisa are walking along a hiking trail in Jasper National Park and they see some imprints on the trail. Travis examines them closely and says he recognizes them as bear tracks, saying. "A bear has been here." Lisa replies, "How do you know those imprints are bear tracks? They don't look big enough to be bear tracks." Travis replies, "They are the tracks of a small bear. In fact, they are the tracks of a small grizzly bear, as we can see by these very long claw imprints."

In this case, Travis has presented an argument to Lisa. She has expressed doubts that the imprints they saw are bear tracks. Travis has used argument from sign to give her a reason to accept the conclusion that they are bear tracks. Argument from sign is a presumptive type of argument based on a premise that, generally, findings, as observed in a case, are characteristic of some type of object, event, or action. The other premise is that these characteristics or signs are present in the given case. The conclusion is that the particular event or object in question will occur or has occurred in this particular case.

The argumentation scheme for argument from sign is the following, where *A* and *B* are taken as these two propositions.

ARGUMENTATION SCHEME FOR ARGUMENT FROM SIGN

SPECIFIC PREMISE: *A* (a finding) is true in this situation.

GENERAL PREMISE: *B* is generally indicated as true when its sign, *A*, is true.

CONCLUSION: *B* is true in this situation.

It is easy to see why argument from sign, in the scheme displayed above, is defeasible. The general premise is not an absolute universal generalization. The one proposition being true generally (but not necessarily) indicates that the other will be true as well. Yellow skin may be sign of liver dysfunction. But there are cases where a patient will have yellow skin but will not have liver dysfunction. The presence of yellow skin coloration is just a preliminary indicator or symptom. It may have evidential value. But the presence of other known factors in a case may rule it out, defeating the initial inference to the conclusion that this patient has liver dysfunction.

Argument from sign proceeds from a finding of some data in the form of a sign or indicator. The sign is some sort of observed finding. A conclusion is then drawn that the sign indicates the presence of something else that it is connected to. The conclusion drawn can be expressed as a proposition that some event will or has taken place or that some object or factor is present. A finding is known or taken to be a sign of some proposition inferred from it for various reasons. It could be that one type of event is usually causally connected to the other. Or it could be that a finding of the presence of some other factor, because of some identifiable characteristic of that factor, is made apparent in the sign. For example, the presence of dark clouds is a sign of rain because one is commonly associated with the other and because dark clouds can be cited as a cause of rain. For the purposes of the argumentation scheme, the two things that are connected, the finding and the conclusion drawn from it, can be expressed in the form of propositions.

In evaluating argument from sign, the following two critical questions are appropriate.

1. What is the strength of the correlation of the sign with the event signified?
2. Are there other events that would more reliably account for the sign?

Quite often, argument from sign is a weak form of argument that cannot be relied on uncritically. Even so, it is a presumptive form of argument that can sometimes help point an investigation or chain of reasoning to a plausible conclusion.

In some cases, arguments from sign are predictive. For example, dark clouds or high winds might be a sign of a particular kind of weather that will occur in the future, such as a storm. In some cases, arguments from sign are used in a retroductive fashion, as in the bear case where the existence of the bear prints are used to reason backward in time to the conclusion that, in the past, the bear was present at this location. The presence of the bear is used as a basis for explaining the presence of the tracks.[15]

If we look at argument from sign as a form of defeasible reasoning, we can easily see its presumptive nature. The bear tracks could be taken as a sign of something else, depending on what was observed and where the observations were made. Perhaps someone, using some sort of gadget, cleverly planted the bear tracks there to mislead us or give us the impression that there are bears in this region. But since in Jasper National Park, normally there are bears present, we would take the presence of these bear tracks as a pretty good argument that there was a bear in this

[15] Sometimes the kind of argumentation exhibited in the bear tracks example is called inference to the best explanation. The importance of this form of argumentation in scientific discovery was established by the American philosopher Charles S. Peirce.

region. However, if we were to find bear tracks in a university classroom, we would be much less inclined to leap to the conclusion that there must have been a bear present in this classroom. We would probably expect that these bear prints were the result of some student prank or would try to find some other explanation, because it would not be normal for a bear to be present in a university classroom.

Characteristically, argument from sign provides a basis for making an initial intelligent guess or hypothesis, which leads to a fuller explanation once the fuller context of a case is filled in. For example, in the following case[16] two initial signs of footprints and tusk-shaped wounds led to an explanation of several rhinoceros deaths.

> When conservationists at South Africa's Pilanesberg game reserve discovered a series of systematically killed rhinos, they had two clues to the culprits: tusk-shaped wounds on the corpses and elephant footprints in the vicinity. Although an elephant does not normally attack a rhinoceros, the game reserve has a number of unsupervised, adolescent males who would normally be kept in line by bulls. Without adult role models to test themselves against, the animals have become juvenile delinquents.

Here the tusk-shaped wounds and the elephant footprints offered clues on a basis of argument from sign. Two signs suggested that elephants were the killers. But further evidence led to an even more specific hypothesis. The initial hypothesis was thereby confirmed, once the fuller context of lack of supervision of the juveniles by role models was filled in.

In some cases, there is a sequence of signs, each one of which, by itself, gives only a small weight of presumption for a conclusion. But when you put the sequence together, there is an evidence-accumulating argument. This argument uses a chain of reasoning containing several arguments from sign to build up to a much more plausible weight of presumption in favor of the conclusion. In the following tale from *A Study in Scarlet*, Dr. Watson, looking for accommodations in London, has just been introduced to Sherlock Holmes. Holmes used the following sequence of reasoning to arrive at the conclusion that Watson has just returned from Afghanistan:

> Here is a gentleman of a medical type, but with the air of a military man. Clearly an army doctor, then. He has just come from the tropics, for his face is dark, and that is not the natural tint of his skin, for his wrists are fair. He has undergone hardship and sickness, as his

[16] Michael Kesterton, "Social Studies," *Globe and Mail*, October 13, 1994, p. A20.

> haggard face says clearly. His left arm has been injured. He holds it in a stiff and unnatural manner. Where in the tropics could an English army doctor have seen much hardship and got his arm wounded? Clearly in Afghanistan.[17]

Holmes made a guess, in this case. It was only a plausible hypothesis. But as the individual instances of argument from sign built up evidence as his sequence of reasoning proceeded, the accumulation of evidence made his conclusion a plausible one to draw (at least, according to the story). The context of the case also played an important role here, because Holmes was aware that there had recently been a war in Afghanistan in which many British men of that era had taken part. Hence the best explanation of all the phenomena that Holmes observed – the tanned skin, the injured arm, and so forth – would be that Watson had been a participant in the Afghanistan campaign. Of course, it was only a hypothesis. But Holmes's conclusion drawn by argument from sign was a clever bit of reasoning, characteristic of the fictional detective's careful observations and power of drawing inferences from them.

EXERCISE 3.6

Analyze the following arguments by identifying the argumentation scheme involved. Identify the premises and conclusion of the argument. If there are any questionable aspects of the argument that should be considered, identify critical questions that should be asked.

1. Barbara had a runny nose, fever, cough, and nasal congestion. On the fifth day, red spots appeared on her body. Therefore, Barbara has the measles (or rubeola).
2. Jane had a runny nose, swollen glands, and a slight fever. On the third day, red spots appeared on her face and neck, and then faded after two days. The physician suspected Jane had German measles (rubella). He gave Jane a blood test that confirmed his diagnosis.

SEVEN Argument from Commitment

In argument from commitment, the proponent takes as premise a proposition that the respondent is committed to and uses it to press the

[17] Arthur Conan Doyle, *The Complete Sherlock Holmes*, vol. 1 (New York: Doubleday, 1932), p. 11.

respondent to concede another proposition that follows by inference from that premise. An example is the following case.[18]

Bob: Ed, you are a communist, aren't you?

Ed: Of course. You know that.

Bob: Well, then you should be on the side of the union in this recent labor dispute.

In this case, let's say, Ed has frequently advocated communism in the past and has often been known, for example, to shout, "Power to the people!" in demonstrations. Also, in this case, when asked, Ed admitted to Bob that he is a communist. So the conclusion may be drawn that Ed is a communist or that he committed to communism, as we might put it. Given this general commitment of Ed's, Bob draws the plausible conclusion that Ed sides with the union in a particular labor dispute. Of course, Ed might not, but since a communist would normally be strongly in support of the union side in a labor dispute, it can be inferred defeasibly that Ed is on the union side. Of course, if the dialogue went on, and Ed declared that in this particular case he was not with the union, Bob's conclusion would have to be withdrawn, on the balance of considerations.

Argument from commitment has the following general form, where *a* is a participant in a dialogue, and *A* and *B* are statements, as usual.

ARGUMENTATION SCHEME FOR ARGUMENT FROM COMMITMENT

COMMITMENT EVIDENCE PREMISE: In this case it was shown that *a* is committed to proposition *A*, according to the evidence of what he said or did.

LINKAGE OF COMMITMENTS PREMISE: Generally, when an arguer is committed to *A*, it can be inferred that he is also committed to *B*.

CONCLUSION: In this case, *a* is committed to *B*.

There are two critical questions that are appropriate for responding to the use of argument from commitment.

1. What evidence in the case supports the claim that *a* is committed to *A*, and does it include contrary evidence, indicating that *a* might not be committed to *A*?

[18] Douglas Walton, *Argumentation Schemes for Presumptive Reasoning* (Mahwah, N.J.: Erlbaum, 1996), p. 55.

2. Is there room for questioning whether there is an exception in this case to the general rule that commitment to *A* implies commitment to *B*?

In examining the second critical question, one should ask whether proposition *B*, as cited in the linkage of commitments premise, is identical to the proposition *A* as cited in it. If not, some discussion on what exactly is the nature of the relationship between the two propositions can be helpful.

If the respondent in the dialogue asks either critical question, where the proponent has just used argument from commitment at the last move, then the burden of proof is shifted back to the proponent's side. Unless the proponent can answer the critical question adequately, the argument from commitment is defeated.

In the example dialogue above, it is pretty clear from the evidence of his words and actions that Ed is committed to communism, so the first critical question can easily be answered. But Ed could possibly reply, using the second critical question, by explaining that in this particular case, he thinks the union is wrong, because their demands are excessive and will bankrupt the company, putting everyone out of work. So it is possible to reply to an argument from commitment by saying that normally you would be committed to a particular policy, but that this particular case is an exceptional one for you. There is the possibility of an exception to the rule. The bringing forward of such evidence in asking the second critical question would defeat the argument.

The second critical question has to do with what the respondent is committed to in the premise, in relation to what he is committed to in the conclusion. In some cases, the same commitment can be involved both in the premise and in the conclusion. For example, consider the following dialogue.

Bob: Ed, you are a communist, aren't you?

Ed: Of course. You know I am passionate about that.

Bob: Well, then I assume you advocate the communist position, taking the union side in the recent labor dispute.

In this example dialogue, the proposition *A*, Ed's being a communist, is identical or at least very close to being identical to *B*, in both the premise and the conclusion of the inference. By contrast, in the previous example dialogue, there is much more of a difference in the relationship between the two propositions. In examining any case, a careful look at the actual wording of the two propositions is helpful.

One way that argument from commitment can be abused is through the committing of the straw man fallacy of distorting or exaggerating an opponent's position, in order to make it easier to attack and refute it as implausible. Environmental debates provide classic cases of such arguments, as the following example will indicate.

Stewart and Margo are having a dispute on environmental issues, where Margo has taken a moderate position to the effect that development should be allowed only if it is sustainable and efforts are made not to pollute the environment. Stewart replies, "I see that you are one of those extreme protectionists who think that the earth should be a pristine wilderness where all industrial development is forbidden."

Much here depends on the prior context of the dialogue, and the particular propositions that Margo has committed herself to accepting as her position. But suppose her commitments are not as extreme as the radical view portrayed by Stewart and that her form of environmentalism is moderate. In such a case, her point of view has been misrepresented by him and made to appear more extreme than it really is. This kind of argumentation is merely a tactic to make it easier to refute her argument. As shown by this case, the second critical question is extremely important. The proposition that the proponent is committed to might not be the same as the proposition attributed to her by the respondent. If there is a difference between the two propositions, there has to be a reason to draw the inference from the one to the other. Thus the use of argument from commitment is sometimes dangerous. It can even be used as a misleading and erroneous move to attack an opponent in a dialogue.

Argument from commitment can be used in an even stronger way to infer that a respondent is inconsistent in his commitments. Suppose that in another case, Ed had actually taken the side of the management in a recent labor dispute. In such a case, Bob might use argument from commitment in a negative fashion to draw the conclusion that Ed's conduct implies an inconsistency. Consider the following dialogue.

Bob: You are a communist, aren't you?

Ed: Of course. You know that I have often said so.

Bob: Well, you say you are a communist, but you were against the union side in the recent labor dispute, showing that you are not a communist.

In this example dialogue, Bob is drawing the conclusion that Ed's commitments are inconsistent. Or at least he is arguing that they appear to be inconsistent and that the apparent inconsistency raises doubts about whether Ed's professed commitments are really his commitments after all. Bob says, "Well, you say you are a communist," suggesting that Ed may not really be a communist at all, because "actions speak louder than words" when it comes to revealing one's commitments. This kind of attack can be used to make an arguer appear to be illogical or even hypocritical, as is shown in the analysis of various kinds of personal attack arguments in section 9 below.

To reply to this kind of negative use of argument from commitment, as in his response to the third critical question, above, Ed has to offer some kind of account giving his reasons why he did what he did, showing how this case was exceptional. Ed has to go further into the details of the case to restore the consistency of his commitments. This negative use of argument from commitment, called argument from inconsistent commitment, has the following general form.

ARGUMENTATION SCHEME FOR ARGUMENT FROM INCONSISTENT COMMITMENT

INITIAL COMMITMENT PREMISE: *a* has claimed or indicated that he is committed to proposition *A* (generally or in virtue of what he said in the past).

OPPOSED COMMITMENT PREMISE: Other evidence in this particular case shows that *a* is not really committed to *A*.

CONCLUSION: *a*'s commitments are inconsistent.

To reply to the use of an argument from inconsistent commitments, a respondent may need to go further into the details of the case or the nature of his commitment to show why the inconsistency is only apparent and not real. Alternatively, if he admits the inconsistency is real, he must somehow explain how the conflict arose.

The critical questions matching the argument from inconsistent commitments are the following.

1. What is the evidence supposedly showing that *a* is committed to *A*?
2. What further evidence in the case is alleged to show that *a* is not committed to *A*?

3. How does the evidence from 1 and 2 prove that there is a conflict of commitments?

The problem generally with arguments from inconsistent commitments is that an action attributed to someone might suggest that they are not committed to a policy, but how an action is interpreted in a particular situation, as expressing a commitment, is often highly subject to dispute. If I am a professed vegetarian but eat beef on one occasion, does that action mean that I am now committed to a policy of eating beef? Maybe not, because I may just have slipped up on one occasion or been very hungry when no vegetarian food was available. What an action implies, as a commitment, may not be so easy to judge and may require looking at a body of evidence in a given case.

EXERCISE 3.7

Analyze the arguments in the following dialogues by identifying the argumentation scheme of the argument put forward by one party. Identify the premises and conclusion of the argument. If there are any questionable aspects of the argument that should be considered, identify critical questions that should be asked.

Dialogue (a)

RON: Rose, you are a Catholic, aren't you?

ROSE: Yes, you know that.

RON: Well, then you must be voting against the Democrats in the next election, because they support abortion on demand.

Dialogue (b)

TINA: You believe in the theory of evolution, don't you, Tom?

TOM: Well yes, I suppose I do accept that theory.

TINA: So you are one of those godless materialists who rejects equal rights on the grounds that all life should be a struggle where only the fittest should survive.

Dialogue (c)

BRUTUS: You said you were a supporter of free enterprise, right, Barbara?

BARBARA: That's what I maintained, yes.

BRUTUS: But last week you said you approved of the new policy of tightening controls over emission of industrial pollution in the Bay Area. So you are not really committed to private enterprise at all, in that instance.

Dialogue (d)

SENATOR S: Back ten years ago, you condemned our policy on the grounds it contributed to inflation.

SENATOR T: Well yes, I did.

SENATOR S: But while your party has been in power, there has been more inflation than ever.

EIGHT Ad Hominem Arguments

In any of the kinds of conversational frameworks in which people reason with each other, despite the opposition and partisanship characteristic of many kinds of dialogue, there must also be a presumption that in order to achieve collaborative goals, participants must observe rules of polite conversation. Arguers must be able to trust each other, to some extent at least, to be informative and relevant, to take turns politely, and to express their commitments clearly and honestly. Without this kind of collaboration in contributing to a dialogue, argument, of a kind that uses reasoning to fulfill its goals of dialogue interaction, would not be possible. For these reasons, attacking the other party's honesty or sincerity in argument is a powerful move. Such an argument leads one to the conclusion that such a person lacks credibility as an arguer who can be trusted to play by the rules. This argument is so powerful because it suggests that such a person cannot ever be trusted and that therefore whichever argument they use, it may simply be discounted as worthless. Thus the person attacked cannot meaningfully take part in the dialogue any longer, no matter how many good arguments they seem to have. Because they are so powerful and dangerous, ad hominem arguments have often been treated in the past as fallacious. Their use in negative campaign tactics in political argumentation is notorious. But they can sometimes be reasonable arguments. For example, in legal argumentation in a trial, it can be legitimate for a cross-examining attorney to question the ethical character of a witness. The lawyer may even argue that the witness has lied in the past and use this argument to raise questions about his character for honesty. But before we can evaluate such ad hominem arguments, it is necessary to know what form they take.

The simplest form of the ad hominem, or personal attack, argument is the direct or personal type, often called the abusive ad hominem argument in logic textbooks.

ARGUMENTATION SCHEME FOR THE DIRECT AD HOMINEM ARGUMENT

CHARACTER ATTACK PREMISE: *a* is a person of bad character.

CONCLUSION: *a*'s argument should not be accepted.

In this type of argument, *a* is the proponent of an argument that has been put forward. The premise that is alleged is that *a* is a person of bad character. What is normally cited is some aspect of *a*'s character as a person, and often, character for veracity is the focus of the attack. For example, the allegation may be, "He is a liar!" The attack is directed to destroying the person's credibility, so that his argument is discounted or reduced in plausibility because of the reduction in credibility of the arguer. Thus this type of attack is particularly effective where a person's argument depends on his presumed honesty or good character for its plausibility.

The critical questions appropriate for the direct ad hominem argument are the following.

1. How well supported by evidence is the allegation made in the character attack premise?
2. Is the issue of character relevant in the type of dialogue in which the argument was used?
3. Is the conclusion of the argument that *A* should be (absolutely) rejected, even if other evidence to support *A* has been presented, or is the conclusion merely (the relative claim) that *a* should be assigned a reduced weight of credibility as a supporter of *A*, relative to the total body of evidence available?

How these critical questions work can be illustrated by the following case.

Paul Johnson, in his book *Intellectuals*[19] wrote biographical accounts of several famous intellectuals showing the persons in question to be disorderly and unethical in their private lives. Of Karl Marx, Johnson wrote that Marx was lazy in collecting facts, and often dishonest in reporting them (pp. 68–71), and therefore he could not be trusted to use factual evidence in an objective way (p. 69).

[19] London: Weidenfeld and Nicholson, 1988.

To evaluate this use of the direct ad hominem argument, the three critical questions need to be asked. First, was it true that Marx was lazy in collecting facts and often dishonest in reporting them? To answer this question, we have to look at the cases in point cited by Johnson and ask whether the incidents he cites show that Marx was lazy or dishonest. To answer the second critical question, we have to ask what the purpose of Johnson's book is. The purpose of the book is to attack the credibility of several intellectuals, and intellectuals generally, by showing that they had bad character, as shown by their inability to run their own personal lives in an ethical way. Johnson's attack on Marx is relevant, then, in the sense that it contributes to this purpose. (A later chapter examines in greater depth the question of what relevance is generally.)

The third critical question can be put as follows. Is the conclusion of Johnson's argument that Marx's theory of economics should be absolutely rejected, or is Johnson's conclusion merely that Marx should be assigned a reduced weight of credibility, as a supporter of his theory, relative to the total body of evidence available? It would seem that the latter is the better interpretation of Johnson's argument. He is claiming not that Marx's theory is false or has been absolutely refuted as an economic theory by his ad hominem argument. He is claiming only that Marx is not a credible supporter of his theory. But even this weaker form of argument represents a serious attack on Marx's advocacy of his theory.

The weakest aspect of Johnson's ad hominem argument against Marx is on the count of the first question. But generally, his argument used to question Marx's credibility carries weight as a plausible argument, provided support can be given to Johnson's claim that Marx was lazy and dishonest in specific instances. If a person has a bad character in certain respects, it is perfectly legitimate for a biographer to argue that he had a bad character, by citing facts to support her thesis.

In many textbooks, the direct ad hominem argument is called 'abusive', suggesting that it is a fallacious argument and is always wrong. However, as the example above shows, sometimes direct ad hominem arguments can be reasonable, if they are based on facts that support them and if character is relevant as an issue in the dialogue. Still, it is true that the direct ad hominem argument is little more than 'mud slinging' or use of personal attack to try to discredit someone, often merely by innuendo or suggestion, with no facts presented to back up the allegation. Thus, care is needed in dealing with ad hominem arguments.

The circumstantial ad hominem argument is a variant on the direct one based on argument from inconsistent commitment. The allegation of inconsistent commitment is used to suggest that the arguer is not sincere in following the conclusion of his own argument. As in the following classic case of the circumstantial ad hominem argument, the allegation can be expressed by the saying, "You don't practice what you preach."

Parent: There is strong evidence of a link between smoking and chronic obstructive lung disease. Smoking is also associated with many other serious disorders. Smoking is unhealthy. So you should not smoke.

Child: But you smoke yourself. So much for your argument against smoking!

In this dialogue on smoking, the child's argument against the parent is an argument from inconsistent commitment, but it is also a circumstantial ad hominem argument. Indeed, the circumstantial ad hominem argument is a special subtype of argument from inconsistent commitment that has the following form.

ARGUMENTATION SCHEME FOR THE CIRCUMSTANTIAL AD HOMINEM ARGUMENT

ARGUMENT PREMISE: *a* advocates argument α, which has proposition *A* as its conclusion.

INCONSISTENT COMMITMENT PREMISE: *a* is personally committed to the opposite (negation) of *A*, as shown by commitments expressed in his or her personal actions or personal circumstances expressing such commitments.

CREDIBILITY QUESTIONING PREMISE: *a*'s credibility as a sincere person who believes in his own argument has been put into question (by the two premises above).

CONCLUSION: The plausibility of *a*'s argument α is decreased or destroyed.

The circumstantial ad hominem argument is a chain of argumentation based on combining argument from inconsistent commitment with the direct ad hominem argument. The first two premises represent an argument from inconsistent commitment. Together they lead to the third premise, the credibility questioning premise, which is the conclusion of the argument from inconsistent commitment. But this conclusion questions the arguer's character as a sincere person. Thus it functions, in turn, as a premise that leads to the final conclusion of the circumstantial ad hominem argument above. If the arguer *a* is a person of bad character, and his argument depends on his good character (because it depends on his credibility), then the plausibility of his argument is weakened or destroyed by the inconsistent commitment found in it.

The thrust of the child's argument in the smoking case is based on the perception of the parent's inconsistent commitments, as expressed in combining the argument premise and the inconsistent commitment premise. The parent advocates nonsmoking, but at the same time, she herself smokes. This combination of premises leads to the credibility questioning premise. If the parent is inconsistent in this way, it plausibly follows that the parent's belief in her own argument is open to doubt. That is, the parent lacks credibility in the child's eyes. Therefore, the child reasons, the parent's argument can be rejected.

There are many critical questions appropriate for the circumstantial type of ad hominem argument, but in this case, the following four are the most important ones to consider. Credibility of a participant in dialogue is an important notion in the third premise. An arguer's credibility is enhanced by showing that she has good character of a kind that makes her a cooperative and trustworthy participant who helps a dialogue. Conversely, an arguer's credibility can be attacked or destroyed by showing that she has bad character – for example, if she has lied or if she is not sincere in believing what she says. Thus, credibility can enhance the plausibility of an argument or detract from it.

1. Is there a pair of commitments that can be identified, shown by evidence to be commitments of *a*, and taken to show that *a* is practically inconsistent?
2. Once the practical inconsistency is identified that is the focus of the attack, could it be resolved or explained by further dialogue, thus preserving the consistency of the arguer's commitments in the dialogue or showing that *a*'s inconsistent commitment does not support the claim that *a* lacks credibility?
3. Is character an issue in the dialogue, and more specifically, does *a*'s argument depend on his or her credibility?
4. Is the conclusion the weaker claim that *a*'s credibility is open to question or the stronger claim that the conclusion of α is false?

Now let's see how the scheme applies to the smoking example. With respect to the first critical question, the practical inconsistency is easily identified: The parent claims you should not smoke (as a general practice), but the parent smokes herself. The second critical question is how serious the inconsistency is. In this case, the parent could reply, "Yes, I smoke, but I am trying my best to give it up. Once you start, it is hard to stop." If the dialogue were to be extended in this way, the parent could take some of the sting out of the claim of inconsistency. The third question is whether, as a result of the above considerations, the parent lacks credibility. The answer is, to some extent, yes. But some credibility can be restored by the kind of explanation cited above.

In this case, the most important critical question is the fourth one. The problem with the child's reaction is that he appears to reject the parent's conclusion (that smoking is unhealthy) outright, declaring, "So much for your argument against smoking!" This response is an overreaction, because it could quite possibly be that the parent has presented good evidence to support this conclusion. By throwing the whole argument out the window, the child could be making a big mistake. But if the child's ad hominem argument is only the weaker claim that the parent's credibility is open to question, on grounds of her being a smoker, then his standpoint could be quite a reasonable one.

EXERCISE 3.8

Analyze the following arguments by identifying the argumentation scheme involved. Identify the premises and conclusion of the argument. If there are any questionable aspects of the argument that should be considered, identify critical questions that should be asked.

(a) Bob Smith was once accused of sexual harassment. So it would be a mistake to take the views of this reprehensible pervert seriously. Therefore his theory about the disappearance of dinosaurs from the earth should be rejected.

(b) Child to Parent: Your argument that I should stop stealing candy from the corner store is no good. You told me yourself just a week ago that you too stole candy when you were a kid.

(c) Senator X: High taxes and too many regulations on business are the worst things for the economy, and these things are not under reasonable control at all.
Senator Y: When your party was in power, you drove taxes up to record levels, and introduced many new regulations on business. So you are either illogical or, more likely, a hypocrite who doesn't believe a word he says.

(d) A sign on a bumper sticker reads, "What's more ridiculous than an anti-hunter who eats meat?"

(e) Mr. S. denounced investors who take advantage of tax loopholes in the law, arguing that these bad practices ruin the economy for the average person. Mr. T. replied that S. himself had recently taken advantage of a "quick-flip" tax reduction scheme that was technically legal but was really a clever device for tax avoidance.

Mr. S. replied that you shouldn't condemn anyone for taking advantage of the law and that what he did was legal. So he, like any citizen, should be able to take advantage of legitimate deductions.

(f) A politician in office charged that government policy is unduly influenced by corporations that give money to the party. Critics pointed out that private companies had donated millions of dollars in contracts and grants to her own leadership campaign. Citing a list of such donations she recently received, they argued that her condemnation of business donations contradicted her own solicitation and acceptance of such funding. Her spokesperson replied that she was only speaking philosophically about an ideal world when she called for a political party system funded only by public money.

NINE Argument from Verbal Classification

Argument from verbal classification concludes that a particular thing has a certain property on the grounds that this thing can be classified under a general category of things that have this property. A simple example is the following argument.

All dolphins are classified as mammals.

Flipper is a dolphin.

Therefore, Flipper is a mammal.

In this case, the classification of dolphins as mammals is determined by the science of biology. To the extent that the classification of all dolphins as mammals is not subject to exceptions or to borderline cases, the inference in this example may be classified as deductively valid.

But arguments from verbal classification often rest on classifications based on word usage in everyday (non-scientific) speech. Consider the following example.

Anyone with net assets of over two billion dollars is wealthy.

Sarah has net assets of over two billion dollars.

Therefore, Sarah is wealthy.

The term 'wealthy' is vague in ordinary usage. But it is uncontroversial to classify anyone with net assets of over two billion dollars as wealthy. For such a total of net assets is beyond the gray area where there would be disputes about whether someone would rightly be classified as wealthy or not. Thus despite the vagueness of the word 'wealthy,' the argument from verbal classification in the example above can also be evaluated as being deductively valid.

However, some cases of classifications are more subject to doubt. Suppose the first premise in the example just above was the statement, "Anyone with net assets of over a million dollars is wealthy." Whether this statement is acceptable depends on the context of its use. In some countries, it would be true to say that anyone with net assets of over a million dollars is "wealthy." But in Saudi Arabia, for example, this classification would not be accepted as plausible. It not only would leave room for doubt, it would be rejected as a correct account of the way the word 'wealthy' is used.

Classification may be set in place by conventions of scientific terminology or by common usage of terms in everyday discourse. But in some cases, it can also be set in place by legal definitions of terms such as 'murder' or 'capital gains.' In any event, although some terms on which classifications are built are clearly defined in a way that is well established, other terms are highly subject to disputation. In these latter cases especially, it is important to raise critical questions about arguments based on a verbal classification.

The argument from verbal classification has the following general form, where a is an individual entity, x is a variable ranging over such entities, and F is a property.

ARGUMENTATION SCHEME FOR ARGUMENT FROM VERBAL CLASSIFICATION

INDIVIDUAL PREMISE: a has property F.

CLASSIFICATION PREMISE: For all x, if x has property F, then x can be classified as having property G.

CONCLUSION: a has property G.

The critical questions appropriate for the argument from verbal classification are the following.

1. What evidence is there that a definitely has property F, as opposed to evidence indicating room for doubt on whether it should be so classified?
2. Is the verbal classification in the classification premise based merely on a stipulative or biased definition that is subject to doubt?

A stipulative definition is one that is invented, as opposed to representing an established or widely accepting meaning. For example, the term 'quark' was introduced in physics to name a special type of subatomic particle. Or in economics, a recession may be stipulatively defined as two quarters of negative growth in GNP. This stipulative definition may not agree completely with the way the term is used in everyday speech, but it could arguably be put forward to represent a technical use of the term in economics as a discipline. These stipulative definitions seem reasonable, in context, but in some cases such definitions are more questionable because they have a value aspect, a kind of bias or spin that makes one's viewpoint look good or an opposed viewpoint look bad. Such use of emotionally loaded terms often needs to be critically questioned.

An example showing the importance of critically questioning argument from a verbal classification could occur in the case of the dialogue on tipping where Helen might use the following argument to support her viewpoint.

Tipping is elitist.

Therefore, tipping should be discontinued.

This argument from verbal classification is quite dangerous for Bob's side of the dispute. If Bob accepts the premise that tipping can be classified as an elitist practice, then by argument from verbal classification, Helen's thesis that tipping should be discontinued directly follows by a structurally correct inference. Unless Bob critically questions this use of argument from verbal classification, he loses the dispute. Bob has two ways to go. He can directly challenge Helen's premise that tipping is elitist, by asking the first critical question. Or he can pose the second critical question by arguing that even if tipping is elitist to some degree or in certain respects, this kind or degree of elitism is not necessarily a bad thing. In other words, he can question whether a practice ought to be discontinued just because it can be classified as elitist.

Arguments from verbal classification frequently lead to verbal disputes about the real meaning of a term. But they can be quite hard to defend against if the term in question has strong negative connotations of some sort in everyday usage. Once a stigma of this kind is affixed to a thesis, it has a staining effect that is difficult to remove. In the dialogue above, for example, Bob may try to turn the tables by calling Helen's thesis communistic or using some other term to describe it that is generally perceived to be pejorative. In some cases, then, it is not hard to see how argument from verbal classification can lead into name calling and ad hominem attacks.

Another important thing about argument from verbal classification is that this type of argument is frequently used in an aggressive way to bring pressure to bear against an opponent by the use of an argument from a verbal classification that is biased to one side of a dialogue. Suppose that two people are having a theological dialogue on the issue of whether God is a trinity or a unity, and the proponent of the trinity thesis argues against the unity defender using the following argument.

> Your thesis is heresy.
>
> Therefore, your thesis is wrong.

This use of argument from a verbal classification seems to have the unity defender on the ropes, assuming (as seems plausible perhaps to the disputants) that anything that can be classified as heresy sounds pretty bad and must have something wrong with it. This implication could stem from the negative connotations of the term 'heresy' – it sounds like something bad. But it should be questioned, by asking the first critical question above, whether the thesis in question really can be classified as heresy. And even if it can, it should be questioned, by asking the second critical question above, whether all heresy is really all that bad. After all, 'heresy' seems to be stipulatively defined as any view that is against church dogma. What needs to be recognized, then, is that 'heresy' is a kind of biased term, as used in the theological dialogue above. For any view that departs from the trinity arguer's view in the dialogue above can be classified as heresy. Heresy is used not only as a derogatory term, or at least it is meant to be, by the proponent of the argument in the dialogue above. Any view opposed to his own (the official church view) is thereby automatically classified as heresy, permitting no opposition to this view in the dialogue. What a respondent needs to do is to challenge the classification of his thesis under this derogatory term by questioning the biased use of this stipulative term.

Disputes about arguments from verbal classification are sometimes portrayed as trivial. But it is important to recognize that such arguments can be extremely powerful and significant, because their consequences can be enormously important. Such arguments can also be disputed at great length and, in some instances, at great cost in the courts. Consider the following example of this sort.

A private corporation wants to build a new housing development in area X. However, there is a law that if any area is classified as a wetland, no commercial development of any sort can take place on it. Any area that has wildfowl on it and that has over two hundred square meters of water surface during the month of July is classified as a wetland. An environmental group claims that area X meets these criteria and is therefore a wetland.

In this example, the environmental group uses the argument from verbal classification to make their case that area X is a wetland. If they win this case in court, the corporation will not be able to go ahead with their plans for developing area X.

EXERCISE 3.9

Analyze the following arguments by identifying the argumentation scheme involved. Identify the premises and conclusion of the argument. If there are any questionable aspects of the argument that should be considered, identify critical questions that should be asked.

(a) All kangaroos are marsupials. Jumper is a kangaroo. Therefore, Jumper is a marsupial.

(b) Anyone who believes in hiring people strictly on merit is taking an elitist viewpoint. Ben believes in hiring people strictly on merit. Therefore, Ben is an elitist.

(c) At issue in a trial was whether a man who had driven a bicycle while intoxicated had violated the law against drunk driving. The key question was whether a bicycle could be considered a vehicle. The court decided in the negative.

(d) Your argument supports free trade. Therefore, it is a globalist view that supports the big corporations that are against human rights.

TEN Summary

Below are listed all the argumentation schemes covered in this chapter, with the set of critical questions corresponding to each form of argument.

ARGUMENTATION SCHEME FOR ARGUMENT FROM POSITION TO KNOW

POSITION TO KNOW PREMISE: a is in a position to know whether A is true or false.

ASSERTION PREMISE: a asserts that A is true (false).

CONCLUSION: A is true (false).

1. Is a in a position to know whether A is true (false)?
2. Is a an honest (trustworthy, reliable) source?
3. Did a assert that A is true (false)?

ARGUMENTATION SCHEME FOR APPEAL TO EXPERT OPINION

MAJOR PREMISE: Source E is an expert in subject domain S containing proposition A.

MINOR PREMISE: E asserts that proposition A (in domain D) is true (false).

CONCLUSION: A may plausibly be taken to be true (false).

1. *Expertise Question*: How credible is E as an expert source?
2. *Field Question*: Is E an expert in the field that A is in?
3. *Opinion Question*: What did E assert that implies A?
4. *Trustworthiness Question*: Is E personally reliable as a source?
5. *Consistency Question*: Is A consistent with what other experts assert?
6. *Backup Evidence Question*: Is E's assertion based on evidence?

ARGUMENTATION SCHEME FOR APPEAL TO POPULAR OPINION

GENERAL ACCEPTANCE PREMISE: A is generally accepted as true.

PRESUMPTION PREMISE: If A is generally accepted as true, there exists a presumption in favor of A.

CONCLUSION: There exists a presumption in favor of A.

1. What evidence, such as a poll or an appeal to common knowledge, supports the claim that A is generally accepted as true?
2. Even if A is generally accepted as true, are there any reasons for doubting it is true?

ARGUMENTATION SCHEME FOR ARGUMENT FROM ANALOGY

SIMILARITY PREMISE: Generally, case C_1 is similar to case C_2.

BASE PREMISE: A is true (false) in case C_1.

CONCLUSION: A is true (false) in case C_2.

1. Are there differences between C_1 and C_2 that would tend to undermine the force of the similarity cited?
2. Is A true (false) in C_1?
3. Is there some other case C_3 that is also similar to C_1, but in which A is false (true)?

ARGUMENTATION SCHEME FOR ARGUMENT FROM CORRELATION TO CAUSE

CORRELATION PREMISE: There is a positive correlation between *A* and *B*.

CONCLUSION: *A* causes *B*.

1. Is there really a correlation between *A* and *B*?
2. Is there any reason to think that the correlation is any more than a coincidence?
3. Could there be some third factor, *C*, that is causing both *A* and *B*?

ARGUMENTATION SCHEME FOR ARGUMENT FROM POSITIVE CONSEQUENCES

PREMISE: If *A* is brought about, good consequences will plausibly occur.

CONCLUSION: *A* should be brought about.

ARGUMENTATION SCHEME FOR ARGUMENT FROM NEGATIVE CONSEQUENCES

PREMISE: If *A* is brought about, bad consequences will plausibly occur.

CONCLUSION: *A* should not be brought about.

The following three critical questions match the argumentation schemes from either positive or negative consequences.

1. How strong is the probability or plausibility that these cited consequences will (may, might, must) occur?
2. What evidence, if any, supported the claim that these consequences will (may, might, must) occur if *A* is brought about?
3. Are there consequences of the opposite value that ought to be taken into account?

ARGUMENTATION SCHEME FOR THE SLIPPERY SLOPE ARGUMENT

FIRST STEP PREMISE: A_0 is up for consideration as a proposal that seems initially like something that should be brought about.

RECURSIVE PREMISE: Bringing up A_0 would plausibly lead (in the given circumstances, as far as we know) to A_1, which would in turn plausibly lead to A_2, and so forth, through the sequence $A_2, \ldots, A_n$.

BAD OUTCOME PREMISE: A_n is a horrible (disastrous, bad) outcome.

CONCLUSION: A_0 should not be brought about.

1. What intervening propositions in the sequence linking up A_0 with A_n are actually given?
2. What other steps are required to fill in the sequence of events to make it plausible?

3. What are the weakest links in the sequence, where specific critical questions should be asked about whether one event will really lead to another?

ARGUMENTATION SCHEME FOR ARGUMENT FROM SIGN

SPECIFIC PREMISE: *A* (a finding) is true in this situation.

GENERAL PREMISE: *B* is generally indicated as true when its sign, *A*, is true.

CONCLUSION: *B* is true in this situation.

1. What is the strength of the correlation of the sign with the event signified?
2. Are there other events that would more reliably account for the sign?

ARGUMENTATION SCHEME FOR ARGUMENT FROM COMMITMENT

COMMITMENT EVIDENCE PREMISE: In this case it was shown that *a* is committed to proposition *A*, according to the evidence of what he said or did.

LINKAGE OF COMMITMENTS PREMISE: Generally, when an arguer is committed to *A*, it can be inferred that he is also committed to *B*.

CONCLUSION: In this case, *a* is committed to *B*.

1. What evidence in the case supports the claim that *a* is committed to *A*, and does it include contrary evidence, indicating that *a* might not be committed to *A*?
2. Is there room for questioning whether there is an exception in this case to the general rule that commitment to *A* implies commitment to *B*?

ARGUMENTATION SCHEME FOR ARGUMENT FROM INCONSISTENT COMMITMENT

INITIAL COMMITMENT PREMISE: *a* has claimed or indicated that he is committed to proposition *A* (generally or in virtue of what he said in the past).

OPPOSED COMMITMENT PREMISE: Other evidence in this particular case shows that *a* is not really committed to *A*.

CONCLUSION: *a*'s commitments are inconsistent.

1. What is the evidence supposedly showing that *a* is committed to *A*?
2. What further evidence in the case is alleged to show that *a* is not committed to *A*?

3. How does the evidence from 1 and 2 prove that there is a conflict of commitments?

ARGUMENTATION SCHEME FOR THE DIRECT AD HOMINEM ARGUMENT

CHARACTER ATTACK PREMISE: *a* is a person of bad character.

CONCLUSION: *a*'s argument should not be accepted.

1. How well supported by evidence is the allegation made in the character attack premise?
2. Is the issue of character relevant in the type of dialogue in which the argument was used?
3. Is the conclusion of the argument that *A* should be (absolutely) rejected, even if other evidence to support *A* has been presented, or is the conclusion merely (the relative claim) that *a* should be assigned a reduced weight of credibility as a supporter of *A*, relative to the total body of evidence available?

ARGUMENTATION SCHEME FOR THE CIRCUMSTANTIAL AD HOMINEM ARGUMENT

ARGUMENT PREMISE: *a* advocates argument α, which has proposition *A* as its conclusion.

INCONSISTENT COMMITMENT PREMISE: *a* is personally committed to the opposite (negation) of *A*, as shown by commitments expressed in his or her personal actions or personal circumstances expressing such commitments.

CREDIBILITY QUESTIONING PREMISE: *a*'s credibility as a sincere person who believes in his own argument has been put into question (by the two premises above).

CONCLUSION: The plausibility of *a*'s argument α is decreased or destroyed.

1. Is there a pair of commitments that can be identified, shown by evidence to be commitments of *a* and taken to show that *a* is practically inconsistent?
2. Once the practical inconsistency is identified that is the focus of the attack, could it be resolved or explained by further dialogue thus preserving the consistency of the arguer's commitments in the dialogue or showing that *a*'s inconsistent commitment does not support the claim that *a* lacks credibility?

3. Is character an issue in the dialogue, and more specifically, does *a*'s argument depend on his or her credibility?
4. Is the conclusion the weaker claim that *a*'s credibility is open to question or the stronger claim that the conclusion of α is false?

ARGUMENTATION SCHEME FOR ARGUMENT FROM VERBAL CLASSIFICATION

INDIVIDUAL PREMISE: *a* has property *F*.

CLASSIFICATION PREMISE: For all *x*, if *x* has property *F*, then *x* can be classified as having property *G*.

CONCLUSION: *a* has property *G*.

1. What evidence is there that *a* definitely has property *F*, as opposed to evidence indicating room for doubt on whether it should be so classified?
2. Is the verbal classification in the classification premise based merely on a stipulative or biased definition that is subject to doubt?

FOUR Argument Diagramming

This chapter is concerned with the task of taking an argument as given in a particular case as a text of discourse and identifying the argumentation as a set of premises presented as reasons to accept a conclusion. Identifying the structure of such a chain of argumentation by means of an argument diagram can be extremely useful prior to criticizing the argument by finding gaps or problems in it and evaluating the argumentation as weak or strong. In this chapter, we do not tackle the problem of how to evaluate argumentation found in a text of discourse. We only confront the prior problems of how to identify and analyze the argument. Of course, some arguments are easier to identify and analyze than others. In an abstract philosophical text, in a complex text of discourse containing technical scientific argumentation, or in a legal case where there is a mass of evidence on some highly contested issue, it may be extremely difficult to analyze the argumentation in any very clear and simple way by using a single diagram that is not filled with complexities. The problem with tackling real cases of arguments in a natural language text of discourse is that there can be gaps, ambiguities and uncertainties about what was really meant. Here we consider only some relatively simple cases that are fairly easy to diagram. Only toward the end of the chapter do we address some of the problems posed by harder cases. The method begins with the actual text of discourse of a case and, using the textual evidence given, builds a diagram representing the sequence of argumentation expressed in the case. Toward the end of the chapter, parts of this method are developed to distinguish carefully between propositions actually stated by an arguer in a case and unstated propositions that need to be attributed to the argument in order to make it possible to analyze it carefully and evaluate it fairly.

ONE Single and Convergent Arguments

An important error pointed out at the beginning of this chapter is that of mistakenly treating something as an argument that is not really an argument, but only something that looks like one. For example, as shown in chapter 1, it can be easy in some cases to confuse explanations and arguments. The ultimate goal of critical thinking is, of course, to evaluate arguments. But the problem is that once this skill is learned, there is a danger of misapplying it to tests of discourse that are not really meant to put forward an argument. It would be a serious error to judge something to be a bad argument when it is not really an argument at all. In chapter 1, some advice was given on how to avoid this error. The concepts of argument and explanation are defined by contrasting them. The purpose of offering an argument in a dialogue is to give the other party a reason or some reasons to accept a conclusion. Conclusion indicator words, such as 'therefore' and 'thus', and premise indicator words, such as 'for this reason', are important clues to identifying an argument. These terms are not always present, but in this chapter some additional means are given for identifying and analyzing arguments of different kinds.

There are several basic types of argument structures that can be identified, depending on how the inference is linked together in a chain of reasoning in a given case. The simplest type, the single argument, has only one premise given that is used as the basis for inferring a conclusion. For example, consider the following text of discourse.

> Diseased cattle can transmit fatal diseases to humans who consume beef products. Therefore inspection of cattle for such diseases is essential for human safety.

This text clearly conveys an argument, in the sense of that term defined in chapter 1. The conclusion, the second statement, is indicated by the word 'therefore' in front of it. The other statement, the premise 'Diseased cattle can transmit fatal diseases to humans who consume beef products', gives a reason to support the conclusion. Thus, this argument can be classified as a single argument.

Many of the arguments encountered in everyday argumentation have two premises.

> Suppose that in the dialogue on tipping, Helen had argued as follows: "I think that tipping is a bad practice. For one thing, it makes the party receiving the tip feel undignified. For another thing, it leads to an underground, black-market economy."

In this argument, each premise functions as a separate reason for supporting the conclusion that tipping is a bad practice. Each stands on its own as a separate argument. Both have the scheme called argument from consequences (chapter 3). And we can see that Helen has put forward two separate arguments from consequences. The argumentation scheme helps us to see that there are two separate arguments given.[1] Another bit of evidence is the wording used by Helen. She says "one thing" and then "another thing" when she presents the two statements, indicating two separate reasons. Yet another bit of evidence is that the one statement can function as a reason without the other. For example, making people feel undignified is quite a strong reason for thinking tipping to be a bad practice, whether the argument from negative consequences of the black-market economy is taken into consideration or not.

The pattern of argumentation that is present when there is more than one premise and where each premise functions separately as a reason to support the conclusion is called a convergent argument. In defending a convergent argument or using it to respond to the doubts expressed by an opponent in a dialogue, you can take your choice of using one premise or the other. Each is an independent evidential route for supporting the conclusion by offering a reason. A convergent argument is really like two separate arguments. In fact, it doesn't really matter whether you call it two separate arguments or one convergent argument. We will see, once the method of argument diagramming is developed below, that both structures are diagrammed the same way.

Another example of a convergent argument is provided by the following text of discourse quoted from a political speech given by Michael Dukakis during a presidential election campaign.

[1] For the present we ignore the unstated premises involved in both arguments, as the issue of unstated premises is not dealt with until a later part of the chapter (section 6). Making the party who received a tip feel undignified is taken to be bad consequence of tipping. And leading to an underground, black-market economy is also taken to be a bad consequence of tipping. That these consequences are bad could be added as unstated premises in the argument.

> I've opposed the death penalty all of my life. I don't see any evidence that it's a deterrent and I think there are better and more effective ways to deal with violent crime.[2]

In this case, very little of the exact context in which the argument was used is given, except that it was part of a political speech in an election campaign. Even though no indicator words of a convergent argument are given (as in the previous example), we can clearly tell that the argument is of the convergent type. Dukakis was giving two separate reasons for his opposition to the death penalty. Even if one premise was strongly argued against or even refuted by the opposition (then the George Bush, Sr., camp), Dukakis would still have a leg to stand on in his argument. The other premise would still give a strong line of support for his opposition to the death penalty. It provides an independent line of argument. Thus, the argument clearly fits the convergent pattern.

EXERCISE 4.1

Determine whether each of the following arguments is single or convergent. Briefly state your reason for your classification.

(a) All swans are white. Therefore, no swans are not white.

(b) Contamination of rivers is a problem of huge proportions. Nearly all the rivers in North America are poisoned by sewage dumped into them.

(c) My pen is probably on the desk. One reason is that's where I normally leave it. Another is that I was just working at the desk before I left.

(d) Making students memorize dates in history promotes drudgery. It also stifles the creative spirit of inquiry. For these reasons, making students memorize dates in history is not a good teaching practice.

(e) Desert mountain peaks make good sites for viewing the stars. Being high, they are closer to the stars. Being dry, they are relatively free of the obstruction so often created by the clouds.

TWO Linked Arguments

Not all arguments with multiple premises are convergent. In other cases, for example, in the kind of argument we were preoccupied with in the

[2] Then Governor Michael Dukakis, in the Bush-Dukakis presidential debate, Los Angeles, October 15, 1988.

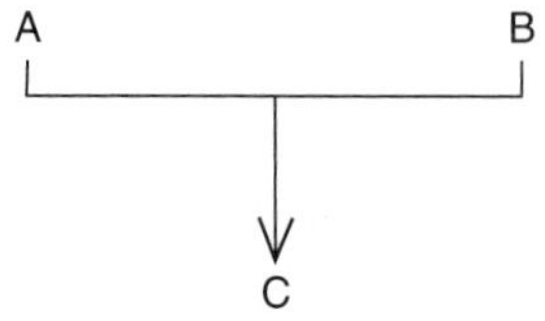

Figure 4.1 Linked argument.

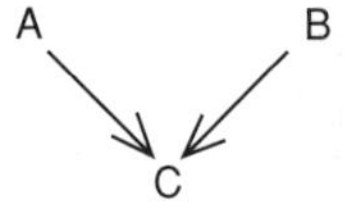

Figure 4.2 Convergent argument.

three preceding chapters, there are many examples of arguments where two premises are jointly used to provide support for a conclusion. In such cases, the two premises depend on each other, and it would be a mistake to view the argument as convergent. Consider the Tweety example once again.

Birds fly.

Tweety is a bird.

Therefore, Tweety flies.

This argument is of a very common type. It has two premises, and the two function together to give a reason to support the conclusion. For this reason it is called a linked argument, meaning that the premises function together to give a reason to support the conclusion. Here we can see the argument is linked because it is in the presumptive form studied in chapter 2. The first premise functions as a defeasible generalization that, with the aid of the second premise, offers a reason to accept the claim that the conclusion is true. Given the way the premises fit together in a known form of inference, we can classify the argument type as linked.

In making an argument diagram, the Tweety example is represented as linked argument, of the kind shown in Figure 4.1, where A is the premise 'Birds fly', B is the premise 'Tweety is a bird', and C is the conclusion 'Tweety flies'.

The diagram for the convergent type of argument is shown in Figure 4.2. An example is the argument from the dialogue on tipping on page 140. A is the premise 'Tipping makes the party receiving the tip feel undignified' and B is the premise 'Tipping leads to an underground, black-market economy'. The conclusion C is the proposition 'Tipping is a bad practice'.

There are certain common and readily identifiable kinds of multiple-premise arguments that are always linked. All the arguments with argumentation schemes given in chapter 3 are linked. But to consider another kind of example, let's reconsider the following deductive argument from chapter 2.

All residents of Tutela Heights reside in Brant County.

Ned is a resident of Tutela Heights.

Therefore, Ned is a resident of Brant County.

This argument, as indicated in chapter 2, is deductively valid, meaning that if the two premises are true, the conclusion must be true. Thus, if both premises are accepted, that gives a strong reason for accepting the conclusion. Thus, the two premises depend on each other for support. If the first premise were to be omitted from consideration, the second, just taken by itself, would provide only a very little support for the conclusion. To see this, consider the argument with the first premise omitted.

Ned is a resident of Tutela Heights.

Therefore, Ned is a resident of Brant County.

Even if the premise of this argument is held to be true, by itself that provides only a little support for the conclusion. For all that is known, Tutela Heights could be anywhere, once the first premise is omitted from consideration and no longer assumed or known to be true. The same effect of support lessening occurs when the second premise is omitted, yielding the following argument.

All residents of Tutela Heights reside in Brant County.

Therefore, Ned is a resident of Brant County.

As long as the other premise is omitted, this argument is very weak, for it can no longer be assumed that Ned is a resident of Tutela Heights. In the absence of this premise, it no longer follows that he has to be a resident of Brant County. Thus the argument is linked.

The reason that this argument is a linked one is comparable to that given above in the analysis of the argument in the Tweety example. In both types of case, the two premises are linked to the conclusion by an identifiable argument structure. The first premise is a generalization, and the second premise is a particular instance that fits the generalization. Thus, the two propositions fit together, supporting the conclusion by an interlocked structure. That is typical of many linked arguments. You can see by the structure of the argument that it is linked. If you take either premise away, the support given by the other one, by itself, for acceptance of the conclusion is much weaker. So by recognizing the structure of the argument, you can immediately see it is a linked argument, as opposed to a convergent one. A typical syllogism, of the kind studied in chapter 2, always has two premises and is a linked argument. Both premises are required for such an argument to be deductively valid. If either one is omitted, such an argument would be very weak.

Here is another example that shows the linked configuration very clearly.

> Suppose that in the dialogue on tipping, Bob had argued as follows: "I think that tipping is good for a healthy economy, because it rewards initiative, and anything that rewards initiative is good for a healthy economy."

Here Bob has advanced two premises in support of his conclusion, and they function together to provide a base of support for his conclusion. One premise, 'Anything that rewards initiative is good for a healthy economy', is a broadly general (universal) proposition. It could be analyzed as a universal conditional of the form, 'For all x, if x rewards initiative, then x is good for a healthy economy'. The other premise, 'Tipping rewards initiative', fits into the conditional of the first premise as the antecedent part. So by *modus ponens*, we are warranted in inferring the conclusion, 'Tipping is good for a healthy economy'. Hence the argument, as used by Bob in the dialogue on tipping, is linked. If you pulled either premise out, the other would, by itself, give much less of a basis for strong support of the conclusion. Clearly, the two premises function together.

In many cases, recognition of an argumentation scheme clearly shows that an argument is linked. For example, if the argument is an appeal to expert opinion, it may be clear that three premises, fitting the premises represented in the scheme, go together to support the conclusion. In other cases we may not know anything about how the premises fit together as a structured type of inference we are familiar with, but the wording of the argument in its context of use makes it clear that the argument is of the linked type.

> Competent individuals are at liberty to make their own medical treatment decisions; incompetent individuals are not. Thus, competence and liberty are inextricably interwoven.[3]

In this argument, there is no familiar argumentation scheme (evidently) used so that we could use this structure to identify the argument as linked.

[3] George J. Annas and Joan E. Densberger, "Competence to Refuse Medical Treatment: Autonomy vs. Paternalism," *Toledo Law Review* 15 (Winter 1984): p. 561.

But even so, it is clear from the context and wording that the two premises are meant to function together in support of the conclusion.

In many cases, more than two premises need to be linked together, to see how an argument supports its conclusion. For example, consider the following argument on government spending. It has the form of dilemma, a type of argument that is be analyzed in chapter 8.

> If we increase government spending, the increased deficit will weaken the dollar. If we decrease government spending, the homeless and unemployed will suffer. We must either increase or decrease government spending. Therefore, either the increased deficit will weaken the dollar or the homeless and unemployed will suffer.

In this case, it is clear that all three premises are functioning together to support the conclusion and therefore that the argument is of the linked type. The evidence from the text of discourse backing up this reconstruction is that all three premises are explicitly asserted prior to the assertion of the conclusion, which is preceded by the word 'therefore,' and all four propositions fit into the structure of the dilemma.

EXERCISE 4.2

The following two-premised arguments are all linked. Briefly explain how the two premises function together to support the conclusion.

(a) All textbooks are books meant to educate. And some logic books are textbooks. Therefore, some logic books are meant to educate.

(b) Dogs retain implicitly a lot of the qualities of wolves. Wolves are pack animals. Therefore, dogs are implicitly pack animals.

(c) My goal is to get to Minneapolis. Highway A4 is the way to get to Minneapolis. Therefore, I should take Highway A4.

(d) If Jane has agreed to run, Dick will not be elected. Jane has agreed to run. Therefore, Dick will not be elected.

(e) Any action that lessens human suffering can be morally acceptable. Euthanasia lessens human suffering. Hence, euthanasia can be morally acceptable.

(f) My notes must be in the lecture theater, because I had them with me when I gave the lecture there a few minutes ago, and I didn't have them when I left the room.

(g) Paul is either close to graduation or has just graduated. But we know he has not graduated. Therefore, Paul is close to graduation.

THREE Serial and Divergent Arguments

In chapter 1, chaining of argumentation, where the conclusion of one argument functions as the premise of another, was identified. When chained argumentation is used, the type of structure is classified as a serial argument. For example, in the following argument, the conclusion of the first single argument functions also as the premise of the second single argument:

> Customers often tip just because it is the accepted practice. Therefore a customer's tip is not necessarily a good criterion of excellent service. Therefore, you can't argue that tipping is good just on the basis that it rewards excellence of service.

The serial structure of this argument is clearer if we write out its three component statements vertically, as follows.

> **A:** Customers often tip just because it is the accepted practice.
>
> **B:** Therefore, a customer's tip is not necessarily a good criterion of excellent service.
>
> **C:** Therefore, you can't argue that tipping is good just on the basis that it rewards excellence of service.

The middle proposition in the sequence has two functions. First, it acts as the conclusion drawn from the premise above it. But then, in a second step of argument, it functions as a premise from which a new conclusion is drawn (the third statement in the sequence). This type of dual function is characteristic of the serial argument.

Another example is the following argument.

> Psychology is the religion of the modern era. If people are unhappy, guilty, or confused about life, they go to see a psychologist. Last year, two million people in North America visited a psychologist because of personal and emotional problems.

This argument is composed of three propositions in the following sequence.

> **A:** Last year, two million people in North America visited a psychologist because of personal and emotional problems.
>
> **B:** If people are unhappy, guilty, or confused about life, they go to see a psychologist.
>
> **C:** Psychology is the religion of the modern era.

Figure 4.3 Serial argument.

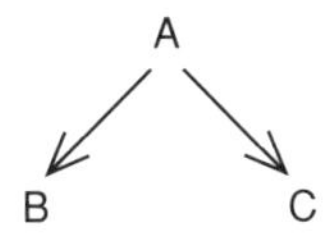

Figure 4.4 Divergent argument.

The bottom proposition, C, is a thought-provoking and somewhat controversial statement that needs justification in order to be plausible. Such justification is provided by the middle statement, B, which acts as a premise to support C. But then support for B is provided by putting forward A as a premise. The top statement, A, is a more specific proposition, used as a premise to back up the more general middle proposition, B.

In Figure 4.3, a diagram of the structure of the sequence of reasoning in an argument, the circled numbers stand for propositions and the arrows joining the numbers stand for steps of inference from one proposition to another.

Another type of argument that sometimes occurs is the divergent argument, where two propositions are inferred as separate conclusions from the same premise. For example, consider the following argument.

Smoking has been proved to be very dangerous to health. Therefore, commercial advertisements for cigarettes should be banned. And also, warnings that smoking is dangerous should be printed on all cigarette packages.

In this sequence of reasoning, three propositions are involved.

A: Smoking has been proved to be very dangerous to health.

B: Commercial advertisements for cigarettes should be banned.

C: Warnings that smoking is dangerous should be printed on all cigarette packages.

The divergent structure of the argument is represented by the diagram in Figure 4.4.

Now we have seen how serial and divergent argument structures can be represented in a diagrammatic form. Serial arguments are very common, as shown by the argument chaining exhibited in the dialogues in chapter 1. The chaining (serial) pattern of argumentation is the glue that holds longer arguments together. Divergent arguments are less common. We could easily dispense with the divergent pattern by representing two conclusions as a single statement in which the two conclusions are joined by the word 'and'. But we have included the divergent structure for treatment here as it is often encountered in textbook accounts of argument diagramming.

EXERCISE 4.3

Exhibit the structure of the reasoning used in the following arguments by drawing a diagram of the argument.

(a) Flatulence from cows emits a noxious sulfur gas that is a major cause of thinning of the ozone layer. Therefore, to prevent global warming, we need to set to work to solve the problem of bovine flatulence. Therefore, we ought to commission a scientific inquiry into the problem of bovine flatulence.

(b) Teenagers are growing more prone to extreme violence. Therefore, we should try more juvenile offenders in adult court. And also, we should expand our treatment centers for juvenile offenders.

(c) Because the greatest genetic variations are observed in African people, it can be concluded that they had the longest evolutionary history, indicating the probability of an African origin for modern humans.

(d) These senators voted against their party on the gun control bill. So they ought to be punished for violating party solidarity. Therefore, they should be removed from key party committees. And they should be reprimanded for their reckless actions.

(e) The deficit is out of control. Therefore, we should reduce government expenditures or raise taxes. But we can't raise taxes, because it would put a brake on the economy. Therefore, we must reduce government expenditures.

FOUR Distinguishing between Linked and Convergent Arguments

One of the difficulties most often encountered when beginning to use the method of argument diagramming is that in some cases, it seems hard to judge whether an argument is linked or convergent. In some cases it is very clear that the premises are independent means of support for a conclusion and do not depend on each other. Such an argument is clearly convergent. In other cases, such as syllogisms and many other examples, the argument is clearly linked. However, in some cases, it is not possible to determine whether the argument should be classified as linked or convergent, because there is not enough information given to judge fairly how it should be understood. Consider the following argument.

> I promised my girlfriend I would take her to see *Schindler's List*, and she would be really disappointed if I did not take her, so I guess I should take her to see that movie.

Is the reasoning in this argument linked or convergent? Here you could give reasons for interpreting the argument either way. Initially, each premise does seem like a separate and independent reason to support the conclusion. Each offers a reason that would have considerable weight as a justification for taking her to the movie, even in the absence of the other premise. On this view, the argument is convergent. But the two premises do seem to be connected, even if somewhat loosely. If a person would be disappointed if a promise to her were not kept, then keeping that promise is even more important than it would otherwise be. Given this connection, it seems that the two premises together have somewhat more strength as a unit than if the two of them were taken as separate reasons. On this view, the argument is linked.

In a case like this, where there are no indicator words telling us that the argument is linked or convergent, what should we do? The policy in such a case should be to diagram the argument as convergent. If we are not sure there is a linking of the premises, it might make the argument stronger if it were taken as linked. But if in doubt, it is best to interpret the argument in the weaker way and not to assume a link is operative if we are unsure about it. Fortunately, in many cases, there are four kinds of evidence bearing on the question of whether an argument should be taken as linked or convergent in a given case. The best policy in a case where such evidence is available is to back up your classification of the argument as linked or convergent by citing the evidence.

The most important kind of evidence is the following test, called the blackout test, which can be applied in the simplest kind of case, where an argument has only two premises, as follows. Black out the one premise, for example, by putting your finger over it, and assume that it is not being considered as part of the argument to support the conclusion. Then ask whether the strength of support for the conclusion by the newly reduced one-premise argument has dropped considerably, compared with the support furnished by both premises together. If support has dropped considerably, then that is evidence that the argument is linked. It was the blackout test that we (in effect) used in classifying the first argument in section 2 above as linked.

All residents of Tutela Heights reside in Brant County.

Ned is a resident of Tutela Heights.

Therefore, Ned is a resident of Brant County.

We classified this argument as linked because the two premises depend on each other for support of the conclusion. Now we can see how the blackout test applies to it. Suppose the first premise were to be blacked out. Then the second premise, taken by itself, would provide only a very little support for the conclusion. To see this, examine the argument once again with the first premise omitted, as we did above.

Ned is a resident of Tutela Heights.

Therefore, Ned is a resident of Brant County.

Even if the premise of this argument is true, it provides only a little support for the conclusion, because if the other premise has been blacked out, Tutela Heights could be anywhere. Now examine the argument with the other premise blacked out.

All residents of Tutela Heights reside in Brant County.

Therefore, Ned is a resident of Brant County.

It can no longer be assumed that Ned is a resident of Tutela Heights, given the blackout, and so it no longer follows deductively that he has to be a resident of Brant County. The blackout test applied to the other premise has also shown that support is weakened considerably. Thus, the argument is clearly linked.

Next let's apply the blackout test to another earlier example, where Helen had argued as follows in the dialogue on tipping: "I think that tipping is a bad practice. For one thing, it makes the party receiving the tip feel undignified. For another thing, it leads to an underground, black market economy." We classified this argument as convergent, because each premise provides a separate reason to support the conclusion. Let's see how the blackout test might apply to it. First we black out one premise and examine the argument with only the other premise appearing.

Tipping makes the party who received the tip feel undignified.

Therefore, tipping is a bad practice.

In this argument, the premise still gives a fairly strong reason to support the conclusion, even though it gives somewhat less support than if the other premise were to be considered as well. A similar finding is produced by deleting the other premise, yielding the following argument.

> Tipping leads to an underground, black-market economy.
>
> Therefore, tipping is a bad practice.

Once again, the displayed premise still gives a fairly strong reason in support of the conclusion, even without the other premise. Using the blackout test helps to offer evidence why this argument should be classified as convergent rather than linked. Of course, in this case, there is also other, even stronger evidence that the argument is linked. It is provided by the indicator words, 'for one thing' and 'for another thing'.

What we have seen is that there are different kinds of evidence that can be used to help judge, in a given case, whether an argument should be viewed as linked or convergent. This evidence can be put into four categories.

1. **Indicator Words.** Words such as 'my other reason' or 'in addition' indicate a convergent argument. Words such as 'along with this' or 'also required' indicate a linked argument.
2. **Inference Structure.** If the argument fits into a familiar deductively valid form of argument, such as *modus ponens*, or an argumentation scheme, such as argument from consequences, that is evidence that the argument is linked.
3. **Blackout Test.** Try blacking out one of the premises. If the basis of support for the conclusion drops radically, then that is evidence that the premise is part of an argument with a linked structure. If the basis of support goes down only slightly or not at all, that is evidence that the argument is convergent.
4. **Context of Dialogue.** The more text of discourse that is given in a particular case indicating how the argument is being used to contribute to a goal of dialogue as part of a larger sequence of argumentation, the more evidence will be given indicating whether the reasoning is used in a linked or convergent argument.

The blackout test is not sufficient by itself to determine, in every case, whether a given argument is linked or convergent. Indeed, even all four kinds of evidence together are not sufficient in every case. Still, it is often useful to know whether an argument is linked or convergent, when it comes to analyzing and evaluating it critically. Thus, one can often make a provisional determination, based on the evidence, and give reasons why one is interpreting the argument as linked or convergent. In many of the most common cases, the evidence makes it very clear which way the argument should be taken. If doubt remains, the best policy is to treat the argument as convergent.

EXERCISE 4.4

1. Classify the following arguments as linked or convergent, giving evidence from the text or context of discourse to support your interpretation.

(a) The mail delivery by the post office is not very good because the time of delivery is not predictable, the service is often slow, and the packages are often banged up or damaged.

(b) Mail delivery by private courier service is very good because it is fast, and you can track your package to prove it was sent.

(c) Mail delivery by private courier service is better than post office mail delivery because post office deliveries tend to be slow, whereas the courier service is fast.

(d) Bob was at fault in the accident, because he was on the wrong side of the road and he went through a red light.

(e) *Schindler's List* was a compelling movie to watch, because the acting was superb, and the atmosphere conveyed by the scenery portrayed in the film conveyed a chillingly realistic historical ambiance.

(f) Kevin took the money without the owner's consent and spent it for his personal use. Therefore, it is reasonable to conclude that Kevin embezzled the money.

(g) Global warming is the cause of the recent floods in Europe, China, and North America. How do we know that? Professor Tusk has informed us, and he is a geography specialist at the University of Arizona in the area of climate changes.

(h) Either this marble is black or red. It is not black. Therefore it is red.

(i) This one marble is red. This other marble is also red. Therefore both marbles are red.

(j) Newborns should be screened for HIV infection. If screening is done, a better diagnosis for other illnesses, such as pulmonary illness, is made possible. Counseling on the risk of breast feeding can be given to the mother. And finally, education for the prevention of additional transmission is made possible.

2. Classify the reasoning used in the following arguments as linked, convergent, or undetermined, citing the evidence from the text of discourse used as your criteria.

(a) Getting people off welfare requires giving them job skills. Giving them work-related education is the way to do this. Therefore, funding for programs offering work-related training to welfare recipients ought to be increased.

(b) Education is a right that cannot be exercised if serious obstacles stand in the way. Financial need is the worst obstacle preventing people from getting a higher education. Therefore, tuition fees must be reduced by greater government support for universities.

(c) Research done by universities is an important source of innovative technique, new ideas, and scientific discoveries that are useful for government and industry. Learning from a professor who is engaged in research in an academic field makes a course much more interesting and informative for students. For these reasons, university research should be supported.

(d) The number and use of motor vehicles has increased so much that improvements in pollution control have not been enough to protect citizens from elevated levels of fine particles in the air. These fine particles are very dangerous to human health. So we must find ways to decrease the number and use of motor vehicles.

(e) Polio is a problem for North America, even though it has been eradicated for a number of years. For there are strains of the virus in countries such as China, India, Africa, and Eastern Europe. And with modern jet travel, this virus can easily be transmitted from one population to another, even in a faraway country.

(f) It would not be practical to try to control free speech on the Internet. Government regulations to police all the millions of messages every year would be prohibitively costly. Also, any set of regulations would inevitably hinder legitimate research and transmission of data in subjects such as science and history.

(g) It is necessary to control free speech on the Internet. Increasingly, Web sites and chat rooms are being used to lure children into pornography. This criminal activity is a form of speech that needs to be controlled by the police.

FIVE Complex Arguments

Now we have four different kinds of argument structures – linked, convergent, serial, and divergent – extended reasoning in a text of discourse can be analyzed by combining these structures in a case. To take a simple example, suppose that Helen presents the following argument to Bob, during the course of the dialogue on tipping. Here the individual propositions are numbered for convenience.

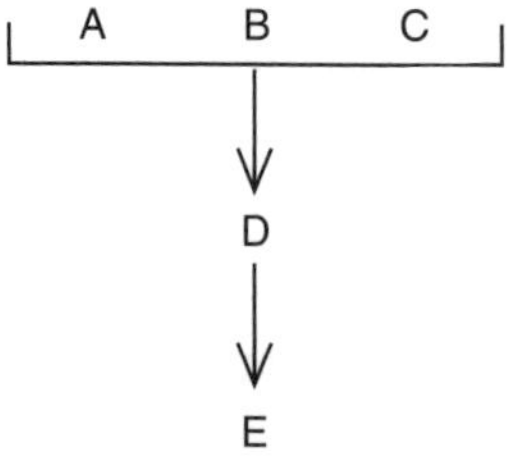

Figure 4.5 Linked and single argument.

> (A) Either you have to decide what is fair pay for a job on an individual basis, like tipping, or you can have a government committee decide the worth of the job as a contribution to the economy. (B) A government committee can make an objective assessment. (C) An individual customer makes a subjective decision that could be biased by personal favoritism. (D) Therefore, a government committee should decide the worth of a job as a contribution to the economy. (E) Therefore, tipping should be discontinued as a practice.

The first job in analyzing any argument in a given text of discourse is to scan over the text and determine which proposition is the ultimate conclusion being argued for. In this case, the final conclusion is E, as represented in the diagram in Figure 4.5.

It appears that premises A, B, and C are linked together to support the intermediate conclusion D. A presents a disjunction, or choice between two alternatives. B gives a reason for preferring the one alternative, and C gives a reason for dispreferring the other alternative. D acts as the conclusion for the disjunctive inference, but then, it also acts as a premise for a further conclusion, E. Hence in this case, the reasoning in the argument combines a linked structure with a single structure.

To consider another example, suppose Bob were to argue as follows in the dialogue on tipping.

> (A) Many students can pay their tuition costs only by getting tips in their part-time service sector jobs. (B) So if you abolished tipping, these students would not be able to stay in school. (C) Therefore, abolishing tipping would have a severe impact on a vulnerable segment of the population. (D) Also, it would affect university enrollments in a negative way.

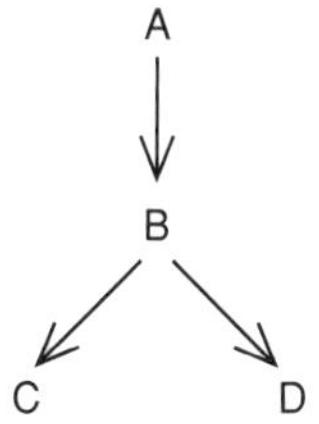

Figure 4.6 Single and divergent argument.

In this case, the argument combines a serial structure with a divergent structure, as shown in Figure 4.6. In many cases, a recurring difficulty is that it may require some thought to decide whether an argument is linked or convergent. Suppose, for example, that in the dialogue on tipping, Bob were to argue as follows.

> (A) I don't think that having government guidelines to decide on fair salaries for different jobs is a good idea. (B) Government guidelines are highly inefficient as a practical way of deciding on these questions. (C) Also, not only that, but government bureaucracies are often frustratingly unfair. (D) Look at the favoritism, patronage, and pork barreling that goes on in present government operations. (E) If you have favoritism, patronage, and pork barreling going on, then bureaucracies are going to be frustratingly unfair.

Scanning over this case, we first of all select out the proposition that is the final conclusion of the argument, and it appears to be A. All the rest of the sequence of reasoning is directed to backing up A. First, premises B and C are premises used to back up A, in a convergent argument. The most evident indicator that the argument is convergent is the word "also," used to preface premise C. But also, premises B and C give two separate reasons in support of A. The one is that government bureaucracies are inefficient. The other is that they are often frustratingly unfair.

Then we come to propositions D and E. Evidently, they are used to back up C. But is this argument linked or convergent? Here the indicator is the structure of the inference, which has a *modus ponens* form. Hence, in the diagram in Figure 4.6, the same number is used on both arrows going from D and E to C. In contrast, to show the convergent nature of the other subargument, different numbers are used to label the arrows from C to A and B to A.

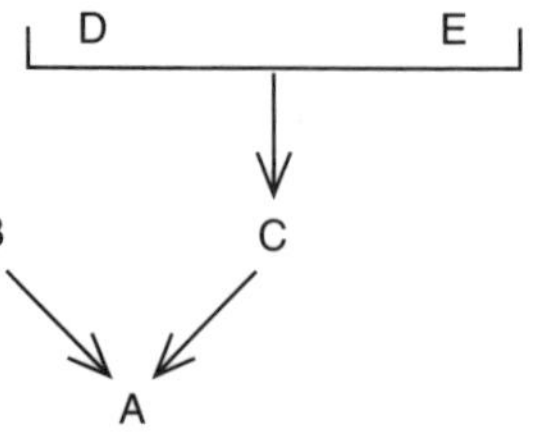

Figure 4.7 Linked and convergent argument.

The argument diagram in Figure 4.7 shows a structure that combines a linked argument with a convergent argument. The two inferences are joined together by the common proposition C. It is a conclusion in the first argument, but then it serves as a premise in the next one.

In some cases, it would not be particularly important or necessary that the diagram indicates that an argument is linked or convergent. As noted above, if it is hard to judge clearly whether the argument is linked or convergent, just diagram it as convergent. Where making such a distinction is possible and important, however, a written justification should be added to the argument diagram, citing the evidence from the text of discourse used to back up the claim that it is linked or convergent.

EXERCISE 4.5

Exhibit the structure of reasoning used in the following arguments by drawing an argument diagram. In instances where a part of an argument is either linked or convergent in structure, justify your choice of classification by giving a reason.

(a) Giving my two children a clothing allowance turned out to be a good idea. For one thing, it took the pressure off me to buy them clothes that I considered too expensive and too ugly. Also, it taught them some good lessons in economics. When I give them their money, it's up to them to decide what to buy. When their money doesn't stretch as far as they want to get the desired items, they get a realistic idea of what things cost. No longer do they need to convince me of their need to have something, so I don't have to fight with them anymore about what we can afford.

(b) Equity initiatives seek to redress existing inequalities of power and resources between groups by redistributing power and resources on a fair basis. Redressing existing inequalities is necessary, because some groups have been dominant in the past, and have oppressed other groups by a process of victimization. This oppression was very bad for the victimized groups. Therefore, equity initiatives ought to be supported by everyone who believes in justice and equality.

(c) Equity initiatives are very bad for a productive economy because they pit one interest group against another in an endless conflict over claimed rights. Such endless conflicts are disruptive to productive, collaborative effort in a country because they constantly fuel resentment and envy among citizens who perceive themselves as belonging to one group opposed to another. This type of conflict pulls people apart instead of bringing them together, and the constant quarreling disrupts any kind of collaborative effort on a large scale.

(d) "There are a lot of computers that claim to do multimedia. But when you try to do something as simple as loading a CD-ROM, it can get pretty scary. So, if you want a multimedia computer that actually works, there really is only one choice. Apple Macintosh. It's the easiest computer to set up, learn, and – most important – use. Plus, every Mac comes with built-in sound and video capabilities. That's not true of most PCs. So visit an authorized Apple Canada Dealer today" (ad for the Apple Macintosh Computer, *Globe and Mail*, April 10, 1995, p. A7).

(e) In his book *Fingerprints of the Gods* (Toronto: Doubleday Canada, 1995), Graham Hancock argued for the existence of a previously unidentified high civilization of distant antiquity.

> The Sphinx is supposed to have been built by Khafre around 2500 BC, but since the beginning of dynastic times – say 3000 BC onwards – there just hasn't been enough rain on the Giza plateau to have caused the very extensive erosion that we see all over the Sphinx's body. You really have to go back to before 10,000 BC to find a wet enough climate in Egypt to account for weathering of this type and on this scale. It therefore follows that the Sphinx must have been built before 10,000 BC and since it's a massive, sophisticated work of art it also follows that it must have been built by a high civilization. (pp. 419–420)

SIX Unstated Premises and Conclusions

Suppose that once again in the dialogue on tipping, Bob were to put forward the following argument to Helen: "Any practice that rewards excellence of service is a good practice; therefore tipping is a good practice." This argument would have the form of a syllogistic inference, except that Bob did not explicitly state the proposition 'Tipping rewards excellence of service' as a premise. Would it be reasonable to assume that this proposition could be taken to be an assumption of Bob's argument? In the context of the dialogue on tipping, it seems as if it would be reasonable to assume that Bob is using this premise as a premise in his argument, for three reasons. The first reason is that without this premise, Bob's argument would have a gap, and unless this gap is filled, the argument would not be deductively valid. Indeed, without this premise being assumed as part of the basis of Bob's argument, it would be of no use in getting Helen to accept the conclusion that Bob needs to prove. Thus, without this premise, the argument would not only be invalid, it would even be useless in the dialogue on tipping. The second reason is that when the unstated assumption above is inserted into the gap, the argument becomes valid and useful to prove Bob's thesis in the dialogue. The third reason is that the missing assumption seems to be a proposition that Bob is committed to, and that fits with what we know of his viewpoint in the dialogue. We know from the previous sequence of argumentation in the dialogue that Bob is committed to the proposition that tipping rewards excellence of service. Certainly, it is a proposition that is compatible with and even supports his point of view in the dialogue. So there is plenty of contextual evidence that this proposition is a commitment of Bob's. For these three reasons, then, an unstated proposition can sometimes be assumed to be a premise in a given argument. Inserting such a missing premise is justifiable in critical argumentation as long as it is recognized that it is being inserted only as an assumption or hypothesis that makes it possible for us to identify the whole argument. For if the argument were to be left incomplete, we have no way to identify the weak points in it by asking the appropriate critical questions. Thus, we can't properly criticize the argument unless the whole thing is represented.

The missing premise we have filled in is merely an artifact needed for criticism of an argument. It is not something that necessarily represents what the arguer really believes in his heart. Suppose Bob is questioned on this point and denies that he accepts the proposition 'Tipping rewards excellence of service', or means it to be a premise in his argument. In that case, we would have to retract our assumption that this proposition can be plugged in as the missing premise in Bob's argument. But unless Bob indicates his disagreement at any point in a dialogue, it would be a reasonable presumption to adopt that this premise should be taken as an unstated premise of his argument. But we must remember that Bob never actually said it. It is important to emphasize the distinction between an explicit premise, one that has been stated by a participant in a dialogue, and an unstated premise that has been attributed to his argument. To claim that a participant stated a proposition, he must be quoted as having asserted this proposition in so many words in the dialogue. Thus in an argument diagram, the distinction between a stated and an unstated premise needs to be indicated and kept in mind.

Now there is a small complication to be added. It is not just premises that are missing and need to be inserted in order to complete an argument. Sometimes conclusions can be unstated parts of arguments as well. Suppose, for example, that during the course of the dialogue on tipping, Helen were to argue as follows.

> If a practice makes one person in a social exchange feel less empowered, then it is a bad practice that should be discontinued. Tipping makes one person in a social exchange feel less empowered. I can tell you that from personal experience.

There are no indicator words here. Helen puts forward only two statements. The third statement is merely an affirmation that the first two can be backed up by Helen's personal experience. So we can ignore or delete that and concentrate on the first two statements. They seem to imply a conclusion. In the context of the dialogue on tipping, it is clear that these are not just two random statements. They are put forward by Helen as premises in an incomplete argument that she is offering. What is missing is the conclusion. There are reasons to think that Helen's argument is incomplete. It looks like the unstated conclusion is the proposition 'Tipping is a bad practice that should be discontinued'. What evidence supports this hypothesis? First, we know that Helen's thesis in the dialogue on tipping is this very proposition. Thus, Helen is certainly committed to it, and indeed, her aim in the dialogue is to prove it to Bob. Second, this conclusion does follow by a *modus ponens* inference from the two premises she asserted. When that conclusion is plugged in, the argument is valid. Thus it would be fair to presume, subject to correction by Helen, that this proposition is her (unstated) conclusion.[4] As a basis for identifying and criticizing what Helen said, we are justified in taking the

[4] Traditionally in logic, for quite a long time, an argument that has a nonexplicit premise or conclusion has been called an enthymeme. We continue to follow this long-established tradition, even though there is evidence that the founder of the field of logic, Aristotle, used the term 'enthymeme' (in Greek, *enthymema*) to mean something else. In light of this evidence, it might be better to use the term 'incomplete argument.' But the use of enthymeme to stand for an argument with nonexplicit premises or conclusions has been taught in logic textbooks for so many generations that it is hard to resist it.

step of viewing it as an argument with the unstated proposition inserted as conclusion.

In some cases, unlike the dialogue on tipping, we don't know anything about the argument or the dialogue it is part of except for what was said in a few words. However, even in these cases, it can be useful and necessary to insert an unstated assumption as part of the argument needed to complete it. For example, consider a case where a mother, trying to offer nutritional advice to her son, says, "You want to grow up to be big and strong, don't you? Eat your vegetables!" In this case, there are only two sentences. One is a question, and the other is a directive. But what the mother said can be taken to express an argument. And indeed, it is clear that she is arguing to her son, giving him a reason to accept the view that eating his vegetables is a good thing, something he should do. Her first sentence is a rhetorical question, meaning that its real function is not that of a question but a statement. Her first sentence gives a premise, and her second one states a conclusion that, she alleges, should be drawn from that premise. She is using an argument to try to persuade him to eat his vegetables.

In this case, the mother's argument can be identified and made complete by adding an unstated premise.

STATED PREMISE: You want to grow up to be big and strong.

UNSTATED PREMISE: If you don't eat your vegetables, you won't grow up to be big and strong.

CONCLUSION: You should eat your vegetables.

Once the argument has been completed in this way, we can see it is a linked argument because the two premises fit together to support the conclusion. The son wants to grow up to be big and strong. His mother is telling him that he can achieve this goal only by means of eating his vegetables. Presumably, the son would understand that what his mother is saying is that eating vegetables is necessary in order to grow big and strong. And all the rest of us understand that as well. For it is a commonly accepted assumption that eating vegetables is necessary for a child's proper nutrition and healthy growth. Thus, there are reasons for adding the unstated premise to make the argument complete. The argument would make no sense or would not be plausible without this premise. And not only the mother but the rest of us as well can easily accept this statement as a commitment that would not be disputed, because it is so widely accepted.

In still other cases, the missing assumption in an argument is not a commonly accepted proposition of a kind that could be called general knowledge. It may be a proposition that is special to a case. For example, consider the following argument.

The burglar was under five feet tall, so Sean was not the burglar.

In this case, the missing premise is the statement, 'Sean is not under five feet tall'. How do we know this? It is not a matter of common knowledge. For, presumably, we do not even know who Sean is, and we aren't told how tall he is. Still, it is relatively clear, from what is stated, that the unstated premise is that Sean is not under five feet tall. The reason is that this proposition is what is needed in order to get a linked argument that is valid and that offers a reason to support the conclusion that Sean was not the burglar.

In filling in unstated assumptions in incomplete arguments, it is best to remember that our purpose should be normative and not psychological in nature. Our purpose is not the psychological (or psychiatric) one of trying to determine what this person really meant, at some deeper psychological level. Perhaps, in the example above, the arguer knows that Sean is six foot seven. But we do not need to know that. All we need to know is that to make the argument complete, it needs to be assumed that Sean is not under five feet tall. Our purpose in filling in a missing part of an argument in critical argumentation should be to complete the argument (subject to correction or rebuttal), based on the evidence given in the text of discourse of a dialogue. The unstated premise or conclusion that is inserted into the explicitly given assertions should be treated as an artificial (conditionally acceptable) construct, as a presumption that can be based on (or refuted by) evidence. This approach is both useful and necessary for critical argumentation.

In everyday dialogues, premises and conclusions are often left unstated, because stating them explicitly is not necessary, would even be tedious, and would make the argument unnecessarily complicated. Thus incomplete arguments are often useful for communication generally, and for criticizing an argument. Generally they can be used by an arguer to facilitate communication by allowing her audience to fill in gaps for themselves, because the arguer takes for granted that the audience does not dispute the unstated assumption. The audience can construct an argument out of an incomplete message that, when completed, is relevant as a contribution to the goal of the dialogue. And filling in unstated parts can be useful for criticism of an argument, because criticism needs to find the weak points in the argument. The purpose of constructive criticism should be to fill in the gaps in the way that makes the argument complete as a contribution to a dialogue. In critical argumentation, criticizing an argument is not just attacking it by any means possible. Criticism should be seen as constructive. The purpose of criticizing an argument is, of course, to try to find its weak points. But this can be carried out in a helpful and collaborative manner that will enable everyone, including the arguer herself, to identify these weak points and correct them.

EXERCISE 4.6

Fill in any unstated premises or conclusions needed to complete the following arguments. Give your main reason for selecting the missing assumption by citing evidence from the text and/or context of discourse.

(a) Jenna and Rupert are having a critical discussion on the issue of whether euthanasia is a good practice or not. Rupert, who is against euthanasia, argues: "Anything that leads to loss of respect for human life is a dangerous practice. Therefore, euthanasia is a dangerous practice."

(b) Jason should know the streets of Manhattan, because every cab driver in Manhattan should know the streets of Manhattan.

(c) A roadside sign reads: "The bigger the burger, the better the burger. The burgers are bigger at Burger King."

(d) All physicians are college graduates, so all members of the American Medical Association (AMA) are college graduates.

(e) A social scientist who has just finished a survey on the knowledge of North American college students is quoted speaking to an audience as follows: "There are college students who think that Africa is in North America. But anyone who thinks that Africa is in North America has no knowledge of the basic facts of geography."

(f) Members of a political party are deliberating on the question of whom to elect as the next party leader. One participant suggests Brown as a candidate. Another participant replies: "Brown has been low in the polls lately, so she would not make a good leader."

SEVEN Diagramming More Difficult Cases

So far the cases examined have been relatively easy to diagram. In many cases, however, considerable interpretation and reorganizing of the material in a text of discourse needs to take place before the structure of the argument can be identified. In some of these cases, however, missing premises or conclusions can be more easily found by using argumentation schemes. Consider the following argument: 'The corporate income tax should be abolished; it encourages waste and high prices'. The missing premise in the corporate income tax argument is the statement, 'Whatever encourages waste and high prices should be abolished'. This statement could be analyzed as stating the defeasible generalization, 'In general, if a practice encourages waste and high prices, that is a reason to abolish it'. So analyzed the argument can be represented as follows.

UNSTATED PREMISE: In general, if a practice encourages waste and high prices, that is a reason to abolish it.

STATED PREMISE: The corporate income tax is a practice that encourages waste and high prices.

CONCLUSION: The corporate income tax should be abolished.

Notice that the second premise has been reworded slightly so that the corporate income tax is classified by including the phrase 'is a practice that'. The analysis so far is fairly obvious, but the example could be analyzed even more deeply by using argumentation schemes.

In chapter 3, section 5, the argumentation for argument from negative consequences was defined.

PREMISE: If action *A* is brought about, bad consequences will plausibly occur.

CONCLUSION: *A* should not be brought about.

With this argumentation scheme in mind, it is easy to see the rationale of the corporate income tax argument. The rationale behind it is the unstated assumption that waste and high prices are bad consequences. Since it was stated that the corporate income tax encourages waste and high prices, another implicit assumption follows, namely, that the corporate income tax has bad consequences. Putting the whole chain of argumentation together, we can see that five statements are involved.

(A) The corporate income tax should be abolished.

(B) The corporate income tax has bad consequences.

(C) The corporate income tax encourages waste and high prices.

(D) Waste and high prices are bad consequences.

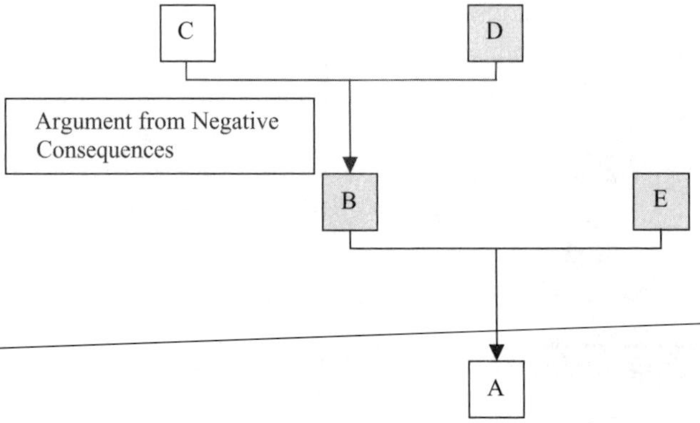

Figure 4.8 Diagram of the corporate income tax example.

(E) Any practice that has bad consequences should (other things being equal) be abolished.

The only explicit statements are (A) and (C). The other statements, B, D, and E, are unstated assumptions in the original corporate income tax argument.

The whole sequence of argumentation can be represented by the argument diagram in Figure 4.8. Statements B, D, and E have been darkened to indicate they represent unstated assumptions, while A and C are shown as propositions that were explicitly stated in the given argument. This argument was still fairly easy to diagram, once the argumentation scheme was used to help, but many other cases of arguments in natural language discourse can prove to be more difficult.

When confronting a particular case, such as an argument expressed in a newspaper editorial, a letter to the editor, or a magazine article, much work may need to be done to re-express the argumentation in a form that is amenable to diagramming it. This process of preparing the text of discourse for diagramming is called transformation. There are four kinds of transformation that may have to be made.[5] Deletion is selecting out items in the text that are not part of the argument or not needed to represent the premises and conclusions in it. For example, much of the material in a text may consist of descriptions, explanations, clarifications, and so forth, which perform no role as premises or conclusions in the argument. Quite a

[5] Frans H. van Eemeren, Rob Grootendorst, Sally Jackson, and Scott Jacobs, *Reconstructing Argumentative Discourse* (Tuscaloosa: University of Alabama Press, 1993), pp. 61–62.

lot of the text in realistic cases can be non-argumentative in nature. Addition is the finding and inserting of unstated premises and conclusions required to make the argument complete. Permutation is the re-ordering of the propositions into an orderly sequence that supports the conclusion. Substitution involves a clarification of the function and format of a move in a dialogue, and re-expressing a move as part of an argument. For example, the question in the example above "You want to grow up to be big and strong?" was said to be a rhetorical question. A rhetorical question performs the function of making a statement. In the argument above, we re-expressed this rhetorical question as a statement used by the mother to 'You want to grow up to be big and strong'. In this transformation, the sentence in the given text of discourse is in the form of a question, but its real function is to make a statement used as a premise in the argument.

The following example is an argument that is moderately difficult to diagram, even though some indicator words are given. You have to think through the argument to see how the statements presented function as evidence that gives reasons in support of the conclusion. You also have to decide which parts of the text can be usefully represented by an argument diagram. Thus, you have to determine which parts are best deleted.

Recently, there has been some controversy about the prevalence of the habit of eating junk food that is of poor nutritional value, and the impact that has on health. It has often been assumed that public education about making wise nutritional choices can solve the problem. But it may be a lot harder to reverse the trend of eating junk food than could be achieved by education alone. It's cheaper and easier for people to eat junk food rather than nutritious food. At the store where I shop, a candy bar costs less than a dollar and is ready to eat. Fresh fruits and vegetables tend to be inconveniently packaged and cost more. It's also a lot more profitable for manufacturers to market junk food than nutritious food, because junk food has a longer shelf life in the retail outlet.

To analyze this argument, we have to begin by determining which parts of it represent an argument supporting a conclusion and which parts have some other function. The first statement fills in the context of dialogue by telling us what the controversy in the case is about. It poses a problem that has been discussed. The second statement tells us about one solution to the problem that has been proposed. It tells us that there is a widely accepted or commonly argued view that public education can solve the problem. The rest of the argumentation, after the word 'but', opposes this commonly accepted view by offering a set of reasons for thinking that it is not justified. It is this part of the argumentation that we can usefully diagram by the methods learned so far. For our present purposes, we can simply delete both of the first two statements.

However, as well as deletion, we also have to perform the operation of addition. We need to fill in some missing premises that are not explicitly stated but that are meant to be part of the argument. One is the statement that candy bars can be classified as junk food. Another is the statement that fresh fruits and vegetables can be classified as nutritious foods. Let's insert these statements as premises and number each of the statements in the argument.

(A) It may be a lot harder to reverse the trend of eating junk food than can be achieved by education alone. (B) It's cheaper and easier for people to eat junk food rather than nutritious food. (C) At the store where I shop, a candy bar costs less than a dollar and is ready to eat. (D) Candy bars can be classified as junk food. (E) Fresh fruits and vegetables tend to be inconveniently packaged, and cost more. (F) Fresh fruits and vegetables can be classified as nutritious foods. (G) It's also a lot more profitable for manufacturers to market junk food than nutritious food, because (H) junk food has a longer shelf life in the retail outlet.

In this argument, A is the ultimate conclusion. Statement A is supported by statement B. The arguer then goes on to give a number of reasons supporting B. Statements C, D, E, and F all go together to support B. Thus C, D, E, and F can all be diagrammed as premises in a linked argument supporting B. G gives an additional reason to support B, and H gives a reason to support G. Thus G can be drawn as a premise that is part of a convergent argument leading to B. Finally, H is a single argument supporting G. This analysis is shown in Figure 4.9.

It is possible to supplement this analysis with an even deeper one. If we wished to go into a bit more depth, we could add another missing premise that goes along with H to support G. It is the statement that food that has a longer shelf life in the retail outlet is more profitable for manufacturers to market. This would add a statement I to the diagram that

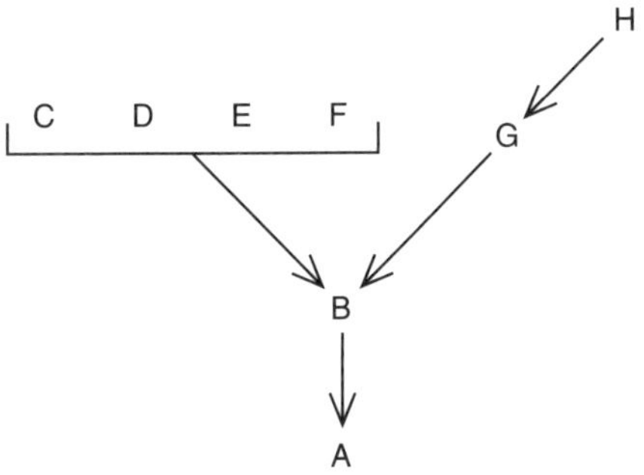

Figure 4.9 Linked, serial, and single argument.

would go along with H in a linked argument supporting G. It is often a matter of how much depth you want to go into in analyzing an argument that determines whether it is useful to add additional assumptions that were not explicitly stated in a case but that might play some role in how the argumentation in the case is to be criticized or evaluated.

In this textbook, we can't go any further into the four techniques for cleaning up a text of discourse prior to diagramming the argumentation in it. Suffice it to say that such an operation is based on the critic's understanding of natural language discourse. There is no mechanical set of rules that can be given. Thus, below, some cautionary remarks about the process are added. What needs to be seen is that without some process of transforming the natural language discourse, with all its idiosyncrasies, into an argument diagram, there is no possibility of applying critical argumentation methods to real cases of everyday arguments of the kinds encountered in magazines and newspapers.

Normally, an argument in a media text has the format of a dialogue as its normative structure even although the intended readership or audience has no active role as respondents in the dialogue. But the structure of the argument is a dialogue, normatively speaking, because the reader (or audience member) should raise critical questions about the argument he or she has been presented for acceptance. However, care is needed in reconstructing such texts of discourse. In many cases, the media discourse is not itself a direct argument but a report of someone else's argument that the media text may then support or endorse (or argue against). Care is needed to separate, in such cases, the original argument and the media report of it – a second-hand account that may be highly selective. And remember, you may not have access to the text of discourse of the original argument.

EXERCISE 4.7

Apply the process of transformation in order to identify the premises and conclusions in the following natural language texts of discourse. Draw an argument diagram to represent the ultimate conclusion and the reasons given to support it. Cite evidence from the text of discourse to support each step in your process of transformation.

(a) Spray Nine claims that it kills the HIV virus on a dry surface in thirty seconds. But Bob Howard, of the Centers for Disease Control, says that the HIV virus would die in thirty seconds on a dry surface even if nothing was put on it. It seems, then, that you aren't really getting any additional safety by using Spray Nine. I don't think I am going to buy this product to protect me from HIV transmission.

(b) "Don't you wish we could just do away with CFCs? In a way we can – if we cool our buildings with natural gas. Natural gas absorption cooling equipment cools with water, rather than with CFCs, which deplete the ozone layer. It also has fewer moving parts than conventional cooling systems, which means maintenance costs are lower. And, because it costs much less to operate, it cuts the energy costs of cooling – by up to 50%. There's another big benefit, too. It saves electricity during the heat of the summer, when demand is at its highest. As a result, we can help our cities avoid brownouts. And help reduce the need for power plants. Best of all, we can help America balance the use of its energy resources. No doubt about it, natural gas is a high-tech, low-cost way to keep cool without CFCs. It's a cool way to help save our ozone layer, too" (American Gas Association, *Wall Street Journal*, April 10, 1995, p. A19).

(c) "The Japanese are not simply masterful adapters of other people's works. They make them their own, contributing flair in design and efficiency in manufacture. These qualities derive in part from a desire for simplicity. From chairs to soy sauce bottles, Japanese designs offer a clean, minimalist profile. Space is precious in Japan, so products that don't waste it are particularly valued. The most obvious example is in the miniaturization of electronic devices. Thirty years ago, Sharp Corporation introduced the first solid-state calculator. It was described as desk-top even though at 25 kilograms it weighed nearly as much as the desk on which it sat. Today the calculator is small enough to fit in a pocket. Then there is craftsmanship. Japanese cars began to outsell their competitors not only because of their pleasing designs but also because they were very well made. In objects as disparate as sewing machines, household furniture and motorcycles, the Japanese have achieved visual harmony and elegance. Anyone acquainted with rollerblading has the Japanese to thank, or blame. In 1969, Yoshisada Horiuchi designed a booted skate with four wheels mounted in a line. An American invented an in-line skate in the 19th century, but his design didn't catch on, apparently lacking the Japanese elegance" ("Japan Excels by Design," *The Economist*, reprinted in the *Globe and Mail*, April 10, 1995, p. A9).

EIGHT Summary

There are four basic types of argument structure central to argument diagramming. A single argument presents only one premise that is used all by itself as the basis offered to support the conclusion. In a linked argument, the premises function together to support the conclusion. In a convergent argument, each premise functions by itself to fulfill the probative function. Thus a convergent argument can be viewed as several different arguments used to support the same conclusion. In a serial argument, the conclusion of one argument becomes a premise of the next argument used in the sequence of reasoning. In a divergent argument, two propositions are inferred as separate conclusions from the same premise. In some cases, it is not a straightforward matter to tell whether the argument is linked or convergent. As a basis for determining whether the argument is linked or convergent, four kinds of evidence are used: indicator words, inference structure, the blackout test, and the context of dialogue. In cases where there is insufficient evidence to determine firmly whether an argument is linked or convergent, it is best to diagram it as convergent.

An incomplete argument is an argument with a statement, a premise, or conclusion that was not explicitly stated in the text of discourse of the given case but that needs to be made explicit in order to offer a basis for critically evaluating the argument as a whole. The process of filling in unstated premises or conclusions is part of a more general process called transformation. The four kinds of transformations used to make up an argument diagram from a given text of discourse are deletion, addition, permutation, and substitution. Some premises or conclusions that were not explicitly stated may have to be filled in to make the argument useful to prove something that contributes to settling an issue in a dialogue. Such an argument may assume that an audience will fill in these missing premises or draw the unstated conclusions by themselves. If these missing parts are left out, however, the arguer's reasoning may not be properly represented.

An implicit premise or conclusion needs to be marked as such in an argument reconstruction (by using a convention on the diagram, to separate it from explicit premises and conclusions). Thus, such an implicit premise, it must always be remembered, is being attributed to the arguer on a basis of presumption only, when the textual evidence justifies such an addition to the case. But in the end, judging whether a proposition should be inserted as an unstated addition to an argument is best done on a contextual basis of determining how the argument is being used in the context of dialogue in a given case. Judgments of how to complete incomplete arguments are best done on a case-by-case basis, utilizing the evidence from the context of dialogue.

The examples studied before the first six sections of this chapter are meant to be clear and straightforward in exhibiting simple illustrative cases of arguments. But the reality of diagramming natural language argumentation, as indicated in section 7, can be much more difficult. In dealing with difficult cases of the kind that are encountered in many cases of real texts of discourse, arguments need to be re-expressed by transforming them. One needs to identify a set of premises and a conclusion or an orderly sequence of them. But in some cases, this sequence is buried in an unclear and confused text of discourse. It can be very hard in such cases to judge which unstated assumptions are needed to complete an argument or even to identify clearly the premises and conclusions supposedly being explicitly stated.

The reality is that people are often deceptive. They use ambiguity and obscure language to hide their meaning and even to try to disguise it so they won't be held accountable. In many cases, arguers even use innuendo and other clever deceptive techniques of obfuscation to provide 'plausible deniability'. For example, an unstated premise or conclusion may be put forward in an argument to persuade an audience, but then later, when critically questioned, the proponent of the argument may deny that she meant to assert this proposition at all. These techniques of trying to weasel out of one's prior commitments are all too familiar in political argumentation. But there are even cases where arguers try to avoid the fulfillment of this burden in advance of any challenge that may come later. For example, an arguer may say: "I have heard rumors that proposition *A* is true, but it would be unfair of me to repeat these rumors because I can't prove they are true. But just in case they may turn out to be false, I'd like to deny that they are true." In a case such as this, the arguer is trying to get you to accept *A* as a plausible presumption that might be true, without having to accept a burden of proof for having put *A* forward as a claim for your acceptance. Fortunately, not all cases of arguments are put forward in such a tricky manner to evade responsibility for having to support premises and conclusions with evidence. But in critical argumentation, we need to be aware that such cases exist.

Thus a certain cautionary restraint and judgment is called for. It would be counter-productive to always go around plugging in additional premises that would make an argument structurally correct, even if it is clear that the argument is a bad one, and is not being presented in a way that represents structurally correct reasoning or the author's position being advocated in the text of discourse. Such an attribution needs to be seen as subject to repudiation by the proponent of the argument. It is well to keep this limitation in mind because, as we saw in connection with argument from commitment in chapter 3, there can be serious problems with wrongly attributing unstated premises or conclusions to arguers in some cases. The main problem is the danger of committing the straw man fallacy, by misattributing to an arguer some statement he is not committed to[6] and does not represent the position he is arguing for. Despite these dangers, the four transformations, including the technique for the addition of unstated premises and conclusions, are necessary and useful methods of argument diagramming. We could not properly identify, analyze, and evaluate everyday arguments in natural language conversations if we didn't deploy them. But we need to use them cautiously, always backing up an attribution by appealing to the textual and contextual evidence given in the case.

[6] On the notion of commitment as a central concept for critical argumentation, see Douglas N. Walton and Erik C. W. Krabbe, *Commitment in Dialogue* (Albany: State University of New York Press), 1995.

FIVE Dialogues

Dialogues, as we saw in chapter 1, have characteristics such as civility, meaning that the two participants take turns making various moves. This chapter begins by analyzing the different types of dialogue that embody such characteristics in order to make the dialogue successful as an environment for using rational argumentation. Such moves include not only the putting forward of arguments, but also the asking of questions, including critical questions used to respond to arguments. It is the connected sequence of questions and answers, as well as chains of arguments, that make up the dialogues. Thus, asking the right questions in a dialogue and responding appropriately to the other party's questions are important aspects of what makes a dialogue move forward. This chapter classifies the different types of dialogue and examines some of the main properties of questions and how they are used in dialogues. Questioning is obviously very important in law and politics. For example, in a trial, a lawyer has to question a witness and sometimes in cross-examination can do so in quite a probing, even aggressive way. The lawyer for the other side often needs to object to such questions. Questioning is also very important in science at the discovery stage, where hypotheses are formulated.

Asking questions often seems like an innocent and harmless enough activity, you might think, from a viewpoint of critical argumentation. After all, questions don't make assertions, in the way propositions are typically used to do, and questions don't have premises and conclusions, the way arguments do. But questions have presuppositions, and these presuppositions are statements that can often function in a dialogue much the same way arguments do. Questions can be loaded, and they can be complex. Put this combination together and you can ask questions that function as tricky devices of entrapment. So questions, it will turn out, are in many cases not as innocent or harmless as they might seem. In fact, asking the right questions, and being careful to respond to them in the right way, can be enormously influential moves in steering a dialogue in a direction that may go toward (or away from) the goal the dialogue is supposed to fulfill. For all these reasons, learning skills of questioning and answering is one of the most important aspects of critical argumentation. The skills taught in this chapter include learning to recognize different kinds of questions, learning how to answer them, and learning how to reply when an answer is not appropriate. Also taught are skills of learning how to detect hidden and tricky implications of questions and how to respond in a rational and constructive way to such questions.

ONE Persuasion Dialogue

At the beginning of this book, in chapter 1, section 1, we saw that five main characteristics of any dialogue containing argumentation can be identified: the issue, the viewpoints of the participants, the characteristic of civility, the opposition of viewpoints, and the use of arguments. Chapter 1 illustrated all these characteristics with the dialogue on tipping. It is shown below that there are different types of dialogues, but we begin with the persuasion dialogue, since it is of central importance for critical argumentation. The dialogue on tipping is a persuasion dialogue, meaning that Bob and Helen have opposed viewpoints on the tipping issue, and each is trying to persuade the other to accept his or her viewpoint. Helen is against tipping. It is her opinion that it is a bad practice that should not be continued. Bob is for tipping. He thinks that it is a good practice that should be retained. What each party is doing in the dialogue is using rational argumentation to try to get the other to give up his or her old viewpoint and come to accept a different viewpoint instead, namely, that advocated by the arguer.

We can see that the dialogue on tipping, like all persuasion dialogues, represents a mixture of opposition and collaboration. Helen's and Bob's viewpoints are opposed to each other. They have opposite opinions about tipping. Each is an advocate of her or his own viewpoint, and it is important that each should put forward the strongest and most persuasive arguments that she or he can, and to question critically and try to refute the arguments of the other as well as she or he can. The issue is examined by looking at the reasons for and against on each side. As shown in chapter 1, if both sides do this, the dialogue can be successful by throwing light on the issue, bringing out the reasons for and against each view, and enabling us to resolve or clarify the issue.

A persuasion dialogue is about a central issue; each party has a viewpoint on that issue, and the viewpoint of the one party is opposed to that of the other. As is shown in chapter 6, a viewpoint or point of view is made up of two components, a proposition (statement) and an attitude (pro or contra) to that statement. In a persuasion dialogue, one party has a pro attitude to some proposition, while the other doubts that proposition, as in a dissent. Or one has a pro attitude to some special proposition and the other has a pro attitude to the opposite proposition, as in a dispute (see chapter 1, section 9). This special proposition was called the arguer's thesis in chapter 1. In a dispute, the thesis of the one party is the opposite of the thesis of the other. In a dissent, one party doubts that the thesis of the other is true, and the first party offers arguments designed to remove the other's doubt. In a dissent, the role of the proponent is to put forward an argument, using reasoning to remove the respondent's doubt about some particular proposition (the conclusion of the reasoning). The role of the respondent is to express doubt about this particular proposition or, in some cases, even to express the opinion that this proposition is false. Thus every persuasion dialogue, whether dispute or dissent, is characterized by an opposition between two parties, meaning that there is a particular proposition that one accepts and the other does not. In a case of strong opposition, the thesis of the one party is the opposite (negation) of the thesis of the other party, and this type of dialogue is called a dispute. In the case of weak opposition, the one party has a particular proposition as her thesis, and the other party does not accept that thesis but does not hold the opposite proposition as his thesis. In this kind of dialogue, the dissent, the respondent is successful if he can merely question the proponent's defense of her thesis, by throwing doubt on it. Thus, the careful asking of questions is an important method of arguing.

Such opposition in a persuasion dialogue, whether it be a dispute or a dissent, can represent a factual disagreement or a disagreement about whether some action or kind of action is a good policy or not. For example, we might have a dispute about whether mercury is heavier than lead or not. This would be factual dispute about whether the proposition 'Mercury is heavier than lead' is true or false, and you might try to persuade me that your view of the matter is right by citing evidence. For example, you might quote a passage in a chemistry textbook. The dispute on tipping, in contrast, represented a disagreement on whether a kind of action, namely, tipping, is generally a good policy or not. This too is persuasion dialogue, even though it is about actions and about whether some specific course of action or policy for action is good or not. The reason is that the sentences 'Tipping is a good policy that should be retained' and 'Tipping is a bad policy that should not be retained' can both be classified as statements that are true or false. And so persuasive arguments giving reasons why each is true (or false) can be given. It is important to make this point about persuasion dialogue, even though it may seem like a minor one in itself, because below a distinction is drawn between persuasion dialogue and another type of dialogue called deliberation.

The most important characteristic of a persuasion dialogue is that the two parties each try to persuade the other that his or her thesis is true (in the case of a dispute). But what is meant by 'persuasion'? What is referred to is not just psychological persuasion but what could be called rational persuasion. As noted above, the concept of argument has a rationality component. The proponent of an argument tries to get the respondent to accept the conclusion by using premises that the respondent already accepts or can be convinced to accept through using further arguments. The proponent uses argument for this purpose by using a chain of reasoning. But the specific way she uses such a chain of reasoning is characteristic of persuasion dialogue. She tries to use an argument that meets two requirements. One is that the argument is structurally correct as a deductive, inductive, or plausible inference. The other is that the argument has premises that the other party accepts or can be convinced to accept. If the proponent uses an argument successfully in such a case, the respondent is obliged to accept the conclusion. The reason is that both participants in a persuasion dialogue must respect a rational argument. That is part of what they agree to when they enter into this type of dialogue. If the proponent presents an argument that meets these two requirements and the respondent cannot refute or critically question the argument, then he should accept it. He should be rationally persuaded to accept the conclusion. Even though he did not accept it before, he should now accept it. In other words, an arguer in a persuasion dialogue should be open to changing his opinion if presented by an argument that gives good reasons to support its conclusion. If he refuses to budge, even though presented with a compelling argument, he has in effect opted out of the persuasion dialogue. In other words, it is important in a persuasion dialogue to be open-minded. To be dogmatic or to ignore evidence is a bad thing.

In one special type of persuasion dialogue, called the critical discussion, the goal of the dialogue is to resolve the central conflict of opinions by proving that the one party's viewpoint has been successfully defended and the other party's has not. In this type of dialogue, there has to be winner and loser, or the dialogue has not been successful. However, in other persuasion dialogues, even though neither side succeeds in proving her thesis or refuting that of the other side, the dialogue is still reasonably successful. For example, a philosophical discussion on some issue such as free will or euthanasia can be successful even if one side was not proven right and the other wrong. A persuasion dialogue, like a philosophical discussion, for example, can be successful if each participant gains insight into the reasons why the other party held his view, as well as deeper insight into the reasons why she herself held the view she did. Some see critical insight as less important than who won the dialogue, but such insight is valuable because it can clear the way to knowledge by exposing arguments that are questionable or even fallacious.

Of course, we are already familiar from chapter 1 with the kind of dialogue in which there are two different and opposed viewpoints and where each participant uses rational argumentation to try to get the other to come to accept her or his viewpoint, but in the end the thesis of one side is not shown to be true and that of the other side false. The dialogues in chapter 1, such as the tipping dialogue and the genetically modified foods dialogue, are of this type. Such a dialogue can be worthwhile and can throw light on an issue even though it doesn't resolve the issue. However, to illustrate how persuasion dialogue is governed by rules that regulate each move, the example of the critical discussion has been chosen here. The critical discussion is one of the most easily recognizable types of persuasion dialogue, and its resolution requirement is strict and definitive. For a critical discussion to be successful, one side must win while the other side loses. The conflict of opinions must be resolved, making the outcome go to one side or the other. In some ways, this type of persuasion dialogue is the easiest for the beginner to grasp and appreciate.

Below a version of the ten dialogue rules that govern moves made by both participants during the argumentation stage of a critical discussion is presented.[1]

[1] The rules for the critical discussion have been set out by the Amsterdam School of argumentation theory, including the rules for the argumentation stage presented above. A version of this set of rules can be found in Frans H. van Eemeren and Rob Grootendorst, *Argumentation, Communication and Fallacies* (Mahwah, N. J.: Erlbaum, 1992), pp. 208-209. The version represented above is not quoted verbatim. It has been re-expressed and modified to suit the needs and language of this book.

Rules for a Critical Discussion

Rule 1: Parties must not prevent each other from advancing or casting doubt on each other's viewpoints.

Rule 2: Whoever advances a viewpoint is obliged to defend it if asked to do so.

Rule 3: An attack on a viewpoint must represent the viewpoint that has really been advanced by the protagonist.

Rule 4: A viewpoint may be defended or attacked only by advancing argumentation that is relevant to that viewpoint.

Rule 5: A person can be held responsible for the unstated premises he leaves implicit in his argument.

Rule 6: A viewpoint is regarded as conclusively defended only if the defense takes place by means of argumentation based on premises accepted by the other party, and it meets the requirement of rule 8.

Rule 7: A viewpoint is regarded as conclusively defended only if the defense takes place by means of arguments in which an argumentation scheme is correctly applied.

Rule 8: A viewpoint is regarded as conclusively defended only if supported by a chain of argumentation meeting the requirements of rules 6 and 7 and if the unstated premises in the chain of argumentation are accepted by the other party.

Rule 9: A failed defense must result in the proponent withdrawing her thesis and a successful defense must result in the respondent withdrawing his doubt about the proponent's thesis.

Rule 10: Formulations of questions and arguments must not be obscure, excessively vague, or confusingly ambiguous and must be interpreted as accurately as possible.

From these rules the reader can get a pretty good idea of how the critical discussion works as a distinctive type of dialogue. And one can get an idea of how it represents a normative model of argumentation, meaning that certain kinds of moves and arguments are excluded as inappropriate or incorrect by the rules. To make this point, let's examine each of the rules.

Rule 1 forbids the use of force or threats in a critical discussion or other tactics used to try to get the other party to 'shut up'. Rule 2 expresses the requirement of burden of proof, as defined in chapter 6. Rule 2 means that if you make a claim that a particular proposition is true, you must present an argument with that claim as its conclusion, if the other party questions the reason for your making such a claim. Rule 3 is directed toward dealing with the straw man fallacy. It requires that if you attack or question the other party's viewpoint, you must direct your criticism to the real viewpoint he advocated and not to some exaggerated or distorted version of it. Rule 4 requires relevance, a factor that is studied below in chapter 7. Rule 5 has to do with enthymemes, or arguments with missing premises of the kind studied in chapter 4, section 6. Rule 6 (as well as rule 5) shows clearly why the critical discussion is a type of persuasion dialogue. A successful argument used by a proponent has to be based on premises that the respondent is committed to, as judged by what she has previously gone on record as saying in the dialogue so far. Rules 7 and 8 add structural requirements on the chain of argumentation used to argue from the respondent's premises to one's conclusion. Each step must be based on a correct form of argument, that is, an argumentation scheme or a form of argument that is deductively valid or inductively strong. Rule 9 states the requirement for winning and losing that is characteristic of the critical discussion as a special type of persuasion dialogue. Rule 10 adds a linguistic requirement. Because dialogues representing real cases of conversational argumentation occur in natural language discourse, clarity of expression is required. Thus, avoidance of obscurity, or excessive vagueness and ambiguity, is necessary if the argumentation is to be successful.

Persuasion dialogue is not the only type of dialogue in which argumentation can occur. In the next section, we see that there are other types of dialogue, with different characteristics and different rules. Since the dialogues studied in chapter 1, such as the tipping dialogue and the Santa Claus dialogue, are persuasion dialogues, it is easy to appreciate why the persuasion dialogue is so common and so characteristic of a good deal of everyday argumentation. Thus, it is clearly a good place to start in studying how a type of dialogue can have rules that govern the rational argumentation used in it. The critical discussion is a good type of persuasion dialogue to use to introduce the reader to persuasion dialogue. Although the rules are not stated in an exact formulation of the kind that could be used in computing, they are easy to understand without using technical notation, and they clearly represent a normative model of argumentation, meaning a model that represents correct use of argumentation and excludes certain kinds of argumentation moves, ruling them incorrect in the model.

EXERCISE 5.1

1. Review the dialogue on genetically modified foods in chapter 1, and judge how well the moves made in the dialogue conform to the rules for a critical discussion.

2. Sit down with a partner and engage in a brief critical discussion on the issue of tipping. Decide which side of the issue you support most strongly and find a partner for the discussion who supports the other side. Record the dialogue. Identify three of the most persuasive arguments that were used on each side. Show how each of these three arguments (on one side or the other) was linked to other arguments in the discussion.

TWO Commitment in Dialogue

One of the central notions of any type of dialogue is commitment. As arguers in a dialogue make various claims and put forward arguments or make moves of any kind, these moves incur commitments for them. For example, if an arguer agrees to the proposition that tipping leads to bad consequences, she becomes committed to that proposition. Each participant in a dialogue has a commitment set, sometimes called a commitment store, in which all the commitments of each participant are recorded. When a participant incurs a commitment, it is inserted into her commitment set. Thus each commitment is stored in a kind of data base containing a list of propositions that a participant in the dialogue has gone on record as accepting. Ideally, such commitments are kept track of in a data base. In real life, participants often forget their commitments or sometimes even try to hide them. Sometimes people will argue about them. For example, one person might say that another person once maintained that capital punishment is justified, while he (the second person) might insist that he never said that. Since there is no public record of what he said or didn't say, there is no way of checking. However, ideally, in a dialogue, there should be a record of the previous moves in the dialogue and a record of the commitments of both parties.

When a participant in a dialogue has committed herself to a certain proposition then she is bound to acceptance of that proposition if the issue arises again later in the dialogue. Let's take an example from the dispute on tipping. Suppose Helen has, previously in the dialogue, agreed to the proposition that any practice that rewards excellence of service is a good practice. And suppose that, at some other point in the dialogue, she agreed to the proposition that tipping rewards excellence of service.

Then it would be appropriate for Bob to use the following argument in the dialogue on tipping.

> Any practice that rewards excellence of service is a good practice.
>
> Tipping rewards excellence of service.
>
> Therefore, tipping is a good practice.

Bob points out, let's say, that this argument is deductively valid and that Helen is committed to both premises. Because the structure of the argument is valid, once Bob has pointed out that Helen is committed to the premises, she also has to accept the conclusion of this argument as a commitment of hers. What is shown here is that once you are committed to some propositions in a dialogue, you may also be committed to others, even if you did not realize it. You may become committed to other propositions that follow logically from ones you previously accepted as true.

One can certainly see why Helen should have to accept the proposition 'Tipping is a good practice' as a commitment of hers once Bob has put forward the argument above. If she denies this proposition is true, she has been shown to be inconsistent in her commitments. And as shown in chapter 1, section 1, inconsistency is a very bad thing in logic. If you contradict yourself, then everything you have said cannot be true. Inconsistency is an important sign of error in critical argumentation. As things stand, Bob has shown that Helen has inconsistent commitments in the dialogue on tipping. Thus, Helen has to respond somehow and deal with Bob's criticism.

When Bob used the argument above, however, it posed another problem for Helen in the dialogue on tipping. Acceptance of the conclusion would mean that she has conceded that Bob is right that tipping is a good practice. But in the dialogue, she does not agree with that proposition at all. She is against it. Indeed, if she were to accept it, such a commitment would mean that she has lost the critical discussion on tipping. This concession would mean that in the dialogue, Bob has been successful in proving his thesis. So Helen is in a pickle here, unless she can retract her commitment to one of the premises. Should she be allowed to do this? The answer is that in a persuasion dialogue, it should be allowed. Helen can do it by explaining why she changed her mind. Suppose, for example, she decides to retract her commitment to the proposition that tipping rewards excellence of service, saying, "That's not really right, and although it looked right at first, I now think it is wrong and I reject it."

Helen might even give some reasons why she thinks this proposition is not true. This kind of move seems generally very reasonable in a persuasion dialogue. In such a dialogue, when confronted by a rational argument that is logically reasonable and persuasive, you are supposed to accept the conclusion, even if you previously did not accept it. Retraction of this sort is part of being open-minded in a persuasion dialogue. You have to be open to new evidence and to changing your mind if your previous position was shown to be wrong. Thus, retraction of commitment should sometimes be allowed in a persuasion dialogue.

The central technical problem in formal models of persuasion dialogue is to define the precise conditions under which retraction should be allowed. This is not an easy problem, and we shall not try to solve it here. Suffice it to say that there can be different kinds of persuasion dialogue, some with stricter rules, including rules of retraction, and some with more permissive rules. There are three general requirements on commitment in dialogue that can be stated, however, and that participants should be held to.

Three General Requirements on Commitment in Dialogue

1. If a proponent is committed to a set of statements, and the respondent can show that another statement follows logically as a conclusion from that set, then the respondent is committed to that conclusion.
2. The respondent has the right to retract commitment to that conclusion, but she must also retract commitment to at least one of the premises. For otherwise it has been shown that she has inconsistent commitments.
3. If one party in a dialogue can show that the other party has inconsistent commitments, then the second party must retract at least one of those commitments.

As shown in chapter 1, inconsistency is generally a bad thing in logic. If a set of statements is inconsistent, they cannot all be true. At least one must be false. Thus if an arguer tries to maintain a set of commitments that is inconsistent, it means that there is something not right in her position. Thus the other party can use such a finding of inconsistency as a criticism.

Indeed, in chapter 3, section 7, the argumentation scheme for Argument from Inconsistent Commitment was presented. It is a negative form of argument from commitment. When confronted with such an argument, a respondent must reply by dealing with the criticism. But it is possible for him to do this without losing the dialogue just because an inconsistency has been found in his commitment set. He can go further into the details of the case, and he may be able to show why the inconsistency is only apparent and not real. In some cases, it can look as if an arguer's position is inconsistent, but further clarification may show that there is not really an inconsistency there or that it can be dealt with by making some corrections. If an argument has been going on for quite a few moves, a party's viewpoint in the dialogue may consist of many single commitments, and the logical relationships among these commitments can be quite complex. Also, in realistic everyday argumentation, it can be quite hard or even impossible to keep an exact record of all an arguer's commitments she incurred in the past. Thus as a matter of general policy, commitment sets do not always have to be consistent. However, if one party in a dialogue points out correctly that the other party's commitments are inconsistent, the party accused of inconsistency has to deal with this criticism at her next move.

To give another illustration of how these rules concerning commitment work, let's go back once again to the dialogue on tipping. Suppose Helen gets Bob to agree that tipping has bad consequences in at least some cases, citing the time a waiter spilled soup on her husband's suit, because there was a misunderstanding over tipping. In the chapter on argumentation schemes, it was shown that the following form of argument is reasonable.

ARGUMENTATION SCHEME FOR ARGUMENT FROM NEGATIVE CONSEQUENCES

PREMISE: If *A* is brought about, bad consequences will plausibly occur.

CONCLUSION: *A* should not be brought about.

Since Bob has agreed that tipping has bad consequences, it follows from this form of argument that he is also committed to the conclusion that tipping should not be brought about. In other words, he is committed to the statement that tipping is the sort of practice that should not be continued. His commitments imply that it is a bad practice of a kind that ought to be stopped. But this commitment is inconsistent with Bob's point of view in the dialogue. He is pro-tipping. In other words, he is committed to the proposition that tipping is a good practice of a kind that should be continued. So Bob is now in a pickle of the same kind that Helen was in above. He must retract at least one of his commitments. This example shows how argumentation schemes can be binding in a dialogue and how they can be used to criticize an arguer's position. Such a criticism of inconsistency gives rise to the need for retraction of a commitment.

EXERCISE 5.2

In exercise 1.7, four sample dialogues were presented in which there was a problem regarding the consistency of an arguer's commitment set. Analyze each dialogue to show how the problem should be resolved in accord with the three general requirements on commitment in dialogue.

THREE Other Types of Dialogue

So far we have been concerned only with the rules for commitment management in persuasion dialogue. But there are other types of dialogue as well in which argumentation can occur, and each of them requires different kinds of commitment rules. In addition to persuasion dialogue, there are five other basic types of dialogue for argumentation: negotiation dialogue, inquiry, deliberation, information-seeking dialogue, and eristic dialogue. The main characteristics of each type are summarized in Table 5.1.

Each type of dialogue has its collective goal as a framework governing both participants and all their moves. But then, each participant also has an individual goal. An argument is useful in a framework of dialogue to the extent that it contributes to the collective goal of the dialogue. Thus, an argument, as the term is used in this chapter, presupposes a conversational framework where there is a verbal exchange between two parties and

TABLE 5.1 TYPES OF DIALOGUE

Type of dialogue	Initial situation	Participant's goal	Goal of dialogue
Persuasion	Conflict of opinions	Persuade other party	Resolve or clarify issue
Inquiry	Need to have proof	Find and verify evidence	Prove (disprove) hypothesis
Negotiation	Conflict of interests	Get what you most want	Reasonable settlement that both can live with
Information seeking	Need information	Acquire or give information	Exchange information
Deliberation	Dilemma or practical choice	Coordinate goals and actions	Decide best available course of action
Eristic	Personal conflict	Verbally hit out at opponent	Reveal deeper basis of conflict

where reasoning is used by the two parties for some purpose relating to this conversational exchange. Thus, all of the types of dialogue require collaboration. Each party must take turns making its moves and must make each move according to the rules for the dialogue to be successful. But within this collaborative framework, there is also room for opposition. For example, in a persuasion dialogue each party advocates his or her own viewpoint and attacks the opposed viewpoint using the strongest arguments and criticisms she or he can find.

Every dialogue in which argumentation is used has four stages. At the confrontation stage, the thesis of one party is stated, and the nature of the opposition of the other party to that thesis is determined. At this stage, the issue of the dialogue is formulated and agreed to by both parties. At the opening stage, the arguers decide to begin the discussion, and agree to follow the rules appropriate for that type of dialogue. At the argumentation stage, the two sides put forward their arguments to defend their views, and each critically questions the arguments put forward by the other. At the closing stage, the discussion is terminated, and if one party has fulfilled its goal, the other side must concede.[2] Whether an argument or a question is appropriate depends on what stage of a dialogue it occurs in. For example, a question about how to formulate the issue of the dialogue may be relevant at the confrontation stage, but that very same question might be irrelevant if asked during the argumentation stage.

For example, in a critical discussion, each party must state its point of view on the issue to be discussed, and it must be made clear whether the dialogue is a dispute or a dissent. At this stage, the burden of proof that each side has taken on is made clear. At the opening stage, both sides must agree that the dialogue they will take part in is a critical discussion, as they agree to abide by the rules for a critical discussion. During the argumentation stage, as illustrated by the dialogue on tipping and the other dialogues in chapter 1, each side puts forward arguments in support of its own viewpoint and critically questions the arguments put forward by the other side. At the closing stage, the side that had the weaker argument given to support its viewpoint must give in to the side that had the stronger argument. At this stage in a successful critical discussion, the conflict of opinions is resolved.

The second type of dialogue that is a framework for argument is called the inquiry. The inquiry stems from a kind of unsettledness that is the lack

[2] See van Eemeren and Grootendorst, *Argumentation, Communication and Fallacies*, pp. 34–37.

of a decisive proof of some claim where there is a need to definitely, one way or the other, prove that this claim is true or false. Now it may be the case that, even after an exhaustive collection of evidence, this particular proposition cannot be either proved or disproved. But that finding can be a useful outcome of the inquiry, too. If it can be shown that, despite a collection of all the relevant data, the proposition can neither be proved nor disproved, then at least it can be shown that it should not be taken for granted that the proposition is settled or accepted as true.

The inquiry is a highly collaborative framework of argument in which high standards of proof are adopted. A group of investigators collect all the relevant data that are available both for and against a particular proposition that is at issue. They then organize the evidence, once it is collected, and reach a stage where they agree that this is all the evidence that can be found. They then reach an argumentation stage. They attempt to draw out conclusions in an orderly way, built on the solid foundation of premises provided by the given evidence, so that the proposition at issue can be definitively proved or disproved. Thus, the goal of the inquiry is to prove that a particular proposition is true or false or, if that fails, to show very definitely that existing evidence is insufficient to prove it or disprove it. In a persuasion dialogue, participants are fairly free to change their minds and retract a previous commitment. Indeed, as noted above, open-mindedness is quite an important property in a persuasion dialogue. If a strong argument based on new evidence is found that goes against a proposition an arguer was previously committed to, then the participant in a persuasion dialogue should retract his previous commitment. The purpose of the inquiry is to minimize or even eliminate the need for such retractions. The method of the inquiry is to proceed carefully by accepting as premises only propositions that are definitely established by strong evidence as true or false. The reason is that there will be no need in the future to have to go back and retract these premises, and then start a whole new line of reasoning based on different premises.

The inquiry is often associated with a philosophy of foundationalism, where the use of reasoning is compared to the construction of a building where the builders start with firmly established foundations and then build upward on them. Scientists and philosophers have often portrayed reasoned argument in science as taking the form of the inquiry. Aristotle felt that what he called demonstration (or inquiry, in our terms) was the best model for scientific reasoning. Descartes, a scientist as well as a philosopher, was a strong exponent of the inquiry as a kind of argument appropriate for both scientific and philosophical reasoning. He even argued that premises in an inquiry should be indubitable, or beyond all possibility of doubt. Other foundationalists have not been this extreme. But they emphasize that evidence should be firmly established before scientific conclusions are drawn from it. Whether these claims for the structure of reasoned scientific argument are true, however, is the subject of much controversy. It seems generally that, at the later stages of scientific research, where results are solidified and presented to colleagues and the public, scientific reasoning does take a form of argument very similar to the inquiry. However, at the earlier stages, where a lot of creative guesswork is involved in arguments about scientific hypotheses, the inquiry is probably not a very useful model of scientific argument. The American philosopher and scientist Charles S. Peirce argued that there is an initial discovery stage in scientific reasoning. At this discovery stage, abductive inference is used to construct plausible hypotheses. These hypotheses can later be verified or falsified as deductive or inductive arguments, once they are tested by experiments and other kinds of scientific evidence. But the use of plausible hypotheses at the discovery stage can lead to better results more quickly by cutting down on the time and expense of testing all the possible hypotheses that could be constructed.

The third type of dialogue is the negotiation dialogue. In negotiation dialogue, matters of the truth and falsity of a proposition are secondary. Instead, the purpose of a negotiation dialogue is for both parties to "get a good deal," that is, to reach an agreement that both parties can find acceptable even if it involves some gains and losses for both. The kind of unsettledness that is characteristic of negotiation dialogue is a conflict of interest. This is a kind of conflict that frequently involves financial interests – that is, each party has something to lose or gain monetarily by the outcome of the argument. In the type of negotiation dialogue called distributive bargaining, there is a conflict of interest between the two parties, and the dialogue is a zero-sum game in the sense that one party's gain is the other's loss. However, there are also other negotiation dialogues where the issue is not purely economic but concerns relationships and has to do with personalities and motivations.

Some of the rules for negotiation dialogue are different from those of persuasion dialogue. For example, rule 1 of the critical discussion banned the use of threats as arguments by stating that parties must not prevent each other from advancing or casting doubt on each other's viewpoints. Making a threat to use physical force of some sort against the other party would be highly inappropriate in a persuasion type of dialogue. However, threats of various kinds are common in negotiation dialogue. In a union-management negotiation about wages, the union may threaten to go on strike if management does not agree to their demands. As their argument, management may then threaten to cut wages or let employees go. In extreme cases, management may even threaten to declare bankruptcy, dissolving the company, with the result that everyone in it will lose their jobs. Such uses of threats in argumentation are not necessarily wrong or inappropriate as part of a negotiation, even though using a threat can be a risky tactic in some instances. When used excessively, inappropriately, or in an unconvincing way, threats can be counterproductive in a negotiation. Even so, a threat that might be highly inappropriate in a persuasion dialogue might not be so in a negotiation dialogue. For example, if two parties were having a critical discussion of the abortion issue in a philosophy class, and one threatened to beat the other up if he did not immediately accept her viewpoint, everyone would recognize such a move as highly inappropriate. It would be unethical and possibly even illegal. But even over and above that, it would be inappropriate in the critical discussion on the abortion issue. It would not help the discussion reach its goal and might even prevent it from doing so.

The fourth type of dialogue in which argument is used is called information-seeking dialogue. In this type of dialogue, the one party presumably has some information that the other party needs or wants to get. The role of the party who has this information is to transmit it to the party who lacks it. This type of dialogue tends to be collaborative and non-adversarial in nature. It starts with an initial situation where one participant has some information that the other party lacks. The kind of unsettledness that is characteristic of this type of argument is a lack of information or an imbalance of information between two parties. The one party wants or needs to get the information that the other party is assumed to have. A common example is asking for directions when one is lost.

A person needs to get to a meeting in Lockhart Hall but has arrived as a stranger at the university and does not know where Lockhart Hall is located. Encountering a passerby who appears to be a student who would be likely to be familiar with the campus, she asks him, "Where is Lockhart Hall?" He points in a particular direction and says, "It's just behind that building over there. You just have to walk around this pathway and then turn to your right. Then you'll see the sign for Lockhart Hall."

In this kind of case, the informant does not have to be an expert on building locations or architecture. But he is someone who is thought to be familiar with the area and thus be in a position to provide the needed information. But in some cases, the informant needs to be an expert. A special type of subcase of information-seeking dialogue is where the one party is an expert in some domain of knowledge or is in a special position to know something. For example, if I am consulting with my financial adviser, I might ask her different questions about which are the best buys among the stocks presently available, what are the latest government regulations on income tax, and so forth. In this kind of dialogue, the adviser tries to give you relevant information you need to arrive at a decision on what to do. So deliberation may ultimately be involved. But the primary purpose of the dialogue is not for the two parties jointly to arrive at a decision on what to do but for the one party to give information to the other. Then later, in a separate dialogue or a separate sequence of reasoning, the other party can arrive at a decision on what to do. Appeal to expert opinion is an important kind of reasoning used here. It is also very important as a form of witness testimony in legal argumentation. Ballistics experts or experts on DNA are commonly asked to give legal testimony.

The fifth basic type of dialogue in which arguments are used is called deliberation. Deliberation could be typified, for example, by the arguments in a town hall meeting where a group of citizens have gathered together to discuss some practical problem in their local area. They discuss different solutions or ways of solving the problem, and, normally, the participants divide into different factions or hold points of view and then argue against the position of an opposed point of view. Ultimately, however, their aim is to come to agreement on some line of action that they can take in order to deal with the problem. Although one can deliberate alone, looking at different sides of a problem, in other cases there can be a large number of people involved in deliberating together, as in a town hall meeting. Nevertheless, in the simplest type of case, which we will consider as our model, there are just two parties involved in the deliberation, representing two opposed points of view on how to solve a problem.[3] At the opening stage, an issue or 'governing question' about

[3] The model presented here is that of David Hitchcock, Peter McBurney, and Simon Parsons, "A Framework for Deliberation Dialogues," in *Argument and Its Applications: Proceedings of the Fourth Biennial Conference of the Ontario Society for the Study of Argumentation* (*OSSA 2001*), ed. H. V. Hansen, C. W. Tindale, J. A. Blair, and R. H. Johnson, compact disk. Also available on Peter McBurney's Web page at the University of Liverpool, Department of Computer Science: http://www.csc.liv.ac.uk/~peter.

what should be done is posed. The subsequent discussion of this question will include suggesting various proposals or possible action options. Arguments for and against the various proposals are discussed. Finally, the participants, after examining all the relevant arguments, will come to agreement on some recommended course of action as the best choice to solve the problem.

The unsettledness characteristic of the deliberation type of dialogue is a difference of opinion on what the two parties consider a prudent course of action would be in order to solve a problem that they are confronted with, which requires some sort of action. It is also characteristic of argument in deliberation that knowledge is insufficient to determine clearly the choice that needs to be made. So, although knowledge based on probability is frequently relevant in deliberation, this kind of knowledge by itself is generally insufficient to resolve the issue. In the simplest kind of case of deliberation, there is a direct conflict between two possible courses of action, and a choice needs to be made between these two courses. This type of case is frequently called a dilemma in philosophy. Examples would be the abortion dispute or the dispute on euthanasia, where the arguments on both sides focus down to two strongly opposed choices or possible courses of action.

Practical reasoning is the type of reasoning most frequently used in arguments in deliberation dialogue. And, as we will learn in chapter 8, practical reasoning tends to be presumptive in nature. Argumentation in a deliberation dialogue typically takes the form of practical reasoning, chaining together goals and possible courses of action that would be means to implement those goals in a particular situation. The conclusion of such a chain of argumentation states that a practically wise (or prudent) person ought to select some particular course of action designated as the conclusion of the argument.

The sixth type of dialogue in which argument commonly occurs is the eristic dialogue. It is essentially a quarrel where each party attacks the other party by any means of argument that seems available. In the quarrel, unlike the critical discussion, the reasoning skips from one topic to another very rapidly. So, in the quarrel, a high degree of irrelevance is tolerated. The kind of unsettledness that is characteristic of argument in a quarrel is an antagonism between two parties, each of whom has a perceived grudge or grievance against the other that is deeply felt. In a quarrel, one party often lashes out at the other in personal attacks. In polite conversation, for example, in normal business affairs, it would not be regarded as appropriate to bring up such grudges or grievances. In fact, normal, smoothly functioning, polite conversational argument is made possible by suppressing the urge to give vent to quarreling. When the quarrel does arrive, it is often like a sudden thunderstorm. It is unanticipated and arrives on the scene quickly. The deeply held grudge then emerges to the surface. Consider the following case.

> A married couple is having an argument about who should take out the garbage, who forgot to take out the garbage on a particular day, or some relatively trivial incident like this. But then suddenly, one of the parties brings up some deeply held grievance and begins to attack the other party as being guilty of some wrong act. In reply, the attacked party begins to engage in what is called counterblaming.

What is very characteristic of argument in a quarrel is the ad hominem, or personal attack, type of argument. Each party blames the other for some supposedly bad act that occurred in the past and offended the other party deeply.

The individual goal of each party in the quarrel could be described as "hitting out" verbally at the opponent. This description suggests that the quarrel is a trivial adversarial exchange that has no real value as an argument. However, in some instances, the quarrel can have a very valuable benefit of allowing powerful feelings to be vented. This cathartic function is valuable because, in a serious quarrel, deeply internalized emotions can be vented, based on grievances that have been repressed for too long, and it can be very valuable to express them overtly to the other party who is involved in these supposed grievances. Thus, each party can get insight into feelings that are deeply important to the other party but would not normally be appropriate subjects for polite conversation. The resulting insight can be a good basis for facilitating personal relationships on a long-term basis. For example, one party may have an annoying mannerism that the other person does not want to mention because it could give offense. But during a quarrel, it could become apparent how much the one person in the past has been offended by this habit she perceives as being so detestable. The other party then may say something like, "I didn't realize how important that was to you or how much it bothered you, so in the future, I will try very hard not to indulge in this habit."

Eristic dialogue is the most adversarial and least collaborative of all the six basic types of dialogue. You could almost say it is purely adversarial, except that in order to have a quarrel, participants must at least collaborate in following some minimal rules. For example, they must take turns. If one party blocks the other party from taking its turn to attack, we don't really have a quarrel. A quarrel has to go back and forth. Of course, the quarrel is still very adversarial and in many instances highly chaotic. One party will often try to dominate the dialogue by continuing to argue loudly, thus blocking the other from speaking. Or one party will tell the other to "shut up or else" and so forth.

Often, quarrels seem silly and pointless. And in many cases, they are. But in some respects, quarrels as arguments do have a serious side. Contrary to initial appearances, then, the quarrel is a conversational framework that can be useful in giving us insight into the evaluation of arguments. Generally, however, quarrels generate more heat than light, and the prognosis on the quarrel, from a point of view of logic, tends to be generally negative. One particular factor to note is that the quarrel typically exhibits an attitude of closed-mindedness on the part of both participants. In other words, a participant in a quarrel tends to be highly unwilling to admit that she is wrong or could be shown to be wrong, no matter how strong or how revealing the arguments of the other side turn out to be. As noted above, the persuasion dialogue requires participants to remain open-minded. In this respect the quarrel stands in sharp contrast with the persuasion dialogue. Thus, if an argument shifts from a persuasion dialogue (or any other type of dialogue, for that matter) to a quarrel, it is a pathological sign of deterioration of the argument. Once the argument has degenerated into a quarrel, the arguers become dogmatic and unalterably fixed in their positions. It may be impossible to get them out of this mode, once they are there. Thus the onset of the quarrel is a danger to the other types of dialogue.

EXERCISE 5.3

Give a brief example of each of the five types of dialogue described in section 2, either from your own experience or from an account of an argument found in a media source. Show how the example you cite exemplifies the characteristics of that type of dialogue generally.

FOUR Simple and Complex Questions

Dialogues are made up of various kinds of moves, in addition to the putting forward of arguments. One type of move stressed in chapter 1, section 8, is that of criticizing an argument by asking questions. But various kinds of questions can be asked in a dialogue. We need to begin by identifying several different types of questions and their important properties. Examples of four important types of questions are given below.

WHETHER QUESTION: Is Bob conservative or liberal?

YES-NO QUESTION: Is Bob conservative?

WHY QUESTION: Why is Bob attracted to socialism?

CONDITIONAL QUESTION: If Bob is a conservative, how long has he been a conservative?

A whether question, also called a disjunctive or multiple-choice question, poses a number of alternatives, and the respondent is supposed to select one of them as the answer. A yes-no question admits of only two direct answers, 'yes' or 'no,' and may be seen as a restrictive type of whether question that offers only these two alternatives. For the purposes of this chapter, there are two different kinds of why questions that need to be distinguished. One type is a request for an explanation. The other is a request by the questioner that the respondent furnish a proof (or argument) for some proposition that is queried. Here it is important to be alert to the distinction between an explanation and an argument. Finally, a conditional question contains a conditional, or if-then, proposition of the kind defined in chapter 1. Other kinds of questions are who questions, which questions, and deliberative questions, such as "What shall I do now?"[4]

It is important to make the distinction between an answer to a question and a reply to a question. A reply is any verbal response given in a dialogue following the asking of a question. A relevant reply is one that meets the need expressed by contributing to the dialogue. Relevance of replies is defined in section 7 of this chapter. The reply in the first dialogue below is not a relevant reply to the question.

Thelma: When is Harvey leaving for New York?

Fred: The photocopier is not working, and the repairman should be called.

The response given in the next dialogue is a relevant reply.

Thelma: When is Harvey leaving for New York?

Morris: You'll have to ask his assistant.

[4] A more complete classification of the different types of questions is given by David Harrah, "The Logic of Questions," in *Handbook of Philosophical Logic*, ed. D. Gabbay and F. Guenther, vol. 2 (Dordrecht: Reidel, 1984), pp 715-764.

Note that although Morris gave a relevant reply to Thelma's question in the first example, he did not answer the question. If he had said, "Harvey is leaving on February 3 for New York," that would have been an answer. A direct answer gives exactly the information requested by the question, while an indirect answer (partial answer) furnishes only some of that information. For example, in the second example above, suppose Morris had replied, "I'm not sure, but I think he is leaving next week some time." This reply would be an answer, but only an indirect answer. But if he had said, "Harvey is leaving on February 3 for Bali," that would be a direct answer. Both direct and indirect answers are relevant, but a questioner prefers a direct answer if it can be given.

All questions have presuppositions. For example the question 'When is Harvey leaving for New York?' presupposes that Harvey is leaving for New York. In other words, asking the question 'When is Harvey leaving for New York?' assumes a dialogue in which both questioner and respondent are committed to the proposition that Harvey is leaving for New York. The question also has a lot of other presuppositions, such as the propositions that Harvey exists, that New York exists, that there is a way of leaving for New York that can be assigned some time or date, and so forth. Asking this question presupposes that both parties to the dialogue are already committed to all these statements. For the question to be appropriate and to work properly as a useful question to ask at that point in the dialogue, the respondent must be committed to all these statements. This observation leads to a technical definition of the notion of a presupposition of a question in a dialogue. A *presupposition of a question in a dialogue* is a proposition that a respondent becomes committed to in the dialogue in virtue of giving any direct answer to the question. For example, if Morris gives the direct answer "Harvey is leaving on February 3 for New York," he becomes committed to the proposition that Harvey is going to New York. So in the context of the dialogue, given what little we have been told about the case, the proposition 'Harvey is going to New York' counts as a presupposition of the question "When is Harvey leaving for Bali?" The asking of questions is also based on presumptions about a dialogue that take the form of implicatures, of the kind described in chapter 6. For example, if I ask you, "When is Harvey leaving for New York?" there is a presumption that you (the person to whom the question was put) might plausibly be expected to know the answer. At least it is presumed that you might be able to give some useful reply that would lead me toward an answer. Such presumptions can also be described as presuppositions of a question, because the answer becomes committed to them when any direct answer is given. For example, by giving any direct answer to the question 'When is Harvey leaving for New York?' a respondent becomes committed to the proposition that he knows when Harvey is leaving for New York.

There tend to be a lot of presuppositions to a given question, but for purposes of critical thinking, some are more important to identify than others. Generally, a presupposition is important to identify in a dialogue if it is controversial in that dialogue. Suppose that in the dialogue on tipping, the following exchange occurs.

Bob: Tipping raises a person's self-esteem by rewarding excellence of service.

Helen: How could any practice that treats a person like an object raise that person's self-esteem?

The important presupposition of Helen's question in this case is the proposition, 'Tipping is a practice that treats a person like an object.' Before Bob gives any direct answer to Helen's question, he should be aware that this proposition is a presupposition of the question and a controversial one in the dialogue. It is a proposition that he should challenge, from a point of view of supporting his position in the dialogue. In contrast, the proposition 'A practice can raise a person's self-esteem' is also a presupposition of Helen's question, but an important one (relative to the context of the case).

Now we have dealt with simple questions and need to go on to examine some examples of complex questions. A complex (multiple) question is one that has more than one proposition as its presupposition and where it is important, in a dialogue, for the respondent to sort out these separate propositions and be aware that they are different. When a respondent gives any direct answer to a complex question, he becomes committed to more than one significant proposition, and therefore he may need to accept one and repudiate the other. An example of a complex question is given in the following dialogue.

Rita: If you are still going to Singapore on Sunday, will you contact Fred Simpson and inform him that the deal is off?

Ted: OK.

The question in this case is complex, as indicated by the fact that it has a conditional in it as well as a conjunction. Ted's reply indicates that he agrees to everything in the question. But he might have wanted to separate out the individual propositions and agree to some but not to others. For example, Ted might have replied, "I'm not going to Singapore on Sunday after all," indicating that the proposition that is the antecedent, 'I (Ted) am going to Singapore on Sunday,' is not true. Or he might want to agree with the antecedent of the conditional but separate out the propositions in the conjunctive part of the question. For example, he might reply, "I will contact Fred Simpson, but it is not my responsibility to tell him the deal is off. I think, as a courtesy to Fred, you ought to phone him and tell him personally." In this reply, Ted indicates that he agrees to one of the propositions in the conjunctive consequent of the conditional but not to the other.

In fact, most questions used in everyday conversations are complex. But an example of a simple (non-complex) question would be, 'Are you Bohemond Smith?' To answer this question, a simple 'yes' or 'no' will suffice, and a respondent has no need to break the question into parts, in order to say 'yes' to one part and 'no' to another. Even this simple-looking question is complex in certain ways. It is a yes-no question, and the presupposition of the question is the disjunctive proposition, 'Either you (the respondent) are Bohemond Smith or not'. This proposition is a tautology, a proposition that is logically true, independently of the component propositions in it. It is like saying, 'Either it will rain tomorrow or it will not'. Of course, such a prediction could never turn out to be false, no matter what actually happens tomorrow, because it is a tautology, and makes no real prediction at all (that could ever turn out to be false). However, such a proposition is complex, because it is a disjunction. Even so, however, the question in the example above is not complex, in the sense that there are two or more different propositions in it that are important for the respondent to separate. Presumably, the respondent should be satisfied to answer 'yes' or 'no', without dividing the question.

Despite the tradition of calling 'complex question' a fallacy, there is nothing intrinsically wrong with asking complex questions. In many cases, asking a complex question is necessary in order to communicate in a dialogue successfully. For example, if two people are trying to fix a photocopier machine, they might have a dialogue of the following kind.

Laura: How do you fix a paper jam of the kind that happens when that red light at level one goes on, as just now happened when I tried to copy a document?

Trevor: I can't quite figure out what the instructions are telling me to do. If I lift the top part of the machine, push the yellow release catch, empty the paper in the roller, and then click the release catch back into place, would that clear this kind of jam, provided I turn the power off, and make sure not to stick my fingers in where the roller engages with the teeth?

In this case, since Laura and Trevor need to deal with complex matters relating to procedures for maintaining a complex machine, they need to ask each other complex questions. If they had to break every complex question down into simple, single questions, it would make the kind of dialogue required in this case difficult, or perhaps even impossible.

So there is nothing intrinsically wrong with complex questions, but they can get us into difficulties in certain kinds of cases, where splitting up the question is important in light of a respondent's commitments in the dialogue. Consider the following example.

> A new health care bill transferring responsibility for health care funding from the federal to the state governments has been put forward in the Legislative Assembly for a vote. A Democrat, Representative Munson, would very much like to vote against this bill. However, attached to the bill is a "rider" – a piece of legislation that would retain a strong form of affirmative action as policy for the federal government. Representative Munson is in a pickle. Which way should he vote? If he votes against the health care bill, he also has to vote against affirmative action. But in order to vote for the proposal strengthening affirmative action, he would also have to vote for the health care bill (which he is against).

Because of the way voting on the bills put forward is structured, Representative Munson does not have the choice of doing what he really wants to do, which is to vote for the one bill and against the other. So he must make up his mind on the basis of his priorities which of the two policies is most important for him to support, by voting one way or the other. No matter which way he votes, however, he goes against his commitments on one proposition or the other. So here, the complex nature of the question is a problem for him.

This problem of having to vote on a complex bill that may have several propositions in it is common to all legislatures, parliaments, and congresses that allow amendments to be "tacked on" to bills. A legislature may require that such an amendment must be relevant, or 'germane', to the bill being considered. However, the U.S. Senate allows for non-germane amendments to be added to a bill. What this means is that anything can be added to a bill to be voted on, whether it is relevant to the bill or not.

> What this means, in effect, is that any matter, whether it has been previously introduced or not, whether it has been referred to committee or not, and whether it is germane to the pending business or not (except general appropriation bills) may be introduced as an amendment. This was, in fact, the manner in which the 1960 Civil Rights Bill was brought to the floor in the Senate. Senator Lyndon B. Johnson, then majority leader, in motioning up an obscure bill to aid a school district in Missouri which was federally impacted, announced that the bill would be open to civil rights amendments.[5]

The problem of having to vote on complex propositions is not unique to the U.S. Senate. But the most dramatic cases of having to vote on complex legislation, where the voter's commitments are sharply divided on different issues, occur there, because there is no requirement of relevance on amendments.

Another way that complex questions can pose a problem is that they can be too complex or more complex than is necessary, with the result that the question is very confusing. In political debates, use of these highly complex questions is common. The following example, from the *Oral Question Period of the House of Commons Debates of Canada* (*Hansard*, February 16, 1976, p. 10956), concerned a union's right to appeal to a government tribunal against a decision of the Anti-Inflation Board.

> In view of the fact that this right of appeal which the government spoke of so glowingly when the legislation was going through the House, is increasingly becoming a farce since the person aggrieved cannot appeal to the administrator except with the consent of the Anti-Inflation Board or the government, and now cannot appeal the decision of the administrator to the appeal board and since they cannot take the matter to the federal courts unless they have been before the appeal tribunal, has the time not come for the minister to introduce legislation immediately to give any person who is affected by a decision of the Anti-Inflation Board the right to go directly to the appeal tribunal, and if not satisfied, to go directly to the courts?

[5] Lewis A. Froman, Jr., *The Congressional Process* (Boston: Little, Brown, 1967), p. 132.

You might say that this case is similar to the previous one. For, surely, the matter of the union's right to appeal to a government tribunal against a decision of the Anti-Inflation Board is a highly complex matter of administrative procedures. And so the asking of such a complex question as the one in the example above can be justified by the complex nature of the subject matter itself.

But there is an additional problem evident in the example above. The complex question in this case contains a certain slant or bias in some of its clauses, indicated by the use of loaded terms, such as 'glowingly' and 'farce', and by its pushing for one side by using the phrase, "has the time not come...?" The problem here is like the one posed by the following question: 'Are you going to be a nice boy and go to bed now?' It is a complex question, and the first part, before the 'and', puts a certain pressure on the respondent. If he says 'yes', all is well, but if he says 'no', he is committed to the proposition that he is not being a nice boy. So there is nothing inherently wrong with asking complex questions, but problems can arise in three kinds of cases. (1) The dialogue may be structured so that the respondent cannot separate the questions. (2) The question may be so complex that it is confusing. (3) The complex question may be combined with loaded terms or other forms of slanting that give it a push to one side. This third kind of problem case is examined further below when certain tricky kinds of questions are analyzed.

EXERCISE 5.4

1. Consider the following questions asked in the context of a debate on cannibalism. One party is arguing for the thesis that cannibalism is always morally wrong, while the other party argues for the thesis that cannibalism could be morally acceptable in some cases – for example, in an emergency where somebody is starving. Identify the type of question, and identify one important presupposition of the question.

   (a) Is cannibalism practiced in some cultures?
   (b) Why is cannibalism contrary to respect for a human body?
   (c) Why do you advocate a practice that has been condemned by every civilized society?
   (d) What could a person do to survive if she were a plane crash survivor in the Andes and had no source of food other than the bodies of the crash victims?
   (e) Should human bodies be treated with respect?
   (f) If human bodies should be treated with respect, then wouldn't eating one be morally wrong?
   (g) What's more important, saving a human life or treating a human body with respect?

(h) Is cannibalism a distasteful subject?

(i) What would you do in a situation where you were starving and there was no food other than a human body: (1) eat the body, (2) die of starvation, or, (3) hold off as long as possible and eat the body only to prevent your own death?

2. Analyze the following questions to judge whether the question is complex. Identify the important presuppositions of the question. Comment on whether the complex nature of the question could pose a problem.

(a) Are you the man from the mayor's office who called us on the phone yesterday?

(b) Do you agree that human bodies should be treated with respect and never eaten?

(c) If I push the red button, and then do not punch in the code, will the burglar alarm go off immediately, or will I get a chance to disarm it?

(d) The following question on the topic of the economy was asked in the Questions Without Notice section of the Parliamentary Debates of the House of Representatives of Australia (*Hansard*, June 6, 1991, p. 4939): "My question is directed to the Prime Minister. Since the failed Treasurer has moved to the back bench, is it a fact, as reported in today's press, that the Prime Minister is now receiving disturbing economic advice which indicates that the honourable member for Blaxland gilded the lily and that Australia's economic position is much worse than he had previously led the Prime Minister to believe?"

(e) The following question on the use of Australian security intelligence organization information was asked in the Questions Without Notice section of the Parliamentary Debates of the House of Representatives of Australia (*Hansard*, June 6, 1991, p. 4939): "If the Prime Minister continues to rely selectively on the convention of neither confirming nor denying such damning allegations in order to suit his own self-interest and, given that he is chronically unable to tell the truth, will he – in the national interest – agree to establishing a judicial inquiry so that the Parliament and the people of Australia will have the truth exposed once and for all?"

FIVE Loaded Questions

A loaded question is a question asked by a questioner at some move in a dialogue that has one or more presuppositions contained in it that the respondent is not committed to at that move. Typically, the presupposition contained in a loaded question is also a dangerous one for the respondent to become committed to. It is often a commitment that will make him look bad or even might lead him to lose the dialogue once the questioner uses it to defeat him. The concept of a loaded question depends on what the respondent's commitments are, or are not, at any particular stage that the sequence of argumentation has reached in a dialogue. For example, suppose at some move in the dialogue on tipping Helen asked Bob the question, 'Why does tipping someone treat that person like an object?' And suppose that prior to that move in the dialogue, the question of whether tipping treats persons like objects had never been discussed. Helen's question is loaded, at the move where it was asked in the dialogue on tipping, because at that point, Bob was not committed to the proposition that tipping someone treats that person as an object. Moreover, it could easily be used to prove (or argue plausibly for) the contention that Bob's thesis, 'Tipping is a good practice that should be continued' is false. Thus, it would be very dangerous for Bob to give any direct answer to this question. Any practice that treats someone like an object is generally taken to be bad practice, ethically speaking. So if Bob gave a direct answer to the question, Helen would have a very strong argument available that could easily be used to defeat Bob in the dialogue on tipping.

Asking loaded questions is generally allowed in everyday conversational argumentation, and so it is certainly a useful and important skill of critical argumentation to be able to identify them. One must be very careful, because of the dangers of answering such a question too hastily. Consider the following example as an extension of the dialogue on tipping in chapter 1.

Helen: Why does the practice of tipping treat a person like an object?

Bob: I don't agree with the presupposition of your question, namely the proposition that tipping treats a person like an object.

In this case, from a critical argumentation perspective, Bob has made the right type of reply. If he had given any direct answer to the question, he would automatically have become committed to the proposition that tipping treats a person like an object. As pointed out above, such a reply would be a very dangerous move, from a point of view of Bob's side of the dialogue on tipping. For it could easily be used, along with some other plausible assumptions, to prove that tipping is a bad practice, of the kind that ought not to be continued. It is for this reason that loaded questions of this sort, often called 'leading questions' in law, can be objected to in a trial and are often struck down by the judge.

Helen's why question in the example above asked for an explanation of why tipping treats a person like an object. But when a questioner asks for an explanation of why a proposition *A* is true, the presumption inherent in the question is that *A* is in fact true. So in this example, Helen's question presupposes that tipping is in fact a practice that treats a person like an object. Therefore, as soon as Bob gives a direct answer to Helen's question, he becomes committed to this proposition, and it is a very damaging admission for him to make, given his position in the dialogue. One of the most important lessons of this example is that it is not always obligatory or even in many cases a wise thing to do to give a direct answer to a question. Sometimes it is better to question the question, or even, as in this example, to repudiate a presupposition of the question by clearly and emphatically denying your commitment to that proposition. In fact, replying to a question with another question is quite a common and legitimate sequence of dialogue in everyday conversational exchanges. In many cases, asking a questioner questions about her question is necessary for the dialogue to carry on constructively.

The most important critical argumentation skill with respect to loaded questions is to be able to spot the loaded nature of the question so that you won't commit yourself to propositions that may be used against you, without even realizing what you are conceding. In many cases, even though we aren't told or don't know the fuller context of dialogue in which a question was asked, we can determine, simply by identifying some loaded terms used in the question, that the question is loaded. For example, consider the following question: What are your views on the token effort made by the government to deal with this monstrous oil crisis? In this case, nothing is known about the dialogue surrounding this question, but the loaded terms 'token' and 'monstrous' are easily spotted. That does not mean the question is fallacious or was unfair or inappropriate as used in a dialogue. Much depends on whether the respondent was previously committed to the propositions that the effort was "token" and that the oil crisis is "monstrous" (and is indeed a "crisis"). But still, it is useful, from a critical thinking point of view, to spot the bias in the question.

One problem with loaded questions that is very important to be aware of, from a critical thinking point of view, is that unless they are responded to in the right way, they can easily leave the impression that the respondent has lost ground in a dispute. A loaded question shifts a presumption onto the respondent's side, and this presumption will be lodged into place unless the respondent makes a special effort to dislodge it. Questions such as the following one are loaded in the sense that they impute guilt to the respondent: 'How could an innocent-looking person like you be driven to commit such a vicious crime?' The problem here is that if the respondent doesn't react to this question sufficiently vigorously, by showing righteous indignation at the impertinence of the question, he is likely to appear to be guilty. What he must do is to dispute the presuppositions of the question he disagrees with. Otherwise there will tend to be a lingering presumption that they are likely to be true. In fact, then, a loaded question is really very much like an argument and needs to be treated like an argument by the respondent. He must question the question itself and attack its presuppositions by demanding that the questioner prove such allegations.

But on the other hand, the strategy of vigorously arguing against the question can easily backfire. For people react with suspicion to a person who protests his innocence too vociferously when accused of a crime.[6] So one has to be very careful in reacting to a loaded question that implies guilt for wrongdoing. If the respondent is innocent or at least wants to rebut the allegation, the best approach is to respond appropriately to the severity of the accusation, as the context of dialogue indicates. The best strategy is to either question or attack the presuppositions of the question as strongly as is required to shift the burden of proof back to the other side. This approach requires the adoption of a critical attitude toward the question. The first step is to identify the loaded statements that are presupposed by the question and subject each of them to critical questioning or counter-argumentation appropriate for the dialogue. In most cases it is quite sufficient to demand that the questioner prove the loaded statements, and then leave it at that. Then if she does try to prove them, you can go on to engage these arguments in the subsequent dialogue.

EXERCISE 5.5

Identify any presuppositions in the following questions that could make the question loaded, as used against a respondent in a dialogue.

(a) About how much money did you spend on vacations away from home in the past year?
(b) In the past three weeks, how often did you buy coffee, tea, bottled water, diet soda, or regular soda?
(c) Do you think we should continue to use tax money to support frivolous art programs?

[6] B. Yandell, "Those Who Protest Too Much Are Seen as Guilty," *Personality and Social Psychology Bulletin*, 5, (1979): 44–47.

(d) Why do you keep trying to justify a view that is so obviously racist?
(e) Do you think Bob is innocent of the most vicious crime known to man?
(f) The following question on the topic of the Women's Conference in China was asked in the Senate Parliamentary Debates of Australia (*Hansard*, August 23, 1995, p. 196): "My question is directed to the Minister for Family Services and it relates to next week's Beijing women's conference. Why was Aus AID's Dr. Ware appointed as a delegate to that conference after that official, on 23 June at estimates, refused to accept as coercive the official Shanghai policy to impose a fine of three times the family annual income payable over six years where a woman refused to have her second pregnancy aborted?"

SIX Responding to Tricky Questions

When a question is both complex and loaded, it can be used as a device of entrapment, typified by the following case, used as an example by the leading traditional logic textbooks for many years to illustrate the problem.

Have you stopped using mind-altering drugs?

This question is a kind of trap, because it is a yes-no question, and no matter which direct answer is given, the respondent becomes committed to having used mind-altering drugs. If the respondent answers 'yes,' then he admits having used such drugs in the past. But if the respondent answers 'no,' he admits that not only has he used them in the past, but is continuing to do so. Thus the 'no' option is even worse, but the point is that no matter which way the hapless respondent answers, he commits himself to having done something that makes him look bad and probably destroys his credibility.

Asking a loaded question has sometimes been called fallacious. Note, however, that even this question, as tricky, dangerous, and deceptive as it seems, could be reasonable to ask in some cases. For consider the following dialogue, where Bruno is the defendant in a trial in which he stands accused of murder, and he is being questioned by the prosecution.

Prosecutor: Do you admit using mind-altering drugs in the past?

Defendant: Yes.

Prosecutor: Have you stopped using mind-altering drugs?

In this case, in virtue of defendant's prior response, in which he freely admitted he had used mind-altering drugs in the past, the prosecutor is justified in asking Bruno the question, 'Have you stopped abusing your spouse?' at the next move in the dialogue. So in this case, asking the so-called fallacious question is appropriate in the context of dialogue of the case. Nevertheless, it is quite possible to see, from the classic case of the question used in this example, how this tricky type of question can be, and typically is used, to unfairly browbeat a respondent, and try to trap him into damaging admissions. So it is a questioning tactic that is well worth being aware of.

Another tricky aspect of the spouse abuse question is its negative format. 'Stopped' means 'discontinued,' a negative idea, meaning 'not doing something you did before.' Research has shown that a negative accusatory question, such as "Isn't it true that your work is poorly regarded by your colleagues?' – asked in cross-examination of an expert witness in court – tended to be "presumptuous" in suggesting guilt.[7] The role of negation in tricky presumptuous questions has been known since ancient times. Eubulides, an ancient philosopher who lived around the same time as Plato, was known for inventing several paradoxes. One of these, called the horned man, involves the following question.

Have you lost your horns?

The trick in this question is similar to that in the mind-altering drugs question. No matter which direct answer is given – 'yes' or 'no' – the respondent concedes that, at one time, he did have horns. This commitment makes him look silly. But part of the trick is explained by a certain ambiguity in the negative term 'lost', brought out when the question is paraphrased into the form of an argument where 'lost' is negated. The following version of Eubulides' paradox is in the form of an argument.[8]

What you have not lost you still have.
But you have not lost horns.
So you still have horns.

One meaning of 'not lost' presupposes you had something before. This meaning makes the first premise true. The other meaning of 'not lost' does not require that you had the thing before. This meaning makes the second

[7] S. M. Kassin, L. N. Williams, and C L. Saunders, "Dirty Tricks of Cross-Examination: The Influence of Conjectural Evidence on a Jury," *Law and Human Behavior* 14 (1990): 373–384, p. 376.
[8] William Kneale and Martha Kneale, *The Development of Logic* (Oxford: Clarendon 1962), p. 114.

TABLE 5.2

Proponent	Respondent
Did you use mind-altering drugs?	Yes.
Have you stopped using them?	

premise true. So there is a subtle ambiguity in the negation, revealing a kind of equivocation implicit in the horned man type of question. So the fact that the spouse abuse question, and comparable tricky questions, is expressed in a negative way is an additional dimension of trickiness to watch out for.

Questions like the horned man question and the spouse abuse question are not always fallacious, as noted above, so the problem is to know how to evaluate them when they are used in a given case. The best method is to apply a profile of dialogue, a sequence of questions and replies representing the context of dialogue in a case. For example, in a case such as the example above where the spouse abuse question has been correctly used, the profile of dialogue can be represented as in Table 5.2.

If the respondent's answer had been 'no' at the first move, then the questioner should not have gone ahead with the next question. If she did, then her asking of the question at her second move would be inappropriate. The problem with such a loaded question is that it can be used in a case where the respondent never took mind-altering drugs, or did not want to admit it, to try to force an admission of guilt. It does this by balling up a sequence of questions into one complex question in a way that leaves the respondent no way open to reply 'no' at moves in the profile of dialogue. What the critical arguer must do, then, when confronted with this kind of tricky question, is to challenge its presuppositions. To give a direct answer would be to fall into the trap set by the question. Instead, the critical respondent must reply to the question by questioning its presuppositions. The respondent should ask the proponent how she can prove the allegation made in the presupposition of the question, and he can also deny the allegation, depending on what sort of strength of critical reaction is appropriate for the accusation and how it has been brought forward in the dialogue.

The exact reply that is appropriate is a function of the type of dialogue, the commitments already made by the respondent at that point in the dialogue, and other factors of the particular case. For example, in the following case, from a debate on job cutbacks at a national park, the respondent replied quite well to a tricky question.

Questioner: Since the policy of this government is to eliminate jobs, can the respondent confirm the bad news and explain in unequivocal terms why my constituents are the targets of such savage and unacceptable cutbacks?

Respondent: It is true that the park service is reducing some jobs because of economic necessity. But we are doing our best to ease the situation and to help retrain employees who can be given other duties; we are proceeding as humanely as possible.

Although the respondent did not answer the question directly, she did take the sting out of the accusations made in the question that the cutbacks were "unacceptable" and "savage" and that the policy of the government is to reduce jobs. As critical arguers evaluating the question asked in the example above, we would not be able to predict this reply or to suggest a better one because we do not have the information on the particulars of the case known to the respondent. It is up to her to give the reply. But we are in a position to evaluate critically the question identifying the complex structure of the question, its presuppositions, and the loaded nature of these presuppositions. By doing so, we can expose the trickiness of the question, showing why a critical questioning of the question is a more rational approach than trying to answer the question.

Loaded and complex questions are often given an additional dimension of trickiness by containing an ad hominem attack on the respondent. This type of ad hominem attack is particularly dangerous because, posed in the form of a question, the allegation does not seem to require any proof, even if it is only based on suggestion and innuendo. The classic case[9] concerns a dialogue between someone who is against hunting and a hunter. In the exchange, the critic of hunting has been accusing the hunter of engaging in barbaric practices of sacrificing hares or trout, just for her own amusement. The hunter then replies with the following question: "Why do you feed on the flesh of harmless animals?" Here the hunter has turned the tables on the critic. Of course, if the critic is a vegetarian, he can easily rebut the presupposition of the question. But if he does eat meat occasionally, he appears to be stuck in a circumstantial inconsistency. He is criticizing the killing of animals, but by buying and eating meat, he is supporting this very practice himself. So the question in the classic case is a tricky question that contains a circumstantial ad hominem argument.

The question in the classic case is a tricky one indeed, for it has some genuine basis for the ad hominem argument. Eating meat is genuinely

[9] Richard Whately, *Elements of Logic* (New York: William Jackson, 1836), p. 196.

connected to the killing of animals. But what the critical respondent must point out is that eating meat is different from killing animals for amusement, which is what the critic has accused the hunter of doing. To turn the tables on the hunter and reply adequately to her tricky question, the respondent must point out that eating meat is not the same as the action of killing animals for sport (or amusement). The two things are related, but they are not the same things. And then he must repeat that he is accusing the hunter of killing animals for amusement.

An ad hominem attack posed in a question like that in the classic case is a highly effective tactic used to put the respondent on the defensive. And one can see why. The question conceals a use of argument from commitment to attack the integrity, and hence the credibility, of the respondent. By forcing the respondent to admit that he himself engages in a practice that contributes to the killing of animals, the question used by the hunter in the classic case makes the respondent appear to be a hypocrite. The respondent appears to take the morally high ground in posing such an accusation of barbarity against the hunter. But the question challenges whether the respondent is really such a moral person himself. A question that is quite aggressive or potentially damaging, particularly one that accuses the respondent of blame for something bad, is often replied to by an ad hominem question directed back to the questioner, saying, "You are just as bad." This type of ad hominem reply is sometimes called the "two wrongs" argument. The back-and-forth dialogue of ad hominem questions and ad hominem replies is characteristic of a lot of political debating. For example, when one candidate in an election campaign resorts to "negative ads" or "character attacks," the opposing candidate frequently feels that he must reply with equally damaging ad hominem attacks or otherwise he will lose ground in the polls. Such a pattern of attack is illustrated by the following political debate.

Politician *A*: Can you assure the people that there will be no increase in interest rates tomorrow?

Politician *B*: This is a ludicrous question coming from this person whose party was pushing interest rates up to 20 and 25 percent per annum when they were in power.

In this case, the question is not an explicit ad hominem attack, although it does imply a responsibility for high interest rates (presumably, a bad thing for people generally). But the reply attacks the question, using a circumstantial ad hominem argument to make the questioner appear to be inconsistent and suggest that she is hypocritical. In this case, the question is far from reasonable, and the use of the circumstantial ad hominem to reply seems both justifiable and effective.

Use of an ad hominem reply to respond to an ad hominem question or any question implying guilt can be reasonable. But such dialogue sequences need to be analyzed carefully. As in the classic case, such a reply can be legitimate and have justification, but the cases of the questioner and the respondent may not be exactly the same, or similar. The following describes a *60 Minutes* news story, "What Killed Jimmy Anderson?" (March 2, 1986).

A news program investigated evidence that the deaths of several schoolchildren in a small town could have been due to toxic chemicals that came to be in the water system through industrial waste disposal. The interviewer asked a corporate representative about the possibility that his company had violated the law by dumping toxic chemicals. The representative replied that the interviewer was "an interesting person to raise that question" in relation to the fact that his network was recently cited for some contamination problems. The interviewer countered this reply by pointing out that unlike the corporation's case that was the subject of the program, in the case of the network citation there were no deaths or illnesses reported, no lawsuits, and no criminal investigation.[10]

Here the interviewer accused the corporate representative (or his company) of being responsible for dumping toxic chemicals. But then the corporate representative replied that the interviewer's own television network has done the same thing. This *ad hominem* reply throws the burden of guilt back onto the interviewer's side, suggesting he is a "fine person" to be asking such questions.

But what is especially interesting about this case is the interviewer's reply, pointing out several differences between his situation and that of the corporate representative. The interviewer is pointing out just what we observed in the hunter case, namely, that the situation on the one side is different from that on the other. Still, just as in the hunter case, the ad hominem reply does have some sting and some justification, for it counters that the attacker is involved in the same kind of practice that she accuses the other party of being guilty of. So evaluating ad hominem

[10] Douglas N. Walton, *Question-Reply Argumentation* (New York: Greenwood Press, 1989), p. 179.

answers to ad hominem questions or to any questions that are loaded or imply guilt or blame of some sort needs to be undertaken carefully. The reply needs to be judged in relation to the question, and the two situations need to be compared carefully, to see whether they are the same or similar or in which respects they might be different.

In question-reply sequences, ad hominem attacks can occur in the initial question, in the reply given to the question, or in both. Where the ad hominem attack is made in the question the critical thinker needs to identify the question as a loaded question, and to identify the precise nature of the loading as being an ad hominem attack. Where the ad hominem attack has been made in the reply, the critical thinker must evaluate the situation of the questioner as compared with that of the respondent, in the respects related to the ad hominem exchange, as far as information about these two situations is given in the case. By comparing the two situations, an evaluation can be made of the extent to which the ad hominem reply is justified or not. But even recognizing a question as loaded because it contains an ad hominem attack is an important step in critical argumentation.

EXERCISE 5.6

1. Analyze the following questions, citing the important presuppositions and showing how an attempt to answer them could be tricky. Show what sort of reply would be appropriate for the question.
   (a) Did your sales increase as a result of your misleading advertising?
   (b) Why have your sexist views so often been considered offensive in the past?
   (c) Do you and your communist pals think that your efforts to suppress freedom of speech can be used to force everyone to live in a police state where everyone is depressingly at the same level of mediocrity?
   (d) The topic of the following question in the *Question Period of the House of Commons Debates of Canada* (June 10, 1982, p. 18304) was the government's position on unemployment: "How long is the minister prepared to condemn 1,200 more Canadians every day to job loss and insecurity because he is too stubborn and too uncaring to change his policies?"
   (e) The topic of the following question in the Question Period of the House of Commons Debates of Canada (June 20, 1986, p. 14760) was government expenditures.

   Mr. Don Boudria (Glengarry-Prescott-Russell): "Mr. Speaker, my question is directed to the Prime Minister. On a daily basis the media are reporting the excessive abuse by the Prime Minister in spending taxpayers' money on hotels, airplanes, videos, limousine rentals, caviar, and champagne, as if he had won the 649 Lottery. Will the Prime Minister now put a stop to the spending orgy of taxpayers' money?"

2. Evaluate the argumentation in the following question-reply exchanges.

(a)

REPORTER: If you, as an elected representative, are in a position of public trust, where you are not supposed to be in a conflict of interest situation, how can you have accepted a free fishing trip given by an airline, which is a private corporation?

POLITICIAN: What about you? The travel writer for your newspaper roamed the world for years on free airline passes. Isn't that a conflict of interest situation?

(b) The following extract is from *Hansard* (*Canada: House of Commons Debates*, May 3, 1985, p. 4380).

QUESTIONER: Mr. Speaker, my question is directed to the Deputy Prime Minister. It concerns junkets on board the sacred instruments of travel of the Government. In the face of massive cut-backs in the arts, the CBC [Canadian Broadcasting Corporation], and other valuable areas of government activities, could the Deputy Prime Minister tell the House what could have possibly possessed his colleague, the Minister of Communications, to fill a government jet with family and personal staff members to fly off to Algeria, Greece, and other exotic places, at a cost of $57,000 to the Canadian taxpayers, at a time when he and his colleagues are preaching restraint and telling us how to tighten our belts? How does he intend to stop this kind of activity in the future?

RESPONDENT (Deputy Prime Minister and Minister of National Defence): Mr. Speaker, as I recall it, the specific journey that the Hon. Member talks about was one which was made in the vital interests of Canada's international trade in one of the leading areas of our technology, namely, telecommunications. The Minister visited several countries in the Middle East on missions to improve markets and establish markets for the sale of Canadian manufactured products and goods. When I saw the article to which the Hon. Member refers, I, who have that responsibility now, looked very carefully at that trip. I see every justification for the use of government aircraft in that instance. It has nothing but benefit. Certainly it is a far greater advantage to Canada than the example that was portrayed by his

> Party when it was the Government a couple of years ago, when three government aircraft, with three separate Cabinet Ministers, arrived at roughly the same time in the City of Winnipeg, unbeknownst to each other. All of them could have taken commercial aircraft.

SEVEN Relevance of Questions and Replies

In any sequence of question-reply argumentation, the reply needs to be evaluated in relation to the question. And both the question and reply need to be evaluated in the larger sequence of exchanges in a dialogue, of which they are a part. Questioning and replying moves are best judged in relation to how both questioner and respondent take part collaboratively in helping a dialogue move forward toward realizing its goal. The questioner should ask relevant and probing questions that are not too complex or aggressively loaded, in an order that allows for helpful and accurate responses. The respondent should answer a question or, if he cannot, at least give a relevant reply. In some instances, questioning the question can be a relevant reply, if that is the best way for the argumentation to move ahead in the dialogue.

It is an interesting experiment to watch news interviews or other kinds of interviews shown on the media, such as interviews of sports and entertainment celebrities and other persons of interest to the public, to see which replies given were relevant to the question asked. Examples are common where the reply is not relevant. To say that the reply is relevant means that it either answers the question or deals with it constructively in a way that contributes to the moving forward of the dialogue toward its goal. A typical example is the following dialogue.

Questioner: Did you try drugs when you were in college?

Respondent: I've always been against the ingesting of illegal substances.

In this case, the reply seems to suggest that the answer given is 'no'. But if you look at it more carefully, you can see that the reply does not really answer the question at all. The reply is really an answer to a different question, the question of whether the respondent is against "the ingesting of illegal substances" or not, as a general question of policy. It does not commit him on the question of whether or not he personally ever ingested illegal substances and does not answer the specific question of whether he took drugs (legal or otherwise) in college. Giving relevant replies to questions is extremely important for a successful dialogue, but the failure to do so, as illustrated by the example above, is frequently overlooked. The other aspect of this example that needs comment is the issue of whether the question itself was relevant or appropriate in the dialogue. If it was not relevant to the supposed issue or topic of the interview, the respondent should point that out. Then questioning could get back to a constructive or more informative and relevant line of information-seeking dialogue.

The problem cases are those where the reply given looks like a relevant answer, because it is an answer to some related, similar question, but does not really answer the question that was asked and is evasive. For example, consider the following sequence in the dialogue on tipping.

Bob: Would you agree that if some fair method of judging when a tip is appropriate could be devised, tipping could be a valuable way of rewarding excellence of service?

Helen: There is no fair method of judging when a tip is appropriate.

In this case, it may look like Helen has answered the question. But the question is a conditional one. Helen replied by denying the antecedent (assumption) of the conditional. That is not an answer, and it does not really deal with the issue posed in Bob's question. In this case, Bob needs to reply: "That's not what I asked you. I asked whether if such a method were to be devised, would it follow, in your opinion that tipping could be a valuable way of rewarding excellence of service." Helen still may not want to answer the question, but it won't do to deny the antecedent of the conditional, either as an answer or as a constructive reply in the dialogue.

On the other hand, the critical thinker must not be too quick to condemn any reply to a question as 'irrelevant' if it does not answer the question. For as we have seen above, in cases of loaded and complex questions, it is not only legitimate but even helpful to question a question critically instead of answering it. A better reply to the conditional question in the example above would have been to answer it, but along with the answer, to add on a clarification that would defeat a potentially misleading implication of the question. Helen might have replied: "Yes, I'll concede that if some fair method of judging could be devised, then tipping could, as you say, be a valuable way of rewarding excellence of service. But I don't think a fair way of judging when a tip is appropriate could ever be devised. So your question is purely hypothetical. And the fact that I answered it in the affirmative should not be taken to imply that I in any way agree to the proposition that tipping could be a valuable way of rewarding excellence of service." This reply gives a relevant answer, but at the same time deals critically with a possibly misleading suggestion implicit in the question that Helen (rightly) wants to avoid.

In some cases, however, replying to a question with a question is evasive, because the question is not an appropriate critical question that contributes to the moving forward of the dialogue. Instead, it is a tactic of distraction used to cover up evading giving an answer by sending the dialogue off in a different direction. In the following example, the issue was a controversy about using for-profit hospitals to treat teenagers with drug or alcohol dependency problems. Controversy arose because it was alleged that the teenagers were not being adequately supervised.

Parent: Why weren't you looking after my child properly?

Hospital Director: How can we look after thirty-six when you can't take care of one?

The problem in this case is that the hospital director, instead of answering the question, is trying to evade it by shifting a burden back onto the parent. The question appears to be a reasonable one, in the context of the controversy in the example. But the hospital director avoids having to answer it by using an emotionally distracting question in reply. The parent is understandably concerned about the problems he had with the child, and there is probably a feeling of some guilt on his part. So it would be difficult for him not to be distracted by this clever reply to his question. When evaluating relevance of a reply, the first task is to judge whether the reply answered the question. And if not, then it must be decided whether the reply moves the dialogue toward its goal or sends it in a different direction (away from the goal).

EXERCISE 5.7

Evaluate whether the following replies were relevant to the question asked, as far as can be judged from the context given.

(a) In this case, the mayor of Detroit was interviewed by a media reporter on the topic of No Crime Day in Detroit.

INTERVIEWER: The murder rate this year so far is over three hundred people murdered in Detroit. More people were murdered last month in Detroit than in the whole year in Toronto so far. Do you feel that this represents a failure or problem, from your point of view as mayor?

MAYOR: You are asking me questions about this high murder rate in Detroit. That is not the question. Other cities like New York also have high rates. The topic is No Crime Day. This murder rate question is not relevant.

INTERVIEWER: Well, yes, it really is relevant.

(b) In this case, a reporter was interviewing a politician about an upcoming election.

INTERVIEWER: What went wrong in your last four years in office?

POLITICIAN: Let's put that in perspective: What went right? Unemployment has been down, the deficit has been reversed, and high interest rates are no longer a problem. In the last four years, the country has been more prosperous, there has been economic renewal, and greater social justice.

(c) The topic of the following question in a magazine article in which a political leader was interviewed was teenage pregnancies.

QUESTIONER: Figures indicate that there are up to eighty unplanned teenage pregnancies every week in Manitoba. Do you think a strong sex education program would help to solve this problem?

RESPONDENT: I think that there are a number of reasons for teenage pregnancy. Quite frankly, we discover over and over again that many of the children, and they are children at that age, know that they should be using birth control and choose not to use birth control. That's why the responsibility component of family life education is so very very important.

(d) The topic of this interview of a politician was capital punishment.

QUESTIONER: Do you think that if capital punishment is brought back there will be fewer murders of police officers and prison guards?

RESPONDENT: Capital punishment will definitely be brought back because the people are outraged by the current state of affairs and are solidly behind the death penalty in capital cases of murder.

(e) The following exchange (no topic given) took place in a debate in the Questions Without Notice section of the Parliamentary Debates of the House of Representatives of Australia (June 6, 1991, p. 4947).

QUESTIONER: I ask the Minister for Community Services and Health: in administering his portfolios, is it his practice as Deputy Prime Minister and Minister for Community Services and Health to mislead or otherwise deceive the Australian people if he finds it politically expedient to do so? Is deliberately misleading the Australian people acceptable political behavior?

RESPONDENT: I thank the honorable member for the question, which I would have thought called for an obvious reply. I certainly do not intend to spend any time on it. But if the honorable member wants to go to the question of integrity, I believe, frankly, that the Opposition perhaps ought to look at its own house.

QUESTIONER: What is your answer?

RESPONDENT: In terms of the performance of Opposition members in relation to policy questions, frankly, they seem to back away from every commitment they make, and for the Opposition to make a statement in this Parliament is not to establish any credibility.

EIGHT Summary

This chapter began by identifying one type of dialogue that is centrally important in critical argumentation called the critical discussion, a subtype of a more general type of dialogue called persuasion dialogue. Not all persuasion dialogues are of the critical discussion type. For a persuasion dialogue it is not necessary for the conflict of opinions (the issue) to be resolved definitively one way or the other, by showing that the one party wins the dialogue and the other loses. Although persuasion dialogue is important, it is only one kind of dialogue that contains argumentation. The five other types of dialogue are listed in Table 5.1 (p. 183), along with their main characteristics. How questions are asked and answered is a central part of the structure of any type of dialogue.

Among the most important types of questions defined were disjunctive (multiple-choice) questions, yes-no questions, why questions, and conditional questions. There is an important distinction between a reply and an answer. An answer is a special type of reply that supplies the information requested by the question. A direct answer furnishes exactly the information requested by the question. A presupposition of a question was defined as any proposition that a respondent becomes committed to in virtue of giving any direct answer to the question. From the perspective of a particular dispute about some issue, once the dispute has reached a given stage where a particular question has been asked, certain propositions are especially important to identify, because they play an important role in the exchange. From a viewpoint of critical thinking, in evaluating a question-reply exchange in a given case, it is these presuppositions that are important to identify and be aware of. A question may have many other presuppositions that are of lesser importance.

A complex question is one that has several, that is, more than one, of these significant presuppositions. In effect, a complex question really contains two (or more) questions in one. To reply to it in a way that contributes to the goal of a dialogue, these two questions may have to be separated and then replied to individually. However, there is nothing inherently wrong with complex questions. They are often necessary in order to communicate successfully about complex subjects or deliberations where several connected propositions need to be considered together. A loaded question is one that has one or more loaded statements as presuppositions of the question. There is nothing inherently wrong with using loaded questions in a dialogue, any more than there is anything inherently wrong with using loaded statements. But what is important is to realize that loaded statements and questions both function in a dialogue very much as do arguments used in a biased way to support the user's side and to argue against the respondent's side. They do have an argumentative weight, and a respondent must be alert to the need to deal with them carefully, and, in many cases, also fairly aggressively. Loaded questions often need to be challenged strongly by a respondent, and it is vital for a critical thinker to be aware of the loaded propositions contained in the question.

A tricky question is one that is both complex and loaded, used to trap a respondent by being structured so that no matter which direct answer the respondent gives, he becomes committed to a proposition that is loaded against his side of a dispute. Tricky questions, such as the spouse abuse question, are typically used to make accusations that the respondent is guilty for some blameworthy act, or otherwise to make the respondent appear to be on the losing side in a dialogue. As noted in the case of the spouse abuse question, the very same question can be used as a tricky tactic of entrapment in one case, yet be quite reasonable, and no trap at all, as used in another case. So it is no good simply condemning all questions that are both complex and loaded or banning such questions altogether. Each case needs to be evaluated on its merits, by constructing a profile of dialogue that exhibits the right order of asking and replying to questions in a case. In a fallacious case of the use of a tricky question, it can be shown that the right sequence of questioning and replying has been balled up into one question, in a way that obstructs the constructive progress of the dialogue toward its goal. What the critical thinker must do is to question the question by challenging its presuppositions. And such a challenge, when justified, should be judged to be a relevant reply to the question.

Another thing to watch for in dialogues is a reply that looks relevant to a question but is not. In many cases, a reply is topically relevant, but it does not really address the question as posed. In some cases, replying to a question with another question is not a relevant reply and is merely an attempt to evade answering the question. But in other cases, replying to a question with a question is a relevant reply, because, in many cases, the question has important presuppositions that need to be critically questioned or even rebutted by the respondent. Such a reply is relevant if it contributes to the goal of the persuasion dialogue by aiding the progress of the argumentation through a sequence of questions and replies that elicit the real commitments of both parties on the issue.

SIX Detecting Bias

The detection of bias, or a slant to one side in an argument, is an important skill of critical thinking. There are definite indicators of bias, studied in this chapter, that can be detected in an argument in a given case. Most of this chapter is devoted to showing how to recognize indicators of bias present in a given case. In some cases, a mass of evidence, indicating a persistent pattern of bias in a series of arguments in a dialogue, can be overwhelming. But the problem in many cases is that it is hard to identify a bias because it is concealed in the language used. Someone who is trying to persuade an audience may use emotive language in the form of loaded terms that puts a "spin" on the argument. Such use of loaded terms in natural language can often make it look like a simple statement of fact is being made. This appearance tends to disguise the real function of the discourse, which is to put forward an argument.

People typically feel that verbal disputes are trivial and that how a term is defined is of little or no importance, compared with the job of proving a point by "hard" observational evidence collected by statistics. But problems about language and verbal disputes are often far from trivial. Biased language is a powerful tool of persuasion on important issues of public policy. In some cases, billions of dollars are involved in lawsuits, social policies, and government regulations that turn on issues of how a key term should be defined. In many cases, merely identifying a bias by realizing that the language used conceals an argument is all that needs to be done in order to criticize the argument effectively. The best critical response is to reconstruct the discourse as an argument, and then ask for the speaker to give reasons to support her argument. When a respondent makes such a best critical response, the next move in the dialogue is often the offering of a definition of a key term by the proponent. As noted above, the dialogue may then shift to a verbal dispute about words and definitions of words. Thus the first part of this chapter is concerned with definitions of words and phrases, especially words and phrases that have a concealed emotional and persuasive spin.

If bias in an argument is concealed in the language used, a critic or someone who wants to evaluate the worth of what is said may not know how to respond. But it is important to know how to identify such a bias and how to respond to it by making an allegation of bias. One problem is that when an argument is criticized as biased, the arguer will often dispute the claim. Such counter-arguments often lead to verbal disputes about the meaning of words that may be hard to disentangle. Another problem is that not all bias is bad or of a kind that should be condemned. In many cases, a bias in favor of one's own viewpoint is quite normal, because an arguer in a dialogue is trying to advocate her own point of view. Unfortunately, however, in some cases, bias is part of such a strong commitment to one's own viewpoint in a dialogue that there is a closure to all opposed argumentation. This can be a serious problem, representing a troublesome kind of bias, because an arguer should be open to critical questioning and should have to give reasons to support a claim made. We rightly expect critical argumentation to be two-sided and balanced in a dialogue. Thus in the last section of this chapter, indicators are given for distinguishing between normal and troublesome bias.

ONE Loaded Terms

A distinction is often drawn between the emotive meaning of a term and the descriptive or factual meaning.[1] The descriptive meaning is the core factual or cognitive content of a word, while the emotive meaning represents the feelings or attitudes (positive or negative) that the use of the word suggests to respondents. The emotive meaning of a word is a kind of implicit suggestion contained in the word that triggers a positive or negative response in an audience. Whether the factual meaning of a term used in everyday language can ever be cleanly separated from its emotive meaning is disputable. Emotive meaning is present in many, if not most, terms used in everyday language. And because it is emotional in nature and can

[1] The phrase "emotive meaning" was coined by Ogden and Richards in their book, *The Meaning of Meaning* (1923), according to Junichi Aomi, "Persuasive Definitions in Social Sciences and Social Thought," in *Man, Law and Modern Forms of Life*, ed. Eugenio Bulygin, Jean-Louis Gardies, and Ilkka Niiniluoto (Dordrecht: Reidel, 1985), pp. 187–190. Charles Kay Ogden and Ivor Armstrong Richards, *The Meaning of Meaning* (1923; New York: Harcourt Brace, 1959).

vary from audience to audience or even from individual to individual, it is hard to define or isolate it precisely. But the distinction between factual and emotive meaning is an extremely useful one to be aware of in critical argumentation, if only because it heightens awareness of the role of emotive terminology in argumentation. In many cases, a statement is loaded to support one side of a dispute and refute the other side in virtue of a term used in the statement that has positive or negative emotive connotations. Some words in particular have strong positive or negative emotive connotations. For example, in reporting on a military conflict, our side may be described as 'freedom fighters' and the other side as 'terrorists'. A laudatory term, such as 'treasure' or 'masterpiece', evokes a positive or favorable feeling toward the thing described. A derogatory term, such as 'crook' or 'pollution', evokes a negative or unfavorable feeling.[2] So if, in the dispute on tipping, Helen makes the statement 'Tipping is demeaning', this statement is loaded against Bob's side of the dispute, simply in virtue of its use of the derogatory term 'demeaning' to describe tipping.

Bertrand Russell cited the following classic 'emotional conjugation' to illustrate shades of emotive meaning of words and how they reflect bias.

> I am firm, you are obstinate, he is a pig-headed fool.
>
> I am righteously indignant, you are annoyed, he is making a fuss over nothing.
>
> I have reconsidered the matter, you have changed your mind, he has gone back on his word.[3]

Terms such as 'obstinate' and 'pig-headed' are derogatory, and as such, they are not neutral but carry with them an evaluation. Accordingly, such terms are called 'loaded terms'. A loaded term is a label attached to something in a way that makes the statement containing the labeling either debatable or false.[4] A loaded term then has a certain slant or "spin" that supports one side of a disputable issue by making the other side

[2] Monroe C. Beardsley, *Thinking Straight*, 4th ed. (1975; Englewood Cliffs: Prentice-Hall, 1950), p. 181.

[3] According to *The Cambridge Dictionary of Philosophy*, ed. Robert Audi (Cambridge: Cambridge University Press, 1995), p. 223, Russell used the "pig-headed" example in a BBC Radio "Brains Trust" program in 1948. The *New Statesman* newspaper then ran a competition for other examples that brought in 2,000 entries like the other two cited.

[4] Ralph H. Johnson and J. Anthony Blair, *Logical Self-Defense*, 2nd ed. (Toronto: McGraw-Hill Ryerson, 1983), p. 129.

look wrong or bad. The use of loaded terms in argumentation is a very powerful technique, indeed, as we know from the current deployment of terms such as 'racist' and 'sexist' on controversial social issues. If some practice is described as 'racist' or 'sexist', it is automatically seen as very bad, given the conventional emotive suggestions that these terms have taken on in current usage. Such words have such strong implications that if our point of view is described as 'racist' or 'sexist', whether justifiably or not, it makes it almost impossible to defend. Your view is made to appear so offensive and bad that whatever you say next will probably be discounted.

The classic case of loaded terms is illustrated by the following example.

Bill and Hilda are having a dispute on the abortion issue. Bill is pro-life and Hilda is pro-choice. At one point in the dialogue, Bill makes the statement that abortion is murder.

The problem here is that in one brief sentence, Bill has classified the practice of abortion under the term 'murder'. This term has highly negative emotive implications, implying an act that is very bad. It is perhaps the worst crime a person can commit. If abortion is murder, it is certainly wrong as a practice, and this conclusion is in fact Bill's thesis in the dispute. It is also the opposite of Helen's thesis. Thus, when Bill made the statement that abortion is murder, it functioned as an argument that implied the conclusion that abortion is a kind of action that is wrong and indeed is horrible, just like murder.

In many cases, emotive terms are used to gain support from an audience. The proponent of the argument may simply use terms that are positive for the audience in order to persuade the audience to accept her conclusion.

This country's employment insurance program is a necessary protective shield for working men and women to give them an equal chance to find productive employment in times of need as patriotic citizens who just want a chance to do a day's work.

Arguments such as this one are very common, because so many terms in natural language tend to have positive emotive connotations. There is nothing wrong with using terms with positive emotive connotations to support your argument, in general. But from a point of view of critical argumentation, it is important to realize that such terminology does express an argument. The example above looks like a statement or proposition. It does not have the surface form of an argument, with a word such as 'therefore' or other evidence that an inference is being drawn or proposed. But under the surface, it is evident that the statement is really being used to put forward an argument. The statement is conveying the message that employment insurance is a good thing. It is being recommended as a good policy that is associated with good goals and values, such as being a patriotic citizen. But if the statement in the example is an argument, then it has a burden of proof. Anyone presented with it has a right to demand some support or justification for it before accepting it. Thus, the most important thing about the emotive use of terms in critical argumentation is that it tends to disguise the putting forward of an argument. A critic should always realize that she can, and often should, challenge such an argument.

Of course, if language with positive emotive terms can be used to support a claim, language with negative emotive terms can be used to attack a claim. Consider the following example.

> This country's unemployment insurance program is a legalized form of theft and escape from work for Cadillac-driving welfare bums who manipulate the system to rip off the rest of us legitimate taxpayers who contribute to the system.

Like the previous example, on superficial reading, this bit of discourse looks like an instance of the act of making a statement. But when examined more critically, it is evident that not only is a claim being made, but reasons are being given to support that claim. The discourse is telling us that the unemployment insurance program is a bad thing. It is described negatively as an 'unemployment' program rather than an 'employment' program. It is described as 'theft', something wrong or bad. It even uses highly emotive terms such as 'rip off', 'manipulate', and 'Cadillac-driving welfare bums'. Very clearly, the wording of the statement is conveying the message that the unemployment insurance program is a bad policy that should not be continued in its present form. Use of emotive terminology in argumentation can be powerfully persuasive, not only because of its emotional impact, but also because it tends to be concealed. In a verbally presented speech that is televised rather than written down, for example, the audience tends to not be very aware of the choice of terms and of the emotive aspects of the language being used. The speech seems to go by very fast, and the audience is not likely to even remember the exact wording of the speech. But even so they will be strongly influenced by the emotional impact of the speech, just as we are often influenced by the words of a popular song. Thus, using emotive terminology is an easy way to get your argument across without it even being challenged or examined critically. Once the speech is written down, and the language in it is scrutinized more carefully, however, the argumentation in it can be recognized and analyzed.

To cite another example, suppose that Bob and Helen are having a critical discussion about capital punishment, and Bob argues, "The death penalty is a *cruel* and *inhuman* form of execution in which the prisoner is *slaughtered* to satisfy the *bloodlust of revenge*." What is immediately evident is how many emotive terms Bob has used, such as 'cruel', 'inhuman', and 'slaughtered', in his statement. Each of these terms used to describe capital punishment is highly negative, in the sense that they imply that capital punishment is a bad thing. Thus, Bob's statement is highly argumentative. By virtue of the wording used, his statement implies that Helen's viewpoint in the dialogue is wrong. For after all, she is defending capital punishment. For these reasons, Bob's statement could be called a loaded proposition. What this means is that, in the context of the dialogue between Bob and Helen, Bob's statement takes sides. It implies that his viewpoint is right and Helen's is wrong. There is much we could say about Bob's statement and how it uses emotive terminology. But the most important lesson for critical argumentation is the following observation. Bob's statement is not just a proposition that is true or false. It is in fact a concealed or covert argument. In context, it functions as an argument. Why? The answer is that the use of negatively loaded terms implies that Helen's thesis in the dialogue is wrong.

What needs to be made clear is that Bob's use of emotive terminology is not inherently wrong. After all, he is taking one side in a dialogue about capital punishment. He is simply expressing the point of view that he advocates in the dialogue, and that is normal and reasonable. But in critical argumentation, we need to be aware that Bob's statement should not just be treated as a proposition that is true or false. It should be treated as an argument. Part of such a challenge concerns Bob's choice of definitions. Bob is doing more than just stating a fact about the death penalty. He is, in effect, defining the expression 'death penalty' in a certain way. In the same way, the use of loaded terms in the abortion example can shift to a verbal dispute about definitions. As the dialogue continues, Bill and Hilda may then have a dispute about how the term 'abortion' should be defined. Bill might want to define 'abortion', for example, as 'the murder of a baby'. Hilda might retort by saying that the fetus is not a person and that, therefore, it is incorrect to describe it as a baby. She may then define 'abortion' as 'the termination of an unwanted pregnancy'. How they might then go on to dispute this issue – a verbal dispute – would represent a continuation of the dialogue.

The problem with the use of emotive terminology in argumentation is not that the use of such language is inherently wrong. Terms used in natural language often have emotive implications, meaning that they imply that something is good or bad, positive or negative. And it is perfectly legitimate to argue that something is good or bad. That is just expressing your point of view. But you also should be able to defend your point of view, to justify it with an argument. The problem is that putting forward a statement that contains such emotive terminology may conceal the fact that a conclusion is being drawn or advocated from the statement and that the statement with the conclusion is an argument. The respondent faced with such an argument may not realize this need for support. As shown in the next section, many arguments are put forward covertly through a process called innuendo, in which the conclusion is not explicitly stated but only suggested by what was left unsaid.

EXERCISE 6.1

What is the problem with the following arguments? In each case, identify the emotive term or terms being used and show how the claim made represents an argument.

(a) Johnson and Blair (*Logical Self-defense*, p. 127) cited the following case of an argument used in the debate about capital punishment (Sandra Precop, "No Answer in Noose," *Windsor Star*, February 1976).

> Canada needs to abolish the death penalty. The arguments from both sides have been repeated so loudly and for so long that it would be a waste of ink to go over them again. To me it always comes down to one basic equation: a murder plus a murder does not equal justice.

(b) Henrietta and Ralph are having a dispute on whether adding Spanish-language classes to the school curriculum would be a good idea. Ralph, who is against the idea, says: "Adding Spanish language classes would be a deterioration of the curriculum."

(c) Kate is trying to persuade Heinrich to stay in school. He replies: "What a waste of time my staying in school would be."

(d) Boris and Anna are arguing about whether a whale sanctuary, to save whales from being harpooned, would be a good idea. Boris says, "This precious creature is worth saving."

(e) Two people are discussing a recent news report on a controversial issue. One says he thought the report was pretty good. The other replies, "It was pure propaganda."

TWO Point of View and Burden of Proof

As stressed in the previous section, there is nothing inherently wrong in using emotive terminology to advocate your own point of view or to attack the point of view of an opponent with whom you disagree on an issue. But as we see below in chapter 7, there are two sides in a dialogue. Although you have the right to advocate your point of view by argumentation as strongly as possible, your opponent also has the right to ask critical questions and to ask you to give reasons to support the claims you have made. The notion of an argument, as explained in chapter 1, has two aspects. First, an argument is a claim with reasons offered to support it. But second, an argument has more than one side. An argument is put forward to offer reasons to support a claim that is open to doubt or questioning. The respondent to whom the argument is directed has a right to question it. As we saw in the dialogues in chapter 1, each party has a point of view. For example, one may be against tipping, while the other may be for it. But if a claim is made by either party, the respondent to whom the claim was made has a right to ask which reasons can be given to support it. You can't just demand that the other party accept your point of view without giving some reasons why he should change his point of view on the issue. If no such reasons can be given by the proponent of the argument, she must withdraw it. But what exactly is a point of view?

Using the Santa Claus dialogue from chapter 1 as an example, we are in a position to define the important notion of a point of view (or viewpoint or standpoint). A viewpoint is made up of two components. One is a proposition and the other is an attitude. The notion of a proposition was already defined in the last section. An attitude can be one of three types: for (pro), against (contra), or neutral (neither pro nor contra). In the Santa Claus dialogue, the central issue is whether lying to the children about Santa Claus is wrong. The proposition is the statement, 'Lying to the children about Santa Claus is wrong'. Alice was for this proposition, meaning that she took the view that it is true. Bob was against it. He held that it is not true. Thus, the points of view are opposed, meaning that the proposition contained in the one is the opposite of the proposition contained in the other.

The notion point of view is thus defined in the following formula.

Point of View = Attitude + Proposition

At the beginning of a dialogue, it should be clear what the point of view of each participant is. Only then can it be determined at the end of the dialogue whether the original difference of opinions was resolved or not.

As shown in the previous section, use of emotive language can often express a point of view. If someone describes abortion as "murder" or an action as "racist," that means he or she is against it and is making a claim that such a practice is wrong and that everyone should be against it. In the case in the last section, Bob described capital punishment as "a cruel and inhuman form of execution in which the prisoner is slaughtered to satisfy the bloodlust of revenge." We can certainly take this language to imply that Bob is against capital punishment and thinks that it is a wrong practice that everyone should be against. That is the point of view Bob is advocating in the dialogue. As noted above, however, Helen has taken the opposite point of view. Thus, Bob's use of language implies that Helen's point of view is wrong or incorrect. Instead of having merely to accept defeat by Bob's use of language, however, Helen should have the right to challenge Bob's argument by demanding that he give a reason to back it up. All Bob needs to do is to reformulate his claim as an argument by saying, "In my opinion, capital punishment is wrong for several reasons: First, it is a cruel form of execution; second, it is inhuman; and third, it is carried out for revenge." Helen can then question each of these arguments and challenge Bob to support them with reasons.

The reasonableness of Helen's move in such a case is based on a notion called burden of proof. Bob has a right to say what he did. But anyone who doubts his claim should have a right to ask Bob to give a reason to support it. Unless Bob can offer such a reason, in the form of an argument that supports the claim as a conclusion, he should withdraw the claim. The precise rationale of such a requirement of critical argument will not become fully apparent until later in this chapter, but here we need to see that it reflects the notion of dialogue in chapter 1, in which there are two sides to a dialogue. One side is opposed to the other, and thus each side should have to give up its own viewpoint and come to accept the viewpoint of the other side only if presented with arguments that give a reason to do so. Otherwise, an arguer should have the freedom to remain doubtful about an opposed point of view and to question it critically. It is an important requirement of rational argumentation in dialogue that when an assertion is made, a critic can question it. The requirement that if a critic does question the assertion, the claimant must give some reason to support the claim if she continues to maintain that it is true is called the burden of proof.

Asking a question normally does not incur a burden of proof to any claim made, but there are many exceptions. Some questions do contain statements within them. Some questions can be highly argumentative. So-called leading questions in law, for example, have assumptions built in that try to get a jury to accept a proposition contained in the question. Tricky questions such as, 'Have you stopped engaging in child abuse?' are, in effect, arguments that implicitly contain propositions. No matter which way you answer, 'yes' or 'no', you become committed to the proposition that you have engaged in child abuse. And this may be a proposition you want to deny. Thus, you may have to challenge such a question or demand that the questioner prove the allegation contained in the question or retract it. In general, questions are different from assertions. You should be free to ask a question at any time and to expect a reasonable answer or reply. But if you make an assertion, there is a burden of proof. An assertion can and often should be challenged by asking for an argument to back it up. In principle, then, making an assertion is a different kind of speech act from asking a question. Questions can certainly contain propositions, but not in the same direct way that assertions do.

When a proponent makes a statement that contains emotive language supporting her own viewpoint and attacking the opposed viewpoint, such a move is legitimate, in general. However, the critical arguer has a right or even an obligation to point out that such a claim represents an argument and to insist that the requirement of burden of proof be met. Thus, while bias, in the form of commitment to a viewpoint, is perfectly normal in argumentation, it is also a phenomenon that is important to recognize and to respond to in a properly critical manner. But a problem about bias is that it is often hidden in the language in which a claim is made, so that we are not ready to deal with it. Bias may not only be hidden in the emotive words used to make a claim, it may also be hidden because the claim itself is not even stated, only implied by what was not said.

Innuendo can be a powerful method of conveying a conclusion because it leaves a lot to the viewer's imagination in drawing a conclusion. One of the most famous cases in the history of political ads was the ad produced by the Democrats in 1964 to suggest that Barry Goldwater, the Republican candidate for U.S. President, was "trigger-happy."[5] The ad showed a child plucking petals from a daisy, while an ominous countdown began in the background, followed by a nuclear explosion. Lyndon Johnson was shown, saying, "We must love each other or die." But there was no explicit partisan content in the ad at all, until the final message to vote for President Johnson. This ad was so effective because such a frightening message was conveyed entirely by innuendo. Nowhere was any explicit claim made that Goldwater was dangerous. The argument to that conclusion was based solely on innuendo.

In many cases of innuendo, the conclusion is drawn by a process called implicature, meaning that the conclusion is suggested by what the proponent says (even if she did not state it explicitly), and the respondent can presumptively infer the conclusion, based on assumptions about the type of conversation that the two are supposed to be engaged in. In the following classic case, a professor, A, has been asked to write a letter of reference on behalf of a student, Mr. X.[6]

> A is writing a testimonial about a pupil who is a candidate for a philosophy job, and his letter reads as follows: "Dear Sir, Mr. X's command of English is excellent, and his attendance at tutorials has been regular. Yours, etc."

In this case, the reader of the letter will draw the conclusion that A is stating that Mr. X is not a good candidate for the position. The implicature is drawn because A says less than is expected. What conclusion does the reader of the letter draw from this absence of expected information? It would appear that the only reason why A says so little is that he is of the opinion that Mr. X is not a good candidate for the job but does not want to come right out and say this, by stating any bad characteristics that he thinks the candidate has. So by saying nothing, except for a few

[5] Kathleen H. Jamieson, *Dirty Politics* (New York: Oxford University Press, 1992), pp. 54–55. Jay Newman, *Fanatics and Hypocrites* (Buffalo: Prometheus, 1986).

[6] H. Paul Grice, "Logic and Conversation," in *Syntax and Semantics*, vol. 3, ed. Peter Cole and Jerry L. Morgan (New York: Academic, 1975), pp. 41–58.

trivial remarks, he is suggesting by implicature that Mr. X lacks any good characteristics that would make him a suitable candidate for the job.

The assumption often made in a dialogue is that if a particular proposition is expected to be mentioned but is not, that must mean that it is being claimed (by implicature) to be false. In other words, the message is that Mr. X does not have any of those good qualities that are normally mentioned in a letter of reference of this kind. One can see in this case that the presumptive inference used to draw the implicit conclusion has the form of an argument from ignorance, of the kind studied in chapter 8, section 7, because it was based on what was omitted, as opposed to a positive assertion. By innuendo, basing his inference on what was not said, the respondent draws various conclusions without the proponent having to state them.

The really clever thing about innuendo is that it leaves an avenue of plausible deniability to an arguer, enabling an arguer to get across her conclusion while being able to deny later that she said anything of the sort. Ironically, the proponent of the innuendo can even add that, in his opinion, the proposition she put forward is false. Of course, the ironic thing is that once the innuendo has been made, the damage has been done, and it doesn't matter at all whether the proposition is later retracted. In the following case,[7] Andy Rooney of *60 Minutes* commented on an allegation by Senator Alan Simpson that a reporter was a "sympathizer" of Saddam Hussein because he continued to give TV reports from Baghdad all during the Gulf War. Simpson apologized later for the allegation, and Rooney offered a comparable apology to Simpson, quoted below:

> Senator Simpson did go to Baghdad to see Hussein last April 13th and at that time, he comforted Hussein for things being written about him in our newspapers by saying that American reporters were "pampered and haughty." That's why I've been calling Senator Simpson "Saddam Hussein's friend." Well, now I feel sort of bad about it. I shouldn't have done that. Senator Simpson says that the *Wall Street Journal* has suggested he's a racist, too. I certainly wouldn't suggest he's a racist because I simply don't know. I've heard rumors that, if he could, he'd repeal the 1st Amendment guaranteeing freedom of the press. I've heard rumors that he's one of our dumbest senators. It would be unfair of me to repeat those rumors because I'm not sure they're true. I've never even met him. Neither can I prove that Senator Simpson is a friend of Saddam Hussein. It is not certain that

[7] Douglas Walton, "Plausible Deniability and the Evasion of Burden of Proof," *Argumentation* 10 (1996): 47–58, quoted from p. 52.

> they're friends and, unless the facts prove otherwise, I apologize to him for having said they are friends. I hope you take this apology in the spirit in which it's intended, Senator – unless you can prove otherwise.

This ironic series of "apologies" by Rooney perfectly conveys how the technique of innuendo can be used to pass on allegations that are never proved and even later denied, but still do the job of getting the audience to draw a conclusion that is conveyed to them.

Innuendo is an important indicator of bias because the conclusion advocated by the proponent is not explicitly stated. Thus, the argumentation is concealed and can do its work without a respondent audience being aware that the message has a particular slant. This type of bias is hidden and harder to detect. The audience may be unaware that a viewpoint is being advocated and that there is a burden of proof attached to it. Hence, innuendo can be manipulative, deceptive, and misleading. While it may appear that suggestions based on implicature are mild and harmless, in fact they can often work much more powerfully as "hidden persuaders" to get an argument across without the respondent being aware of it. The power of suggestion, so used, can have a lasting effect on an audience, even if they are unaware of the bias that has affected their view.

EXERCISE 6.2

1. Identify the two viewpoints in the dialogue on tipping in chapter 1. What proposition is contained in each viewpoint? What attitude is contained in each viewpoint? How are the two viewpoints opposed?

2. Examine the dialogue on tipping to find instances where a burden of proof has been incurred by one side or the other.

3. Analyze the use of innuendo in the following cases:

(a)

> Captain L had a first mate who was at times addicted to the use of strong drink and occasionally, as the slang has it, "got full." The ship was lying in a port in China, and the mate had been on shore and had there indulged rather freely in some of the vile compounds common in Chinese ports. He came on board, "drunk as a lord," and thought he had a mortgage on the whole world. The captain, who rarely ever touched liquors himself was greatly disturbed by the disgraceful conduct of his officer, particularly as the crew had all observed his condition. One of the duties of the first officer [i.e., the mate] is to write up the "log" each day, but as that worthy was not able to do it, the captain made the proper entry, but added: "The mate was drunk all day." The ship left port the next day and the mate got

"sobered off." He attended to his writing at the proper time, but was appalled when he saw what the captain had done. He went on deck, and soon after the following colloquy took place:

"Capt'n, why did you write in the log yesterday that I was drunk all day?"
"It was true, wasn't it?"
"Yes, but what will the owners say if they see it? 'T will hurt me with them."
But the mate could get nothing more from the captain than "It was true, wasn't it?" The next day, when the captain was examining the book, he found at the bottom of the mate's entry of observation, course, winds, and tides: "The captain was sober all day" (Charles E. Trow, *The Old Shipmasters of Salem* (New York, 1905), pp. 14–15).

(b) "[The makers of] Anacin, a headache pain reliever, made the claim in their advertisements, 'Only Anacin has this formula.' This claim was technically true, because no other headache reliever combined aspirin and caffeine, but the implication it suggests is misleading, because caffeine made no contribution to pain relief" (Ivan L. Preston, *The Tangled Web They Weave: Truth, Falsity and Advertisers* (Madison: University of Wisconsin Press, 1994), p. 43).

(c) "A 1971 pamphlet published by the Manufacturing Chemists Association (forerunner of the Chemical Manufacturers Association) celebrates the 'fairyland' of modern food products and packaging made possible by chemical technologies; the association suggests that many people will be surprised to learn that 'not only food but the elements that go into clothing and shelter, and even the earth itself and all its inhabitants, can be described in terms of chemicals.' Fredrick J. Stare is cited cautioning consumers against letting 'any food faddist or organic gardener tell you there is any difference between the vitamin C in an orange and that made in a chemical factory.' The chemicals-are-natural theme was the centerpiece of Monsanto's Chemical Facts of Life public relations campaign in the late 1970s and early 1980s; hundreds of Monsanto TV and magazine ads reminded consumers that chemicals were a fact of life; indeed, 'without them, there would be no world.' The AIHC similarly reminds us that 'life is essentially a chemical process'" (Robert E. Proctor, *Cancer Wars: How Politics Shapes What We Know and What We Don't Know about Cancer* (New York: Basic Books, 1995), p. 126).

(d) During a hard-fought election campaign, the one candidate includes the following message as part of a televised ad:

> If you knew that one of the candidates in this race was receiving money from illegal sources, would that affect your voting decision? Look into the matter and see where the campaign funds of my opponent are coming from. Of course, I am not saying that he is taking money from illegal sources, and if accused of making that allegation, I would deny it.

THREE Biased Argumentation

We often discount an argument when we find that it is biased. When this happens, the argument is devalued to some extent, meaning that it is judged to be less plausible. For example, suppose a salesperson is selling a car to some potential buyers in the showroom. She keeps emphasizing all the good qualities of the car. Whenever the buyers mention a drawback of this particular type of car, she always counters by arguing that the drawback is not really as bad as it looks. In such a case, the buyers would get the impression that the salesperson's arguments are biased, because she always supports the arguments for buying the car and finds some reason to discount any arguments that seem to go against buying the car. On the other hand, you expect a salesperson to be biased. The salesperson's job is to sell the car and to present it in a good light. She is probably paid on a commission basis. So a buyer should not generally be under any illusion that a salesperson is offering neutral advice on whether the car is a good buy, versus other cars that are available, or not. The buyer would be naïve to think that all the salesperson is doing is giving him advice or information on the qualities of the car. She may be doing that, but she is also trying to persuade him to buy the car. This is not a discussion of an issue by two parties, where each party is trying to bring forward the strongest possible arguments to support her side in order to throw light on the issue. Instead, what the salesperson is trying to do, or at least what it is supposed to be her job to do, is to use any arguments that will get the other party to buy the car, preferably at a price that is favorable to the dealer. The salesperson definitely has a strong interest at stake in the outcome.

Of course, a good salesperson will show some signs of looking at the arguments on both sides, and fairly taking them all into account. But still, it would be a mistake to take this evidence of two-sidedness as being, in itself, a conclusive indicator that the salesperson's arguments are not biased. Given that you expect a salesperson to try to sell you a product, the bias in her argument is not deceptive or misleading. But other situations contain even more potential for deception. In a type of television program called an infomercial, the opening of the program gives the appearance of a news format or talk show, but once the viewer is drawn in, it turns out to be a half-hour commercial advertisement or sales pitch for a specific product. In the following case, the program was an ad for a health product.

According to a *20/20* report (September 20, 1990, "It's Really a Commercial," p. 16), a television program, "Rediscover Nature's Formula for Youth," used terms like "investigative team" to suggest it was a news program. One presenter on the program even introduced himself as "your Inside Information investigator" (p. 15). When confronted with the charge that he was pretending it to be a news program to sell a product, the producer replied (p. 16), "Come on John, it's the real world" (to interviewer John Stossel). (Douglas Walton, *One-Sided Arguments: A Dialectical Analysis of Bias*? (Albany: SUNY Press, 1999), p. 178).

In this type of case there is a deception involved, because the program purports to be a news report, presumably presented as a kind of information-seeking dialogue that is balanced, presenting all sides of an issue. The viewer's normal expectations are exploited by introducing the program in a format and style of delivery that suggests a news report. But as the program progresses, there is a gradual shift to an outright sales pitch. In a case such as this one, the criticism of bias is rightly used to evaluate the argument by giving a reduction in the weight of plausibility initially accorded to the argument. It was supposed to be part of a news report that (presumably) has certain standards of objectivity in the collection and presenting of facts. But once it is revealed that the argument is really a sales pitch, its plausibility should be reduced.

One of the most obvious and most important indicators of bias is the factor that an arguer has something to gain by advocating a particular argument. This something to gain is usually an interest that is financial in nature, but it could also be a gain in something like prestige, which may not have an exactly specifiable or immediate monetary value that can be given to it. It could be an interest in promoting one's career, for example, that might not have an exact dollar value at a given time but that could certainly turn out to be of financial value and to have a definite interest for a person.

In the following example of a dialogue, one should look at the argument from the point of view of the audience.

Two people, Wilma and Bruce, are participants in a televised public debate on the issue of acid rain. The question being debated is whether or not acid rain is causing serious harm to the environment. Wilma argues at length that reports on the extent and seriousness of the damage caused by acid rain have been greatly exaggerated. She also argues that the costs of taking action to prevent these damages are prohibitive. After Wilma has been presenting arguments along these lines for a while, Bruce points out that Wilma is on the board of directors of a major U.S. coal company and that therefore her arguments should not be taken at face value.

In this case, Bruce's argument is that because Wilma has a connection with a coal company, a group that has a definite financial interest at stake in public policies to control environmental pollution, her arguments should be discounted. What exactly does this criticism amount to, and how should it be evaluated? The first thing to notice is that once Bruce has made this point, the result will surely be that the audience who is following the arguments will discount Wilma's arguments on the acid rain issue. Once it has been pointed out that she has something to gain, they will see her arguments in a different light. Is this shift in evaluation justified, and why does it occur? It is because argument from bias has been used, but why is this argument so effective, and why should the plausibility of Wilma's argument be reduced on this basis?

Initially, the audience saw Bruce and Wilma as being two participants in a debate on the acid rain issue. So they were supposedly engaging in a persuasion dialogue of the critical discussion type, each putting forward strong arguments to support the side he or she accepted, and interacting argumentatively with the strong arguments put forward by the other side. The presumption behind this idea of the critical discussion of the issue, however, was that each would be open to the arguments put forward by the other side and not automatically discount or reject them just because they were put forward to support the other side. While we might not expect either of the participants to change his or her viewpoint in the end, we still expect each to acknowledge good evidence when it is brought to his or her attention and to react to an argument based on plausible evidence making some concessions modifying a view previously expressed or otherwise showing a willingness to take the argument into account. Otherwise, the persuasion dialogue would fail in its goal of deepening and enriching the positions taken on both sides of the issue.

Bruce's use of the argument from bias suggests that Wilma may have made up her mind on the issue of acid rain before the debate even started. Or at any rate, she certainly had a reason to push strongly, wherever possible, for the argumentation on the one side, given her interests in a company that has much to lose by environmental restrictions that would likely be brought in if there were to become a strongly held public opinion that acid rain is a serious problem that needs to be addressed. The bias alleged by Bruce's argument makes us doubt whether Wilma is really taking part in the dialogue, in the right sort of open, honest, and balanced way that is appropriate for contributing to a critical discussion. We suspect that Wilma may be covertly engaging in a kind of dialogue that might be better described as interest-based bargaining.

Note, however, that Bruce's argument from bias is not a complete refutation of Wilma's argumentation. Even though she has something at stake financially in the outcome, her arguments might still be good ones, or at least worth listening to and judging on their merits. The argument from bias is a presumptive type of criticism that is defeasible in nature, which needs to be weighed as part of the larger body of evidence in a case. As a criticism, it should result in a reduction of plausibility with respect to the argument criticized. The outcome should not be that the argument is dismissed as entirely worthless. Notice also that evidence of concealment can be a big factor in how we judge an argument from bias in a given case. If Wilma had announced her coal company affiliation at the beginning of the debate, Bruce's later use of the argument from bias would not have such a sting. But when he made the allegation, and then she had to admit that she had such an affiliation, it may have seemed to the audience that she was hoping to conceal her connection with the coal company. This aspect of the place of the argument from bias in the dialogue, in relation to what was previously known or announced, makes a big difference in the impact of the argument. So here there can be an aspect of deceptiveness, as in the case of an infomercial, where an argument turns out to be something it did not initially appear to be.

If a finding is announced as an outcome of scientific research, a carefully controlled type of investigation with high standards of evidence, we rightly accord it a much higher degree of plausibility than a proposition we would accept on the basis of just anyone's report or claim. But scientific research, which used to be done mainly by governments and universities, is more and more being paid for by private companies. They have a commercial interest in the outcomes of that research and how they are presented. It has become more and more necessary for the critical thinker to ask who has funded the scientific research that has produced a study.

One major factor is that there is a huge industry in the United States of advocacy communication supported by trade associations that are in the business of supporting, conducting, and reporting on scientific research on specific substances. The reports issued by these agencies – on subjects such as global warming, workplace hazards, and health aspects of products like tobacco, styrofoam, and disposable diapers – are portrayed by the agencies as based on genuine scientific research (and in many cases they are), but the problem is that they are conducted by advocacy groups who definitely have something to gain (or lose) by the outcome of the research. The following quotation from a book on public information about cancer indicates the extent and power of these trade associations.

> There are thousands of such associations in the United States, promoting everything from asbestos to zinc. The Beer Institute defends brewers against the charge that drinking causes crime or traffic accidents; the Lawn Institute (representing grass-seed producers and pesticide manufacturers) works to assure consumers that it is okay "to ChemLawn." The Asbestos Information Association cautions consumers against a hysterical "fiber phobia"; the Calorie Control Council defends artificial sweeteners such as cyclamate and saccharin against charges that they cause cancer. In 1986, according to one estimate, trade associations and their member corporations spent nearly $2 billion on what has come to be known as issues management, advocacy communication, or image advertising. Washington, D.C., alone is headquarters to some 1,700 trade associations, making trade association business the second-ranking private industry in the nation's capital, after tourism. (Robert E. Proctor, *Cancer Wars: How Politics Shapes What We Know and What We Don't Know about Cancer* (New York: Basic Books, 1995), p. 110)

The problem with the media reports issued by these trade associations is what Proctor (p. 104) calls "science as advertising." The reports claim to be scientific studies or to be reporting the findings of scientific research. But what they are reporting and the way they are reporting has a certain slant on it. They are hoping to raise questions or to get public goodwill, of a kind that will forestall government regulation of their industry, and thereby to increase their corporate profits and minimize the damage posed by alleged health hazards of their product. A case in point is one trade industry that has been active and highly visible in recent years.

Founded in 1954, the Council for Tobacco Research was established by tobacco manufacturers, growers, and warehousers to promote research by "independent scientists into tobacco and health" (Proctor, *Cancer Wars*, p. 106). Since the late 1950s the council has spent more than $240 million on this research, leading to the publication of over 5,000 scientific papers. In 1983, during a congressional debate on a bill requiring warnings on cigarette packages, the Tobacco Institute, an offshoot of the Council for Tobacco Research, announced the following scientific findings (Proctor, *Cancer Wars*, p. 106).

1. The vast majority of smokers do not get lung cancer.
2. Smoking cannot explain the ethnic and geographic patterns of lung cancer mortality.
3. Studies linking smoking and disease do not adequately control for other variables.
4. Some animal studies show that smokers actually live longer than non-smokers.

Some of these claims are plausible and some are not. Initially, once we are told that they were based on scientific research, the claim would be found more plausible. But once it was revealed that this scientific research was funded by the Council for Tobacco Research, this former weight of plausibility should be lowered. The reason is that this is a trade association group that is paid for by tobacco interests. Of course, the Council of Tobacco Research would defend its credibility by arguing that the research it supports is done by "independent scientists." But how independent are these scientists really if their income comes from the Council of Tobacco Research? That is the key question, and each case must be evaluated on its merits. But one should rightly be very skeptical if the scientific finding announced just happens to support the commercial interests of the agency who has paid for that research. Scientific research, particularly on complex matters where a study of one aspect does not tell the whole story, for example, on questions of nutrition, health, and the environment, can go one way or the other, as new evidence comes in. So there can be a lot of selectivity involved in which outcome is reported or not or judged to be significant at any particular time. So it may be prudent to take the latest scientific finding "with a grain of salt" before acting on it.

Before accepting any argument at face value, it may be extremely useful to question whether the argument has a bias and, if so, to criticize it as a biased argument. In such a case, the critic is mounting a counter-argument against the original argument. The kind of argument used by the critic in such a case, called the argument from bias, has the following form of inference:

> If a sequence of argumentation used in a dialogue shows indications that it is not taking the evidence on both sides of the issue into account, then that argumentation is biased.
>
> The sequence of argumentation in this case shows such indications.
>
> Therefore the sequence of argumentation in this case is biased.

The critical questions appropriate for use in responding to the argument from bias are the following:

1. What is the context of dialogue, and in particular, is it a type of dialogue that requires an argument to take evidence on both sides of an issue into account?
2. What is the evidence for the charge that the argument is biased?

How the argument from bias is properly used in evaluating an argument in a given case is by giving a reduction in plausibility to the weight of plausibility initially accorded to the given sequence of argumentation. The criticism assumes that the argument was supposed to be part of a particular type of dialogue, such as a critical discussion. In certain types of dialogue, such as a persuasion dialogue, it is important that an arguer takes the arguments on both sides of an issue into account and does not just automatically push ahead with the arguments for the side she advocates, completely ignoring or routinely discounting and rejecting the arguments for the other side. In other words, an argument is more plausible if it is based on a consideration of all the evidence in a case, on both sides of the issue, than if it is pushing only for one side and ignoring all the evidence, even if it may be good evidence, on the other side. So if an argument is biased, that is, if it pushes only for one side, we discount that argument as being of less worth. But we have to be very careful to realize that just because an argument is one-sided, it should not mean that it is worthless or that we should always or completely reject it. Even so, recognition of bias can be very important in how we judge an argument.

EXERCISE 6.3

1. Evaluate the argument in the following case.

   A videotape on trees and the environment was distributed free to teachers in the public school system as an educational tool for use in classes on geography and the environment. However, the video was produced by a logging company that had a large financial stake in the geographical regions covered in the program, and it clearly expressed a point of view on environmental issues favorable to the interests of the loggers. After the video was played to one class for a while, one observant child said, "Hey, it's a commercial!"

2. Evaluate how one should react critically to the claims made in the following cases.

(a) During the dialogue on tipping, let's suppose that Helen argues as follows.

> HELEN: Look, Bob, I happen to know that you are a public relations consultant who has been hired by the Union of Restaurant Service Providers as part of their campaign to promote tipping. Your arguments in favor of tipping as a good practice should not be taken at face value.

(b) A scientific report predicted staggering economic losses and unemployment if a ban on whiskey bottles made from vinyl chloride was put into effect by the U.S. Government. The report was produced by Arthur D. Little, a company hired by polymer industry officials (Proctor, *Cancer Wars*, p. 103).

(c) A scientific policy research study based on a computer model showed that if advertising were taxed in Minnesota, not only the advertising industry but the state's entire economy would be damaged. The study was sponsored by the Communications Industry Coalition, an industry group (Cynthia Crossen, *Tainted Truth: The Manipulation of Fact in America* (New York: Simon & Schuster, 1994), p. 139).

FOUR Verbal Disputes

In a dialogue the point of view of the one side is opposed to that of the other side. The dialogue is supposed to resolve this disagreement by having each side put forward arguments. But in some instances the disagreement can be impossible to resolve this way because their parties are not arguing about the same thing. Their disagreement is merely verbal, meaning that they are using a key word differently. For example, consider the following dialogue.

Carly: Derek finally got rid of that old Toyota of his and bought a new car. He's driving a new Honda now.

Levon: No, Derek didn't buy himself a new car. That Honda is a good three years old.

In this dialogue Carly and Levon disagree. She thinks that Derek is driving a new car now. He says that Derek did not buy a new car, implying that the car he is driving is not new. Their disagreement, however, does not stem from the facts of the matter. It stems from how each of them uses the term 'new'. When Levon uses the term 'new' he means a car that is the model that appeared in that year. For example, in the year 2003, a car is 'new' only if it is a 2003 model (manufactured in the period designated by the automakers for a 2003 vehicle). When Carly uses the term 'new', she means a car that is new to Derek, that is, different from his 'old' one and perhaps one that is a more recent model than the old one. It could be true that Derek's car is a new one, in Carly's meaning of the word, but false that it is a new car in Levon's meaning of the word. In other words, Carly and Levon have a merely verbal disagreement, as opposed to a substantive disagreement about what the facts are. They have both seen Derek's new car, and so they agree about the facts of the case. What they disagree about is the meaning that the term 'new' should have in describing those facts.

Now let's contrast this dialogue with another one.

Leshandra: Derek finally got rid of that old Caprice Classic of his and bought a new car. He's driving a new Mustang now.

Ben: No, Derek didn't buy himself a new car. It's his uncle's new Mustang that he's driving.

In this dialogue, Leshandra and Ben disagree about a factual issue. Leshandra sees Derek driving a new Mustang, and from this fact she draws the conclusion that Derek bought it, replacing his older car with it. It follows from what she says that in her view Derek owns the new Mustang. Ben thinks differently. Evidently, he has some information that she does not. He says that it is his uncle's new Mustang that Derek is driving. If so, Derek does not own the new Mustang. In this dialogue, there is an opposition of viewpoints, just as in the previous one. But here the difference is not merely verbal. Leshandra thinks that Derek owns the new Mustang, but Ben does not think so. They disagree about the factual issue of who is the owner of the car. This disagreement is said to be factual, or substantive, to use another word, because it can be settled by bringing forward arguments based on the facts of the case. For example, if Ben and Leshandra talk to Derek, he might admit that the car belongs to his uncle. Or if the dispute about who owns the car were to become serious, they could investigate at the motor vehicles office to see in whose name the car was registered.

Such verbal disagreements may seem trivial and harmless, as in the example above, but in many cases they can be quite serious. For example, suppose the representatives of two countries in the U.N. General Assembly are arguing about whether a third country should be admitted to the United Nations as a member country. One might object that this third country is not democratic, because it is run by a dictator, and argue that it should not be admitted on the ground that only democratic countries qualify for membership. The other might disagree, arguing that the so-called dictator is the president of the country who was elected when a majority voted for him. According to the point of view argued for by this side, if the president was elected by a majority vote in an election, the country is a democracy. In a case like this, the two representatives are having a verbal dispute. It is reasonable enough and quite common to have such a verbal dispute about the meaning of a key term that participants do not agree on. The problem is that the nature of the dispute may be disguised if the participants think it is based on a substantive disagreement about the facts of a case when the disagreement is merely verbal. The use of the word 'merely' here should not suggest that verbal disputes are trivial, however, or that they are always easy to resolve. In many cases, one side uses emotively loaded terms to express his or her point of view, while the other persists in using emotively loaded terms that reflect the opposite point of view. Until they either desist from using such terms or come to agreement on how to define them in a way they can both live with, the dispute may never be resolved.

It was shown in section 1 above how the use of loaded terms in a dispute can easily lead to arguments about how a key term should be defined. In the one example, Bill and Hilda were disputing on abortion when Bill, the pro-life advocate, said to Hilda, "Abortion is murder." His use of argument from verbal classification in this instance is a case of a loaded term – 'murder' has highly negative implications – implying that the pro-choice side is advocating something highly immoral, namely, murder of a human being, and also illegal. This use of a loaded term may then lead to a verbal dispute about how 'abortion' should be defined. Hilda might start by retorting that a fetus is not a person and therefore cannot be "murdered." She might follow up by presenting her definition of 'abortion' as 'termination of an unwanted pregnancy'. Hilda and Bill might then go on to have a verbal dispute about how abortion should be defined.

In response to Hilda's definition, Bill might go on to advance his own definition of 'abortion', as illustrated in the following dialogue.

Bill: I define 'abortion' as the murder of a baby.

Hilda: You can't define the term that way. For one thing, 'murder' is a value-laden term. For another thing, the fetus is not a person. In my view, it is improper to call the aborted fetus a 'baby'. So as I said before, abortion cannot be a 'murder'. That's ridiculous.

In response, Hilda objects not only to Bill's use of the loaded term 'murder' in his definition, but also to his assumption that the fetus is a person. What has occurred in this case is that the argument has shifted from an ethical discussion on the abortion issue to a verbal dispute about the meaning of a key term. When this kind of shift occurs, there is often a kind of tightening up of the dialogue and a concentration on fine shades of meaning of words and phrases. Some see such a verbal dispute as trivial or 'quibbling', but it is not necessarily a bad thing if terms can be agreed on or the nature of the dispute clarified. However, if the verbal nature of the dispute is masked or hidden, that can be a big obstacle in the resolution of the conflict of opinions. Verbal disputes of this kind can turn essentially on hidden differences of opinion about the meaning of a word or phrase or on an ambiguity, where two participants use the same word or phrase in different ways. It can be a problem if disputants think they are arguing about the facts of a case when, in reality, under the surface, they are having a verbal disagreement.

In short, the shift from a substantial dispute to a verbal dispute may need to be clarified and brought to the surface before a persuasion dialogue can proceed in a productive way toward the resolution of the conflict of opinions that is the basic issue. A terminological diversion, in the form of a verbal dispute contained within the main dialogue, is not necessarily a bad thing. But if the participants are unaware of the shift, so they have no idea they are really arguing about words, the persuasion dialogue can become bogged down without, apparently, being able to move along any further.

In the last two cases, there has been a shift from a substantial dispute on some particular issue to a subdialogue where the argumentation has become a verbal dispute about the meaning of a key word or phrase. What is needed, if the original dispute is to be resolved or at least put back on track toward its eventual resolution, is the recognition that a term can have more than one meaning assigned to it, and a distinction needs to be made between the various senses of the word. Then the next step is some clarification of these meanings. The usual way of dealing with the problem is for a definition of some sort to be proposed, and then for some agreement on the definition to be made or at least some evaluation of the definition to take place in the dialogue.

Another factor to be aware of in such cases of argumentative use of emotive terms is that powerful interests can be at stake. Not only are definitions non-trivial, but millions of dollars can be spent using professional public relations techniques to put a "spin" on a controversy. The term 'wetland' came to prominence in the environmental debates of the late 1960s and early 1970s. It refers to an area saturated by water to the extent that only specially adapted plants can grow in it. Wetlands are very valuable to the ecology, according to scientists. Environmentalists, concerned about the disappearance of wetlands, especially due to building, have lobbied to protect these areas from development. Large amounts of money are at stake, and developers have engaged in many widely publicized legal actions and debates on the issue with environmentalists. Starting in the 1970s efforts were made to introduce a standardized ecological definition of the term 'wetland'. A 1979 definition cited features such as the kind of soil, the kind of vegetation, and the way water is present. In 1989 a definition of this kind was codified in a federal government manual for identifying wetlands. In the presidential election campaign of 1988, George Bush committed his administration to a policy of 'no net loss' of wetlands. By 1990, it became clear that if Bush kept to this commitment, he was in danger of alienating many of his pro-business, pro-development constituents. Accordingly, in August 1991, a document produced by a vice presidential task force proposed a redefinition of the term 'wetland', making the criteria stricter than those given in the 1989 manual. According to studies by scientists and environmentalists, under the new definition, 50 million acres previously designated 'wetlands' would now be excluded. This so-called codification of the definition in the 1989 manual was implemented in federal agencies without approval by the White House or Congress and without inviting public comment, even though it met with intense opposition from environmentalists.[8] It is important to recognize that this dispute over definition was a matter of powerful competing interests. It may seem that 'wetlands' is a scientific term that should be defined by the scientific experts and that the matter is one of scientific description of the facts. But this approach allows a 'technological elite' to be granted 'definitional hegemony' to advocate their own views and interests under an appearance of scientific neutrality. The real issue is not so much about science as about competing interests of opposed advocacy groups. Money is involved, and cause advocacy is involved. Those financially involved in land development, building, real estate, logging, and so forth are on the one side of a dialogue. The environmentalists and their

[8] This classic example is summarized below from the account presented by Edward Schiappa, "Wetlands and the Politics of Meaning," in *Environmental Pragmatism*, ed. Andrew Light and Eric Katz (London: Routledge, 1996), pp. 209–230.

supporters, who often also use professional public relations experts and are well funded, are on the other side. Both sides are trying to convince the public, the media, and the politicians to go along with them in adopting policies, drafting laws, or taking actions on land and building projects.

EXERCISE 6.4

1. Analyze the following dialogues to determine whether each is a substantial dispute or a verbal dispute, giving your reasons.

(a) Toban: Before the battle of the Milvian bridge, the Roman emperor Constantine had the symbol of the cross painted on the shields of the Roman soldiers.
Julia: That's a bit of historical fiction that is incorrect. He had the chi-rho symbol (an X with a vertical stroke through it curved downward at the top) painted on their shields.

(b) Kenny: Microsoft is having a good year. Their sales are considerably up from last year.
Jennifer: I wouldn't say so. Their profits are only very slightly up from last year, and are way down from previous years.

2. Discuss any problem in the following case that may be hindering the dispute from proceeding to a resolution by a discussion of the issue.

(a) The issue of a debate between two people was whether or not euthanasia should be legalized. One party argues that it is morally justified, and should therefore be legalized, because it offers terminally ill patients who are enduring unbearable suffering an opportunity to die with dignity. She argues that such a patient should be able, on request, to be taken off life-support systems when aggressive or heroic treatments are no longer doing any good to save her life. The other party disagrees, arguing that euthanasia is murder and that any physician who gives a patient a lethal drug is killing that person, even if the patient agrees to it. The one party keeps insisting that euthanasia is murder, while the other denies that it is murder at all, saying that it is 'letting nature take its course', without high-tech interference.

3. The following example describing a dialogue that took place is from William James's lecture, "What Pragmatism Means."[9]

> Some years ago, being with a camping party in the mountains, I returned from a solitary ramble to find every one engaged in a ferocious metaphysical dispute. The corpus of the dispute was a

[9] William James, *Pragmatism: A New Name for Some Old Ways of Thinking* (London: Longmans, Green, 1907), pp. 43–45.

> squirrel – a live squirrel supposed to be clinging to one side of a tree-trunk; while over against the tree's opposite side a human being was imagined to stand. This human witness tries to get sight of the squirrel by moving rapidly round the tree, but no matter how fast he goes, the squirrel moves as fast in the opposite direction, and always keeps the tree between himself and the man, so that never a glimpse of him is caught. The resultant metaphysical problem now is this: Does the man go round the squirrel or not? He goes round the tree, sure enough, and the squirrel is on the tree; but does he go round the squirrel? In the unlimited leisure of the wilderness, discussion had been worn threadbare. Every one had taken sides, and was obstinate; and the numbers on both sides were even. Each side, when I appeared, therefore appealed to me to make it a majority. Mindful of the scholastic adage that whenever you meet a contradiction you must make a distinction, I immediately sought and found one, as follows: "Which party is right," I said, "depends on what you practically mean by 'going round' the squirrel. If you mean passing from the north of him to the east, then to the south, then to the west, and then to the north of him again, obviously the man does go round him, for he occupies these successive positions. But if on the contrary, you mean being first in front of him, then on the right of him, then behind him, then on his left and finally in front again, it is quite as obvious that the man fails to go round him, for by the compensating movements the squirrel makes, he keeps his belly turned towards the man all the time, and his back turned away. Make the distinction, and there is no occasion for any further dispute. You are both right and both wrong according as you conceive the verb 'to go round' in one practical fashion or the other." Although one or two of the hotter disputants called my speech a shuffling evasion, saying they wanted no quibbling or scholastic hair-splitting, but meant just plain honest English 'round,' the majority seemed to think that the distinction had assuaged the dispute.

Analyze the argumentation in this case, showing what the disagreement was, how it appeared to the participants to be a substantive dispute, and how the third party was able to resolve ("assuage") it by showing it was a verbal dispute.

FIVE Lexical, Stipulative, and Persuasive Definitions

There are many different kinds of definitions. Each kind has a function, when put forward in a dialogue exchange that itself has a purpose. One party puts forward or presents a definition to the other party for some purpose in the dialogue. Let's call the first party the proponent or definer and the second party the respondent. One of the most familiar types of definition is the lexical definition, of the kind found in a dictionary, used to explain the meaning of a word (or phrase) to someone who looks it up in that dictionary. The definer writes the definition, and then the respondent, who presumably does not understand the meaning of the word or wants to have it clarified, looks it up, seeking help.

A lexical definition gives an account of a word that has a conventional meaning in a language. Thus, a lexical definition is a kind of report on how native speakers of a language use a term in everyday speech (or in special contexts, like in a scientific field). A lexical definition is an explanation of how the word is used, and it is successful or not to the extent that it (1) accurately represents actual usage and (2) explains that usage in a way that helps the respondent to understand the meaning of the word, as it is used. The usual way of finding a lexical definition of a term is to look it up in a dictionary. Dictionaries are particularly helpful with words that are uncommon or unusual. For example, if we look up the word 'hauberk' in *Chambers Twentieth Century Dictionary*, the following entry is found.

> hauberk, hö′bark, n. a long coat of chain-mail sometimes ending in short trousers: originally armour for the neck. [O.Fr. hauberc-O.H.G. halsberg-hals, neck, bergan, to protect.]

This entry explains the term 'hauberk' quite well. But if you look up the word 'good' in the same dictionary (p. 561), the entry is very long (almost a full page) but is not really all that helpful. 'Good' is defined as 'having suitable or desirable qualities', and a long list of synonyms, such as 'virtuous,' 'commendable,' and 'benevolent,' is given. This would probably not be terribly enlightening if you did not already know what 'good' meant. So that is the way of dictionaries. They assume you already have a native speaker's level of skill or at least a fair level of comprehension of the language and many of the common words in it. And then they build on this assumption to present explanations of the less common and less familiar words.

In contrast to a lexical definition, a stipulative definition is purely arbitrary, and the definer is even free to invent a new word and to assign any meaning to it that she chooses. Consider the following two definitions.

Driving over 30 mph on a city street (unless otherwise designated) is defined as 'speeding,' or driving too fast.

A 'tigon' is defined as the offspring of a male tiger and a female lion.

Stipulative definitions look normal and harmless, but sometimes people will get into disputes about them, as shown in the following dialogue.

Helen: I define an 'excessive' tip as any tip over 15 percent of the bill.

Bob: That is arbitrary. I would say that a tip is "excessive" if the amount is more than was merited by the quality of the service.

In this case, Helen stipulated an exact figure as defining an excessive tip, but Bob criticizes the definition as 'arbitrary.' He might add, "I don't see any real difference in excessiveness between 14.9 percent and 15.1 percent in a tip."

Most other definitions are a mixture of lexical and stipulative definitions. They start off using a familiar term and use the conventionally accepted meaning of that term as a base line, but then develop it in a certain direction. In wills, contracts, and negotiations, for example, many terms that have a generally accepted conventional meaning familiar to anyone are defined more precisely, in a way that is partly stipulative. The following example is a stipulative definition.

> 'Blind' means, for federal income tax purposes, either the inability to see better than 20/200 in the better eye with glasses or having a field of vision of 20 degrees or less.

Similarly, a discipline such as science will take a term like 'acid' or 'number', which has a familiar conventional meaning in everyday usage, and then give it a more precise definition that fits into the methodology of that particular discipline. These kinds of definitions could be called precising definitions, in that they take a familiar term and then propose a stipulative counterpart that is more precise (often using numerical criteria for the purpose).

A persuasive definition takes a term that has a conventional lexical meaning in normal usage, and then presents a partly stipulative definition of a kind that supports one side and goes against the other side of an issue in a persuasion dialogue. An amusing example is the following definition.

> 'Football' means a sport in which modern-day gladiators brutalize one another while trying to move a ridiculously shaped 'ball' from one end of the playing field to the other.

The persuasive definition puts a certain 'spin' on a word by redefining it in a positive or negative way. In this example, the purpose of offering this negative definition of 'football' is to make the sport appear to be pointless, silly, and brutal. The definition takes up a definite viewpoint or commitment that provokes or continues a dispute on football, representing a persuasion dialogue in which there are two sides. Precisely because they give a new meaning to a term that already has an established usage, persuasive definitions are deceptive. The problem is that a persuasive definition masquerades as an honest assignment of meaning to a term while condemning or approving the thing being defined.[10] But persuasive definitions are not inherently bad or illegitimate as such. They are normal in persuasion dialogue and have a place in that type of dialogue. On the other hand, they can be deceptive and tricky in some cases and are well worth being aware of.

Words have positive and negative emotional connotations, as well as descriptive content. Many words, as noted above, have a laudatory or derogatory spin, because of their positive or negative connotations in everyday speech. A persuasive definition typically changes the conventional meaning of a term by taking it in a direction that suits the purpose of the definer. But the emotional connotation of the word tends to stay in place. By an "inertia" effect, the word tends to retain the same laudatory or derogatory spin it always had. Thus, there can be a certain subtle deception in some cases, because the respondent may not realize he is being manipulated. In other cases where a persuasive definition has been used, productive dialogue may be blocked off.

In many cases, people in a dispute appear to come to a kind of impasse when they can't seem to get any further because the argumentation just goes back and forth in a terminological tennis match. The verbal dispute that ensues then requires some terminological clarification or introduction of definitions. For example, Helen and Bob might have the following exchange in the dialogue on tipping.

Helen: Well, you know tipping is so elitist, it is a kind of oppression.

Bob: Are we talking about the same thing? I don't see tipping as bad at all.

Helen: Well, how would you define tipping, anyway?

Bob: Tipping is a major factor in the gross national product that is a function of commercial transactions as payment for human services.

[10] Charles L. Stevenson first developed the concept of a persuasive definition and showed its importance for critical argumentation in *Ethics and Language* (New Haven: Yale University Press, 1944), and in an earlier article, "Persuasive Definitions," *Mind* 47 (1938): 331–350.

In this dialogue, Helen and Bob recognize that their dispute requires some sort of verbal clarification or definition. But when Bob attempted to supply the required definition, his attempt was not successful. The purported definition of 'tipping' he offers is just too obscure to be helpful in clarifying the term or enabling the dispute to go any further in a productive dialogue.

Bob and Helen may then try again to introduce some definition of the disputed term 'tipping.'

Helen: Your definition is pretty useless. It's too obscure. Let me offer a clear and precise definition: Tipping is a gratuity given to an inferior person performing a menial task for a superior person.

Bob: That definition is clear, all right. But it uses emotionally loaded language that implies that tipping is inherently bad. I object to that.

At this point, Helen and Bob have again reached an impasse. Bob simply refuses to accept Helen's definition. What should be done here? Bob has a right to refuse the definition that Helen has offered, apparently. But she presented the definition in good faith, when a definition was needed. And her proposed definition is certainly much clearer and more precise than the one Bob offered.

On the other hand, Bob is right that Helen's definition is loaded with negative terms, portraying tipping in a derogatory fashion. If he accepts this definition, he will find it extremely difficult or even impossible to argue successfully for his thesis in the dispute that tipping is a good practice. Bob may then offer a definition of his own.

Bob: Let me propose an alternative definition of tipping.

Helen: All right. If you like.

Bob: Tipping is a reward for excellence of service given to someone who deserves it by someone who rightly appreciates and wants to acknowledge excellent work.

Helen: Well, Bob, how can I accept that? It makes tipping sound so positive and upbeat that it pretty well defeats my side of the argument.

Here then, we have reached another impasse in the dispute. Both Helen and Bob have now offered definitions of tipping. The one definition, however, is opposed to the other. One makes tipping appear to be very positive in nature, while the other makes tipping appear to be highly negative.

Bob and Helen have several options in continuing their dialogue on tipping. One is to continue the verbal dispute, in the hope of resolving it. Helen might propose a counter-example to Bob's definition of tipping.

That is, she might cite a case of tipping where a tip was given, but the person who got the tip did not really deserve it. She could then point out that Bob's definition of 'tipping' is different from the accepted lexical meaning in a way that shows his definition to be inadequate or defective. Alternatively, instead of continuing the verbal dispute, Bob and Helen might try to collaboratively agree on a neutral definition of 'tipping' that would not have any strong positive or negative connotations built into it. This alternative is a good one in this particular case, because the word 'tipping,' in its conventional lexical meaning, is not a laudatory or derogatory word. Once a non-persuasive or non-biased definition is agreed on, then Helen and Bob could get back to the issue of whether or not tipping (so defined) is a good practice worth continuing.

EXERCISE 6.5

1. Classify the following definitions as lexical, stipulative, precising, or persuasive.

(a) The following definition is included in the description of a scholarship in a university calendar: "For the purposes of this scholarship, 'full-time student' shall mean a student enrolled in six or more semester-length courses in a given calendar year."

(b) A gullible person is a person who is easily fooled.

(c) 'Monocracy' means government by one person.

(d) A liberal is a do-gooder who basks in a rosy glow of self-adulation while advocating government rules that support approved causes in the short term but lead to long-term consequences that everyone has to pay for.

(e) Capitalism is the economic system that allows greedy, aggressive, and cunning schemers to exploit working people in order to amass fortunes used for selfish purposes.

(f) In Western Australia, a driver is legally intoxicated if he or she is found to have a blood alcohol level of .01 parts alcohol in the blood, or over.

(g) A mattock is a kind of pickaxe for loosening the soil, with a cutting end instead of a point.

(h) To mumble is to speak softly and indistinctly.

2. Propose a neutral definition of 'tipping' that Bob and Helen might be able to agree on in the dialogue on tipping.

3. Propose a neutral definition of 'abortion' that Bill and Hilda might be able to agree on in the dialogue on abortion.

SIX Philosophical and Scientific Definitions

In intellectual and philosophical discussions, definition statements are of a certain sort, such as 'The essence of religion is peace of mind' or 'True courage is grace under pressure'. Such statements, which purport to define the most important (or 'essential' property of something), are called essence statements.[11] Essence definitions make claims about the essence of poetry, of art, of friendship, and so forth as part of an intellectual discussion or dispute. The following ways of expressing an essence definition are especially important (x is an individual thing and A is a property said to apply to the individual).

The essence of x is A.

x is by nature A.

True x is A.

Real x is A.

Genuine x is A.

In a philosophical treatise, the author often begins by discussing the lexical meaning of the term, but then argues that the concept, if it is truly to be understood in its "true" or "real" meaning, must be defined in a different way, by giving an essence definition. The problem is that essence definitions of words such as 'love', 'honor', 'culture', 'life', or 'democracy' may carry with them a positive or negative emotive meaning. For example, if something is said about "true love," there may be a positive suggestion that this phenomenon is highly valuable. In such a case, the essence definition has become a persuasive definition, even though its persuasive nature may not be evident. For example, consider the statement 'The essence of religion is love'. This statement puts a positive spin on religion by the emotive meaning of 'love.' The statement 'The essence of religion is a neurotic reaction of anguish' is just the opposite. It puts a negative spin on religion.

The fact that an essence definition is being used as a persuasive definition in an intellectual or philosophical discussion does not necessarily mean that the definition is wrong or misleading or should be criticized as incorrect. For if the intellectual discussion is a persuasion type of dialogue, of the kind studied in chapter 1, the use of a persuasive definition

[11] Soren Hallden, *True Love, True Humour and True Religion: A Semantic Study* (Lund: Gleerlup, 1960).

could be quite appropriate. Even so, from a critical perspective, it can be valuable to recognize that the definition has a certain slant or bias and is being used for the purpose of persuading the reader.

An essence definition is best seen as a kind of hypothesis, or tentative proposal, put forward by a proponent to a respondent in a persuasion dialogue. It is a proposal that represents or supports the proponent's thesis, and the respondent is being asked to respond to it critically. Thus, the essence definition should not be seen as the last word in a discussion or as a statement that is pronounced with absolute finality, leaving no room for further discussion. On the contrary, it is best seen as a statement that represents a particular viewpoint and as a definition that is part of the argument designed to develop that viewpoint, giving a respondent insight into it. If the respondent accepts the essence statement, it should be as a tentative hypothesis used as a basis for further exploration of the issue. But if the statement turns out to have strong arguments against it, the respondent should then feel free to retract his commitment to it, by giving it up as a definition and perhaps opting for some other (opposed or alternative) definition instead, depending on how the discussion has gone. Thus, essence definitions should be seen as having a provocative function of giving rise to arguments that throw a new slant on an issue by opening up a different point of view that was concealed or that you may not have thought of before, because it is different from the conventionally accepted way of looking at it.

A good example of how essence definitions can be questioned critically and treated as hypotheses in a philosophical discussion of ethical values is the Platonic dialogue *Meno*, where the issue is whether virtue (moral excellence of character for living the good life) can be taught or not. The Greek word *arete* is usually translated as 'virtue', but probably 'excellence' is a better word to convey its meaning. In the *Meno*, the participants recognize, early on in the dialogue, that the issue of the discussion depends directly on how the term 'virtue' should be defined. Throughout the dialogue, both Meno and Socrates, the two participants, put forward essential definitions of 'virtue', but they agree that this term cannot be defined in a way that is not open to questioning and objections. But Socrates gets Meno tentatively to accept the definition of virtue as a kind of knowledge, and then using this hypothesis, Socrates develops his philosophical view that all knowledge is a kind of recollection of things that we are already aware of implicitly but that need to be sharpened or articulated by dialogue. At the end of the dialogue (88d), the participants conclude that virtue is a kind of wisdom.

The argumentation in the *Meno* illustrates the right kind of attitude to take toward essence definitions. When a proponent puts forward an essence definition, she is not asking you to accept it as the last word. Nor should she be seeing it as a substitute that replaces the lexical definition of a word. Instead, she should be putting forward the essence definition as an invitation to take part in a persuasion dialogue (or perhaps it is already part of an ongoing persuasion dialogue about some issue) that will throw some light on an issue by putting a different slant on it that you may not have encountered or appreciated before. Thus, you should feel free to accept or reject the definition as you wish. You should not feel bound to have to accept it absolutely, as a kind of stipulation of meaning, but neither should you absolutely reject it, without at least thinking about it, just because you recognize it as a persuasive definition. The best attitude to approach essence definitions with is with skeptical open-mindedness.

You might think that difficulties defining key terms, and problems over the positive or negative connotations of these terms, are unique to ethical or political disputes about values and conduct and do affect reasoning in scientific research. But an examination of the problems encountered by sociologists in defining the word 'gang', for example, would indicate that such an assumption is not true. Because of the importance and frequency of statistical claims made about gangs in the media and in studying and dealing with crime, there will be all kinds of misleading statistical data (see chapter 3 on definitions in statistical surveys) unless the problem of defining the term 'gang' can be solved. It might also be added here that there are some disciplinary conflicts involved as well, for legal definitions are adopted for criminal law purposes, while sociological definitions are adopted for the purpose of scientific research on social groups.

Some researchers have even suggested that the problems of definitions that have confounded gang research could be solved by making a survey of youth service workers, police officers, judges, probation officers, educators, city council members, ex-convicts, past and present members of gangs, and others familiar with gangs to agree on a definition of the term 'gang'. The following definition was composed on the basis of this survey.

> [a gang is] a self-formed association of peers, bound together by mutual interests, with identifiable leadership, well-developed lines of authority, and other organizational features, who act in concert to achieve a specific purpose or purposes which generally include the conduct of illegal activity and control over a particular territory, facility, or type of enterprise. (Walter B. Miller, *Violence by Youth*

> *Gangs and Youth Groups as a Crime Problem in Major American Cities* (Washington, D.C.: National Institute for Juvenile Justice and Delinquency Prevention, 1975), p. 121)

Some argued that definitions based on a vote have no special validity. The feeling was that voting would be an appropriate method to determine a lexical definition but a poor method of establishing the kind of stipulative definition needed for scientific research.

Another contentious aspect of the definition above concerned the clause that the purpose of a gang generally included illegal activity. This characteristic is a negative quality, giving a definite pejorative connotation to the word 'gang', implying that gangs are bad groups. Other researchers went even further, emphasizing that "the key element that distinguishes a gang from other organizations of young people is delinquency; its members regularly participate in activities that violate the law."[12] But this kind of definition is contentious, because it builds a negative evaluation into the very definition of the term 'gang', and it is questionable whether such value-ladenness is appropriate in scientific research. But it might be questioned whether definitions that include illegal activity as an intrinsic defining property of the term 'gang' may include, by definition, the very delinquency that researchers and theorists are trying to explain. The result of such a definition may be to inflate statistics on 'gang-related' violence.

> If the only salient property of a "gang member," for example, is his or her membership in a gang, one result may be that any illegal activity involving such a person is defined as "gang related." This is the case in Los Angeles, where the definition produces twice as much "gang-related" violence as would be produced by the Chicago definition, which acknowledges that gang members may have motives unrelated to their gang membership. (Richard A. Ball and G. David Curry, "The Logic of Definition in Criminology," *Criminology* 33 (1995): 225–245, quoted from p. 233)

The problem of defining the term 'gang' here can be presented as a dilemma. If you do justice to the negative connotations of the term 'gang' by defining a gang as a group that has some illegal or immoral purpose, you have built in, by definition, a value assumption that may make it difficult to explain gang delinquency in a non-circular way. But if you try to define the term 'gang' in neutral terms, without building in any negative

[12] Sandra Gardner, *Street Gangs* (New York: Franklin Watts, 1993), p. 5.

implications, you may not be doing justice to the way the term is really being used.

This same kind of problem is even more evident in ethical reasoning about words such as 'courage' or 'justice' that have positive connotations and words such as 'racism' or 'bigotry' that have negative connotations. In cases like these, it is better to acknowledge that the term in question has a laudatory or derogatory meaning, in its conventional lexical usage, and to try to preserve the implication that the word already has – in one direction or the other – by building an evaluative component into the definition. For example, instead of trying to define 'courage' in a neutral way – as absence of fear or as some cognitive state of motivation – it would be more useful, for purposes of an ethical discussion, to acknowledge that the word 'courage' is used in a positive way to praise conduct as good or worthy. Thus, an expressly evaluative definition of 'courage' is 'pursuit of a good or worthy goal in spite of danger, fear, and/or severe difficulties of a painful nature'. This definition is frankly positive, bringing out the laudatory connotations of the word 'courage' in the definition itself. But does that mean that as a persuasive definition, it should be evaluated as improper, deceptive, loaded, or aggressively one-sided, in a way that should indicate its rejection? No, it should not, because 'courage' is an emotively loaded term to begin with, in its lexical use. So to preserve its positive connotations, as long as this is done in an overt and clearly expressed way, is not deceptive and should not be an obstacle to having a productive ethical discussion on the nature of courage or on some issue in which 'courage' is a key term.

If a given term that has a conventional usage already has a strong positive or negative connotation, then the definition of that term should have the same positive or negative slant clearly expressed as part of the definition. Since a persuasive definition is partly stipulative, however, it can depart from conventional usage and go the other way. For example, a term that has positive connotations in normal usage could be defined in a negative way. But where such a departure occurs, the definition should be open to critical questioning and should be challenged on grounds of such a marked departure from usage. For example, someone might define 'courage' as a powerful force of will used to overcome obstacles by taking strong action to fulfill a goal. But because the term 'courage' normally has positive connotations, it would be proper to point out that according to this definition, someone who uses a powerful force of will to rob a bank by taking strong action is acting courageously. Because the new definition of courage deviates from the positive connotations of the term in normal speech, it can be criticized for its somewhat unexpected and potentially confusing failure to preserve the direction of this slant. Someone who has presented this new definition in a persuasion dialogue could defend it with further arguments, but there would be a burden or obligation on her to defend it as a persuasive definition that is stipulative in this important respect.

The same lesson applies to the term 'gang'. Suppose someone defines a gang as a self-formed association of peers, and so forth, except that there is no clause that expresses the negative connotations of this word. Would that be a legitimate or acceptable definition of 'gang'? It could be, if the definition is meant to be stipulative, but if the definition is also being used to represent the conventional idea of a gang, it is open to objection. One should ask: What about a 'gang' that is a self-formed association of peers, and so forth, who act in concert to achieve the purpose of helping cancer patients? Because the aim of this group is good, it is odd and potentially misleading to call it a 'gang' (in any literal sense). Generally, then, a definition should preserve the positive or negative slant of a term, or there should be a legitimate expectation that the presenter of the definition can explain why it has not done so.

EXERCISE 6.6

1. Identify the elements of persuasive definition in the following essence definitions and discuss each essence definition critically.

(a) Political power, properly so-called, is merely the organized power of one class for oppressing another (Karl Marx and Friedrich Engels, *The Communist Manifesto*).

(b) Art is a human activity having for its purpose the transmission to others of the highest and best feelings to which men have risen (Count Leo Tolstoy, *What Is Art?*).

(c) Pornography is the graphic, sexually explicit subordination of women, especially the portrayal of women as sex objects and the depiction of violence against women.

2. Evaluate the following definitions with regard to how they handle the positive or negative connotations of the term being defined.

(a) A cult is a minority religious group gathered around a charismatic leader blessed with deep spiritual insight.

(b) A noise is a sound that is unwanted or unpleasant.

(c) According to the World Health Organization definition of 'health,' "Health is a state of complete physical, mental and social well-being and not merely the absence of disease or infirmity."

(d) Pornography is the artistic portrayal of the natural human body in emotionally provocative poses.
(e) God is the most perfect being you could imagine.
(f) A liar is someone who intentionally deceives you by telling you something is true (or false) when she knows it is not.
(g) Bribery is giving someone else money to give her or him an incentive to help you carry out some goal that is important to you but requires help to be achieved.
(h) Religion is a method of extorting money out of gullible people who are suffering from deep psychiatric guilt or who are terrified of death.

SEVEN Normal and Troublesome Bias

An arguer's commitment to an identifiable position can sometimes be an important indicator of bias. But it is important not to leap too quickly to the conclusion that commitment to a particular proposition is inalterably fixed. In argument from commitment, as we saw in chapter 3, an arguer can identify some propositions that the other party is committed to, and then use these propositions as premises to persuade the other party. In an example in chapter 3, Bob asked whether Ed was a communist. Ed replied: "Of course. You know that." In this case, Ed has admitted that he is committed to a well-known type of position called communism. Given Ed's commitment to this viewpoint, Bob can make presumptions (subject to rebuttal) that Ed will generally take one side, as opposed to the other, on various issues related to politics, economic policies, and social issues. In this case, since Ed has freely admitted he is a communist, that is pretty good evidence that Ed is committed to the communist position.

Suppose that Ed were to take part in the dialogue on tipping and that he came forward with the following argument.

Ed: My view on the subject of tipping is that such a practice is the exploitation and oppression of workers who should get paid regular wages and receive fair benefits for their labor. They should be treated with dignity as equals.

In this case, Ed's argument shows a distinct bias to one side of the issue of tipping. Given Ed's previous declaration of being a communist, it is a bias that it easy to recognize and identify. Once again, the fact that such a bias has been identified does not mean that Ed's argument is wrong or worthless. It means only that Ed has taken a stance that is clearly recognizable and that supports, in a way that might have been expected, one side of the issue.

In many cases, bias, or a slant to one side of an argument, is perfectly normal and expected. In a persuasion dialogue, for example, arguments are supposed to support one's own thesis in a partisan manner, and there is nothing wrong with that. It is only in cases where we rightly expect an argument to be two-sided and balanced that a finding of bias is negative in the sense that it justifies a reduction in the plausibility value given to the argument. But even in a dialogue like the one in chapter 1, where argumentation is normally partisan and is directed to supporting one's own thesis and trying to get the other party to accept it, bias can become a problem that interferes with constructive progress of a dialogue. It is particularly this counter-productive or negative type of bias that is important to identify, from the point of view of critical thinking.

In some cases, however, as a dialogue proceeds, one can get a pretty good general idea of what sort of position an arguer is committing herself to. We have names for certain well-known types of positions of a typical and familiar sort that are frequently encountered in everyday arguments on issues of the day. For example, if someone is a Catholic, a feminist, a communist, a Republican, or a Democrat, and the evidence in a dialogue shows that person accepts this position generally or in a more specific form of some kind, then a respondent in a dialogue with the person will have a pretty good general idea of how that person is likely to respond to arguments on certain issues.

> Lois and James are having a critical discussion on the issue of abortion. James, who is against abortion, identifies himself in the dialogue as a Catholic. Lois is about to argue that the fetus should not be considered a person, in the sense that the fetus would have any kind of rights, when she remembers that the Catholic viewpoint makes a distinction between potential and actual persons and attaches great ethical value to the potential for human life. She is not sure whether James agrees with all these views, but since he calls himself a Catholic, she thinks it is a pretty good guess that he will not accept the proposition that the fetus is not a person, if the proposition is put to him flatly in that form.

This case shows that judging bias from an arguer's commitments is more subtle than it may initially appear. There are various kinds of Catholic positions that may be taken, some quite strict and traditional but others that are regarded as radical by the church hierarchy and that have been highly controversial. So it would be wise not to prejudge James's position as though it were defined in a fixed way by strict Catholic dogma. And one can always put a question to James to see how he reacts. But still, given that he has taken up what he calls a Catholic position on the abortion issue, this commitment does stake out a bias, so that we could say that a typical Catholic would favor or disfavor this or that view on the abortion issue at some given point in the discussion. Since Catholics are generally against abortion, and since James is a Catholic, we may draw a presumptive conclusion that James is against abortion.

What is called stereotyping, or forming defeasible generalizations based on typical patterns that can be regularly (but not absolutely, or even probably) expected to occur, is not necessarily wrong or fallacious, as it is sometimes held to be. Drawing inferences based on such stereotypes is sometimes necessary when using practical reasoning with any success in fields such as politics, medicine, engineering, and business, in making intelligent deliberations on how to proceed in a variable situation, and in practical matters of everyday life generally. The problem is that the intelligent use of this defeasible kind of reasoning requires the realization that defeasible rules are open to exceptions and therefore have to be treated with flexibility in applying them to particular cases.

Even though James, as a practicing Catholic, is against abortion, as far as his own conscience and personal commitment is concerned, he may recognize instances, such as in the case of rape, birth defects, or diseases, where abortion would be an acceptable policy for him to agree with. Or he may be prepared to argue that he can belong to the Democratic party, even though it has a pro-choice political position on the legalization of abortion. Thus, labels such as 'Catholic' or 'communist' may indicate an arguer's bias that you might be unwise to ignore. But these labels indicate a bias only in the sense that they are signs of a certain commitment that may be specified further or retracted in subsequent dialogue.

Any imputation of bias on the basis of an arguer's commitment should be subject to hesitancy as the discussion of the issue becomes more specific or as the arguer may have indicated her own individual views that diverge from the central paradigm of the typical position identified by a certain term in common use. For example, someone may say he or she is a communist but, as the discussion proceeds, may point out that he or she is a modified Trotskyite kind of communist who disagrees with many of the mainstream Marxist views so often identified with communism. So it would be improper to keep insisting that this person must be committed to typical Marxist views on an issue and could never depart from this position in any way.

Other indications of commitment to a position on an issue are the use of loaded terms and/or persuasive definitions. Neither of these techniques of argument is inherently wrong. Both can be used quite legitimately, and they are a perfectly normal and acceptable part of argumentation in dialogue. But each of them, when used in argumentation, reveals a certain slant or 'angle' in an argument, showing that the argument is being used to promote one side of an issue. The key indicator of this kind of bias is the language used in an argument. The bias is partly concealed by its being built right into the language used, so that instead of seeing the argument in an explicit format of the usual type, where premises are put forward in support of a conclusion, all one sees is a single statement expressed in language that has positive or negative connotations. If abortion is described as 'murder', for example, all one sees is what looks like a descriptive statement about abortion. But because of the highly negative connotations of the word 'murder', what is being implied covertly is that abortion is somehow bad or deeply wrong.

Commitment to a position is perfectly normal in everyday arguments and should not be seen as inherently bad, just because it represents a bias or slanting in an argument. However, in a dialogue like those in chapter 1, a certain balance, or middle way, is appropriate for holding a commitment. If commitments are given up too easily, an arguer will be seen as inconsistent, as too wavering, or as lacking in principles. For if the dialogue is to reach its goal, an arguer must hold to her commitments when the evidence seems to her to merit it. But on the other hand, if an arguer clings too stubbornly to her commitments, she will be seen as too opinionated to be reasoned with. So the thing is to strike the right balance. If you are too free with changing your mind, you can get into the position of holding inconsistent commitments. But if you stick too rigidly to your position, as if you were defending a fort against all attackers, you cease to be open to critical questioning and counter-arguments.

Both sides have to be open-minded, even to the point of conceding defeat when confronted with an argument that refutes one's own thesis, for this refinement of argumentation in a dialogue to take place. An arguer who shows that she is taking part in this progress of the buildup of a dialogue by actually conceding to a good refutation or counter-argument will win a certain degree of credibility, which in turn will bestow a certain degree of enhanced plausibility on her argument. Such an arguer is credible, meaning that she has a kind of positive respect as a person who can be relied on to consider an argument on its merits and be open to conceding defeat when faced by a good argument that goes against her own point of view. When an arguer is credible, then a respondent who hears an argument advocated by that person will give it an added degree of plausibility, just because it was advocated by that arguer. On the other hand, if the respondent observes that an arguer only pushes ahead unilaterally in a dialogue, by never conceding any criticisms of the arguments against her own side and giving any weight only to the arguments that either support her own side or go against those of the other side, the respondent will (rightly) see her arguments as biased. His assessment will be that her arguments are slanted to the one side and do not bend enough or give sufficient weight to the arguments of the other side, when such a concession is called for.

A good test of bias is how an arguer responds to arguments that are opposed to her point of view, and particularly to arguments that challenge commitments that are closely related to her central thesis in the dialogue. It is evidence of bias if the arguer shields off such counter-arguments without really doing them justice or making any real effort to take them into account. The problem with this attitude is that it is immune to new evidence, expressed in a closure to any opposed argumentation in a dialogue. Closure to opposed argumentation is indicated by the use of devices and expressions to forestall disagreement in advance, such as 'it is obvious', 'everybody knows', 'clearly', 'of course', 'as anyone can see'. Forestalling disagreement ranges from mild expressions, such as 'of course we all believe,' to more aggressive expressions used to intimidate opposition, such as 'only a crazy person would take that view'. The use of these expressions in a dialogue to forestall disagreement can be considered a special case of the use of loaded terms. When such devices to forestall disagreement are used, this is a special kind of evidence of bias in an argument. Such bias can be troublesome if it represents closure to opposed arguments.

Another type of evidence of closure to opposed argumentation is the kind of response, particularly to the challenge of a deeply held or cherished view, where the arguer reacts in a strongly emotional way that is not appropriate, or even with violence or threats, like 'You had better shut up, if you know what's good for you'. This response indicates that the arguer is trying to close off all opposed considerations. Another kind of evidence is the evangelical style of discourse, characterized by the use of slogans or propaganda to whip up enthusiasm for a 'cause'. The theme here is typically one of loyalty to the group. Instead of responding to an opposed argument critically or by questioning its basis of evidential support, the argument may be put down as expressing hostility of the typical opponents who are against the group values and loyalties. A response of this type to a prior argument would be: "Oh, we've heard that kind of anti-union attack so often before, we don't pay any attention to that!" The biased arguer has the characteristic of seeing an issue in simplistic, black and white terms, so that little or no room is left for taking account of exceptions to a rule or a stereotype. The fanatic sees everything in absolutes. But as we saw in chapter 1, many of the generalizations on which arguments are based in everyday reasoning are defeasible. They hold normally, subject to qualifications, and are open to exceptions of a kind that cannot always be listed precisely in advance. With respect to handling arguments based on such generalizations in a dialogue, a degree of flexibility is required. As shown in chapter 1, defeasible generalizations are different from the absolute generalizations, marked by the universal quantifier 'all', that support deductively valid inferences. Treating a defeasible generalization as though it were an absolute generalization, of the kind that admits of no exceptions, amounts to committing what was called in chapter 1 the fallacy of hasty generalization. The following example of the fallacy of hasty generalization shows the absolutistic aspect of this kind of thinking.

> I had a bad time with my former husband. From that experience I've learned that all men are no good.

An argument that concludes too hastily to a universal generalization is associated with the attitude of closure to opposed viewpoints. Fanaticism is the extension of this attitude into a hardened position.

Of course, as emphasized in this chapter, bias to one side of an argument is perfectly normal and expected in many cases. In the dialogues in chapter 1, for example, the arguments were supposed to support the advocated thesis on one side, and there is nothing wrong with that, as long as the arguer is open to the arguments of the other side. Closure to critical questioning is a problem from a viewpoint of critical argumentation, because the fanatic will not respond appropriately to a strong and challenging argument that demands some sort of concession or change in her position. Thus, you cannot ever really argue successfully or productively with such a participant in a dialogue. The fanaticism of terrorists fighting for the cause of "political liberation" or the 'overcommitment' to positions such as Marxist dialectical materialism or some racist ideology combine revolutionary fervor with the persecution of members of targeted groups. Fanaticism, then, is an extreme form of closure to opposed argumentation that is often recognizable by dramatic polarization of an issue and use of devices to forestall disagreement in the form of possible counter-arguments.

EXERCISE 6.7

1. Evaluate the dialogue with respect to the management of commitment in the following cases.
   (a) Helen identifies herself as a feminist in the dialogue on tipping. Bob is about to argue that tipping supports human rights by allowing for freedom of choice in the marketplace. But he remembers that Helen has argued that the majority of workers in the service sector are women and that tipping is unfavorable to women by keeping them in low paying jobs and dependent on tips. Bob is not sure whether he ought to present his argument or not, since it is a pretty good guess that Helen does not think that tipping supports women's rights or allows for more freedom of choice for women in the marketplace.
   (b) Helen identifies herself as a feminist, in the dialogue on tipping. Bob argues to Helen: "You could never support freedom of choice in the marketplace because, as a feminist, you think that there should be government quotas that require giving jobs to women whether they are the best candidates or not. As a feminist, you support only policies that give more freedom of choice to women, enforced by government policies that limit the freedom of choice of men."
2. Find any indications of bias in the following cases.
   (a) In the dialogue on tipping, Bob argues to Helen: "Every decent American is in favor of free enterprise, and tipping is free enterprise."
   (b) During the debate on the issue of acid rain, Wilma argues to Bruce: "The intelligent and well-informed audience here today knows that the media has blown this acid rain issue far out of proportion to the real extent of the problem."
   (c) The last mechanic I went to charged me for a part that wasn't replaced by a new one. From that experience, I've come to the conclusion that all mechanics are dishonest.
   (d) The following quotation is a segment of Benito Mussolini's speech "We or They," delivered in 1930.

   > The longer our regime lasts the more the anti-Fascist coalition has recourse to expedients dictated by desperation. The struggle between the two worlds can permit no compromises. The new cycle which

begins with the ninth year of the Fascist regime places the alternative in even greater relief – either we or they, either their ideas or ours, either our State or theirs! The new cycle must be of greater harshness, not of greater indulgence. Whoever has interpreted it differently has fallen into a grave error of interpretation. This explains why the struggle has now become world-wide and why Fascismo has become the subject of debate in all countries, here feared, there hated, elsewhere ardently desired. (Gorham Munson, *Twelve Decisive Battles of the Mind* (New York: Greystone, 1942))

EIGHT Summary

The kind of bias studied in this chapter is dialectical, in the sense that it is a property of how an argument is used in a context of dialogue – a conventional type of conversation that two parties are supposed to be taking part in. For an arguer to have a bias toward her own viewpoint in a dialogue is normal. There is nothing wrong with that. But problems can arise for critical argumentation if that bias is hidden in the emotive language used by an arguer or in innuendo. Because of the possibility of concealed bias there is a danger that one party in a dialogue or both may fail to realize that an argument has been brought forward and that, consequently, its proponent has incurred a burden of proof. Two kinds of dangers are possible in such a case. One is that the respondent may not realize that the argument should be critically questioned and that reasons to support it should be asked for. The other is that the proponent may not only fail to offer any support for the claim made but may even try to avoid the burden of proof. Such an arguer may even try to seal off the possibility of criticism, or of confronting opposed arguments, by claiming there is no need to prove her claim. Such moves represent a dangerous kind of bias.

An arguer who collaboratively takes part in a dialogue needs to consider an opposed argument on its merits and even concede defeat if confronted with evidence that shows her own thesis to be false. Bias can become a problem when it leads to this pathological closure to all opposed argumentation. However, even when bias is normal, it can be valuable for a critic to identify it. But the really serious and worrisome cases of bias are those when an argument seems to be objective and open to criticism, but where this pretense is misleading. Another problem is that bias is often concealed within the language used in an argument. A critic may not even realize that emotive use of language is a form of argumentation that needs to be defended and that should be questioned. Concern with challenging hidden bias in chapter 5 took us into the area of language and meaning. The only way to challenge terminology that contains bias is to ask for a definition of the word or phrase in question. This move often leads to verbal disputes.

It is typical of extended argumentation on controversial issues that it can shift from a dispute about a particular issue to a verbal dispute about the words used in arguing about the issue. Such a shift is not necessarily bad. It can be constructive in clarifying the issue in some cases. However, in other cases the shift to a verbal dispute can block argumentation from proceeding in a constructive manner toward fulfilling the goal of the dialogue. Two kinds of problems in this type of case can be acute. One is the kind of case, like the squirrel around the tree case, where the participants do not realize they are bogged down in an unresolved verbal dispute. The other is the kind of case where loaded terms have been used by one or both sides, and the use of these terms is not acceptable to one side. Before the dialogue can proceed, some agreement on how to define a loaded term may be necessary, once the meaning of that term has been brought into question.

The different types of definitions cited were lexical definitions, stipulative definitions, precising definitions, and persuasive definitions. Persuasive definitions, in particular, require identification of the critical question in a dispute, because if both sides use them, it can lead to a deadlocked verbal dispute in which no further progress is possible. A decision needs to be made whether the term at issue should be defined in a neutral way that both sides can agree to or whether the term has built-in positive or negative connotations that ought to be retained in the definition. A special kind of persuasive definition is the so-called essence definition, which purports to go beneath conventional meanings and popularly accepted opinions to reveal the 'essence', or most deeply important characteristic of something. Essence definitions are typically put forward in intellectual and philosophical discussions that purport to reveal a deeper meaning that makes participants in the discussion think twice about something they had not reflected deeply about before but were familiar with only in a more superficial way.

SEVEN Relevance

In chapter 5 it was shown how replies to questions can be irrelevant, but there is a still more general problem about relevance concerning argumentation. How can arguments, or any moves in a dialogue, for that matter, be judged relevant or irrelevant? This problem is a central one for critical argumentation because many of the emotional appeals commonly used in argumentation, such as appeal to pity or fear or ad hominem arguments, are fallacious because they are irrelevant arguments. They are powerful tactics of distraction that work to throw an arguer off the trail, creating distractions and confusion by arousing powerful emotions. However, appeals to emotion are not always fallacious. Sometimes they are relevant. So there is a problem of judging in any given case when such an appeal should be considered relevant or not. While argumentation schemes are helpful for this purpose, judging relevance often means one also has to examine a more lengthy chain of argumentation in a dialogue. As indicated in chapter 1, a sequence of argumentation in a dialogue should always have a particular proposition it is ultimately aimed to prove as its target. Its target is the issue that the dialogue is supposed to settle. In a critical discussion, the chain of argumentation is aimed at proving or casting doubt on some particular proposition at issue in a dialogue. For example, in order to be relevant in the dialogue on tipping, an argument needs to be aimed at supporting, rebutting, or critically questioning the thesis that tipping is a good practice that ought to be continued.

The problem with irrelevant arguments is that not only do they fail to prove or cast doubt on this ultimate proposition, they go in a chain of reasoning away from the proposition to be proved. The fault is not in the reasoning and its individual links. An irrelevant argument can be quite valid as reasoning. The problem with irrelevant arguments is that they are useless at a given juncture in the context of an argument.

They can be highly distracting, and prevent a dialogue from progressing toward resolution of an issue. The problem lies in how the argument is used for some purposes where two parties participate in an argument with each other. Thus, you cannot prove irrelevance just by looking at a single argument and evaluating it in relation to an argumentation scheme, although that is part of what is involved. You have to judge where a whole sequence of argumentation is going, in relation to where it should be going. To judge this matter, you have to look at the context of dialogue of a case as a whole. You have to first determine where the argument is supposed to go. For example, in the case of a critical discussion you have to determine the thesis that is supposed to be proved or doubted. Then you have to determine whether the argumentation in the given case can be chained forward to reach that thesis or whether it is going in a different direction away from that thesis.

ONE Probative Relevance

Every type of dialogue that is a context for argument begins with an unsettled issue, and the purpose of the dialogue is to settle the issue. A persuasion dialogue has as its issue two opposed propositions. For example, in the dialogue on tipping, Bob's thesis is that tipping is a good practice that should be continued, and Helen's thesis is that tipping is a bad practice that should not be continued. This global issue is what all the reasoning used in the dialogue is directed toward. Bob uses arguments to prove his thesis (or disprove Helen's), and Helen uses arguments to prove her thesis (or disprove Bob's). For an argument to be relevant in the dialogue on tipping, then, it should be part of a chain of reasoning that has one or the other of these theses as its ultimate conclusion.

In some cases, it is extremely dubious whether an argument is in fact relevant, in the sense of being used to prove the conclusion that the argument is supposed to be aimed at. Here is a typical problem case.

> A proposal for a new ordinance on thickness of concrete foundations and safe construction of stairwells is under consideration at City Hall. One councilor, currently running in an election, rises to speak passionately in favor of the bill, arguing only that decent housing for all the people is desirable, failing to mention anything about concrete foundations or safe construction of stairwells.

The failure of relevance in this case can be categorized as an instance of the fallacy of *ignoratio elenchi* (literally, ignorance of refutation), or 'irrelevant conclusion,' committed when an argument 'purporting to establish a particular conclusion is directed to proving a different conclusion.' The kind of tactic so commonly used by political arguers, represented in this example, is quite familiar to us. Judging from the context of the case, we can perceive the fault. The speaker is wandering away from discussing the issue he is supposed to discuss, whether the bill on foundations and stairwells is a good one or not. Instead, he is trying to gain the favor of the audience by arguing for a proposition they all enthusiastically accept. Why would he do this? Possibly to look good for the media, so that he might get coverage that would help him in the upcoming election race. Putting on such a show may seem harmless, but we need to recognize that it is taking up time for discussion in which the arguments for and against the proposal on foundations and stairwells should be considered. If these relevant arguments aren't considered, or even articulated, the vote taken on the bill could be a bad decision.

What, then, makes an argument relevant in a given case? The answer is that the argument must be part of a chain of argumentation that has as its final proposition the conclusion that is supposed to be proved by the arguer. What this proposition is must be known or made evident in the case before an argument in the case can be judged to be relevant or not. In the decent housing example above, we know that the proposition at issue is the thesis that the particular bill on housing should be voted for, or not. Every argument that is relevant in the dialogue on tipping must also have some bearing on the global issue, posed at the beginning of the dialogue by the two opposed theses of Helen and Bob. The argumentation in the dialogue that is relevant can be viewed as a long chain of reasoning that has either Bob's or Helen's thesis as its final end point, or conclusion to be proved. An argument, to be relevant, must have a place somewhere in this chain of reasoning. For example, suppose Bob, at some point in the dialogue, presents the following argument.

> If customers tip wisely, then tipping rewards excellence of service.
>
> Customers tip wisely.
>
> Therefore, tipping rewards excellence of service.

We judge this argument to be relevant in the dialogue on tipping, because it is not too hard to see how it is connected, by a chain of argumentation, to the global issue of the dialogue. It is connected by the following inference.

> If tipping rewards excellence of service, tipping is a good practice.
>
> Tipping rewards excellence of service.
>
> Therefore, tipping is a good practice.

The conclusion of the first inference also functions as the premise of the second inference. The two inferences can then be connected together in a chain of reasoning where the final conclusion is Bob's thesis in the issue to be settled. Hence the first inference is a relevant argument, as used by Bob. When Bob presents the first inference above as an argument, Helen might agree or disagree with the premise that customers tip wisely. If she agrees with both premises, Bob can then use the argument to prove his thesis that tipping is a good practice. If she disagrees with the premise, Bob could still try to find other arguments to support it and to persuade Helen to accept it. Thus, it is not hard to figure out how this argument could be used by Bob as part of a chain of argumentation he could use to prove his thesis. Hence this argument is relevant in the dialogue on tipping.

In making relevance judgments we are most often concerned with the relevance of an argument to its wider context in dialogue, but in some cases we can also be concerned with the relevance of a premise in an argument. For example, in the inference about tipping just above, we can see that the second premise, 'Tipping rewards excellence of service', is not only relevant in the argument as a whole, it is also relevant to the other premise, 'If tipping rewards excellence of service, tipping is a good practice'. The reason is that the two premises function together as parts of a linked argument that supports the conclusion 'Tipping is a good practice'. In such a case, we can judge that the second premise is relevant to the first premise and that both premises are relevant to the conclusion. We can also say that the whole argument is relevant in the dialogue on tipping.

Now contrast this case with the case where Bob used another argument in the dialogue on tipping, as below.

> The Matterhorn is higher than Mount Whitney.
>
> Mount Whitney is higher than Mount Rainier.
>
> Therefore, the Matterhorn is higher than Mount Rainier.

In itself, this argument is quite a good one. It is deductively valid, and the premises are true. Thus, the argument provides a good reason for accepting the conclusion. But the problem is that it is not relevant in the dialogue on tipping. The reason is that there doesn't look like there is any way of putting it into a chain of argumentation that would go toward supporting Bob's thesis in the dialogue that tipping is a good practice that ought to be continued. Of course, Bob's argument might be relevant in a dialogue about the heights of mountains. But it is not relevant in the dialogue on tipping. In that dialogue, it doesn't prove anything, and so we might say that it is not probatively relevant, meaning that it is of no value to prove something, in this case Bob's thesis about tipping. But probative relevance needs to be distinguished from another kind of relevance.

Two propositions are probatively relevant if one can be used to prove the other or to cast reasonable doubt on the other. Two propositions are topically relevant if one shares subject-matter overlap with the other.[1] For example, the pair of propositions, 'Bananas are yellow' and 'Bob ate a banana' are topically relevant to each other, because both contain the common subject matter of bananas. But they are not probatively relevant, because you could not use one to prove the other. However, they could be probatively relevant in the right context of dialogue. The reason is that probative relevance is determined by how propositions are used as premises or conclusions in a chain of argumentation. For example, the proposition 'Bananas are yellow' could be probatively relevant to the proposition, 'Bob ate a banana' if the chain of argumentation were to be extended in the right way. Consider the following chain of argumentation.

> Bananas are yellow.
>
> Bob ate either a banana or some other fruit.
>
> Whatever fruit Bob ate, it had a color.
>
> Therefore, what Bob ate was either yellow or some other color.
>
> Only bananas, of all things that Bob ate, are yellow.
>
> What Bob ate was yellow.
>
> Therefore, Bob ate a banana.

This chain of argumentation began with the statement 'Bananas are yellow' and then moved forward to prove the conclusion that Bob ate a

[1] Richard L. Epstein, *The Semantic Foundations of Logic*, vol. 1 (New York: Oxford University Press, 1995), pp. 99–107, developed a formal logic called relatedness logic that can be used to model argumentation based on topical relevance. This logic is based on assignments of subject matters to statements, as indicated above.

banana. Hence, as used in the argument, the proposition 'Bananas are yellow' did turn out to be probatively relevant to the proposition 'Bob ate a banana'.

Despite this example, there is generally a distinction between probative and topical relevance. It is common that two statements are topically relevant to each other but are not probatively relevant to each other. Of the two notions, probative relevance is the more important one in most cases where irrelevance is a problem in argumentation. In the housing legislation example above, the problem is that the speaker's remarks on decent housing for all the people is not probatively relevant, in relation to the bill being discussed. Even though his remarks are topically relevant, the problem is that they are of no use in the deliberations on whether this particular bill is a good one that should be voted for by the legislature.

Relevance of an argument always needs to be judged in relation to the stage of the dialogue where that particular argument was used. A critical discussion, a special subtype of persuasion dialogue, has four distinctive stages, and relevance of an argument is a function of the stage of the discussion where the argument was used. Frequently, in the middle or beginning sequence of the reasoning used in the argumentation stage, it may not be evident yet whether or not an argument is or will be relevant, once we have gone further along the sequence in the dialogue. For example, in court, if a judge objects that she does not see the relevance of a lawyer's argument, he may reply, "If Your Honor will give me a little latitude, I can show why it is relevant." Thus, relevance typically needs to be judged in light of the stage of dialogue an argument is used in and how far along the sequence of reasoning has progressed at that stage. In many cases of the kind we so often consider in critical argumentation however, the argument in question is part of the argumentation stage of a dialogue.

EXERCISE 7.1

(a) Consider all possible pairs of propositions in the following set and determine whether each pair (individually) exhibits topical relevance and/or probative relevance: (1) Bob ate two bananas; (2) Bananas are yellow; (3) Apples contain vitamin C; (4) Miami is south of Detroit; (5) Detroit is larger than Tampa; (6) Miami and Tampa are in Florida; (7) Detroit is north of Miami.

(b) Fill in a chain of argumentation that could plausibly be used to connect the argument above to the global issue of the dialogue, showing that the argument is probatively relevant. Suppose Helen, at some point in the dialogue on tipping, presents the following argument.

> If customers tip unwisely, persons serving a customer are offended.
> Customers do tip unwisely.
> Therefore, persons serving a customer are offended.

(c) Assess whether the following argument, if used by Helen in the dialogue on tipping, is relevant or not.

> Protestors at a demonstration in Boston in 2000 argued that corporations have put dangerous drugs like thalidomide on the market in the past. You can't trust these big corporations because they profit from the marketing of drugs.

TWO Dialectical Relevance

In ordinary usage, the term 'relevant' is quite broad, but for purposes of critical thinking, a narrower and more explicit definition is needed of the kind of relevance that relates to the uses of arguments. During the 1970s, the era of hippies and love-ins, the phrase, 'Be relevant!' was often used. It was hard to say what was meant by this phrase, perhaps something like 'Express what you feel to be deeply important to you!' Relevance of this kind is hard to define precisely, because it is subjective. Generally, a proposition will be relevant for a person if that person feels that it is deeply important to her or him. This kind of relevance is emotional relevance. It is also sometimes called psychological relevance. It may be contrasted with dialectical relevance. Dialectical relevance is a special type of relevance that refers to the appropriateness of a proposition as part of a dialogue or conversational exchange where arguments are being used. Thus, dialectical relevance is normative, meaning that it is defined by what is appropriate in a framework of dialogue. Dialectical relevance performs a gatekeeping function in logic, by excluding arguments that in a dialogue are of no use for settling the issue that is supposed to be settled by the dialogue. Irrelevant arguments are not always fallacious, but they can slow an argument down or distract the participants from their task by taking the line of reasoning off in a tangential and unproductive direction. Irrelevance is sometimes identified with the use of 'red herring' tactics in hunting: by dragging a strong scent (like a herring) across the trail, someone could send the dogs off in a wild goose chase (to mix metaphors) away from the direction of the fox.

One lesson of chapter 5 was that the context of dialogue is an important factor in judging the usefulness of argumentation in a given case. Relevance of an argument is determined by general factors concerning the type of dialogue the argument is supposed to be part of. One needs to know the purpose that the argument is supposedly being used to fulfill, in a particular type of dialogue, and what stage the dialogue is supposedly in. In a critical discussion, a given argument is supposed to have as its ultimate conclusion the thesis to be proved by the proponent. It is this requirement that essentially makes relevance necessary for all reasoning used in any argument in a persuasion dialogue. As shown in chapter 5, one of the rules of a critical discussion is that participants must use only relevant arguments during the argumentation stage in order to resolve their conflict of opinions. But arguments can occur at other stages as well. Whether an argument is relevant or not in a given case depends on the stage that the critical discussion has reached in that case.

A critical discussion or any persuasion dialogue can go wrong if it begins to turn into a quarrel through both sides using ad hominem arguments or other irrelevant arguments, such as threats or appeals to pity. The quarrel does not restrict relevance much at all. In fact, it is typical of a quarrel in that it skips back and forth over all kinds of apparently unrelated topics. Anything is relevant if it is something a participant feels deeply sensitive about or has some kind of complaint about, to the effect that the other party has been inconsiderate, for example. But in a critical discussion, relevance is a very important property of arguments. If the critical discussion is supposed to be on a particular issue, such as tipping, then if one participant launches into a long argument on the abortion issue, this distraction could confuse everyone and prevent the argument from having any real bearing on the issue of tipping. However, the abortion issue could be relevant in some cases. Suppose that Helen, in the dialogue on tipping, draws a comparison between the tipping and abortion questions, arguing that in both cases, women's rights are involved. In the context of an argument from analogy between the two cases, Helen's argument that introduces abortion as a topic could be relevant.

Another kind of irrelevance occurs where one side tries to force the other party to stop taking part in the discussion altogether by using threats or turns the discussion to a different issue by using appeals to pity. An important requirement of a successful critical discussion is that both parties stick to using relevant arguments that genuinely bear on the issue and refrain from using arguments that are emotionally rousing but do nothing to prove what is supposed to be proved. The other types of dialogue, except the quarrel, also have relevance as an essential requirement for an argument to be useful to contribute to the goal of the dialogue. Like the critical discussion, the other types of dialogue have the same four characteristic stages. Thus, generally to determine the relevance or irrelevance of an argument in a given case, you have to judge where the chain of argumentation is going and whether it is aimed toward the goal of the dialogue. So the two initial questions you need to ask in judging relevance in a particular case are: (1) What type of dialogue is it, and (2) What stage is the dialogue in, as far as one can tell from the given information in the case. As shown in section 1 above, probative relevance needs to be judged by examining the chain of argumentation in a case, to see where this chain is going. A chain of argumentation could go off in any direction. If it is to be useful as a sequence of argumentation, then it needs to be directed toward some purpose. In chapter 6, we saw that each distinct type of dialogue has its own purpose. Hence, whether an argument is relevant or not depends on the type of dialogue it is supposed to be part of, and judging this question in a given case is a function of how the argumentation has been used in that context.

EXERCISE 7.2

Suppose that Bob and Helen are having a critical discussion on the issue of tipping, of the kind sketched out in previous cases where their dispute on tipping has been illustrated. Judge whether the following arguments used by Helen are relevant or not in that context.

(a) I don't agree, Bob, that we should have a critical discussion on tipping. I think we should argue about abortion, because that issue is more important.

(b) Tipping is undignified, because it presupposes a social class system in which one party is presumed to be inferior to the other.

(c) Helen, you are a liar, so your argument on tipping is worthless.

(d) You had better shut up, Bob, because voicing your views on tipping could lead to bad consequences.

(e) Helen, your argument that tipping causes embarrassment should be rejected because I need tips to make enough money to pay my tuition fees. If I don't get these tips, I will starve and my diabetes will flare up.

THREE Relevance in Meetings and Debates

In addition to abstract models of dialogue, such as the critical discussion, it is also necessary in some cases to take account of what is called the speech event, or particular institutional or cultural setting of the dialogue. Let's take the example of argumentation in a trial. In Anglo-American law, there are procedural rules that govern argumentation, and there are even special legal rules of relevance that apply in a given jurisdiction. Or in a congressional or parliamentary debate, rules of order and procedure will be used to at least partly determine when a proposition is relevant or not. Even in an administrative meeting, of the kind that is so often held in universities, for example, the chairman is bound by an agenda, set in advance of the meeting and circulated to all participants. The chairman is also bound by university rules and generally accepted procedures for this type of meeting. The meeting may be a deliberation, and its purpose would be to arrive at decision on what to do about some problem or issue that has arisen. And in such meetings, there is generally a vote on the issue, once the arguments on both sides of a proposal have been discussed. The argumentation in the meeting is also bound by practical constraints, that is, the length of time for the meeting may be limited by the circumstances. Thus, what is or is not judged relevant in a particular case will be partly determined by these special circumstances of the speech event.

As in all cases where relevance is concerned, much depends on what stage the dialogue has reached. In typical cases of problems of relevance that have to be dealt with in meetings, the chain of argumentation may not yet be completed or even very far advanced. Even so, in such a case, some evaluation of the relevance or irrelevance of a given argument needs to be made. Consider the following case.

> The university library committee has called for a meeting, and one of the items on the agenda is the question of how long the library should be open on Sundays. During the meeting, a student launches into a long argument on the problem of student shortages of funds and proposes that tuition costs should be reduced. The chairman of the library committee interrupts to say that she is sympathetic but that the committee has only one hour to discuss several items on the agenda that need to be voted on. She asks for further arguments on the issue of library closing hours on Sundays.

In this case, the student's arguments on shortages of funds could be relevant, because some students cannot afford to have proper study facilities and must rely on being able to work in the library. But generally, the library committee can do little or nothing about problems of student funding. And there are other items on the agenda that do require decisions based on discussion and consensus. Hence, for practical purposes, the chairman can be justified in judging the student's argumentation dialectically irrelevant when he launches into a long digression on questions of student funding shortages. This example shows that the speech event is vitally important in some cases. A meeting of the university library committee is a speech event that has a specific practical purpose within an institution, and it has an arbitrator or chairman, who must impose so-called rules of order on the meeting. Everyone should have a chance to speak, but they must not be allowed to dwell too long on arguments that are not dialectically relevant in this speech event.

In the example in section 1 above, the legislator's speech that decent housing for all the people is desirable was argued in some kind of legislative assembly. This meeting undoubtedly had rules of procedure, perhaps even a specific rule for a moderator to intervene in cases where an argument is irrelevant. To evaluate such a case in more detail, it is necessary to have more information about the speech event that forms the context of dialogue. In certain institutionalized frameworks of argumentation, relevance can be extremely important to limit unproductive debate that could be quite time-consuming and costly. Rules of relevance may be codified in a manual of procedural rules, and a designated official may be responsible for seeing that these rules are followed by participants. For example, there is a rule requiring that participants in the debates in the Canadian House of Commons not use arguments that are irrelevant. The Speaker of the House has to decide whether an argument is relevant or not, based on the issue of a debate, the type of debate involved, and the stage that debate is in. The most dramatic tactic of irrelevance is the filibuster, the technique of filling up the allotted time with purely irrelevant verbiage, in order to block the other side from saying anything at all. For example, a representative from New York once spoke continuously for twenty-four hours to block a bill in the U.S. House of Representatives. In the Canadian House of Commons, so-called guillotine rules allow the government House Leader to chop off the time allotted for debate on a bill. But to deal with cases where a persistent arguer goes on with arguments that are somewhat but not materially relevant to a bill, the Speaker of the House is supposed to intervene and enforce relevance.

In the following case, from a debate in the Canadian House of Commons,[2] the issue of the debate was a bill to amend the Small Business

[2] *Hansard* (Canada: House of Commons Debates, March 20, 1990), pp. 9553–9556.

Loans Act, an act dealing with problems faced by small businesses. In the midst of this debate, a member made a comment that presented a faxed birthday message to the Prime Minister, sent by one of his constituents, recommending that the regulation against demonstrating within fifty meters of the Parliament buildings be expanded, to keep the capital free of demonstrators of all kinds. This argument was irrelevant to the small business bill being debated. The arguer was not chastened by the dismissal of his comment as 'irrelevant' by the speaker, however. He went on trying to prove it was relevant, claiming that the sender of the message is a 'small business person' who also has a few things to say about wasteful government expenditures enforcing nuisance regulations on small businesses. Even though he could be right that the sender of the faxed birthday message was a 'small business person', the argument about demonstrations in the capital failed to give anyone in the debate a good reason to vote for or against any of the amendments to the act that had been proposed.

EXERCISE 7.3

1. Suppose that you are the chairman of a meeting in the following case. How would you respond?

> Your company is having a business meeting scheduled for one hour in which the only item on the agenda is the decision of whether or not to go ahead with marketing a new product that the company has developed: a new burglar alarm system. During the meeting, one of the engineers on the project starts arguing at length that the company needs to have new guidelines on sexual harassment. As time grows shorter, the chairman intervenes to ask whether another meeting could be set up to discuss the question of harassment, because what is relevant right now is the decision of whether to market this new system or not. The engineer replies that the question of harassment is relevant, because it is very important to the psychological adjustment of the employees, and this factor in turn is vital to the successful marketing of the product. He adds that this issue is so important that it must be resolved now.

2. Evaluate any failure of relevance in this case and comment on whether, in your opinion, the Acting Speaker's comment is justified.

> In September 1985, it was reported by the media that nearly a million cans of tunafish in storage had been rejected by the Canadian Fisheries Service as "tainted and unfit for human consumption," but the cans were ordered by the government to be released to market.

> It was never proved that the supposedly rancid tuna was unfit for human consumption, but the Tainted Tuna Scandal was the subject of many attacks on the government by the opposition parties. During a debate in the Canadian House of Commons on a bill to amend the Family Allowances Act, a minister intervened to attack on the tuna scandal.[3] She argued, "We are talking about a million tins of rotting tuna that the Government refuses to take off the shelves." The acting speaker intervened, saying, "Order, please. The Honorable Member knows that we are debating the amendment to the bill on family allowances. I do not know why we are debating tuna fish. I hope the Hon. Member will get back on track." The member replied, "My reference to tuna relates to the health and welfare of Canadians, which is also being dealt a fatal blow as a result of this particular legislation on family allowances."

FOUR Relevance in Legal Argumentation

Courts of law also have rules of relevance that are applicable, for example, in a criminal trial, where the judge is responsible for seeing to it that the attorneys do not use arguments deemed to be irrelevant to the proceedings by the court. One attorney, for example, may object that the other attorney's argument is irrelevant, and the judge will then make a ruling. Relevance is centrally important in evidence law, the branch of law that sets the procedural rules governing the argumentation in trials. Relevance is defined in the American Federal Rules of Evidence (FRE) based on the analysis of it given by the famous and influential evidence theorist John Henry Wigmore.[4] Rule 401 of the FRE offers a criterion of relevant evidence that is widely applicable in American law.

Legal Criterion of Relevant Evidence

"Relevant evidence" means evidence having any tendency to make the existence of any fact that is of consequence to the determination of the action more probable or less probable than it would be without the evidence.

[3] *Hansard* (Canada: House of Commons Debates, September 18, 1985), pp. 6742–6743.

[4] Wigmore's notion of legal relevance was, in turn, based on theories of reasoning of Locke and Bentham, as shown in a very useful book that outlines the history of the subject by William Twining, *Theories of Evidence: Bentham and Wigmore* (London: Weidenfeld and Nicolson, 1985).

The terms 'more probable' and 'less probable' refer to what is called probative weight in law. This refers to the reliance one can put on a statement as legal evidence. To say a statement has probative weight means that reasons can be given to support it as a conclusion drawn from premises that are accepted as factual in a case. The "action" is what is also called in law the ultimate *probandum* in the given case. It is the statement to be proved, rebutted, or cast into doubt by the argumentation used. Putting these two notions together, relevance as defined by the legal definition of relevant evidence could be expressed in terms of critical argumentation as follows. An argument considered as evidence in a case is relevant if it gives more probative weight or less probative weight to the ultimate *probandum* in the case. Thus, relevant evidence in law, judged by the criterion above, is very similar to the notion of probative relevance of an argument described in section 1 above. An argument is held to be relevant, in both legal and everyday sense, if it can be chained forward to boost up or lessen the probative weight of the ultimate *probandum* in a case.

The legal criterion above states that relevant evidence is generally admissible in a trial and that irrelevant evidence is not admissible. This means that the law has a low threshold for relevance. Anything is considered relevant, and is admissible as evidence in a trial, if it has the capability of altering the probative weight of the claim or ultimate *probandum* in the case at trial. However, there are also important exclusion rules in the FRE. Another rule (403) allows for the possibility of excluding evidence that is otherwise relevant according to the legal criterion of relevant evidence.

The Primary Exclusion Rule

Although relevant, evidence may be excluded if its probative value is substantially outweighed by the danger of unfair prejudice, confusion of the issues, or misleading the jury, or by considerations of undue delay, waste of time, or needless presentation of cumulative evidence.

According to the primary exclusion rule, something that might be initially taken as relevant under the general criterion of relevance, might have to be excluded under the exclusion rule. An example would be evidence of previous convictions, which could be excluded as inadmissible in a trial because it might tend to prejudice a jury against the defendant. This rule generally excludes appeals to emotion of a kind that might be powerfully compelling to a jury even though the appeal has little or no probative weight on the issue at trial. For example, appeal to pity or fear might have powerful emotional impact on a jury but might not be relevant as evidence.

In addition to the primary exclusion rule, there is another important rule that can also be used to exclude evidence that might otherwise be considered relevant. According to the character exclusion rule, character evidence is not relevant to prove conduct. This means that you can't argue, 'He is a bad person, therefore he must have committed this crime'. However, there are some exceptions to this rule stated in the FRE.

> Evidence of other crime, wrongs, or acts is not admissible to prove the character of a person in order to show action in conformity therewith. It may, however, be admissible for other purposes, such as proof of motive, opportunity, intent, preparation plan, knowledge, identity, or absence of mistake or accident, provided that upon request by the accused, the prosecution in a criminal case shall provide reasonable notice in advance of trial, or during trial if the court excuses pretrial notice on good cause shown, of the general nature of such evidence it intends to introduce at trial.

As well, the credibility of a witness may be attacked or supported by evidence in the form of reputation for untruthful character.

The character exclusion rule concerns ad hominem arguments that might be used to discredit a defendant or the testimony of a witness. The FRE, recognizing that such arguments can have a powerful persuasive impact on a jury even when irrelevant, try to rein them in. On the other hand, character can be relevant to the issue in some cases. For example, in a civil case where the issue is negligent hiring, the character of the person would be relevant to the issue of whether the defendant was negligent in hiring and entrusting property to him.[5] Another exception to the character exclusion rule is that a defendant in a criminal case can bring forward evidence of his own good character. But once these floodgates have been opened by the defense, the prosecution can introduce evidence of the defendant's bad character, and it is considered relevant. The rationale for excluding character evidence in Anglo-American law has a history. It was found that this kind of character attack was so successful in influencing

[5] James Landon, "Character Evidence: Getting to the Root of the Problem through Comparison," *American Journal of Criminal Law* 24 (1997): 581–615 (reference to p. 584).

juries that trial judges, over hundreds of years, were continually forced to try to restrict its use in courts.[6]

There is another rule in the FRE that is very important to understanding how relevance is defined in law. The conditional relevance rule allows that relevance can be 'conditioned on fact'. This additional clause extends the scope of relevance beyond that defined in the main part of the legal criterion of relevant evidence quoted above. The conditional relevance rule allows evidence as relevant if it satisfies the legal criterion of relevant evidence taken together with additional statements not yet proven to be facts.

The Conditional Relevance Rule

When the relevancy of evidence depends upon the condition of a fulfillment of fact, the court shall admit it upon, or subject to, the introduction of evidence sufficient to support a finding of the fulfillment of the condition.

An argument is conditionally relevant if its relevance is based on additional premises that have not been proved as evidence yet but that can be proved as further evidence is introduced. This notion of conditional relevance has proved to be highly controversial in law because it seems to be quite liberal in allowing evidence as relevant on a conditional basis, even if it has not been proved yet to have probative weight by itself. As the notes of the Advisory Committee indicate, rule 104(b) expresses the notion of conditional relevance. The following famous example illustrates a ruling on conditional relevance.[7]

> If a letter purporting to be from Y is relied upon to establish an admission from him, it has no probative value unless Y wrote or authorized it.

In this example, a letter supposedly from Y could be used as relevant evidence to prove an admission made supposedly by Y in the letter. But such a letter is conditionally relevant, meaning that its relevance is conditional on proving that Y wrote or authorized the letter. Conditional

[6] Ibid., p. 684.

[7] Vaughn C. Ball, "The Myth of Conditional Relevancy," *Georgia Law Review* 14 (1980): 435–469 (reference to p. 437).

relevance allows that one statement might not be relevant only considered by itself, but it could be relevant if, taken together with another statement that might later be proved, it has probative weight. This kind of relevance is conditional in that it depends on the chaining forward of the argumentation and is conditional on further statements that might be proved and used as premises in that chain.

One can see above that relevance as defined in law is very similar to the notion of relevance generally applicable to critical argumentation. It is a kind of probative relevance that depends at least partly on how the argumentation in a case can be chained forward and aimed at the thesis or ultimate *probandum* in the dialogue. In the case of legal relevance as defined by the FRE, the dialogue is the trial. On the other hand, legal relevance is different from relevance in everyday arguments of the kind outside law we have considered previously in this book. A trial is governed by all kinds of relatively precise procedural rules that govern who can speak, when each participant can speak, what arguments are allowed to be used, and how these arguments are judged. We could say that a distinction needs to be drawn between logical and legal relevance. What we have mainly been concerned with is logical relevance of a general kind that applies to all critical argumentation. Legal relevance is partly based on logical relevance, but it is also based on trial rules that are specific to the trial as a legal institution. Trials are very expensive, and so there are special reasons why it is necessary to prevent parties from going on and on taking up time with irrelevant arguments that may be worthless as evidence or might even have a negative impact by introducing confusion and prejudice.

Wigmore drew a careful distinction between legal relevance and logical relevance, fitting the latter into logic generally, or the science of proof, as he called it. Working on the assumption that there is a science of proof in which logical relevance can be defined, Wigmore clarified the relationship between logical relevance and the trial rules used to judge relevance in court. William Twining summarized the main points of Wigmore's account of this complex relationship.[8] Wigmore held that the trial rules of relevance are, broadly speaking, based on the notion of logical relevance, but that the practical conditions of trials bring into play certain special considerations. Thus, the trial rules are not the same as the rules of relevance that would apply in everyday argumentation

[8] Twining, *Theories of Evidence*, p. 156.

outside the law. Hence, the logical rules of relevance do not replace the trial rules, but they do at certain points justify the trial rules or give a basis for criticizing them.

The logical notion of relevance is a general one that applies to dialogues, such as the critical discussion, and other types of dialogue cited in chapter 5. This general model can be applied to other special contexts of argumentation, for example, in a trial or a legislative debate, where specific procedural rules for the speech event govern the dialogue. In these special contexts, it is the job of a judge or "speaker" to see to it that these specific rules governing the dialogue are followed. The distinction is between argumentation used in an abstract normative model of dialogue, as considered in chapter 6, and argumentation used in a speech event representing a special social or institutional setting, such as a trial or a legislative debate. The social or institutional setting is called a speech event because it ties argumentation to specific procedural rules determined by a particular institution. Such rules obviously vary from country to country or from one jurisdiction to another. It is important to recognize that they exist and that they need to be taken into account when any attempt is made to analyze or evaluate critically the relevance of arguments used in these special contexts.

EXERCISE 7.4

In a law court, in attempting to prove the accused is guilty of murder, the prosecution argues passionately that murder is a horrible crime and even succeeds in proving that conclusion. What critical deficiency is evident in this case, and how can it be shown that the prosecutor's argument is deficient in this respect?

FIVE Fear Appeal Arguments

Appealing to fear can be a powerful tactic of distraction in argumentation. It is a kind of argument that one has to be careful with, as it can be powerfully effective even when it is not relevant. In some cases, however, such arguments are reasonable and relevant. Thus, the problem is to judge when they are relevant and when not. The place to begin is to identify the special characteristics of this type of argument. The fear appeal argument is a subspecies of argument from negative consequences where the negative outcome is portrayed in such a way by the proponent as to appeal to the fear of the respondent. Fear appeal arguments are commonly used by government agencies that promote health and safety issues in media ads. Here are two examples.

In a Canadian television ad against drunk driving, a teenager is shown getting into his car with his girlfriend after a party. Then the car is shown crashing, an ambulance arrives, and the dead girl is carried away. The teenager is then shown confronting the situation of informing the girl's parents. He is distraught.

In an Australian television ad, a sad looking young man is shown with one eye that is dark and sightless. He is describing all the difficulties he is experiencing with his disabilities. Then there is a flashback to a scene of the young man being in a car accident, and looking down at his hands that are covered in blood. Again it shows the man with his disfigured face and blinded eye, who says: "I can't work out why I'm being punished, just because I undid my seat belt for a couple of seconds."

Numerous television ads by government health agencies have used fear appeal arguments to try to get teenagers to stop smoking (or not to start). One ad warns of the dangers of secondhand smoke by showing smoke creeping into a room toward an infant in a crib (while eerie music plays in the background). All these ads use the fear appeal argument. By portraying negative consequences in a dramatic way that the target audience is presumed to find especially fearful, the purpose of the ad is to move the audience to a designated course of action (or in the smoking case, inaction).

The fear appeal argument is based on a use of disjunctive reasoning. There are two alternatives involved. For example, in the smoking ad type of case, there is the option of smoking or the option of not smoking. If the respondent smokes, there is short-term pleasure. But balanced against that are the known long-term negative consequences of smoking. The tactic of the fear appeal argument is to portray the danger of these negative consequences with such a dramatic impact on the respondent that the value of the positive short-term consequences are overcome and that that option is ruled out by the respondent. To be successful, then, a fear appeal argument has to have a strong enough "punch" to unseat the positive option.

Because of their use of emotional appeal, it may seem easy at first to dismiss fear appeal arguments as illogical or fallacious. But if you look at them as arguments based on practical reasoning, used to try to persuade a respondent to carry out a particular line of action, such arguments can be judged to be reasonable enough. For example, it appears to be quite legitimate to use fear appeal ads to try to get people to buckle up or to stop smoking, if these actions really are prudent. However, as mentioned in the section on slippery slope arguments in chapter 4, fear appeal arguments are unconvincing if the audience senses that the danger is being 'hyped' or exaggerated.

A fear appeal argument has two premises. In the first premise, a situation is sketched out that is (presumably) very fearful to the respondent. The second premise warns the respondent that if he carries out a particular action, then the consequences portrayed in the situation will happen to him. The conclusion, then, is the message to the respondent that he should not carry out this particular action. In the form of inference below, the respondent is designated by the use of the pronoun 'you'.

ARGUMENTATION SCHEME FOR THE FEAR APPEAL ARGUMENT

FEARFUL SITUATION PREMISE: Here is a situation that is fearful to you.

CONDITIONAL PREMISE: If you carry out A, then the negative consequences portrayed in this fearful situation will happen to you.

CONCLUSION: You should not carry out A.

It is easily seen from this form of inference that the fear appeal type of argument is based on the argument from negative consequences. The critical questions appropriate for the fear appeal argument are the following:

1. Should the situation represented really be fearful to me, or is it an irrational fear that is appealed to?
2. If I don't carry out A, will that stop the negative consequences from happening?
3. If I do carry out A, how likely is it that the negative consequences will happen?

Another issue in evaluating fear appeal arguments is whether they are relevant or not. As mentioned above, there is a tendency to see fear appeal arguments as irrelevant in dispassionate logical reasoning where 'hard evidence' is all that should count. But in judging relevance, what is important is how an argument has been used for some purpose. If the purpose is to promote goals of health and safety, for example, to get respondents to carry out or desist from actions that are harmful to health or safety, then the use of a fear appeal argument, as a species of argument from negative consequences, could be relevant. So it would not be justified to dismiss fear appeal arguments as being inherently irrelevant in any kind of genuine logical reasoning. But, as we see in the next section, some fear appeal arguments should not be judged to be dialectically relevant.

EXERCISE 7.5

Exhibit the structure of the following fear appeal arguments and pose appropriate critical questions.

(a) In a television commercial, two teenage girls are shown grooming in front of a mirror. One comments to the other that it isn't fair that she has such a nice complexion, while her own skin has such a blotchy appearance. The other girl replies, "If you didn't smoke, yours would look much more healthy." The first girl confides that her boyfriend has been thinking of leaving her, because her appearance has declined so much.

(b) An Australian television ad shows a group of men at an outside job site, all drinking beer. One of the men drains off the last of his bottle of beer and tells his young son to get in their utility vehicle. All the other men are still drinking beer, and one of them, between swigs, comments that driving has never been a problem after having a few beers. He says, "I've been driving home a long time mate, and nothing has ever happened to me yet." The next scene shows the man and his son driving through an intersection, after failing to stop, and suddenly their utility vehicle is crushed and completely destroyed by a huge oncoming tractor-trailer. The next scene shows one of the men at the job site answering the phone. He replies, "But he was just here a minute ago."

SIX Threats as Arguments

One very familiar type of argument that is closely related to the fear appeal argument is the use of a threat as an argument. The difference between a fear appeal argument and the use of a threat in argument is that in the latter type of case, the proponent makes a commitment to the respondent that she will actually see to it that negative consequences come about, unless he carries out the course of action that is advocated by her. The use of a threat as an argument has the following form. Traditionally, in logic, such an argument is called the *argumentum ad baculum*, or 'argument to the stick (rod, club).' Here the pronoun 'I' represents the proponent and the pronoun 'you' represents the respondent.

ARGUMENTATION SCHEME FOR THE *ARGUMENTUM AD BACULUM*

CONDITIONAL PREMISE: If you do not bring about A, then consequence B will occur.

COMMITMENT PREMISE: I commit myself to seeing to it that B will come about.

CONCLUSION: You should bring about A.

A threat of this sort is said to be credible to the respondent if the proponent is in a position to bring about B and if the respondent knows it. A credible threat is a powerful sort of argument, not only from a practical point of view, because it represents negative consequences for the interests and safety of the respondent, but also because it can have a lingering fear appeal effect.

There are two types of threats used as arguments, direct and indirect. A direct threat is an argument that has the form above, where the proponent comes right out and explicitly says that she will bring about the negative consequences cited. In an indirect threat, the second premise is not explicitly stated, so that overtly, the argument has the form of a warning. A warning is a speech act that is different from a threat, because the proponent states only what amounts to the first premise of the argument having the form of a threat. That is, when making a warning, the proponent tells the respondent that bad consequences will (might, may) happen if the respondent fails to bring about (or brings about) some particular thing. Indirect threats are very familiar in all kinds of arguments, as can easily be recognized from this example.

Shakey Trembler, the owner of a pizza parlor, is told by Brutus Gunner, notorious gangland figure, that if he doesn't subscribe to the Gunner Protection Agency, all kinds of bad things might happen to him. Brutus says, "Look at the owner of the Dog and Duck Coffee Shop down the street. He didn't join, and his shop was bombed."

Now it could be that Gunner is just warning Trembler and giving him some practical advice. But given Gunner's gangland reputation and his known past history of gang violence, Trembler would be well advised to treat Gunner's message as a threat. There are many practical advantages to making an indirect as opposed to a direct threat. One is that, as long as there was no overtly expressed second premise, there is no definite, reproducible evidence that a threat was made. So the proponent can later deny it: "I never made a threat. All I was doing was giving you some friendly advice." Another advantage is that an indirect threat is often more menacing and has a lingering uncertainty about it that can be worrisome to a respondent.

The four critical questions appropriate for the argument used as a threat are the following.

1. How bad are the consequences?
2. How likely is it that the consequences will occur?
3. Is the threat credible?
4. Is the threat relevant?

With respect to the first critical question, the respondent must weigh the negative factor of the bad consequences against the negative factor of bringing about A (presumably, in the use of a threat type of case, A is something the respondent is against or does not want to bring about). With respect to the second critical question, as in the case of any fear appeal argument, it must be fairly certain or likely that the bad outcome cited will actually come about if the recommended action is not taken. For a threat to be credible, as defined above, it must appear to the respondent that the proponent is actually in a position to carry out the bad consequences cited. Moreover, to make the threat very credible, the proponent must also convince the respondent that he is not only able but willing to carry out the action in question.

The fourth critical question, that of relevance, is more contextual than it may initially appear to be. In some contexts of conversation, threats are definitely irrelevant. For example, consider the following case.

> In a physics seminar two professors are having a discussion on whose theory of nuclear magnetic resonance is better supported by experimental results. In the midst of the discussion, one professor says to the other, "If you don't accept my theory, Brutus Gangland (that big guy just outside the door) will beat you up!"

In this case, the threat would be regarded as not only outrageous, but also highly inappropriate as a kind of argument to carry weight in the discussion. In a word, it would be irrelevant. Indeed, in any kind of critical discussion, using threats such as 'You'd better shut up if you know what's good for you' are best not regarded as relevant arguments.

However, in some cases where two parties are having an argument, threats can be relevant. For example, in argumentation in negotiations, threats (especially the indirect type) are frequently used and are a normal part of the argumentation.

Union and management officials are engaged in a round of talks on the subject of the annual wage and benefits settlement. A union official argues, "Well, if that's the best you can do, the members will be out on strike tomorrow!" The management official replies, "If there is a strike, there will be a negative financial impact, which will necessitate job cuts and salary reductions."

In this case, the threats are relevant arguments used in the process of negotiation. Of course, in many instances, use of threats can also be counterproductive or even obstructive in negotiations. But sometimes, as in the case above, they are relevant. So it would be a mistake to classify all arguments used as threats as irrelevant. Whether the threat is relevant or not depends on the purpose of the conversational exchange in the given case.

EXERCISE 7.6

Evaluate the following arguments and exhibit the structure of each argument.

(a) Personnel manager to employees: "I know that some of you oppose the appointment of Beavis Climber as the new sales manager. On further consideration, however, I am confident you will change your minds. If Climber is not appointed, it may become necessary to make severe personnel cutbacks in your departments."

(b) Assistant to executive: "I'm sure you'll want to raise my salary for the coming year. After all, you wouldn't want your wife to find out about rumors that you have been sexually harassing me."

(c) According to R. Grunberger, author of *A Social History of the Third Reich*, published in Britain, the Nazis used to send the following notice to German readers who let their subscriptions lapse: "Our paper certainly deserves the support of every German. We shall continue to forward copies of it to you, and hope that you will not want to expose yourself to unfortunate consequences in the case of cancellation."

(d) A professor says to two disruptive students who talk loudly during the lecture, "Others can't hear, so if you keep that up, I will bar you from attending the lectures."
(e) A philosophy professor argues in class that abortion should not be paid for by government health funding contributed by taxpayers. A person in his class says, "I find your view offensive, because women are dying because they can't get an abortion. You had better not continue to voice that argument or I will report you for making a remark that I find personally offensive."

SEVEN Appeal to Pity

Appeal to pity is another one of those arguments that is not inherently fallacious but is often suspect, because it is sometimes used as a powerful distraction that is emotionally compelling, even when it is not relevant to the issue under consideration. But in some cases, appeal to pity is materially relevant as an argument. Here is an example.

> An appeal for contributions to help starving children in a disastrous famine, sent out by a relief agency, features an arresting picture of a pathetically starved child with a distended belly. This child's name is given, and the details of his situation are described graphically. The statement is made that if this child does not receive help soon, she will die. A form is enclosed that the recipient of the letter can use to send money.

The argument conveyed in this letter has the form of a sequence of practical reasoning: Here is a bad situation, and if you bring about the designated action, you can help to relieve the bad situation. As such, we do not want to say that this appeal to pity is a fallacious argument, even though it would be prudent to ask some critical questions about the ability of the relief agency to use the money sent in actually to deliver food to the starving disaster victims. But in this case, the appeal to pity is relevant, because it is a legitimate way of evoking a strong enough emotional response so that the respondents will really understand the scope and nature of the bad situation and will therefore make a contribution to help relieve it. Still, a potential donor should ask some critical questions about whether the money will actually get to the needy child. How much of it, for example, will be taken up by administration costs of the charity organizations?

In other cases, however, less of a basis can be found for judging the appeal to pity to be relevant.

> A student missed taking a term test and pleads with her professor to be allowed to take a makeup exam. Her excuse is that if she doesn't get a makeup exam, she will not get an A in the course, and therefore she will not be able to get into law school, and it will all be the professor's fault. She cries and pleads that this failure will ruin her life, and those of her two young children, who both have Crohn's disease.

Is the appeal to pity in this case relevant? One thing to say is that if the pleader has a legitimate excuse, such as a serious illness that can be proved by a note from a physician, then she has the right to a makeup exam. But if she has no excuse other than the story presented, then (according to the rules at most universities), she does not have an adequate basis for a makeup exam. But the thing to notice is that by making such a dramatic emotional appeal, she puts the professor on the defensive by making it appear that somehow he is to blame for her problems. Yet his job is to grade all students' work fairly, on its merit. It would go against his proper doing of his job if he were to give one student an unfair advantage over all the other students who took the test, or who had legitimate excuses, by letting her take a makeup test even if she could have taken the original test and had no good reason for not doing so. What she is doing then is using a powerfully dramatic distraction to try to browbeat him into twisting the proper basis of the decision around so that he comes to a conclusion on the wrong basis. In this case, then, the appeal to pity is irrelevant. It is emotionally powerful and psychologically relevant. But it is not dialectically relevant in the sense that it provides a line of reasoning that can be used to determine the outcome of the professor's decision one way or the other.

In court cases, attorneys often try to portray an accused person of himself being a helpless victim of his circumstances. But whether this kind of appeal to pity is relevant or not depends on how it is used in a given case and what stage the trial is in. If the attorney goes on at length during the trial about the pathetic circumstances of the defendant, the judge may rule the argument irrelevant, on the grounds that it does nothing toward proving whether the defendant is guilty of the crime charged or not. But if an appeal to pity is used at the later sentencing stage – once the trial has already proved that the defendant is guilty – it is relevant for the defense attorney to appeal to pity and to ask for the court to show mercy or compassion. Appeals to pity, then, are not inherently fallacious or irrelevant. But because they are so emotionally powerful, they can often be used to distract an audience away from the main point to be proved.

EXERCISE 7.7

Evaluate the following arguments.

(a) A man applying for a job as a crane operator in an urban renewal job is qualified, except that he is subject to fainting fits. He pleads that he has been unable to get work to support his six children and that his wife was recently blinded in a car accident.

(b) William Makepeace Thackeray, editor of the *Cornhill Magazine* in the 1850s, quotes a letter he received, in an envelope containing some poems (in his essay, "Thorns in the Cushion," printed in the magazine in 1860.

> Camberwell, June 4.
>
> "Sir, – May I hope, may I entreat, that you will favour me by perusing the enclosed lines, and that they may be found worthy of insertion in the Cornhill Magazine. We have known better days, sir. I have a sick and widowed mother to maintain, and little brothers and sisters who look to me. I do my utmost as a governess to support them. I toil at night when they are at rest, and my own hand and brain are alike tired. If I could add but a little to our means by my pen, many of my poor invalid's wants might be supplied, and I could procure for her comforts to which she is now a stranger. Heaven knows it is not for want of will or for want of energy on my part, that she is now in ill-health, and our little household almost without bread. Do – cast a kind glance over my poem, and if you can help us, the widow, the orphans will bless you! I remain, sir, in anxious expectancy.
>
> Your faithful servant,
> S. S. S.

(c) During the trial of two brothers, Erik and Lyle Menendez, who killed both of their parents with fifteen shotgun blasts in 1989, Leslie Abramson, their defense attorney, argued that the Menendez brothers "cannot be held to the cold standards of accountability of a legal system that lags behind social and psychological theories of behavior," as quoted in a *New York Times* report.[9] Abramson argued, "These boys were not responsible for who they turned out to be."

[9] Seth Mydans, "In Brothers' Lurid Trial, One Woman Dominates." *New York Times*, December 20, 1993, p. D9.

She added, "They were just little children being molded. They were never free of the clutches of their parents. When you terrorize people and they react from terror, you pretty much get what you sowed." Abramson called the Menendez brothers "the boys" before the jury, putting her arms around them, suggesting how lovable they were. She portrayed herself as motivated by a "gentler impulse to protect people who have been rejected by society." She went on to say, "I'm drawn to cases where very nice people and very good people are accused of crimes because the law lags behind psychology, like people who have been abused and battered." She called the brothers "delightful clients" and "decent human beings." After killing their parents, "the boys" had gone on a spending spree, one buying a Porsche sports car, and the other taking tennis lessons. Abramson pleaded a history of alleged sexual abuse in a tearful defense that was described by other attorneys as a "cry for help."

EIGHT Shifts and Relevance

One might wonder how people are deceived by irrelevant arguments such as appeals to pity, ad hominem arguments, or arguments using threats. After all, if these arguments are irrelevant, wouldn't everyone see that they are irrelevant? Often they don't, mainly for two reasons. One is that many everyday conversations start up in a natural way, and nobody clarifies what the real issue is or what type of dialogue the conversation is supposed to be. In this kind of case, we lack the information to determine whether an argument is relevant or not. The other reason is that during a sequence of argumentation, there can be a dialectical shift, a changeover from one type of dialogue to another. If one participant doesn't notice the shift, then an argument may seem relevant to her when it is really not. The underlying factor is that the very same argument can be relevant in one context of dialogue but irrelevant in another context of dialogue. If everyone were always clear on what type of dialogue they are supposed to be taking part in when they put forward an argument, problems of irrelevance would not be so tricky. But often there can be a subtle or not clearly marked shift in the same argument, from one type of dialogue to another. When such a shift occurs, an argument may appear to be relevant, because it would have been perfectly relevant before the shift, in the prior context of use.

Threats used as arguments, for example, are clearly and even outrageously inappropriate in a critical discussion. If we are having a philosophy seminar on the nature of knowledge and one participant threatens another to have him beaten up by a large student in the class if he doesn't accept her views on the questions of the nature of knowledge, everyone would rightly regard this *ad baculum* argument as highly inappropriate and irrelevant. But in a negotiation type of dialogue, threats, especially indirect threats to carry out sanctions if the other party does not agree to conditions, are regarded as normal tactics to be used as arguments. A threat in a negotiation dialogue is regarded as somewhat dangerous, because it poses an ultimatum that may be difficult to back down from without appearing to be weak or vacillating. But negotiation is interest-based bargaining, and as such the granting of concessions and the placing of sanctions or penalties on the other party if he fails to comply or grant concessions can be a normal and appropriate part of the argumentation used.

However, in a particular case where two parties are arguing, and it is not exactly clear what type of dialogue they are supposed to be engaging in, a shift from critical discussion to negotiation or vice versa might easily be concealed or might be hard to pin down exactly. For example, in a political debate, the dialogue may supposedly be a critical discussion about some issue. In this context, an argument using a threat would be irrelevant. But given that politics is involved, it may not be possible to rule out self-interested bargaining as what the dialogue is supposed to include, as well. In such a context of negotiation dialogue, a threat could be a relevant argument.

Some dialectical shifts are licit and others are illicit. For example, when Bob and Helen are arguing about tipping, Helen might use the argument that tipping is bad because it leads to an underground economy. Bob might then raise questions about whether we already have an underground economy and what its effects on the economy are. To answer these questions, some source of information, such as a book or report on the underground economy, might be used. In such a case, there has been a shift from the persuasion dialogue to an information-seeking dialogue. But in this case, the shift is licit, because the information on the underground economy, if it is accurate, will contribute to the discussion on tipping by making it better informed. Relevance, in such a case, is transferred from propositions in the one type of dialogue to propositions in the other.

However, a dialectical shift is illicit if the reasoning in the first type of dialogue does not contribute to the goal of the second type of dialogue. For example, a threat may have an appropriate place in a negotiation dialogue, but if there has been a shift to a persuasion dialogue, the threat could be irrelevant as an argument in that context. When a dialectical shift occurs during the sequence of reasoning in an argument, the evaluation of whether the shift is licit or illicit needs to be done by looking backward to determine what type of dialogue the participants were supposed to be taking part in originally. Then the argument should be evaluated with respect to whether or not it contributes to the goal of that original type of dialogue.

Ad hominem arguments used in political debates are best evaluated for relevance on a case-by-case basis. But in election debating, ad hominem arguments are generally relevant or at least can be, in principle, because the character of a candidate is a relevant issue. Voting is based on deliberation, but voters cannot be expected to know all the facts, so they often decide for or against a candidate on her leadership qualities or on how well she represents the voter's viewpoint. Knowing something about the candidate's character may be relevant to this deliberation. On the other hand, too much use of personal attack ads may obscure the real issues, by taking up too much of the debate with sleazy allegations based on innuendo but not proved. Abuse of these irrelevant ad hominem attacks has, unfortunately, become all too familiar in contemporary politics.

EXERCISE 7.8

Identify the type of argument in each of the following cases and discuss whether a dialectical shift is involved.

(a) Two members of the U.S. Senate are discussing a particular bill that is to be voted on during the next session. One presents several arguments against the bill. The other, who happens to be the party whip in charge of discipline, replies: "I wouldn't vote against that bill if I were you. You could find that being a maverick, in our party, means that you will not be appointed to a certain key committee that is very important in determining your future success."

(b) During the course of their critical discussion on the issue of tipping, Bob says quietly to Helen: "I would be very careful about arguing against tipping in front of the group at this dinner party if I were you. That big student with the biceps and tattoos over there is bartender at the Biker's Bar on weekends. Tipping is how he makes his income, and I hear he is a kind of unstable individual who could turn violent in an instant if you say something that he finds disturbing or offensive. Mind you, I'm just giving you some advice, but if you tone down your arguments against tipping a bit, I won't indicate to him how your viewpoint offends his sensitivities on the subject."

NINE Summary

The fallacy of irrelevant conclusion (*ignoratio elenchi*) is committed when an argument that is supposed to prove one proposition as its conclusion is directed to a different conclusion. But how does one determine in a particular case whether this fallacy has been committed or not? That, in a nutshell, is the problem of relevance. One important distinction is that between probative relevance and topical relevance. Two propositions are topically relevant to each other if they share subject matters. Two propositions are probatively relevant if one can be used in a sequence of argumentation to prove the other. A critical discussion is a particular type of persuasion dialogue the purpose of which is to resolve a conflict of opinions. The four stages of a critical discussion are the opening stage, the confrontation stage, the argumentation stage, and the closing stage.

Dialectical relevance is the kind of relevance that refers to the use of a sequence of reasoning in a chain of argumentation that is supposed to contribute to the fulfillment of a conversational goal that two parties are collaborating to achieve. Judging relevance is also often partly a matter of the speech event, or particular institutional or cultural framework of an argument. For example, in a committee meeting in an organizational setting, a chairman or moderator may be expected to cope with dialectical irrelevance by applying rules of relevancy as part of the procedural rules (rules of order) appropriate for the meeting. In political debates in legislative assemblies, rules of relevance are applied by the Speaker of the House, who is supposed to be fair and neutral and to use good judgment in keeping the line of argumentation on track. Politicians, however, frequently try to use irrelevant arguments to score points against the opposition and to get media attention by appearing to be powerful rhetoricians, 'shakers and movers'. Too often, these tactics of diversion work only too well on an uncritical audience, thus subverting the real point of a democracy, which is to give an in-depth discussion of an issue that reveals all the strongest relevant arguments on both sides of the issue. This goal is defeated by the use of irrelevant but entertaining arguments that are the stuff and substance of tabloid journalism.

The fear appeal argument has the following form:

FEARFUL SITUATION PREMISE: Here is a situation that is fearful to you.

CONDITIONAL PREMISE: If you carry out A, then the negative consequences portrayed in this fearful situation will happen to you.

CONCLUSION: You should not carry out A.

It is easily seen from this form of inference that the fear appeal type of argument represents a sequence of practical reasoning based on argument from negative consequences.

There are three matching critical questions for the fear appeal argument.

1. Should the situation represented really be fearful to me, or is it an irrational fear that is appealed to?
2. If I don't carry out A, will that stop the negative consequences from happening?
3. If I do carry out A, how likely is it that the negative consequences will happen?

Fear appeal arguments can be quite reasonable in many instances, despite their reputation as being fallacious.

The use of a threat as an argument (*argumentum ad baculum*) has the following form:

CONDITIONAL PREMISE: If you do not bring about A, then consequence B will occur.

COMMITMENT PREMISE: I commit myself to seeing to it that B will come about.

CONCLUSION: You should not bring about A.

There are four critical questions matching the use of a threat as an argument:

1. How bad are the consequences?
2. How likely is it that the consequences will occur?
3. Is the threat credible?
4. Is the threat relevant?

Whether the *ad baculum* type of argument is relevant or not, in a particular case, depends on the context of dialogue in which it was used. Threats can be relevant in negotiations, but they are irrelevant in the critical discussion type of dialogue.

Appeal to pity is another type of argument that rouses strong emotions and can be used with powerful effect to distract an audience from the real point that is supposedly the issue. However, some appeals to pity, as in cases of charitable appeals, can be relevant to an issue that is being discussed. What is very important in determining whether any of these emotional appeals is relevant or not in a given case is the context of dialogue in the case. And indeed, what often deceives people into thinking one of these arguments is relevant, when really it is not, is the dialectical shift from one context to another during the sequence of argumentation. Judging relevance or irrelevance of arguments, then, is a highly contextual matter. It depends on how the argument is situated in a case, in a context of dialogue for the case. One has to make a global judgment of where the argument is going, whether it is leading toward the thesis to be proved in the dialogue or not, as far as this matter can be judged from the information given in the case.

EIGHT Practical Reasoning in a Dialogical Framework

The argumentation structures analyzed in this chapter are highly typical of the kinds of reasoning commonly used in everyday deliberations. These structures of inference are also used in all aspects of technology, especially in fields such as engineering and medicine, where the objectives are essentially practical in nature, even though the reasoning is based on scientific knowledge. But their root use and their most familiar appearance to us in daily life is in the reasoning we commonly use to decide on which course of action to take, especially where personal choices on how to conduct one's daily life are made and acted on in real situations. As arguments, practical inferences are typically used in the type of dialogue called the deliberation in chapter 6. Deliberation is characterized by the need to arrive at a decision on what to do in a set of circumstances that is not completely known to an agent and that is liable to change in ways that are impossible to predict with certainty. Thus, practical reasoning tends to use argumentation schemes that are neither deductive nor inductive in nature.

We begin with very simple cases of practical inferences, and then, by the end of the chapter, consider so-called real world situations where additional factors need to be taken into account. Such practical inferences are highly familiar and are widely used by everyone. So this book does not introduce you to them – not in the sense of introducing you to something that you are not already highly skilled at using in a practical manner. But by becoming aware of the logical structure of these kinds of inference and studying how they are fitted together in sequences of reasoning used in arguments in deliberation, your critical skills of dealing with reasoned deliberation can be enhanced. Such skills can enable you to 'think twice' in some cases and take a more balanced critical perspective on questionable conclusions you might otherwise have taken for granted.

ONE Practical Inferences

Much of the reasoning used in everyday arguments is neither inductive nor deductive in nature and, instead, is of a kind used to select out from a set of alternative, possible courses of action which line of action is the most practical in a given situation, relative to an agent's goals. A practical inference is based on a premise that states a goal and a premise that states a means to realize the goal and has a conclusion that recommends an action. Practical reasoning is a chaining together of a sequence of practical inferences, where the sequence leads toward an ultimate goal and concludes in a practical directive recommending a course of action to take in a given initial situation, as an agent sees that situation.[1] Practical reasoning is 'practical' because it infers a conclusion representing an action that is the most practical or prudent thing to do in a particular set of circumstances.

The simplest kind of practical inference can be represented as follows, where the first-person pronoun 'I' represents an agent, an entity capable of having goals, of being aware of its circumstances, and of acting on those circumstances and changing them.

> I have a goal, *G*.
>
> Carrying out this action is the means to realize *G*.
>
> Therefore, I ought (practically speaking) to carry out this action.

For example, suppose my goal is to close the door, and the means to close the door is to turn the doorknob and push the door. Therefore, I ought (practically speaking) to turn the doorknob and push the door. Thus, the basic components of a practical inference are three in number. One premise describes or postulates a goal. The second premise describes an action that is a means or way to accomplish the goal. And the conclusion recommends carrying out this action.

The structure of the practical inference can be brought out in a more useful way if we represent the outcomes of actions as propositions, *A*, *B*, *C*, . . . , so that carrying out an action can be described as bringing about a proposition, or "making it true." Using this way of speaking, the

[1] The concept of practical reasoning was originally described by Aristotle (384–322 B.C.), who showed how this type of reasoning is a chaining together of practical inferences, of a kind sometimes called 'practical syllogisms'. However, this terminology can be misleading, because a practical inference is not a syllogism and is quite different from a deductive syllogistic inference.

structure of the practical inference can be represented by the following scheme.

> My goal is to bring about *A*.
>
> Bringing about *B* is the way to bring about *A*.
>
> Therefore, I should bring about *B*.

There are two more specific ways of representing practical inferences, depending on what is meant, more exactly, by 'the way' (or 'the means') to bring about something. Typically, what is referred to is a necessary condition for bringing about something, but in some cases what is referred to is a sufficient condition for bringing about something. For example, paying tuition is a means of graduating, in the sense that it is a necessary but not a sufficient condition of graduating. My killing this fly is a sufficient condition of the fly's being dead. But it is not a necessary condition, because the fly might have died in some other way. The concepts of a necessary and sufficient condition are defined in section 2.

Practical reasoning involves a sequence of practical inferences chained together, in which some inferences in the chain represent necessary conditions, while others represent sufficient conditions. For example, in order to get to the train station by 3 o'clock, my taking the number 9 bus that leaves at 2:30 may be sufficient. But in order to take the number 9 bus that leaves at 2:30, it may be necessary for me to leave my house at 2:15. It may also be necessary for me to have a bus ticket. To get the tram ticket, it may be necessary to walk to the store and to do other things as well. Thus, there is likely to be quite a long sequence of actions I may have to carry out in order to get to the train station by 3 o'clock. Many necessary conditions would be part of the sequence, and if it is long and detailed enough, the whole sequence might be a sufficient way for me to get to the train station by 3 o'clock.

Practical reasoning is generally a defeasible kind of reasoning, subject to qualifications, expressed in various questions. In judging a practical inference, five critical questions are appropriate.

- **(Q1)** Are there alternative means other than *B*?
- **(Q2)** Is *A* a possible (realistic) goal?
- **(Q3)** Are there other goals that might conflict with *A*?
- **(Q4)** Are there negative consequences of bringing about *B* that should be considered?
- **(Q5)** Is *B* the best (or most acceptable) of the alternatives?

Three additional critical questions for more complex cases of practical reasoning are added in section 8. But for the simple kinds of cases considered up to that point, these four are sufficient. For an example of (Q1), it may be that I could ride my bicycle to the train station, instead of taking the bus, and still get there by 3 o'clock. To consider an example of (Q2), it may be that I am so far from the train station at the present time that no means of transport available would get me there by 3 o'clock. As an illustration of (Q3), consider the case where I start to feel very ill, and concern about my well-being (another goal) suggests that it would be wiser to go to the hospital than to the train station. As an example of (Q4), consider the case where I am a rock star and find out that there is a large crowd of my fans assembled at the train, who will still be there at 3 o'clock, so that if I am there at that time, they will recognize me and the crowd will start a riot. These negative consequences should cause me to reconsider. As an example of (Q5), I might find that taking a plane would be faster than taking the train.

Practical reasoning is normally evaluated or weighed on a balance of considerations. The importance of a goal has to be weighed against the negative or positive consequences of carrying out the means to the goal, to the extent that these consequences can reasonably be anticipated. However, because the future is never known with certainty, and most typically not even known with any precise degree of probability, practical reasoning characteristically is tentative and presumptive in nature. A plausible practical conclusion, even one that is strongly indicated, should generally be seen as open to revision should new, relevant information come in.

Some goals are very specific. For example, being at the train station at 3 o'clock is a very specific goal. But some goals are quite general and abstract. For example, if my goal is to be healthy, this is a long-term goal of a general kind, because there might be all kinds of different ways and means of contributing to it, depending on my circumstances at different times. I might get all kinds of advice on which kinds of foods and exercise and which things to do or not do are the most practically wise means of contributing to this goal. It is for this reason that practical reasoning that has to do with general goals is frequently presumptive in nature and is composed of plausible inferences that are relative to changeable conditions. A general goal guides reasoning to steer inference toward a plausible conclusion to accept tentatively as a presumption, based on what is currently known or accepted as representing current conditions.

EXERCISE 8.1

Evaluate the following cases of practical reasoning by showing the structure of the practical inferences involved and citing appropriate critical questions that should be asked.

(a) I need to get to the university by 10:00 A.M., but there is a snowstorm, and my car will not start. The best way is to start walking.

(b) It is necessary for our college students to study Chinese, because trade with China is an increasingly important economic factor in our economy. To trade effectively with China, we need people who can interact culturally with the Chinese. But interacting culturally with the Chinese requires learning their language. Therefore, we should learn Chinese.

(c) Rita is considering staying up all night to study for her calculus exam. The night before the exam, Bruce tells her, "You will be too tired and confused during the exam to think straight."

(d) To deal with crime effectively, we must have tougher sentencing. It is difficult to live productive and peaceful lives with so much crime. Crime must be reduced, and so we must deal with it effectively. Therefore, we must have tougher sentencing.

(e) To be guaranteed job security, it is necessary for the union to go on strike, because if we don't go on strike, the company may decide to have cutbacks. And unless we go on strike, the company will not agree to new clauses in the contract that would make it more difficult to lay off workers. So, the union must go on strike.

(f) The only way I can get into medical school is by performing well on the MCAT. But the only way I can perform well on the MCAT is to take a course on critical thinking. Therefore, I should take a course on critical thinking.

TWO Necessary and Sufficient Conditions

If a particular door is the only exit to this room, and that door is closed, it would be true to say that the only way I can leave the room is by opening the door. To put the same idea in the language of conditions, we might say that opening the door is a necessary condition of leaving the room. Or to put it still another way: No door opening, no room leaving. Another concept in the language of conditions is that of a sufficient condition. If Abraham Lincoln was assassinated by John Wilkes Booth, then Abraham Lincoln is dead. This conditional statement expresses the idea that

Lincoln's being assassinated by Booth is a sufficient condition of Lincoln's being dead. As we see in this case, the conditional, or 'if-then', is normally the way to express the idea that one thing is sufficient for another. But in this case, it can also be seen that the concepts of necessary and sufficient condition are different from each other. Although being killed by John Wilkes Booth is a sufficient condition of Abraham Lincoln being dead, it is not a necessary condition. Lincoln could possibly have been killed by someone else, as might be maintained by a skeptic or by a conspiracy theorist. Similarly, in the case of my leaving this room, opening the door would not (by itself) be a sufficient condition of my leaving the room. I would also have to walk though the door, or find some other means of getting out, once I had opened the door. So being a necessary condition is, in general, not the same thing as being a sufficient condition.

But the two concepts are related. If one thing is a necessary condition for a second thing, then the nonoccurrence of the first thing is sufficient for the nonoccurrence of the second. Consider the statement that it is necessary for there to be fuel in the tank for this car to run. It follows that there not being fuel in the tank is sufficient for the car's not running. The same principle works the other way around as well. If one thing is a sufficient condition for another thing, then the nonoccurrence of the first thing is necessary for the nonoccurrence of the other thing. For example, suppose it is sufficient for Bob's death that he swallows one or more milligrams of cyanide. Then it is necessary for Bob's remaining alive that he not swallow one or more milligrams of cyanide.

These principles concerning the relationship between necessary and sufficient condition statements can be expressed generally as follows, using the negation, or 'not' symbol $\sim$, meaning that $\sim A$ has the opposite truth value of A, that is, if A is true, then $\sim A$ is false, and vice versa.

(T1) If A is a necessary condition of B, then $\sim A$ is a sufficient condition of not-B.

(T2) If A is a sufficient condition of B, then $\sim A$ is a necessary condition of not-B.

Two other general principles can be stated as well. These principles express the idea that the necessary and sufficient condition relationships are converses of each other, as indicated by (T3) and (T4) below.

(T3) If *A* is a necessary condition for *B*, then *B* is a sufficient condition for *A*.

(T4) If *A* is a sufficient condition for *B*, then *B* is a necessary condition for *A*.

An example already used can be used again to illustrate these two principles. Paying tuition is a necessary condition for graduation. By (T3) it follows that having graduated is a sufficient condition for having paid tuition. To illustrate (T4), consider the following example. Burning a candle is a sufficient condition of the presence of oxygen in the atmosphere surrounding the candle. Hence, oxygen in the atmosphere is a necessary condition of the burning of the candle.

You could use (T3) and (T4) to define the concept of necessary condition in terms of the concept of sufficient condition, or vice versa. So we really need to define only the one concept, and then we can define the other in terms of it. And we have already seen that the concept of sufficient condition can be defined in terms of the concept of a conditional. So, in a way, we are not introducing two new ideas here. Even so, it is very important to have a good grasp of the ideas of necessary and sufficient condition in order to understand how reasoning works. Consider as an example of (T1) the statement 'It is necessary that there be fuel in the tank for the car to run'. By (T1), it follows that there not being fuel in the tank is a sufficient condition for the car's not running. Consider as an example of (T2) the statement 'It is sufficient for Bob's death that his brain is deprived of oxygen for an hour'. By (T2), it follows that it is necessary for Bob not to be dead, that is, to be alive, that his brain is not deprived of oxygen for an hour.

Practical reasoning typically involves a sequence of practical inferences chained together. For example, in order to get to the train station by 3 o'clock, I may have to take the 2 o'clock bus. But in order to take the 2 o'clock bus, I may have to walk to the bus stop. And in order to do that, I have to move my feet. Then once I get to the bus stop, I will have to carry out other actions, such as stepping on the bus and paying the bus fare. At each practical inference in the sequence of reasoning, there is a goal premise and a means premise. Usually, the means premise states a necessary condition for the realization of the goal, and then the whole sequence of reasoning, taken together, represents a sufficient condition for the realization of the goal. But in some cases of practical inferences, the means premise can state a sufficient condition for the realization of the goal. The practical reasoning generally is a chaining together of a connected sequence of necessary and sufficient conditions for the bringing about of the goal.

EXERCISE 8.2

Re-express each of the following statements as a necessary or sufficient condition relation between the two propositions (or events or actions). Then re-express it in terms of the other relation. That is, if it is a necessary condition relation, express it by an equivalent sufficient condition relation, or vice versa.

(a) If the union goes on strike, the new jet engine contract will not be completed on schedule.
(b) If Bob wins the chess tournament, Ed will lose.
(c) To pass his geometry exam, Norman must get up four hours early and memorize eight theorems.
(d) If Herman does not get a high score on the LSAT, he will not be admitted to law school.
(e) Unless Lola waters this hibiscus plant, it will not produce flowers.
(f) Studying critical argumentation gives you a critical insight into your own biases and standpoints that you would otherwise lack if you never studied the subject.

THREE Disjunctive Reasoning

One of the critical questions used to evaluate the use of practical reasoning in a particular case was the question of alternative means.

(Q1) Are there alternative means of carrying out the goal in question?

It is normally the case that there is more than one means to carry out a goal, and then the problem is to choose the 'best' means or at least the one that is better (from a practical viewpoint) than the others. The first step in such a case involves considering a number of alternatives. In this kind of practical reasoning, all the alternatives except one are eliminated, and then the last remaining one is selected. This kind of reasoning is disjunctive reasoning, or reasoning to choose one among a set of alternatives, by narrowing them down (optimally by eliminating all except one).

The simplest type of disjunctive reasoning is the following two-alternatives kind, traditionally called the disjunctive syllogism in logic.

(DS) Either A or B

Not-A

Therefore B

The pattern is to eliminate the one disjunct and then select the other as the conclusion to be inferred. The order of the disjunction does not matter. The following form is equally valid: Either A or B; not-B; therefore A. An example of a disjunctive syllogism type of inference would be the following case.

Either the fox went over the hill or in the hole.

The fox did not go over the hill.

Therefore the fox went in the hole.

In this pattern of reasoning, once the disjunct is eliminated that the fox went over the hill (presumably, by observation of the hill), then it is concluded that the fox must have gone into the hole (even though his entry was not observed).

Disjunctive reasoning is not restricted to two alternatives. There can be any number. Generally, disjunctive reasoning has the following form.

(DR) Either A_0 or A_1 or A_2 or... A_{n-1} or A_n

Not (either A_0 or A_1 or A_2 or... or A_{n-1})

Therefore A_n

To make an inference of the form (DR) valid (or strong or plausible, depending on whether the reasoning is deductive, inductive, or presumptive), two general requirements must be met: (1) The list in the first premise must represent all the available alternatives, that is, it must be exhaustive; and (2) all the alternatives except the one designated as the conclusion must be eliminated.

As the matter has been expressed so far, arguments of the form (DR) concern the truth and falsity of propositions. (DR) says essentially the following: At least one of the propositions $A_0, A_1, A_2, \ldots, A_{n-1}, A_n$ must be true; all of the propositions $A_0, A_1, A_2, \ldots, A_{n-1}$, are false; therefore, A_n must be true. However, in many instances, disjunctive reasoning also takes the form of selecting between a set of alternative courses of action. In such cases of practical reasoning, the variables $A_0, A_1, \ldots, A_n$ represent contingent propositions that describe courses of action open to a practical reasoner as potentially prudent or practically reasonable states of affairs to bring about. Consider the following example.

> Suppose that an important goal for me is to be healthy, and my doctor tells me that in order to be healthy, I must lose ten pounds. Also, I know that to lose ten pounds, I must eat meals that have fewer calories and, in particular, less fat. On Friday, I find myself at the deli counter, where there is a range of different sandwiches available: tuna with mayo, chicken with mayo, beef with mustard, Reuben, and corned beef with mayo. Suppose I know that the Reuben is high in fat content, and that all the sandwiches with mayo are high in fat content. By disjunctive reasoning, I can eliminate all except the beef with mustard sandwich as prudent choices. A prudent conclusion, by practical reasoning, would be to select the beef with mustard sandwich.

The practical inference in this case is defeasible, however. If I find out, independently, that the beef with mustard also has high fat content, close or equal to that of the other sandwiches, that new information would defeat the inference. Or if I found out that the fat content of what I am eating is not such a significant factor in weight loss as I once was led to believe, that could influence my reasoning. Another assumption of the inference may be that, at the time of the reasoning, I do not know the fat content of the beef with mustard sandwich or that I have no reason to believe that it is as high as that of the other sandwiches. Another defeating factor in this case might be the cost of the sandwich or other critical questions that might be raised in connection with other goals (other than weight loss) that are important to me.

One way of criticizing a disjunctive syllogism is to attack the first (disjunctive) premise, by arguing that it does not represent all the available alternatives that should be considered. Consider the following example.

> We have a choice between giving in to student demand and teaching what students want, or standing firm and teaching what needs to be taught. Giving in to student demand and teaching what students want is not an acceptable course of action. Therefore, we should stand firm and teach what needs to be taught.

This argument has the form of a disjunctive syllogism and is therefore a structurally correct inference. But the first premise is open to critical questioning, on the grounds that the dichotomy poses a disjunction that is too exclusive a bifurcation of the available alternatives. For in many instances, the choice is not that sharply dichotomous. Being sensitive to student demand is good in teaching, to some degree, but a certain degree of firmness in sticking to what an instructor feels is material that needs to be taught is also good. But the prudence of possible compromises, in this case, defeats the simplistically dichotomous disjunctive premise. It could be that accommodating the interests of the students is compatible, at least in some instances and to some extent, with teaching what needs to be taught. The inference may be valid, or structurally correct as an inference, but its disjunctive premise could be criticized as false or implausible, depending on the particulars of the case.

EXERCISE 8.3

Exhibit the structure of reasoning used in the following arguments by using the form DS or the form DR and evaluate the argument.

(a) Either I must stay in this room or not. If I leave the room, I will not get this chapter written. But I need to write this chapter. Therefore, I must stay in this room.

(b) Either we allow the government to take total control of the field of medicine or we must allow our doctors to be free of governmental restrictions. To allow the government to take total control of the field of medicine is not a prudent course of action. Therefore, we must allow our doctors to be free of governmental restrictions.

(c) The following disjunction was used by Bertrand Russell in 1948 as part of his argument to justify the prudential wisdom of conducting a pre-emptive nuclear strike against Russia: "Either we must have war against Russia before she has the atom bomb, or we will have to lie down and let them govern us."

(d) Child pleading to parent to buy him a new pair of running shoes: "Either you buy me a pair of Nike Air running shoes or my self-esteem will plummet to the level of personal loathing and perceived inferiority. Reducing my self-esteem to this level would be a very bad thing for you to do."

FOUR Taking Consequences into Account

Practical reasoning is about what to do by taking some course of action in the future that appears prudent now, as a way of realizing a goal. But one problem is that we are never really sure what is going to happen in the future, especially in complex situations relating to social and economic policies, political decisions, or business planning. It is best to be flexible, but on the other hand, it is practical and realistic to try to take the foreseeable consequences of one's actions into account, to the extent that one can conjecture or guess what these consequences are likely to be. Indeed, one of the critical questions for the practical inference (cited in section 1) poses the question of side-effects.

(Q4) Are there negative consequences of bringing about the thing in question that should be considered?

When asking this question, one evaluates a course of action being proposed as the conclusion of a practical inference by asking whether there are any foreseeable consequences of this action that ought to be taken into account. If these consequences are negative – that is, if they go against one's goals or tend to undermine them in some way – then that finding provides a basis for doubting, or withdrawing acceptance from the practical inference being considered, as representing a reason for taking what is alleged to be a prudent course of action.

In fact, this form of reasoning toward a conclusion of having reservations about acceptance of a practical inference is so common it has a name. As discussed in chapter 3, it is called *argumentum ad consequentiam*, or argument from consequences (literally, it means 'argument to consequence'). As a form of reasoning, it always uses allegedly foreseeable consequences of a proposed action as the premise, and the conclusion is then inferred that this course of action is recommended or is not recommended. This form of reasoning can be used in a positive or negative way, as an argument to respond to a practical inference that has been put forward when two parties are deliberating with each other on the best course of action. In argument from positive (negative) consequences, a policy or course of action is supported (or argued against) by citing positive (or negative) consequences of carrying out this policy or course of action.

Argument from consequences is often used in economic and political deliberations where two parties (or groups) disagree on what is the best course of action to pursue. To repeat the example used in chapter 3, section 5, two persons, Bob and Helen, disagree on whether tipping is generally a good custom, or a good social policy that ought to be continued. Bob used the following argument.

> If the practice of tipping were discontinued, unemployment would result.
>
> Unemployment is a bad thing.
>
> Therefore, it would not be a good idea to discontinue the practice of tipping.

In this instance, Bob has cited negative consequences of a certain policy or course of action to argue against this policy or course of action. Thus he has used the kind of argumentation called argument from negative consequences in chapter 3.

Argument from consequences can also be used in a positive form, as shown by the example used in chapter 3, section 5. Helen used the following argument.

> If the practice of tipping were discontinued, service providers would have greater self-esteem.
>
> Having greater self-esteem is a good thing.
>
> Therefore, the practice of tipping should be discontinued.

She cited positive consequences of a certain policy or course of action as a reason for supporting that policy or course of action as being a good idea. Thus, she has used argument from positive consequences.

Argument from consequences is frequently used in a deliberation weighing up the pros and cons of a course of action that is being contemplated. For example, in March 1995, voters in the province of Quebec had town hall meetings deliberating on whether to have a referendum giving them a choice to leave Canada and form a separate country or to stay as a province in Canada. Some argued that the economic consequences of separation from Canada would be highly negative for Quebec. Others argued that having a single French-speaking country separate from English-speaking Canada would have positive consequences for French culture in Quebec.

In cases of this kind of political deliberation, typically the argument is about the future outcomes or possibilities of some course of action that is unique, at least in many respects, so that the likely consequences must be guessed or conjectured. The future can never be known with certainty, and guessing can be highly conjectural where many complex and changing variables of a real situation are involved. Hence, argument from consequences is generally presumptive in nature as a kind of reasoning.

In evaluating arguments from consequences, one must be very careful to be alert to the question of which action the alleged consequences are supposedly following from. In the case of the debate on tipping, Bob and Helen are citing the positive or negative consequences of the actions or practices of tipping or not tipping. But in some cases where argumentation from consequence is used, the reasoning shifts to citing the consequences of the action of talking about the actions or practices at issue. For example, suppose Helen were to say to Bob, "You had better shut up if you know what's good for you. Your argument in favor of discontinuing the practice of tipping could result in workers becoming unemployed. And if anyone reported this argument to the union committee on employment equity, you could lose your own job!" Here Helen is citing negative consequences, but they are consequences of Bob's continuing to argue about tipping, not about the consequences of tipping itself.

To take another example that might help, suppose two politicians, Dave and Eunice, are having a critical discussion on the issue of abortion. Dave is supporting the pro-life viewpoint and Eunice is arguing for the pro-choice viewpoint. Dave has just finished putting forward an argument for his thesis that abortion is a bad practice that should be discontinued, on the grounds that the fetus is a person who has a right to life. Eunice replies, "If you take that view, you will not be elected." As a warning or piece of advice, this citing of consequences could be quite accurate and the statement itself might be true. But as a use of argument from consequences, you have to ask the question of it, "Is Dave's not getting elected (which might be quite contrary to his goals) being cited as a consequence of his abortion policy, or is it being cited as a consequence of Dave's talking about the abortion issue in the way he does?" If the latter, the argument from consequence does not go against the practical reasoning on the abortion question that Dave has used as his argument. What it really goes against is the prudence of Dave's saying what he says (or perhaps even of saying anything at all) about the issue. So here the argument does not go against Dave's practical reasoning. Instead, it is being used as an argument to silence Dave and prevent him from taking any further part in the discussion.

Evaluating Eunice's use of argument from negative consequences in this case brings in the concept of relevance (studied in the last chapter). Eunice's argument from consequences may seem relevant because it offers a warning or practical advice to Dave the politician. But Eunice and Dave are supposed to be engaged in a discussion on the issue of whether abortion is, in general, a good practice that is morally justifiable or is not. In the context of this dialogue, Eunice's argument from consequences is not dialectically relevant, in the sense that it contributes to the resolution of the conflict of opinions that is the issue of the discussion. For whether Dave is elected or not will not resolve the general issue of whether abortion is, in general, a practice that is morally justifiable or not.

Of course, Eunice's argument from consequences is relevant to any deliberation Dave may be wondering about with regard to his prospects of being elected. It may be, for example, that Dave is currently a candidate for political office or contemplating such a course of action. But this argument from consequences is not relevant in the discussion on the abortion issue. One must be careful in a case like this because the argument from consequences does seem like a relevant way of raising questions about the practical reasoning advocated by an opponent. But really it is not relevant, in the right way, because it is the consequences of that person's arguing about the issue that are being cited as negative, not the consequences of the policy he is recommending.

EXERCISE 8.4

Evaluate the use of argument from consequences in the following cases.

(a) Pierre and Mary are arguing about the issue of Quebec separating from the rest of Canada. Pierre maintains that separation would be a good thing, because it would preserve the Francophone cultural heritage. Mary argues that if Quebec separates there would be massive unemployment, especially in Quebec, where there are many federal government employees.

(b) Bob is about to try to fix his radio by picking up a live wire. Jane warns him, "I wouldn't do that. You could get a nasty shock!"

(c) Ted and Alice are having a critical discussion on the issue of whether vegetarianism is healthy or not. Ted argues: "Supporting vegetarianism will lead to unemployment in the meat industry, and if you criticize the meat industry, you will get in big trouble!"

(d) Bill and Marcia are arguing whether the United States was right to invade Iraq in Operation Desert Storm. Bill argues: "To even question this U.S. decision will simply encourage those who delay taking action against Saddam Hussein and will lead to more international conflict."

(e) Action Committee Member Eunice and Professor Dave are engaged in a seminar discussion on the abortion issue. Eunice argues, "Women are dying now because they cannot get access to physician-supervised abortion facilities. By arguing against the pro-choice side, you are harming women, and that is a form of abuse that is not tolerated in universities any more."

FIVE The Dilemma

As noted in section 3, practical reasoning involves making a choice between alternative courses of action by judging which one represents the best way to proceed. In some cases, it is very hard to decide, and there may be quite good practical inferences to support both alternatives, where the choice comes down to two courses of action. What to do? In some cases, the decision is particularly painful, because both options have something very painful about them, and you have quite strong reasons to think that each has practical considerations against it as a course of action. This kind of situation is a dilemma, where there are two opposed arguments representing the only two lines of action open, and each of them has strong practical considerations against it as a line of conduct that will contribute to the chooser's goals.

The dilemma is a species of argument from consequences, used very commonly in deliberation where you are confronted with having to make a choice between two alternative courses of action, and both alternatives have known or cited negative consequences. The following example represents a typical dilemma.

> If we increase government spending, the increased deficit will weaken the dollar.
>
> If we decrease government spending, the homeless and unemployed will suffer.
>
> We must either increase or decrease government spending.
>
> Therefore, either the increased deficit will weaken the dollar, or the homeless and unemployed will suffer.

The dilemma in this example has the following form.

> If *A* then *B*
>
> If *C* then *D*
>
> Either *A* or *C*
>
> Therefore, either *B* or *D*

The dilemma is a deductively correct form of inference, so to dispute the conclusion of a dilemma, you have to question the premises.

In any dilemma, there are two conditional premises and a disjunctive premise. In some cases, it is possible to question the disjunctive dilemma. If doubts can be raised about the truth of the disjunctive premise by citing some third alternative, the strategy is called slipping between the horns of the dilemma. For example, in the dilemma above, it would be possible to reply that there is a third alternative: keeping government spending at the current level. To guard against this kind of attack, it would be possible to change one of the conditional premises in the argument above, as follows:

> If we increase government spending, the increased deficit will weaken the dollar.
>
> If we don't increase government spending, the homeless and unemployed will suffer.
>
> Either we increase government spending or not.
>
> Therefore, either the increased deficit will weaken the dollar, or the homeless and unemployed will suffer.

Now the argument has been changed so that it has the following form.

> If A then B
>
> If not-A then C
>
> Either A or not-A
>
> Therefore, either B or C

Now it is no longer possible to slip between the horns because there is no room. The disjunctive premise is a tautology. It is logically true, meaning that it is not logically possible for it to be false.

The proposition 'It will rain tomorrow' is a contingent proposition, meaning that whether the proposition is true or false depends on what happens. In contrast, the proposition 'It will either rain tomorrow or not' is logically true (a tautology), because it is true regardless of what happens tomorrow. The proposition 'It will rain tomorrow' is a contingent proposition, meaning that whether the proposition is true or false depends on what happens. In contrast, the proposition 'It will either rain tomorrow or not' is logically true (a tautology), because it is true regardless of what happens tomorrow. The proposition 'The pen is on the table and the pen is not on the table' is logically false, or a contradiction – a proposition that could not possibly be true. Tautologies and contradictions are not contingent in nature, so they cannot be disputed in the same way that contingent propositions can.

In the dilemma just above, then, we can no longer slip between the horns, so the most straightforward alternative way to attack it is by raising doubt about the argument from negative consequences in one of the conditional premises. This tactic of attacking the argument in one or the other of the conditional premises is called grasping the horns of the dilemma. One might raise questions about the second premise, for example, by arguing that if we don't increase government spending, but keep it at current levels, the homeless and unemployed might not suffer, at least any more than they would have anyway.

Since the dilemma is a structurally correct form of inference, it might seem that the only possible way to attack it is to attack one or more of the premises. However, there is one other way to attack a dilemma that is very clever but is not often used. This method is to construct a counterdilemma: an opposed dilemma that has a conclusion opposite to that of the original dilemma. A famous counterdilemma was used by Euathlus, a student of the philosopher and lawyer Protagoras, who specialized in pleading before juries in Greece in the fifth century B.C. It was agreed by the two of them that Euathlus would pay his tuition fee to Protagoras when Euathlus won his first case. When Euathlus delayed taking up the practice of pleading cases, Protagoras sued him, using the following dilemma as his argument in the trial.

> If Euathlus wins this case, then he has won his first case, and so must pay me, according to our agreement.
>
> If Euathlus loses this case, then he must pay me, according to the court's judgment.
>
> Euathlus must either lose or win this case.
>
> Therefore, Euathlus must pay me.

Euathlus argued for his side by presenting the following counterdilemma.

> If I lose this case, then by our agreement, I do not have to pay Protagoras yet.
>
> If I win this case, then I do not have to pay Protagoras, according to the court's judgment.
>
> Either I must lose or win this case.
>
> Therefore, I do not have to pay Protagoras.

No decision was recorded on who won the case.

Presenting a counterdilemma is a clever way of attacking a dilemma but is not often used, because it requires considerable ingenuity and preparation. The much more usual and readily available methods are those of slipping between the horns or grasping the horns. Generally, then, the dilemma is a species of reasoning that combines disjunctive reasoning with argument from consequences. It is typical of everyday reasoning in deliberation where, in the course of the conduct of our lives, we are faced with situations where all the available options have negative consequences. Despite being torn in such cases, we are often forced, by the dilemma structure of reasoning, to make a choice, one way or the other.

EXERCISE 8.5

Critically evaluate each of the following dilemmas by using either the strategy of slipping between the horns or the strategy of grasping one of the horns. Select one example and mount a counter-dilemma against the original dilemma.

(a) If the instructor aims to please the more able students, some students will be frustrated and claim that his presentation is unclear. If the instructor aims to please the less able students, then some students will be bored and claim that the course is 'Mickey Mouse'. The instructor must aim to please either the less able students or the more able students. Therefore, some will be frustrated and claim that the instructor's presentation is unclear, or some students will be bored and claim that the course is 'Mickey Mouse'.

(b) If high school clinics are to stem the tide of teenage pregnancy, then they must dispense condoms; but if they want to discourage illicit sex, then they must not dispense condoms. Since high school clinics must either dispense or not dispense condoms, either they will not stem the tide of teenage pregnancy or they will not discourage illicit sex.

(c) If physician-assisted suicide is permitted, physicians will contravene their ethical principle not to kill a patient. If physician-assisted suicide is not permitted, some patients will die an undignified death with unnecessary suffering. Either physician-assisted suicide is permitted or it is not. Therefore, either physicians will contravene their ethical principle not to kill a patient, or some patients will die an undignified death with unnecessary suffering.

(d) If we have tariffs and quotes, we will constantly be having international trade wars. If we have free trade, we will constantly be having unfair dumping of subsidized foreign products on our domestic markets. We have to choose. Either we can have tariffs and quotas or we can have free trade. Therefore, we will be constantly having international trade wars, or we will constantly be having unfair dumping of subsidized foreign products on our domestic markets.

(e) If we do not ban the expression of arguments that are 'hateful' to groups of people, then these people will be harmed. If we do ban the expression of arguments that are 'hateful' to groups of people, then we lose freedom of speech. Either we ban such arguments or we do not. Therefore, either we harm people or we lose freedom of speech.

(f) If people are hired for university appointments on affirmative action criteria, then the principle of hiring on merit exclusively is lost. If people are not hired for university appointments on affirmative action criteria, then certain groups who were disadvantaged in the past are not treated equally. Either people are hired for university appointments on affirmative action criteria or they are not. Therefore, either the principle of hiring on merit exclusively is lost or certain groups who were disadvantaged in the past are not treated equally.

SIX The Closed World Assumption

To illustrate how practical reasoning works in a simple type of case, designers of robotic systems constructed to carry out actions are fond of citing certain kinds of problems. Characteristic of such cases is the closed world assumption, where everything is assumed to be held constant other than the facts stated in the case. An example is the blocks world, where there are a number of blocks stacked on a flat surface, like a table, and a robot arm can pick up one block at a time and put it down on top of another block. Each of the blocks has a letter printed on it. The initial (given) situation is that the blocks are stacked in a certain order in one or more piles. The goal is to stack them in a different order. And the means used is the gripping action of the robot arm, which can pick up a block and release it. In the blocks world, there is a clearly stated goal, a finite (usually small) set of alternative means (steps) that can be used to carry out the goal and an ignoring of any intruding factors or external consequences, other than the initial situation, the means, and the goal, as stated. The robot is the only agent being considered, and nothing else matters except what the robot does, or does not do, in the blocks world.

An example is the following simple case of a blocks world problem where the initial situation is represented in Figure 8.1. In this case, the goal is for the robot arm to reverse the two piles of blocks, so that the *ABC* pile is stacked in the right position (in the same order), while the *DEF* pile is stacked on the left, where the *ABC* pile was before. The only

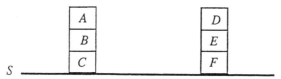

Figure 8.1 Initial blocks world situation.

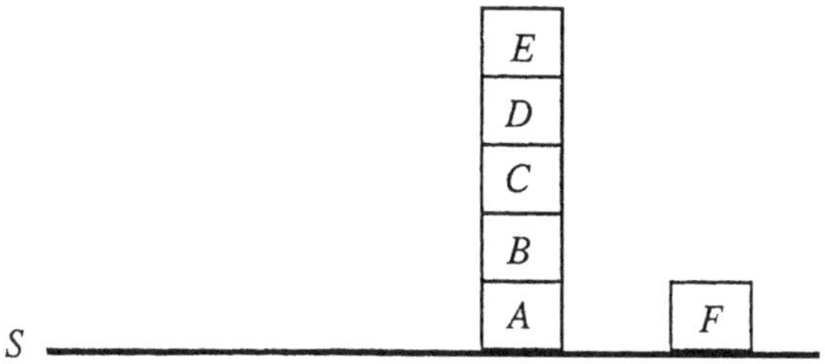

Figure 8.2 New blocks world situation.

action allowed to the robot arm, in order to carry out this goal, is to pick up a block from a pile and set it on the surface, *S*. However, no more than three piles are allowed to occur, at any particular time. So the robot arm is not allowed to carry out the action, for example, of putting block *A* down somewhere on the surface, and then putting block *B* down somewhere else (other than on *A* or *D*). The goal, then, is for the robot arm to reverse the two existing piles without ever producing more than three piles of blocks.

There are only two sequences of actions that can be used to carry out the goal. The first one can be described as follows. Take *A* off the left pile and put it on *S*. Put *B* on *A*. Put *C* on *B*. Put *D* on *C*. Put *E* on *D*. This sequence produces the situation shown in Figure 8.2, with a new pile of blocks located between the locations of the previous two piles. Next, the robot arm must move *F* to the left, to occupy the place on *S* where the *ABC* pile was in Figure 8.1. Then the robot arm must place *E* on top of *F*, and then place *D* on top of *E*. The result, shown in Figure 8.3, is the reverse situation of Figure 8.1. The only other way the goal can be achieved in this case is by carrying out the same kind of sequence of actions, but in the reverse order. That is, the robot arm must begin in the initial situation in Figure 8.1 by putting *D* on *S*, then putting *E* on *D*, and so forth.

In this blocks world case, the situation is simplified by several assumptions. There is a given initial situation, and it can be changed only by making a specified type of action. A sequence of such actions

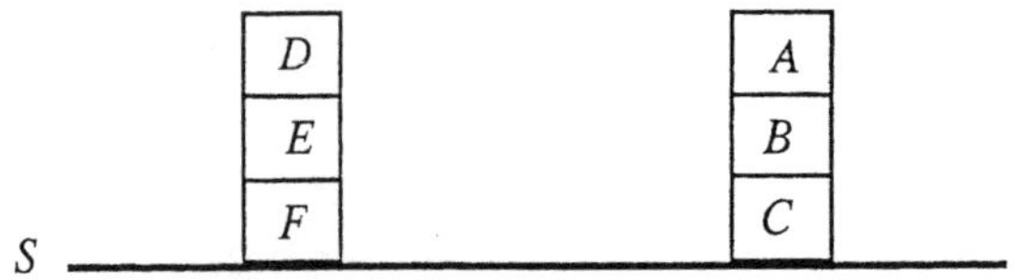

Figure 8.3 Goal achieved in blocks world.

is possible, leading to a clearly specified goal. And most important, the closed world assumption applies – no other external actions or events can intrude by presenting any new developments or obstructions. The closed world is the assumption that any positive fact not specified in a given data base (the knowledge possessed by the agent) may be assumed to be false.[2] In other words, the assumption is that all the relevant information in a situation has been specified, and anything else may be disregarded or assumed not to apply to the situation as known. The following example shows how the closed world assumption is used as the basis for drawing an inference.

> A passenger in an air terminal is scanning the televised flight monitor to see whether there is a flight from Vancouver to New York. She scans over all the flight connections listed on the monitor, and finds no Vancouver–New York flight among the flights listed. She concludes there is no flight between Vancouver and New York.[3]

The closed world assumption is that all the flights one can take from this terminal at this time are listed on the monitor. So if a flight from Vancouver to New York is not listed, one may infer that there is no such flight available. If no such flight is specified as a positive fact in the data base, one may assume that the proposition that there is such a flight is false. Here the inference, based on the closed world assumption, is based on the premise that the data base is complete. So if a proposition is not stated, that lack of knowledge justifies the inference that the proposition is (or may be assumed to be) false.

[2] Raymond Reiter, "Nonmonotonic Reasoning," *Annual Review of Computer Science* 2 (1987): 147–186 (reference to p. 158).

[3] This example was presented by Raymond Reiter, "A Logic for Default Reasoning," *Artificial Intelligence* 13 (1980): 81–132.

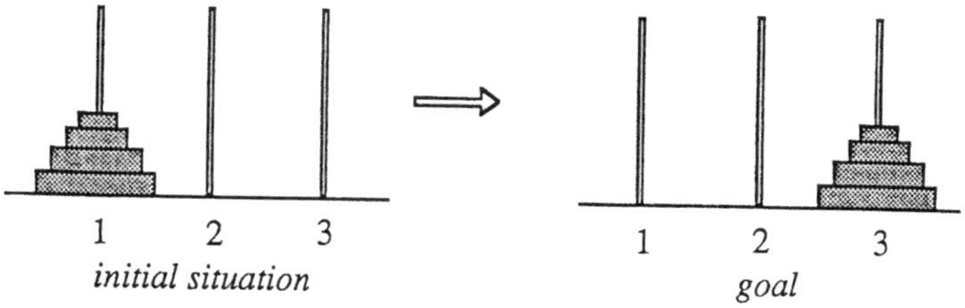

Figure 8.4 The Tower of Hanoi.

The real world of everyday acting and thinking about what to do is not like the simple kind of problem represented in blocks world. In blocks world, everything you need to know to find the best line of action to accomplish our goal is known, the circumstances are not subject to change, and there are no worries about the introduction of new knowledge that could disrupt the situation or indicate a different way of solving the problem. But even despite the uncertainties of real world situations where action is called for, practical reasoning can be applied by basing the reasoning on the closed world assumption, and thereby enabling a conclusion to be drawn, by taking action based on the knowledge one has.

EXERCISE 8.6 Show the sequence of practical reasoning needed to get from the initial situation to the goal, in the case below, where the closed world assumption holds. The left side of Figure 8.4 (initial state) shows three towers and four disks of different sizes piled on the first tower. How can all four disks be moved to the third tower, as shown on the right side (goal state), without ever putting a bigger disk on top of a smaller disk?

SEVEN Lack of Knowledge Inferences

In everyday decision making, in most cases it is not necessary to compile all the knowledge needed to arrive at a maximal decision on the best possible way to do something, by choosing from all the alternative means. In many cases, compiling all this information before taking action would be just too expensive and time-consuming. So much delay would make the situation worse or even make any useful action impossible. Instead, the most practical policy is to be content with bounded rationality, that is, going ahead with practical reasoning on the basis of the information you already have or with enough information, for practical purposes, that can be collected so that you can get a course of action that is good enough to do the job. In such a case, the closed world assumption is just not a practical requirement, and instead you only assume that you know enough to go ahead.

For these reasons, it is often better to draw a presumptive conclusion to go ahead in everyday reasoning on a balance-of-considerations basis, and go with a tentatively adopted line of action, even though the reasons for one alternative, and against the others, are not conclusive. Of course, this is not to recommend acting rashly or impulsively, but often a balance of considerations is a strong enough basis of argument to meet an appropriate burden of proof for a reasoned deliberation to go ahead (tentatively) and commit to a conclusion.

In many cases of the use of practical reasoning in everyday deliberations, drawing a sensible conclusion is a matter of striking the right balance between what is known and what is not known. In some cases, it is even possible to draw a useful conclusion, by a presumptive inference, from what is not known. This type of reasoning, called a lack of knowledge inference (sometimes also called argument from ignorance or reasoning from negative evidence), has the following general form.[4]

> Proposition *A* is not known to be true (false).
>
> If *A* were true (false), it would be known to be true (false).
>
> Therefore, *A* is false (true).

The lack of knowledge inference is a subspecies of *modus tollens* (MT) inference that uses knowledge-based reasoning. An example would be the following case relating to Leona Helmsley, wife of former New York real estate magnate Harry Helmsley. The case of her conviction and imprisonment was a subject of intense public interest and was widely reported by the media at the time. Someone looking for recent news on the story might argue as follows.

> I haven't heard that Leona Helmsley has been released from prison.
>
> If it were true, I would know it (because Leona Helmsley is of intense interest to the media).

[4] Douglas Walton, *Arguments from Ignorance* (University Park: Pennsylvania State University Press, 1995).

> Therefore, Leona Helmsley has (presumably) not been released from prison.

This example illustrates the presumptive nature of this kind of inference. The conclusion can be inferred as the presumptively held proposition asserting that it is highly plausible (as judged from what is known) that Leona Helmsley has not been released from prison yet. However, the argument in this case also depends on whether the arguer has been collecting information from the news media so that she would know that Leona has been released if the media reported it.

Another example will further illustrate how lack of knowledge inferences work. Suppose someone has accused Mr. X of being a spy for a foreign country, and that despite this suspicion, a security investigation by the FBI has revealed no evidence that Mr. X is a foreign spy. What could be inferred from this negative result? The following lack of knowledge inference might be drawn.

> No evidence has been found that Mr. X is a foreign spy.
>
> If there were evidence to be found that Mr. X is a foreign spy, the FBI search would have found it.
>
> Therefore, Mr. X is not a foreign spy.

One might counter that Mr. X is not a foreign spy as far as we know, but isn't it possible that the FBI search just didn't find the right evidence? Isn't it possible, for example, that Mr. X might be a "mole," a deeply concealed spy on whom evidence is very hard to uncover? If so, is the inference above acceptable? Well, of course, it has to admitted that this "mole" alternative is a possibility. So, can we draw the negative conclusion that Mr. X is really not a foreign spy as being true? The answer is that it depends on the purpose of the dialogue in which the inference above is being used as part of the argument and on the stage that the dialogue has reached at the point the argument was put forward.

Arguments from ignorance presuppose a dialogue that is usually of the information-seeking or inquiry type, in which data are being collected in a knowledge base. How strong the argument is depends on how much data have been collected at the given point in the dialogue where the argument was put forward. In the case above, the strength of the argument depends on how much information the FBI collected. If they had undertaken a serious investigation and collected all the knowledge about Mr. X that could be found, so that they could say they knew a lot about Mr. X, then the argument from ignorance about Mr. X could be quite strong.

Thus, one critical question matching the argument from ignorance is the depth-of-search question.

> **CQ1:** How complete is the search for knowledge found in the investigation?

Another question concerns burden of proof.

> **CQ2:** How complete does the knowledge need to be to support the argument adequately?

Suppose, for example, that Mr. X has a job that involves some risk to national security, and Mr. X therefore has to have a certain level of security clearance. Hence a practical deliberation needs to be conducted: Should Mr. X be removed from his job or not? The outcome depends on a balance of considerations: The security risk (the bad consequence of losing state secrets) must be weighed against the bad consequence of harming an innocent person who is not a spy.

In practical terms, then, the lack of knowledge inference about Mr. X above should be evaluated between two alternatives on a balance-of-considerations basis. How serious a security risk is Mr. X in his present job, on the one hand? And on the other hand, how thorough (serious) was the FBI search? Here the assumption is that both premises are true. In particular, it is assumed that the second premise is true, on the grounds that the FBI is a reliable, professional, and competent agency that is experienced in conducting these kinds of security investigations and that in fact they have undertaken a serious investigation into this case. To say that they have done so requires that they have done a search thorough enough so that it can be said that their knowledge is reasonably complete. It needs to be complete enough to warrant that action that is being taken. If these premises are acceptable, then the inference should be judged on a balancing of considerations between the level of security clearance appropriate for the risk in the case of Mr. X versus the completeness of the search. If the search was complete enough to meet the requirements of the level of clearance appropriate for the risk, then it ought to be concluded (presumptively) that Mr. X is not a foreign spy.

Generally, an argument from ignorance is strong (strongly plausible) if (1) the inference has the form of the lack of knowledge inference above; (2) the premises are or can be supported by evidence in the case; and (3) the support given by the premises is strong enough to tilt the balance of considerations in favor of the conclusion. Some might argue for "zero tolerance" and say that Mr. X ought to be fired if there is any risk at all that he is a foreign spy. But would this be a practically wise or sensible conclusion to draw? By parity of reasoning, everyone who is accused of being a spy or about whom there is any suspicion that he or she is a spy, would have to be fired from his or her job. Drawing this conclusion would mean that anyone could be fired, or even that everyone should be fired, of whom it can be said, "There is no evidence he (she) is not a foreign spy." This would be a reversal of the kind of burden of proof normally held appropriate for accusations of criminal misconduct. But more than that, it would not be a way of evaluating lack of knowledge reasoning that would be a sensible or practically balanced way of conducting deliberations of familiar kinds. In the end, then, it is not always practically sensible to keep on collecting all the knowledge you would require to give you absolutely complete information for conclusive reasoning on a case. It might be wiser to tentatively draw a presumptive conclusion on a balance-of-considerations basis, weighing what you know against what you don't know, choosing (on balance) the more strongly supported alternative, if it is well enough supported for practical purposes.

In some cases, however, one of the premises may have little or no real support, but pressure is put on in a dialogue to try to get the respondent of the argument from ignorance to leap to the conclusion uncritically.

In the early 1950's, Joseph R. McCarthy, a senator from Wisconsin, accused many innocent people, in a "witch hunt" interrogation, of being Communist sympathizers. McCarthy would appear with a bulging briefcase at a tribunal that looked like a trial on television, confronting an employee who had been accused of being a "loyalty risk" in his job.[5] He would typically have an impressive-looking bulging briefcase full of files of damaging evidence on the accused, but in fact the papers contained mainly innuendo and slander, and no real evidence.[6] In one case McCarthy declared: "I do not have much information on this except the general statement of the agency that there is nothing in the files to disprove his Communist connections."[7]

What makes the lack of knowledge inference a fallacious argument from ignorance in a case such as this is the highly questionable second premise.

[5] Allan J. Matusow, *Joseph R. McCarthy* (Englewood Cliffs, N.J.: Prentice-Hall, 1970).
[6] Richard H. Rovere, *Senator Joe McCarthy* (New York: Harcourt Brace, 1959), pp. 130–133.
[7] Ibid., p. 130.

In this type of case, the first premise is presumably true, that no evidence was found that the accused person was a communist. But the second premise is highly dubious. For if no real search for evidence was made, and the accusation was simply based on gossip or slander, it is questionable whether such evidence would be found if a serious search for it were to be made. Moreover, the concept of someone's being a 'Communist sympathizer' is vague. It is a hard proposition to prove or disprove. And much of the so-called evidence to support this claim was often based on innuendo and slander reported from the say-so of accusers who were not even called to testify or submit to questioning. There is very much doubt whether the investigative methods used by the tribunals would have found evidence of someone being a 'loyalty risk' even if there were such evidence to be found, in a given case.

EXERCISE 8.7

Identify the premises and conclusion in each of the following lack of knowledge inferences and evaluate the argument from ignorance as strong or not.

(a) Probably no life exists on Venus. Teams of scientists have conducted exhaustive studies of the planet's surface and atmosphere, and no living organisms have been found.

(b) An expert system knowledge base on industrial and agricultural products in South America called SCHOLAR[8] is asked the question, "Is Guyana a major rubber producer?" SCHOLAR does not have the proposition "Guyana is a major rubber producer" in its knowledge base, and all it can positively find, after a thorough search, is that Peru and Columbia are major rubber producers. SCHOLAR answers: "I know enough that I am inclined to say that Guyana is not a major rubber producer in South America."

(c) No one has ever proved that massive federal deficits are actually harmful to the economy. We can conclude only that such deficits pose no real danger.

(d) Extra-sensory perception must be accepted as a fact, because nobody has proved it is impossible.

(e) Randomized clinical trials of the new drug Thoromalozene failed to prove any deleterious side effects. It is reasonable to go ahead with marketing Thoromalozene, now it has been proven safe to take.

[8] Allan Collins, Eleanor H. Warnock, Nelleke Aiello, and Mark L. Miller, "Reasoning from Incomplete Knowledge," in *Representation and Understanding: Studies in Cognitive Science*, ed. Daniel G. Bobrow and Allan Collins (New York: Academic, 1975), pp. 383–415.

EIGHT Real World Situations

The foregoing account of practical reasoning has been simplified in a number of respects. The assumption has been that a single agent is carrying out the reasoning and that this agent has only one goal that is to be taken into account. In any real world situation, however, an agent will have a plurality of goals. In some cases, an agent's carrying out the one goal can even introduce a conflict, by bringing about something that might interfere with the realization of another goal that the agent has. In real world situations, multiple goals are the normal kind of framework a practical reasoner will have to work with. Another complication is that in any real world situation, several independent agents are most likely to be involved in a sequence of practical reasoning. One agent might have goals that are different from those of another agent. Indeed, their goals may even conflict, and the two of them may negotiate with each other by making concessions and trade-offs. A third complication is that practical reasoning may not always be completed once an agent has carried out an action. If the action has consequences the agent perceives, she may decide to change her goals – for example, if she sees these consequences as negative.

In some cases where practical reasoning is used, the situation is a life-or-death dilemma, and any decision, once implemented, is final. However, in many other cases, once an action is taken, the consequences of that action can be observed by the agent, and then on the basis of this new information, the plan of action can be altered accordingly. This feature of practical reasoning, feedback, is the monitoring of the consequences of one's actions, and the modifying of an existing plan of action, based on the new incoming information. Feedback allows an agent to improve practical reasoning, by going ahead tentatively with a defeasible line of action as a conclusion, but then changing that conclusion to accord with new circumstances, as the consequences of that initial line of action are observed. Much practical reasoning, in fields as diverse as medicine, education, and engineering, is carried out on a trial and error basis, where a treatment or a technique is gradually improved over time, as the results of its implementation come to be known and studied. The assumption is that sometimes it is better to go ahead and do something, instead of waiting to collect as much information as possible before taking even tentative steps. The simplest familiar type of machine that uses feedback is the thermostat. When it gets the "message" from a thermometer that the temperature has reached a designated low mark, it turns the heat on. But then when, as a consequence of its action, the heat in the room increases, and the thermometer reaches a designated high mark, the thermostat activates the switch to turn the heat off. The consequences of its action are that the heat will begin to decrease. So the overall outcome is that the thermostat steers a middle course between extremes of heat and cold, as instructed by the "goal" put in place by the setting of the thermostat by a user.

Practical reasoning can continue, in many cases, even after a conclusion is drawn, and action taken, because feedback may occur. But this possibility poses a problem. If practical reasoning can go on and on like this, when is closure achieved? When can the conclusion be drawn that a particular course of action is practical enough to be final? The answer is that no conclusion drawn by practical reasoning on matters of everyday living is ever really final in this sense. Instead, the conclusion is drawn as a defeasible inference that is inherently subject to revision or improvement should new information come in. The closed world assumption can be made, as a basis for action, but it can, in some cases, be later challenged and reversed, if the situation has changed. The best general attitude for a practical reasoner is one of open-mindedness to new information, should it become available in a case.

Another critical question that should always be kept in mind in real world situations is that of multiple goals. An agent should ask, before going ahead with inferring that an action is prudent, whether this action might conflict with other goals the agent has. In real world situations, agents have many goals, and one may conflict with another, in a particular situation. For example, my goal may be to advance in my career, but carrying out this goal may conflict, in some instances, with my goal of being a responsible parent. Suppose my child is sick on a day when an important meeting for my work is being held. What should I do? Any line of action to contribute to the one goal may run contrary to realizing the other goal. As noted in section 5, such practical conflicts often take the form of a dilemma.

The third complication concerns the realistic kind of situation where multiple agents are involved. If you and I have the same goal, we may decide to collaborate, realizing that if we help each other, prospects for carrying out the actions required to realize the goal will be improved. So the two of us may engage in deliberations together, to discuss and seek out ways and means of realizing this common goal. On the other hand, if your goal conflicts with mine, we may enter into negotiations with each other. If I can get the parts of my goal that are most important to me, while giving up other parts that are more important to you, but less important to me, the negotiations could be successful for both of us. Negotiation was treated as a type of dialogue in chapter 1.

In a simple kind of case, such as the blocks world, various complications can be set aside in order to explain the basic elements of practical reasoning. But in a real-world case of a person making decisions on how to act in business, technology, or personal affairs, three complications, in particular, raise critical questions that should be asked.

1. Does new information, particularly in the form of feedback, give good reasons to revise the previous conclusion that has been taken to represent the practical course of action?
2. Does the conclusion that has been taken to represent the most practical course of action (so far considered) conflict with other goals of the agent?
3. Are other agents involved, and if so, does the relation between my goals and theirs indicate that discussion with them before going ahead with my conclusion would be practically useful?

These three additional critical questions apply to the more complex kinds of cases of practical reasoning where feedback, multiple goals, or multiple agents are involved.

EXERCISE 8.8

Evaluate the following cases of practical reasoning by asking appropriate critical questions.

(a) I need to get to the university by 10 A.M., but there is a snowstorm, and my car will not start. The best way is to start walking. However, after walking a few steps, I find that the storm is very intense, and I can make very little progress. I begin to worry about my safety if I proceed further.

(b) It is necessary for our college students to study Chinese, because trade with China is an increasingly important economic factor in our economy. To trade effectively with China, we need people who can interact culturally with the Chinese. But interacting culturally with the Chinese requires learning their language. Therefore, we should learn Chinese. But we also want to preserve our cultural heritage by teaching the French language to as many of our young people as possible. Therefore, we should teach French as well as English in the schools.

(c) To deal with crime effectively, we must have tougher sentencing. It is difficult to live productive and peaceful lives, with so much crime. Crime must be reduced, and so we must deal with it effectively. Therefore, we must have tougher sentencing. But we also want to balance the budget, and keeping a person in jail for a year is very costly. And if we have tougher sentencing, we will have prisoners in jail for a longer time than we have now.

(d) To be guaranteed job security, it is necessary for the union to go on strike, because if we don't go on strike, the company may decide to have cutbacks. And unless we go on strike, the company will not agree to new clauses in the contract that would make it more difficult to lay off workers. So the union must go on strike. But if the union goes on strike it may bankrupt the company, which would mean that not only would the management officials lose their jobs, but the union members would all be out of work as well.

NINE Summary and Glimpses Ahead

Practical reasoning is an agent-based type of reasoning made up of a sequence of practical inferences of the following basic form.

My goal is to bring about *A*.

Bringing about *B* is the way to bring about *A*.

Therefore, I should bring about *B*.

The 'way,' or means, typically refers to a necessary condition for bringing about something, but in some instances a sufficient condition is referred to. Five critical questions are used to evaluate cases where this inference has been drawn.

(Q1) Are there alternative means other than *B*?

(Q2) Is *A* a possible (realistic) goal?

(Q3) Are there other goals that might conflict with *A*?

(Q4) Are there negative consequences of bringing about *B* that should be considered?

(Q5) Is *B* the best (or most acceptable) of the alternatives?

A practical inference can be practically reasonable, in the sense that acceptance of the premises gives a good reason for accepting the recommendation expressed by the conclusion. But this practical rationality is thrown into doubt if any one of the five critical questions is asked and not answered.

The means premise in a practical inference sometimes expresses a necessary condition and sometimes a sufficient condition of bringing about an outcome. To say that one thing is necessary for a second thing is to say that without the first thing being realized, the second thing won't be. To say that one thing is sufficient for a second thing is to say that if the first thing is realized, the second thing will be too. Four general principles express key relationships between necessary and sufficient condition statements.

(T1) If *A* is a necessary condition of *B*, then not-*A* is a sufficient condition of not-*B*.

(T2) If *A* is a sufficient condition of *B*, then not-*A* is a necessary condition of not-*B*.

(T3) If *A* is a necessary condition for *B*, then *B* is a sufficient condition for *A*.

(T4) If *A* is a sufficient condition for *B*, then *B* is a necessary condition for *A*.

Generally, a sequence of practical reasoning is made up of practical inferences that express necessary- and sufficient-condition relationships between pairs of actions.

Practical reasoning always involves selecting from a given set of alternatives, and trying to narrow them down by eliminating some of them as not the best ways to achieve a goal. This kind of selection process of inference is called disjunctive reasoning. In the simplest type of case, there are only two alternatives, and one is rejected. By disjunctive reasoning the other one is accepted. One must be careful, however, because in some cases, insufficient alternatives are represented, and the disjunctive premise should be critically questioned. *Argumentum ad consequentiam* (argument from consequences) is the citing of positive (or negative) consequences as a reason for doing (or not doing) something, based on practical reasoning. Argument from consequences is one of the most frequently used kinds of reasoning in everyday deliberations, in policy-making deliberations in business and politics, and in applications of scientific technology. The dilemma is a species of argument from consequences used to set up two opposed alternatives, each one of which has painfully negative consequences. In every dilemma, there are two conditional premises and a disjunctive premise. Questioning the disjunctive premise is one way of criticizing a dilemma, called slipping between the horns. In some cases, this tactic is not possible or practical, and it is necessary to grasp one of the horns, that is, to attack one of the conditionals. A third tactic is to propose a counter-dilemma.

In simple cases of practical reasoning, such as the blocks world situation, the closed-world assumption is easily applicable, because everything external to the simple world postulated is assumed to be held constant. In a case like that of the listing of data in a data base – such as the listing of flights on a televised flight monitor in an air terminal – the closed-world assumption functions as a convenient device for conveying information to a user. If a flight is not listed, then the user can assume that no such flight is in the data base. The user may then infer that there is no such flight available (from that terminal). An inference of this type, called a lack of knowledge inference, is a commonly used type of reasoning. In evaluating lack of knowledge inferences, how close to closure the search of the data base has been is an important critical question. If no real search of the data base has been made, the argument from ignorance may be used as a fallacious kind of inference in, for example, a witch hunt situation, such as the McCarthy trials. Special care in evaluating this type of inference must be taken where a charge is vague and is hard to disprove (or prove) by concrete evidence.

Complex situations, where the closed world assumption does not apply (or does not apply very easily), include cases where feedback is used to revise a practical inference, cases where multiple goals of an agent are involved, and cases where the goals of more than one agent are involved. In evaluating these more complex cases of practical reasoning, three critical questions are important.

(1) Does new information, particularly in the form of feedback, give good reasons to revise the previous conclusion that has been taken to represent the practical course of action?

(2) Does the conclusion that has been taken to represent the most practical course of action (so far considered) conflict with other goals of the agent?

(3) Are other agents involved, and if so, does the relation between my goals and theirs indicate that discussion with them before going ahead with my conclusion would be practically useful?

In total, then, seven critical questions may be used to evaluate the more complex kinds of cases where practical reasoning has been used. Where the closed world assumption does not apply, the best approach is to evaluate the case on a balance-of-consideration basis, accepting the practical inference tentatively but keeping an open mind for new evidence.

This chapter has offered an account of practical reasoning, or goal-directed reasoning of the kind that fits into the type of dialogue called the deliberation. Real-life cases of dilemmas are often encountered in practical ethics and decision making under conditions of uncertainty in real world situations. In confronting such dilemmas, various kinds of arguments on both sides may have to be considered and weighed. Some of the most common types of arguments of this sort are represented by the argumentation schemes for argument from consequences, argument from commitment, and the sunk costs argument. This chapter on practical reasoning provides a lead-in to the planned volume on persons and ethical argumentation.

This book as a whole has introduced the reader to the forms of various common types of presumptive argumentation, fitting into the types of dialogue introduced in chapter 1. These forms are called argumentation schemes. Examples of schemes we have studied include appeal to popular opinion, appeal to witness testimony, appeal to expert opinion, argument from analogy, argument from correlation to cause, and the slippery slope argument. Each scheme has been presented with a set of matching critical questions. Although we have not gone too deeply into the task of evaluation, saving that for later volumes, the reader has been shown how examples of arguments of many common kinds can be partially evaluated by asking the right critical questions that probe into missing assumptions and weak points. Mention has been made from time to time that some instances of such arguments can be fallacious. But very little discussion is included on exactly how these arguments can be evaluated as fallacious, reserving that subject for the fallacies volume. The focus of evaluation, as far as this first volume has been concerned, is on how these fallible arguments can be used reasonably to shift a burden of proof in a dialogue on a balance of considerations. The central goal of this book has been to get the student to be able to recognize the various common argumentation schemes as representing distinctive types of argument that he or she will often encounter.

Index

Note: Page numbers in italics refer to diagrams; page numbers in bold refer to Exercises sections.